The Educational Psychology of Creativity

edited by

John C. Houtz
Fordham University

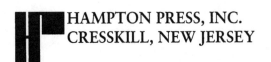

HAMPTON PRESS, INC.
CRESSKILL, NEW JERSEY

Printed in the United States of America

Library of Congress Cataloging-in-Publication Data

The educational psychology of creativity / edited by John C. Houtz.
     p. cm. -- (Perspectives on creativity)
    Includes bibliographical references and indexes.
    ISBN 1-57273-234-2 -- ISBN 1-57273-235-0 (pbk.)
    1. Creative thinking. 2. Creative ability. I. Houtz, John. II. Series.

LB1062 .E345 2002
370.15`7--dc21

2001059360

Hampton Press, Inc.
23 Broadway
Cresskill, NJ 07626

The Educational Psychology
of Creativity

Perspectives on Creativity
Mark A. Runco, series editor

The Motives for Creative Work
Jock Abra

Creative Intelligence: Toward Theoretic Integration
Donald Ambrose et al. (eds.)

Remarkable Women: Perspectives on Female Talent Development
Karen Arnold, Kathleen Noble, and Rena Subotnik (eds.)

No Rootless Flower: An Ecology of Creativity
Frank Barron

Creativity and Giftedness in Culturally Diverse Students
Giselle B. Esquivel and John Houtz (eds.)

Critical Thinking and Reasoning: Current Research, Theory and Practice
Daniel Fasko, Jr. (ed.)

Investigating Creativity in Youth: A Book of Readings on Research and Methods
Anne S. Fishkin, Bonnie Cramond, and Paula Olszewski-Kubilius

Quantum Creativity: Waking Up to Our Creative Potential
Amit Goswami

Educating Creativity: A Primer
John Houtz

The Educational Psychology of Creativity
John Houtz (ed.)

Enhancing Creativity of Gifted Children: A Guide for Parents
Joe Khatena

Style and Psyche
Pavel Machotka

Social Creativity Volumes One and Two
Alfonso Montuori and Ronald Purser (eds.)

Unusual Associates: Essays in Honor of Frank Barron
Alfonso Montuori (ed.)

Creativity Research Handbook Volume One
Mark A. Runco (ed.)

Critical Creative Processes
Mark A. Runco (ed.)

Underserved Gifted Populations
Joan Smutny (ed.)

The Young Gifted Child: Potential and Promise—An Anthology
Joan Smutny (ed.)

forthcoming

Theories of Creativity Revised Edition
Mark A. Runco and Robert S. Albert (eds.)

To my students

Contents

Preface and Acknowledgments

Joe Khatena's (1982) *Educational Psychology of the Gifted* inspired the title of this book. I also must advise the reader that creativity in education is not just a recent phenomenon. Researchers and educators have been advocating the application of knowledge about creativity to schools and classrooms for some time. I recommend to the reader two earlier volumes as background and testimony to the educational psychology of creativity. For example, in 1968, William B. Michael, one of the contributors to this volume, edited a collection of papers in a volume titled *Teaching for Creative Endeavor: Bold New Venture*. In 1970, E. Paul Torrance authored *Encouraging Creativity in the Classroom*, a little book in the series *Issues and Innovations in Education*. These books discuss the traditional theories of creativity available at the time, the methods of assessing creative potential, and what was known about creative personalities, but the majority of the selections and chapters focus on children in schools. Michael's volume contains 13 selections on curriculum planning from preschool through college levels, several entries dealing with school administration and support services for creative pupils, and two articles on parent training. Torrance's book is written for the classroom teacher directly, describing in 10 chapters a variety of teacher knowledge bases and skills applicable to lesson planning and delivery, adapting instruction to pupil differences, modeling creative behavior, and rewarding or reinforcing pupil efforts.

In 1984, Donald and Judith Sanders published *Teaching Creativity through Metaphor: An Integrated Brain Approach*, which capitalized on the growing knowledge of brain functioning and hemispheric specialization. Sanders and Sanders reviewed the current literature and then presented examples of the use of metaphorical strategies with a variety of detailed classroom lessons. Just recently Alane Jordan Starko (1995) published *Creativity in the Classroom*. Starko reviews current theory and knowledge about creativity theory and method, but Part 2 of her book discusses creativity and classroom life: creativity in the content areas, teaching creative thinking skills and habits, motivation and classroom organization, and assessment.

This volume, *The Educational Psychology of Creativity*, continues the tradition of applying creativity knowledge to education practice. This book is designed to be used in a college-level course on creativity and problem solving whose focus is on creativity education. In that regard, this volume distinguishes itself from those just mentioned. A major purpose of this volume is to organize the current knowledge base for educational researchers and individuals responsible for training teachers. Educational reform cannot succeed without the cooperation of teachers who are, in most cases, responsible for implementing the reforms. Thus, to teach for creativity in the classroom requires teachers who are steeped in an educational psychology of creativity, who are informed of the research and knowledge base concerning creativity, who are aware of the factors influencing creativity development, and who believe that they, themselves, can effectively teach for creativity.

The Educational Psychology of Creativity is not directly concerned with geniuses, Nobel or Pulitzer prizewinners, Tony Award winners, or other gifted individuals who have achieved international recognition for their creativity. This book concerns the teaching of creative thinking skills and attitudes to children and adults of so-called "normal" abilities. This volume is based on the assumption that creativity is a normal human process, but, like anything else, it occasionally may need a little help to get started and to keep going. From this assumption, it follows that creativity can be considered a normally distributed trait and, given the right conditions, most people can learn to be more creative. A common understanding of creativity is that it is the production of something novel or original that is useful and that our society values. If we take the meaning of *novel* or *original* to refer only to the ideas and products of those very few creative geniuses that seem to be born to every age, then the *average* person has no need of creativity education. On the other hand, if we consider that each of us in our own *normalcy* can solve a problem for the first time, write a poem, conduct an experiment, build a shelf, follow a new recipe, decorate a room, or do countless other things for the first time and for our own joy and productiveness, then there is a reason for an educational psychology of creativity.

I have organized the book into five sections. The first section is an introduction. In chapter 1, I present a short discussion about the scope and purpose of an educational psychology of creativity. Part II contains two articles addressing theories of the creative process. Part III contains three chapters focusing on recognizing creative potential and ability. Part IV presents five chapters concerned with fostering creativity. The volume concludes with a reflection by Torrance on the state and progress of creativity knowledge. Brief introductions also are provided to Parts II, III, and IV in an effort to integrate the various chapters. At the end of this book, I include brief biographical sketches of the contributors, an annotated list of some popular and comprehensive volumes on creativity, and a list of several creativity organizations.

ACKNOWLEDGMENTS

I wish to thank my contributors, of course, for their energy, creativity, timeliness, and patience.

I owe a special thanks to my colleague, Giselle Esquivel, who contributed two chapters to this book despite a heavy load of teaching, her own doctoral mentoring of students, and administrative duties as a program coordinator.

Many thanks go to Joseph Khatena and E. Paul Torrance for keeping in touch with me during the creative process and encouraging my efforts. The title *Educational Psychology of Creativity* was inspired by Khatena's (1982) *Educational Psychology of the Gifted*.

My mentor, John Feldhusen, underwent an operation during the writing of this volume but continued his efforts and for his dedication and many other things dating since my time with him at Purdue, I owe him a debt of gratitude.

William Michael also contributed despite an illness and his spirit and final product are greatly appreciated.

A number of graduate students and associates helped me during various stages of research and writing: Analise Buonnano, Happy Burdugo, Hiromi Komura, Rosanne Lerner, Dr. Maury Lesser, Lynne McVey, Ruth Okoye, Cathryn Patricola, Kristin Peters, Dr. Ellis Scope, Dr. Fern Sandler, Dr. Patricia Sinatra, Dr. Elaine Singer, and Dr. Ilene Weinerman. Their help ranged from looking up references to listening to me talk to just being interested in creativity and problem solving.

Many other wonderful people contributed in various ways to this book—students, colleagues, friends, family members. I must mention one of my closest friends, Molly Arons, whose creativity in word and deed is often on display. And, Molly, I will always remember Mac.

I also wish to thank Barbara Bernstein and the staff of Hampton Press for their hard work and support.

Finally, let me wish Creed, Kelli, Ashley, Lindsay, and those they care for, a very creative future.

—John C. Houtz

REFERENCES

Khatena, J. (1982). *Educational psychology of the gifted.* New York: Wiley.

Michael, W. B. (1968). *Teaching for creative endeavor: Bold new venture.* Bloomington: Indiana University Press.

Sanders, D. A., & Sanders, J. A. (1983). *Teaching creativity through metaphor: An integrated brain approach.* New York: Longman.

Starko, A. J. (1995). *Creativity in the classroom: Schools of curious delight.* White Plains, NY: Longman.

Torrance, E. P. (1970). *Creativity in the classroom.* Dubuque, IA: Wm. C. Brown.

Part I

Introduction

Part 1

Introduction

1

The Educational Psychology of Creativity

John C. Houtz
Fordham University

Educational psychology is the study of learning and teaching. It is that branch of psychology that is primarily concerned with the factors that influence how children and adults learn or are taught in formal educational settings (Eggen & Kauchak, 1992; Goetz, Alexander, & Ash, 1992; Slavin, 1988). As a field of study, educational psychology has a long—and many agree distinguished—history, but also an extremely wide-ranging one. Because educational psychologists are interested in learning and teaching, their theory and research have taken them into areas also traveled by many other specialists, including developmental, social, experimental, and comparative psychologists, counselors, curriculum developers, evaluators and psychometricians, school administrators, health care specialists, and technologists.

Despite their varied interests, educational psychologists are always guided by the major driving force of their discipline—discovering the conditions under which people best learn from planned instruction. The theories, principles, and practices of educational psychology are, thus, unique to educational psychology. William James (1899/1958), one of the founders of the discipline, clearly described the unique "position" or mission of educational psychology when he wrote that: "Psychology is a science and education is an art, and sciences do not generate arts out of themselves. It requires an intermediary, inventive mind to make the connections" (James, 1899/1958, p. 6).

3

The concept of educational psychology as the intermediary agent or the "linking science" (Grinder, 1989; Thorndike, 1910) has served the discipline well for nearly a century. Current views of the discipline remain essentially unchanged (Shuell, 1990). It is the role of educational psychologists to develop theories and principles that bridge the gaps between the experimental laboratory and the schoolhouse, between the psychologist-researcher and the classroom teacher. It has been a controversial position and an uncomfortable role sometimes. The field has had its share of failures. But, educational psychologists never experience as much criticism as when they stray too far from their original purpose—when their research and writing seem irrelevant to the needs and concerns of educators (Ausubel, 1968).

In 1950, J. P. Guilford addressed the annual convention of the American Psychological Association and called attention to the lack of research on human creativity (Guilford, 1950). What a shame it was, he argued, that psychologists had not given much attention to this important—nay essential—human ability. Creativity was necessary for our survival as a species. Our health, happiness, and futures depended on our individual and collective creativeness. Researchers were conducting too few studies to learn what creativity was about, what helps or hinders it, or how we could make people more creative.

Guilford felt strongly about creativity. He had been involved in manpower training research during World War II. His efforts took him into new areas of human abilities and his developing theory—later to be called the Structure of Intellect (Guilford, 1967)—was leading him to the belief that many abilities of which adults were capable and that were very important to success in life were rarely, if ever, attended to in the formal educational system. As was the concern of the times, these skills could literally mean the difference between life and death.

Guilford, of course, was very much aware of decades of psychological research and theory on human differences. The development of tests of intellectual potential in the early 1900s by Alfred Binet in France and then Binet and Lewis Terman at Stanford University were watershed events (Terman, 1926). Terman's longitudinal studies of "genius" were well known and yielding by the 1940s substantial data about the successful lives of highly intelligent people (Burks, Jensen, & Terman, 1930; Terman & Oden, 1947, 1959). However, what most may have impressed Guilford, Terman, and others was the perception that IQ, alone, was not enough to predict significant accomplishment in life.

Terman's subjects were, in the main, very productive and happy people, which was an important finding. (There are many who continue to believe in links between intellectual giftedness and such negative characteristics as mental instability, poor physical health, and unhappiness.)

But, although Terman's subjects fared well, even outstanding by "normal curve" standards, they had not (and were not to) become the most creative contributors to their respective areas of endeavor. There were no Einsteins or Picassos, for example. Guilford's work during the war, his research, and his developing theory of human intelligence suggested that there were many more abilities than those typically measured by the IQ tests of the day. Similarly, the typical curriculum offered to children and youth in schools included only a small minority of the total possible human abilities.

In the late 1950s and early 1960s, another figure in the study of creativity began research that would come to transform the field. E. Paul Torrance began the Minnesota Studies of Creative Behavior at the University of Minnesota, which led to the development of a standardized measure of creativity potential. First published in 1966, the Torrance Tests of Creative Thinking, as they have come to be known, were based on a clear and concrete definition of *creativity:* "Creativity is the process of sensing gaps or disturbing missing elements; forming ideas or hypotheses concerning them; testing these hypotheses; and communicating the results; possibly modifying and retesting the hypotheses" (Torrance, 1962, p. 16).

The importance of this definition cannot be understated. For the first time, a relatively concrete definition of a very abstract, even mystical, concept was available for people to use to examine their theories and instructional practices. Torrance's definition is the one that leads the thinking behind this text, for it is focused on educable abilities. It speaks of specific skills that can be enhanced through deliberate teaching and other instructional activities. Naturally, not everyone agrees with Torrance's definition, but his tests, in both verbal and figural forms, have provided many researchers and educators with their first useful tool to identify creative potential in "so-called" average people.

The educational psychology of creativity, therefore, is that body of theory, knowledge, and practice concerned with the identification and measurement of creativity, the enhancement of this capacity, and the examination of factors that influence the development of creativity in systematic ways. Over the past decades, numerous writers have characterized the field of creativity research as involving four major foci (Brown, 1989; Dellas & Gaier, 1970; Golann, 1963; Khatena, 1976; Mooney, 1963; Rhodes, 1961; Simonton, 1988): These foci include research on the following:

1. The steps or processes involved in creating.
2. Research on the lives, work styles, or personal histories of creative persons.

3. Research on the measurement of creative products or development of tests or other procedures for identifying the potential for creativity in people.
4. Study of the conditions in the environment that aid or hinder development of creativity; and techniques for deliberately increasing creativity, creative thinking, or creative problem solving.

Rhodes (1961) and Simonton (1988) referred to these categories as the four "p's": person, product, process, and press (Rhodes) or persuasion (Simonton). In each of these areas, different theoretical views, methods of research, and instrumentation have forged a wide range of approaches to the field. From a theoretical point of view, associationists, behaviorists, Gestaltists, cognitivists, developmentalists, and humanists have proposed explanations for creative thinking processes, products, personality development, and environmental influences. Needless to say, different theoretical approaches often disagree on definitions of the phenomena under study, how to properly measure the phenomena, or what factors should be stressed if one is interested in changing the phenomena.

From a methodological perspective, researchers have used both experimental and correlational procedures. Studies have examined the effects of specific environmental manipulations on subjects' creative performance, both in molecular (e.g., individual teaching behaviors or other instructional variables) or molar (whole classroom or school organization) events. Research has correlated numerous measures of personality traits or characteristics, attitudes, interests, or family histories and backgrounds, for example, with measures of individuals' creative performance or creative work styles.

In addition, researchers have used both quantitative and qualitative methods. Obviously, Terman, Guilford, Torrance, and other educational psychologists developed test instruments and procedures to quantify creativity and creative potential. These devices have been widely used. But quite a number of researchers spent their time in detailed case study of creative individuals, their histories and work habits, using extensive interview and observational procedures. In the case of the study of individuals who were deceased, researchers studied their work, read about their lives from autobiographical writings, memoirs, letters, or other records from their estates, or from the writings of their biographers, contemporaries, and historians.

In the area of instrumentation, there is perhaps the greatest diversity of all the areas of creativity study. As previously mentioned, there are tests for creativity or creative potential. Sources claim that there are hundreds of such instruments (Hocevar, 1981; Petrosko, 1978). Besides tests, there are rating scales for people to rate themselves on a host of personal habits, interests, abilities, or activities. There are rating scales and systems developed for one's peers or "expert" judges to use when rating actual creative products of people. As might be imagined, there can be as many of these as there are specific types of creative products (e.g., for rating scientific discoveries, literature, painting, sculpture, music, dance, sports achievements, etc.). Within each of these areas, there are important subspecialties as well (e.g., in literature, different types of poetry, dramatic and comedic plays, science fiction, action-adventure, mystery, romance novels, short stories, biographies, etc.).

The study of creative products has generated much debate among researchers and educators as to what is important in the study of creativity. Despite decades of work, there is no universally accepted definition of creativity or set of criteria for determining in an objective way just how creative an idea or invention may be. Torrance and others have identified such characteristics as fluency, flexibility, originality, elaboration, or resistance to closure. Other qualities that have been used include novelty, social acceptance, transformation, surprise, and, of course, problem solution.

That such variety exists in the study of creativity is both frustrating and encouraging. Recall that educational psychology, itself, is a two-pronged discipline. It is concerned with research and theory on the one hand and reality and pedagogical practice on the other. In its middle person role, educational psychology must constantly try to pull together two different sets of ideas and value systems. Creativity, by most accounts, involves a similar process of pulling together disparate, often opposing, thoughts. Rothenberg (1971), for example, wrote of Janusian thinking to suggest the essential spark of creativity comes from resolving opposite ideas into a new, integrating conceptualization. Koestler (1964) described a bi-associative process to explain how creative ideas come into being. Arieti (1970) wrote of a tertiary process leading to creativity. This tertiary level of thinking enables typically uncompromising or unyielding primary and secondary thought processes to resolve themselves into a productive new formulation.

The creativity literature is replete with reference to or use of conflict resolution in one form or another as a key to the creative process. Studies of the personality characteristics or interest patterns of creative persons show that these individuals have wide-ranging interests and often exhibit conflicting traits or habits (Dellas & Gaier, 1970). Yet, these conflicts do not lead to pathological behavior in most individuals. Despite a commonplace belief that genius, creativity, and mental illness are related (Prentky, 1980), most creative people, as do most individuals at large, lead stable, productive lives. Creativity may require great divergence of thought, but it also requires a perseverance and singleness of purpose sufficient to see a way through conflict, confusion, and insecurity.

Of course, I am not speaking of violent conflicts, such as war or criminal acts or other types of antisocial behavior, but of nonviolent forms of conflict, such as questioning authoritative ideas, seeking alternative viewpoints, making constructive criticisms, wanting to do things differently and expressing those wishes, challenging the current wisdom or reasons for rules and practices. Because the educational psychology of creativity is concerned with understanding and fostering creativity in formal instructional situations, the idea that conflict is key to creative development is very important. Schools (and society, generally) do not, as a rule, tolerate conflict well. In fact, in the main, schools actively discourage most forms of questioning, criticism, and resistance to authority. Controversial views are often ignored or suppressed. Alternative answers to problems are rarely rewarded. School structures, teaching methods, curricular content, and standards of acceptable student conduct are established specifically to prevent or punish ideas or behaviors that deviate too much from what has been determined to be acceptable.

The challenge, then, of an educational psychology of creativity is threefold:

1. To help educators understand the essential nature of creativity.
2. To help educators recognize creativity in themselves and their students.
3. To help educators foster creativity and creative attitudes, through programs, teaching techniques, support services, and other procedures.

I asked the contributors to this volume to write about particular areas of creativity research from the point of view of applications to education. As stated here, this text uses Torrance's definition of creativity. The focus is on understanding, measuring, and developing the creative thinking and problem-solving skills in all students, not simply the intellectually or creatively gifted. From this point of view, for Torrance and many others involved in the study and promotion of creativity, there is much that has been learned. The educational psychology of creativity offers a great deal to educators and policymakers as we attempt to respond to the criticisms directed at our educational system and improve our instructional practices. The knowledge base about creativity can help us meet the needs of schoolchildren as we try to prepare them for today's complex society as well as the projected needs of tomorrow.

REFERENCES

Ausubel, D. (1968). *Educational psychology: A cognitive view*. New York: Holt, Rinehart Winston.

Arieti, S. (1970). *Creativity: The magic synthesis*. New York: Basic Books.

Brown, R. (1989). Creativity: What are we to measure? In J. Glover, R. Ronning, & C. Reynolds (Eds.), *Handbook of creativity* (pp. 3-32). New York: Plenum.

Burks, B., Jensen, D., & Terman, L. (1930). *The promise of youth: Follow-up studies of a thousand gifted children*. Stanford, CA: Stanford University Press.

Dellas, M., & Gaier, E. (1970). Identification of creativity: The individual. *Psychological Bulletin, 73*, 55-73.

Eggen, P., & Kauchak, D. (1992). *Educational psychology: Classroom connections*. New York: Macmillan.

Goetz, E., Alexander, P., & Ash, M. (1992). *Educational psychology: A classroom perspective*. New York: Macmillan.

Golann, S. E. (1963). Psychological study of creativity. *Psychological Bulletin, 63*, 548-565.

Grinder, R. (1989). Educational psychology: The master science. In M. Wittrock & F. Farley (Eds.), *The future of educational psychology* (pp. 3-18). Hillsdale, NJ: Lawrence Erlbaum Associates.

Guilford, J. P. (1950). Creativity. *American Psychologist, 5*, 444-454.

Guilford, J. P. (1967). *The nature of human intelligence*. New York: McGraw-Hill.

Hocevar, D. (1981). Measurement of creativity: Review and critique. *Journal of Personality Measurement, 45*, 450-464.

James, W. (1958). *Talks to teachers on psychology and to students on some of life's ideals*. New York: Dover. (Original work published 1899)

Khatena, J. (1976). Major directions in creativity research. *Gifted Child Quarterly, 20*, 336-349.

Koestler, A. (1964). *The act of creation*. New York: Macmillan.

Mooney, J. (1963). A conceptual model for integrating four approaches to the identification of creative talent. In C. Taylor & F. Barron (Eds.), *Scientific creativity: Its recognition and development* (pp. 331-340). New York: Wiley.

Petrosko, J. (1978). Measuring creativity in the elementary school: The state of the art. *Journal of Creative Behavior, 12*, 109-119.

Prentky, R. (1980). *Creativity and psychopathology: A neurocognitive perspective*. New York: Praeger.

Rhodes, M. (1961). An analysis of creativity. *Phi Delta Kappan, 42*, 305-310.

Rothenberg, A. (1971). The process of Janusian thinking in creativity. *Archives of General Psychiatry, 24,* 195-205.

Shuell, T. (1990). Working in the middle—The nature of educational psychology. *Newsletter for Educational Psychologists, 14*(1), 1, 4.

Simonton, D. (1988). Creativity, leadership, and chance. In R. Sternberg (Ed.), *The nature of creativity* (pp. 386-426). New York: Cambridge University Press.

Slavin, R. (1988). *Educational psychology: Theory into practice* (2nd ed.). Englewood Cliffs, NJ: Prentice-Hall.

Terman, L. (1926). *Mental and physical traits of a thousand gifted children.* Stanford, CA: Stanford University Press.

Terman, L., & Oden, M. (1947). *The gifted child grows up: Twenty-five years' follow-up of a superior group.* Stanford, CA: Stanford University Press.

Terman, L., & Oden, M. (1959). *The gifted group at mid-life: Thirty-five years' follow-up of the superior child.* Stanford, CA: Stanford University Press.

Thorndike, E. (1910). The contribution of psychology to education. *Journal of Educational Psychology, 1,* 5–12.

Torrance, E. P. (1962). *Guiding creative talent.* Englewood Cliffs, NJ: Prentice-Hall.

Torrance, E. P. (1974). *The Torrance Tests of Creative Thinking.* Bensenville, IL: Scholastic Test Service. (Original work published 1966)

Part II

Objective 1:
Understanding the
Creative Process

The first objective of the educational psychology of creativity is understanding the nature of the creative process. Theories of creativity are many and varied and exceptional references exist describing them (Runco & Albert, 1990; Sternberg, 1988). Elsewhere (Houtz, 1994), I have written about four theoretical traditions that have attempted to explain creative phenomena: (a) the associationist-behaviorist approach, (b) the psychodynamic personality approach, (c) the cognitive information-processing approach, and (d) the developmental-humanistic approach. Each approach makes use of different constructs and mechanisms to describe the creative process and each has important contributions to make to the education and development of creative abilities.

For this volume, I have selected two theories: the psychoanalytic-psychodynamic approach to explaining creativity and the cognitive-constructivist approach to explaining creative thinking. In chapter 2, Esquivel writes about the psychodynamic approach. In chapter 3, Runco describes the cognitive view of creativity. These two approaches to creativity explanation were selected for two reasons. First, they represent relatively dominant but diverse viewpoints, each with history and tradition and large followings. Second, the two viewpoints recognize each others' importance in the overall picture of creative performance. No explanation is complete without taking into account both the cognitive and affective dimensions of human behavior. As the psychodynamic and cognitive theories have developed, both have come to discuss the interaction and interplay between mental operations and personality traits, cognitive abilities and cognitive styles, intelligence and emotion.

There are other theorists and approaches, however. The field of creativity theory and research has, as might be suspected, diverse creative people studying it and trying to understand and explain it. But, for the purposes of a simple beginning to this book, the psychoanalytic-psychodynamic and the cognitive-constructivist approaches illustrate the range of constructs and concepts, language, and methods used and useful for studying creative thinking, feeling, and action processes.

REFERENCES

Houtz, J. C. (1994). Creative problem solving in the classroom: Contributions of four psychological approaches. In M. A. Runco (Ed.), *Problem finding, problem solving, and creativity* (pp. 153-173). Norwood, NJ: Ablex.

Runco, M. A., & Albert, R. (Eds.). (1990). *Theories of creativity.* Newbury Park, CA: Sage.

Sternberg, R. J. (Ed.). (1988). *The nature of creativity: Contemporary psychological approaches.* New York: Cambridge University Press.

2

Psychodynamic Theories of Creativity

Giselle B. Esquivel
Fordham University

This chapter examines psychodynamic theoretical perspectives on the creative process and the basis for creative ability within the context of personality functioning. The development of concepts about creativity is traced from its origins in traditional psychoanalytic thinking to more contemporary psychodynamic formulations. An underlying theme of psychodynamic explanations of creativity is the relation between the creative process and pathology, with differing views emerging from the writings of Freud, Jung, Kris, Kubie, and Rank.

In formulating his theory of personality, Freud (1958) described two mental states or levels of consciousness that serve as the context in which personality structures operate. The conscious mind is the state of awareness that gives possibility to rational thinking and to psychological processes of a higher order, referred to as the *secondary process*. The unconscious is that state of mind inaccessible to awareness by ordinary means and characterized by more primitive and symbolic *primary processes*. Freud gave greater emphasis to the unconscious mind as the potential source for both pathological and creative processes.

Freud designated three main personality structures that function at the different levels of consciousness as the id, the ego, and the superego. The id sits in the unconscious mind as an irrational force made up primarily of biologically based instinctual impulses that are governed by the pleasure principle and seek consciousness in the form of wishes and fantasies or symbolically as dreams. The superego is the moral agent or conscience derived from parental and societal values and developed through the process of identification with the parent of the opposite gender. The superego has both conscious and unconscious elements and can range from very harsh to weak or can fail to develop in more pathological cases. The ego is that aspect of personality within the realm of consciousness composed of more autonomous functions such as attention and reasoning. Guided by the reality principle, the ego mediates between the id and the superego and maintains personality balance by a regulatory process that, if successful, is adaptive to the demands of reality. As part of this regulating process, the ego uses various defense mechanisms that serve to ward off anxiety arising from the threat of id impulses and appease the guilt-enducing superego. The three most important defense mechanisms in relation to creativity are repression, regression, and sublimation.

Repression is the mechanism by which unacceptable id impulses, conflicts, and associations are blocked off from conscious awareness and memory. Some extent of repression is needed and viewed as adaptive. However, excessive repression can lead to neurotic symptoms, which are disguised forms of the impulse being repressed, and to personality maladjustment and dysfunction. Someone with a repressed personality style may be limited in spontaneity, fantasy, and creativity.

Regression is the opposite of repression in that through this process there is a weakening of conscious control and a return to earlier less mature modes of behavior or to a breakthrough of id impulses. Although adaptive as a temporary response to anxiety and stress, regression, in its extreme, represents a breakdown of defenses, as found in psychotic functioning.

Sublimation is the most adaptive defense mechanism, giving rise to civilization and to constructive aspects of society. Through sublimation, the energy arising from unacceptable id impulses is channeled into more positive substitutes that both please the superego and allow for impulse release in accordance with reality. Some common sublimated substitutes are contact sports and weight watcher meals that provide overindulgence without guilt. Freud associated sublimation with the creative process.

How did Freud relate his theory of personality to creativity? Freud alluded briefly to the creative process in some of his works, including *Interpretation of Drama* (Freud, 1953) and *Creative Writers and Daydreaming* (Freud, 1959). He saw a similarity between dreams, humor (Freud, 1964), and creativity. In *Creative Writers and Daydreaming*, Freud (1959) traced the origins of creativity to the unconscious mind and to conflictual id impulses that could also set the condition for neurotic symptoms. Although Freud saw unconscious conflict as the preliminary stage for both symptoms of illness and creativity, he pointed to the use of sublimation, rather than repression or regression, as the primary defense mechanism involved in creativity. By using sublimation, the creative person is able to reconstruct the impulse and to divert its energy into more meaningful and acceptable creative activity.

The ability to use sublimation in response to conflict and as part of the creative process may be traced back to childhood. In *Leonardo Da Vinci: A Study in Psychosexuality*, Freud (1957) described how in childhood the tendency to investigate is associated originally with sexual curiosity and can be thwarted by repression of the unacceptable sexual impulse. Another way in which the child may react to sexual curiosity is by becoming a compulsive thinker or intellectualizing in a rigid manner. A more adaptive response is sublimation through which instinctual energy invested in the sexual impulse is transferred to intellectual curiosity, resulting in a reduced need to repress. This type of curiosity is characteristic of creative individuals.

According to Freud (1959), the child learns to use sublimation through play activities. By investing a great deal of time, energy and affect in imaginative and pretending activities, the child is able to express conflicts and rearrange the world in a way that is pleasing. Nevertheless, this reconstruction through fantasy is still tied to reality. Play, therefore, forms the basis for the mechanism of sublimation by allowing the child to develop appropriate ways for dealing with wishes. This concept has been corroborated by other developmental theorists, like Piaget, who describe play as central in affective as well as social and cognitive development.

For adults, the creative process is a substitute for play and a means of fulfilling a basic wish or fantasy in a socially acceptable manner and of reconstructing or correcting unsatisfactory reality. According to Freud (1959), the time element is important in this process. First, some current condition arouses a wish fulfillment, usually of an infantile nature, then a situation is created and projected to the future or to some completed product. In this way, past, present and future are strung together, with the wish, arising from the unconscious, running through it.

To summarize, Freud saw creativity and neurotic conflict as similar processes having the same unconscious basis, except that in creativity sublimation is operant instead of repression. Sublimation develops in childhood and is linked to play and imaginary activity, with some similarity to humor, daydreaming, and the night dreaming process.

Jung (1966) departed from Freud's explanation of creativity as being based on unconscious conflict and with sublimation as the mechanism through which the creative process originates. Jung differentiated between common creative endeavor and true creativity. He agreed with Freud that individual unconscious conflictual experiences may result in certain creative works reflective of symptomatology, but unique creative acts are the result of the collective unconscious. Jung described the collective unconscious as a supra-personality structure within the brain that contains the evolutionary history of mankind in the form of symbolic archetypes or mythological figures that are not available to the conscious mind, but can surface freely and with force as an autonomous complex. Although the autonomous complex can be perceived, it is not subject to conscious control and cannot be inhibited or expressed voluntarily.

The autonomous complex arises when the unconscious region of the psyche is thrown into activity and becomes extended with associations. The energy involved in this process is withdrawn from consciousness, resulting in a weakening of conscious activity, apathetic inactivity or regressive behaviors very commonly seen in artists. From the energy withdrawn from conscious control, the autonomous complex surfaces.

The creative autonomous complex is similar to other autonomous complexes, including those that present themselves in the form of certain types of mental disorders, in the loss of conscious control, but the creative process results in symbolic representations that have universal meaning and purpose. In the creative process, the autonomous complex carries the primordial imagery or archetypes from the collective unconscious into consciousness that are then experienced intensely and shaped by the creative individual into a creative product embedded within symbolic and deep social meaning. Perhaps a good illustration of Jung's concept of creativity is illustrated by Picasso's painting, *Guernica*, in which the depiction of distorted mythological figures makes a powerful social statement about war and the ills of modern society and carries with it universal meaning.

Ernst Kris, an art historian and psychoanalyst, has examined creativity from the perspective of ego psychology, a psychodynamic view that places greater emphasis on the autonomous functions of the ego, extending its role beyond that of mediator between the id and superego. Kris (1952) viewed the ego as playing a major role in the creative process by means of an adaptive regressive mechanism that taps the sources of preconscious and unconscious experience in a purposeful way. Although Freud did not distinguish between conscious and preconscious processes, Kris described preconscious experience as extending beyond logical thought, reflective thinking, and daydreaming to relatively freer and deeper fantasies and symbolic functions that have greater proximity with the unconscious. In essence, the preconscious system stands as a barrier between the ego and the id. In the creative process, the ego relaxes its repressive functions and regulates regression voluntarily and temporarily so that the barrier becomes more permeable, allowing id primary processes to reach preconsciousness more easily. Because these impulses are under ego control, they are not destructive but transformed through preconscious functions. The energy previously invested by the ego in repressing id impulses (as a result of superego demands) becomes available for conscious adaptation and elaboration and enhances reflective thinking and problem solving, and gives meaning to other types of creative activity. Kris termed this self-regulated process "regression in the service of the ego" (p. 138).

According to Kris (1952), the self-regulated regressive process is reflected in clinical observations of creative individuals and introspective reports of creative experiences and may be related to different stages in the creative process. Kris associated periods of intense concentration and deliberation with involvement in preconscious thinking that result in insight and clarification after a period of incubation or rest. At times, an external stimulus may promote this process. For example, Newton attributed the discovery of the law of gravity to the observation of a falling apple. The perception acted as a factor precipitating previously organized preconscious ideas. The inspirational phase may be explained by greater accessibility of id impulses which in becoming conscious are experienced as release of tension. The deep feelings felt are reminders of more passive-receptive experiences of infancy, combined with high intellectual ability. The elaboration phase is associated with greater reinforcement of conscious aspects at the final stage of the creative process. At this stage, more conscious aspects take over, work is slower, and there is greater investment in reality testing and in the formulation of meaningful communication. A sense of mastery in pursuit of creative activity provides functional pleasure. A feeling of satisfaction is achieved when the successful solution of a problem is attained or when preconscious deliberation has led to a satisfactory conscious conclusion.

Kubie (1958) gave even greater emphasis to the role of the preconscious mind in the creative process and rejected the idea of unconscious conflict as the basis for creativity, but saw it rather as drastically interfering with that process. Kubie viewed health and creativity as positively related. Creativity is the ability to be flexible, to learn through experience, to change and to become influenced. Illness or neurosis, characterized by rigidity or "the freezing of behavior into unalterable and insatiable patterns" (p. 144), is the opposite of creativity.

According to Kubie, the preconscious system forms the basis for creative activity and unless preconscious processes flow freely, creativity cannot emerge. Preconscious processes do not operate alone but are under the influence of the conscious and unconscious systems, whose symbolic functions are more anchored and rigid. In the conscious system, the symbols, as represented by thought and language, are under awareness yet limited by reality. These symbolic representations do not allow for free imaginative play and limit the vividness of past and present experiences. The unconscious symbolic processes are even more rigid and fixed representations of repressed experiences that are inaccessible except by special methods or states. Moreover, unconscious processes lead to repetitive and stereotypic patterns that can affect the creative process.

The creative individual shows greater flexibility than others in making an effort to be open to preconscious processes and to reactivate early sensory and emotional experiences. Kubie defined creativity as the ability, therefore, to engage in free play with preconscious symbolic processes. This means, for example, finding new and unexpected connections, relationships, and meanings, or working freely with conscious and preconscious metaphor, slang, puns, double meanings and figures of speech that are not tied into conscious and unconscious areas of personality. According to Kubie, traditional methods of education either tie up preconscious processes prematurely to reality or leave those processes open to the distracting influences arising from unresolved unconscious conflict.

Rank (1960) was initially associated with traditional psychoanalytic thinking but, later, he developed a theory of personality that emphasized the concept of individual will, and consequently, centered his concept of creativity around that theory. Rank's personality typology differentiated between three types of individuals: the artist or productive individual, the neurotic individual, and the average or adaptive individual.

Contrary to Freud's emphasis on the unconscious and extending beyond the concepts of regression in the service of the ego and the role of the preconscious postulated by Kris and Kubie, Rank viewed creativity as a process that involves a greater degree of will and consciousness. Rank described the artist as possessing a personality style that is in conflict with society as a result of his or her high level of awareness and willfulness. The artist type fears ordinary experience and death, wishes to transcend the moment into something meaningful, and seeks immortality through productive work. Rank referred mostly to literary and artistic productions. Artists can draw from internal life experiences, such as romanticists, or from external or naturalistic life sources, such as the classicists, but the attempt is to surpass those experiences. Abstract productions are more objectified and the result of higher degrees of consciousness of the creative purpose. This concept has both similarities and discrepancies with Jung's formulations, which point to the loss of conscious will in transcending abstract creations.

According to Rank, the artistic personality is developed through an internal process that is not totally conscious or willful, but bound up with life experiences. In other words, the creative impulse is manifested chiefly in personality and rooted in life experiences, yet it transcends that experience. For the artist, the will takes the form of a constructive impulse that is quite different from the analytic conception of the biological impulse that is repressed or sublimated. Creativity can be stimulated or influenced by the sexual impulse, but not in a direct way.

The neurotic individual's fear of life is stronger than the fear of death and the will serves as an excessive check on the impulsive life, or a repressive function. In the psychopath, the will affirms the impulse instead of controlling it; therefore, this personality disorder is characterized by a weak will subjected to instinctual impulses. The average individual shows a greater degree of self-acceptance, conventionality and adaptation to ordinary life experiences. However, the artistic individual, despite at times dramatizing his or her pathological features in an attempt to differentiate from the average, shows, according to Rank, the highest level of personality functioning.

DISCUSSION

The psychoanalytic perspective on creativity provided a basic framework for understanding creativity within the context of personality functioning. All of the exponents shared a common basis for explaining creativity in terms of internal psychological processes or mechanisms that operate at various levels of consciousness. Although they differed in their explanations of the specific sources of creativity (in terms of the unconscious, preconscious, and conscious levels), they all saw the qualitative nature of creativity as involving freer, imaginative, playful, flexible, sensorial and childlike features. Moreover, the descriptions they offered were similar regarding the outcome of the creative process as being meaningful, reality based, original, and fulfilling a significant social or universal role.

A central underlying concept tied into the psychoanalytic formulations was the relation that exists between creativity and pathology. This association may have been due to the emphasis placed by early psychoanalytic theory on abnormal personality functioning and its pervasive influence on later psychodynamic conceptualizations of creativity and personality. Based on the theoretical controversy and the views expressed by psychoanalytic writers around this issue, some critical questions may be raised: Do creative and pathological processes share the same psychological basis? Do creativity and pathology involve basically the same processes but with the latter taking a negative direction? Are creativity and pathology two parallel processes that are either similar in some aspects or that can at least co-exist? Are creativity and pathology two incompatible and totally opposite processes?

Do Creative and Pathological Processes Share the Same Psychological Basis? According to Arieti (1976), Freud was mostly concerned with motivational aspects of creativity rather than with the essence of creativity itself. Consistent with his deterministic views, Freud saw both creativity and neurosis as stemming from the same unconscious roots. At the same time, he described the two processes as subsequently becoming quite distinct and differentiated. Psychologically, the creative child is able to develop the ability to sublimate and to turn conflict into imaginative play and creative activity. Although he does not offer an exact explanation as to how this occurs, one may infer from Freud's personality theory that the child's inner experiences, fantasy, and play behaviors, as well as his or her early interaction with parental figures, play a significant role in the development of more creative processes and adaptive defense mechanisms in response to conflict. Nevertheless, there can be no creativity without unconscious conflict. From a different viewpoint, Arieti (1976) emphasized the fact that although creativity and pathology may sometimes share the same motivational basis, the creative process bypasses its origins. Citing the life of Da Vinci as an example, he explained that many people experience frustrations as well as stimulating and encouraging relationships with significant others, yet not all become creative. Thus, there is more to creativity than a conflictual motivational basis.

Do Creativity and Pathology Involve Basically the Same Process But With the Latter Taking a Different Direction? Farley (1981) shared this assumption in relation to individuals or youth who are socially maladjusted. Farley proposed that a low arousal level that leads to stimulation seeking is a characteristic shared by creative and delinquent individuals and that creativity and delinquency are connected by the need for hyperstimulation and the search for variety and intensity of experience. Both creative and delinquent persons reject norms and rules, engage in high energy activities and exhibit risk-taking behaviors. Although the creative person expresses this sensation-seeking motive in constructive creative activities, the socially maladapted person's potential creative abilities are distorted and channeled in negative directions. Farley attributed this discrepancy to detrimental or negative influences, and more specifically to an educational environment that fails to offer opportunities for stimulation of a constructive nature. Farley's view is discrepant with Rank's concept that psychopaths, for example, have very low creative ability and a weak will that is in limited control of instinctual impulses. There is a need to validate also if social maladjustment is the result of thwarted creativity or if other psychological processes are involved. Although there are a number of highly creative individuals who use their creativity toward negative ends, there are many socially maladjusted individuals who are clearly not creative. Moreover, if creativity is defined within a social context or in terms of the social implications and outcomes, it would be difficult to view destructive or antisocial acts, albeit original, as having a similar basis to creativity. Nevertheless, Farley's views pose a challenge in terms of the role of the environment in the development of creativity.

Are Creativity and Pathology Two Parallel Processes That Are Either Similar or Can Coexist? This assumption may be based on observations that many highly creative individuals have manifested characteristics of abnormal behavior (Prentky, 1980). According to Rank (1965), the creative will exists "side to side" or parallel to a neurotic process. The creative will may share some destructive aspects because it is still bound up to personality and experience, and this explains why most productive work involves periods of crises of a neurotic nature and why the relation between creativity and illness has been misinterpreted; nevertheless, Rank viewed creativity as a distinct process. Its function is not an adaptive one as in the average person, but, rather, a meaningful and transcendental one.

In referring to Vincent Van Gogh, Arieti (1976) expressed the fact that the artist was creative "in spite of" his depressed state and that his work deteriorated when suffering from psychotic episodes, but, nevertheless, evolved and flourished in periods of sanity. Similarly, Kris' (1952) concept of "regression in the service of the ego" assumes that regression can have both positive and negative influences on creativity dependent on the extent of the conscious control involved. One might see how a highly creative individual suffering from an emotional disorder might be able to sustain a positive regressive capability while still subject at times to a weakening of the ego and disruptive regressive forces.

Another explanation of the parallel assumptions is offered by McMullan (1976), who described the creative personality as possessing simultaneously incompatible features that work synergistically toward a creative end. (The two-factor characteristics described by McMullan include detached-involvement, mindless-perception, flexible-persistence, disinterested-selfishness, confident-humility, relaxed-attention, constructive-discontent, delayed-closure, and converging-divergence.) The creative person oscillates between the two poles at different times during the creative process. When operating under the more socially negative extremes the creative person may give the appearance to an observer of disturbance. Similar paradoxical attributes have been supported by Prentky's (1980) neurocognitive studies of creative functions.

Are Creativity and Pathology Incompatible and Totally Opposite Processes? Of all the psychoanalytic thinkers, Kubie upheld this view most strongly. According to Kubie (1958), creativity is not only different from pathology but abnormal processes interfere with the creative function. From a greater extension, Schachtel (1959), a psychoanalyst who departed from Freud's theory, defined creativity in terms of allocentric perceptions or the ability to be open to experience on a higher level of consciousness. Similarly, humanists like Abraham Maslow (1963) and Carl Rogers (1954) have described creativity as the epitome of mental health.

STUDY ACTIVITIES

1. Describe how a theory of personality or a specific view of human nature will influence the way in which creativity is conceptualized. Can creativity be explained outside of the context of personality functioning?
2. Examine and explore the basic assumptions made by each of the basic questions discussed in this chapter. Write an essay in support of or against any one of these viewpoints. Discuss the merits or fallacies of each viewpoint.
3. Discuss the concept of "regression in the service of the ego," providing examples from your own personal experience in any type of creative activity.
4. Study the biography of a creative individual in any field or endeavor. Describe his or her creative life and contribution as it relates to personality factors, including adaptive as well as maladaptive characteristics.
5. Compare the following autobiographical excerpts of high IQ and creative adolescents. How would you characterize each in terms of creative qualities (quality of invention, intensity of affect, playfulness, humor, depth of fantasy ideation, introspectiveness, quality of expression)?

> In 1943 I was born. I have been living without interruption ever since. My parents are my mother and father—an arrangement I have found increasingly convenient over the years. My father is a doctor—physician and surgeon—at least that's what the sign on his office door says. Of course, he's not anymore for Dad's past the age where men ought to enjoy the rest of his life. He retired from Mercy Hospital Christmas before last. Got a fountain pen for 27 years of service. . . . (Getzels & Jackson, 1962, p. 101)

> I was born on November 10, 1942 in Chicago. I was the first of three children to be born to my mother and father. Now I have two younger sisters. My grandmother lives with us. One of my earliest experiences was when I was stuck in our neighbor's hallway. I was only two at the time so I couldn't reach the knob. My grandmother finally found me and I got out. She thought I had been lost. . . . (Getzels & Jackson, 1962, pp. 101-102)

6. Write your own autobiography, attempting to be as creative as possible.

7. Examine this excerpt from the autobiography of a creative adolescent (also from Getzels & Jackson, 1962) in terms of the impact of education in the personality development of creative students.

> I entered a public grammar school shortly after coming to Chicago. It was quite regimented in discipline, which I did not like at all. One of the teachers even threatened to suspend me for chewing gum in class. I was very disturbed also, because everything seemed so unconstructive, and to make up for this I took it upon myself to read several hours a day after school. After seventh grade I transferred to this school on the advice of a psychologist. It suited me better after a rough period of adjustment. No teacher made an impression on me.

REFERENCES

Arieti, S. (1976). *Creativity: The magic synthesis.* New York: Basic Books.

Farley, F. H. (1981). Basic process individual differences: A biologically based theory of individualization for cognitive, affective, and creative outcomes. In F. H. Farley & N. J. Gordon (Eds.), *Psychology and education: The state of the union* (pp. 9-31). Berkeley, CA: McCutchan.

Freud, S. (1953). The interpretation of drama. In J. Strachey (Ed.), *The standard edition of the complete psychological works of Sigmund Freud* (Vols. 4-5). London: Hogarth Press.

Freud, S. (1957). Leonardo Da Vinci: A study in psychosexuality. In J. Strachey (Ed.), *The standard edition of the complete psychological works of Sigmund Freud* (Vol. 11). London: Hogarth Press.

Freud, S. (1958). Formulations on the two principles of mental functioning. In J. Strachey (Ed.), *The standard edition of the complete psychological works of Sigmund Freud* (Vol. 12). London: Hogarth Press.

Freud, S. (1959). Creative writers and day-dreaming. In J. Strachey (Ed.), *The standard edition of the complete psychological works of Sigmund Freud* (Vol. 9). London: Hogarth Press

Freud, S. (1964). Jokes and their relation to the unconscious. In J. Strachey (Ed.), *The standard edition of the complete psychological works of Sigmund Freud* (Vol. 8). London: Hogarth Press.

Getzels, J. W., & Jackson, P. W. (1962). *Creativity and intelligence: Explorations into gifted students.* New York: Wiley.

Jung, C. G. (1966). *On the relation of analytical psychology to poetic art.* London: Routledge & Kegan Paul Ltd. & Princeton, NJ: Princeton University Press.

Kris, E. (1952). *Psychoanalytic explorations in art.* New York: International University Press.

Kubie, L. S. (1958). *Neurotic distortions of the creative process.* Lawrence: University of Kansas Press.

Maslow, A. (1963). The creative attitude. *The Structurist, 3,* 4-10.

McMullan, W. E. (1976). Creative individuals: Paradoxical personages. *Journal of Creative Behavior, 10,* 265-275.

Prentky, R. A. (1980). *Creativity and psychopathology: A neurocognitive perspective.* New York: Praeger.

Rank, O. (1960). *Life and creation: Art and artist.* New York: Knopf.

Rank, O. (1965). Life and creation. In H. M. Ruitenbeek (Ed.), *The creative imagination* (pp. 67-96). Chicago: Quandrangle Books.

Rogers, C. (1954). Toward a theory of creativity. *ETC.: A Review of General Semantics, 11,* 250-258.

Schachtel, E. G. (1959). *Metamorphosis: On the development of affect, perception, attention, and memory.* New York: Basic Books

RECOMMENDED READINGS

Fritz, D. W. (1979). *Perspectives on creativity and the unconscious.* Oxford, OH: Old Northwest Publications.

Greenacre, P. (1957). *The childhood of the artist: Psychoanalytic study of the gifted child* (Vol. 12). New York: International University Press.

Hammer, E. F. (1961). *Creativity.* New York: Random House.

Hammer, E. F. (1984). *Creativity, talent and personality.* Malabar, FL: R.E. Krieger.

Jung, C. G. (1966). *The spirit in men, art and literature.* New York: Bollinger Foundations.

Lombroso, C. (1895). *Genius and insanity: The men of genius.* London: Charles Scribner's Sons.

Lombroso, C. (1910). *The men of genius.* New York: Charles Scribner's. (Original work published 1891)

Strean, H. S. (1984). *Inhibitions in work and love: Psychoanalytic approaches to problems in creativity.* New York: Haworth Press.

3

Creativity, Cognition, and Their Educational Implications

Mark A. Runco
California State University

Cognitive approaches to creativity are both intriguing and practical. The intrigue is unavoidable given the importance of creativity—for individuals and for society as a whole—and given the abstract nature of the subject matter. Cognition is virtually never concrete, and cognitive scientists must therefore rely on inference. For this reason, cognition is a difficult and challenging target. Still, because virtually all human behavior has cognitive underpinnings, the theories in this area typically have significant practical implications. Many of these are educational. This chapter emphasizes that practical material; I hope it also captures some of the intrigue.

Cognitive theories of creativity emphasize the intellectual processes and knowledge structures that allow an individual to produce an original and adaptive idea, solution, or insight. This suggests a definition: The processes that generate original and adaptive ideas, solutions, and insights are indicative of *creative potential*. If these processes are put to use, they are likely to produce creative ideas, solutions, and insights. The use of the processes, however, may involve more than cognition. The interplay between cognition and motivation will be discussed later in this chapter (see Runco, 1993, 1994b).

In general terms, cognitive research focuses on how information is obtained, organized, stored, transferred, and transformed. In the classic information-processing model (see Fig. 3.1), there are three information stores, and three processes that transfer information between the stores.

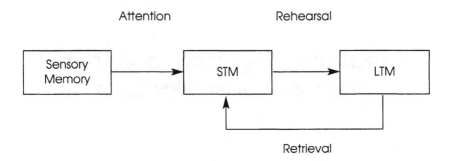

Figure 3.1. The classic information-processing model, with sensory, short-term, and long-term stores, and attention, rehearsal, and retrieval transfer processes

Given this emphasis on information processing, it is not surprising that cognitive theories complement several other general approaches to the study of creativity. The most compatible theories are probably developmental, psychoanalytic, and social. (Complementarity is also suggested by what was just said about an interplay between cognition and motivation.) Cognitive theories are much less compatible with other approaches, such as those suggested by learning and operant theories (cf. Epstein, in press). Complementarity is noted at various points throughout this chapter. Specific disagreements and issues are also mentioned.

One of these can be noted here to help define the coverage of the cognitive approach. It involves the aforementioned reliance of cognitive research on inference and the implied distinction between *potential* and actual *performance*. In the cognitive view, information that has the potential for a behavioral manifestation is at least as important as the actual and observable response. Most operant theories, in contrast, focus on overt responses in an attempt to avoid inference and maximize objectivity. They often examine novel behaviors and responses, and even novelty is defined in an entirely objective fashion. Cognitive research may also examine novelty, but appropriateness or some other facet of creativity are likely to be examined as well, even if the facets in question have a subjective component (e.g., Runco & Charles, 1993). The multidimensional assumption of the cognitive approach fits well with existing theories of creativity that view it as a syndrome or complex (Mumford & Gustafson, 1988; Runco & Sakamoto, in press). Surely research must capture the full range of components within that complex or we will not fully understand creativity. The cognitive research reviewed in this chapter covers a range of components and dimensions.

This chapter begins with a discussion of the role of attention in creative thinking. Memory is also discussed early on, along with divergent thinking and functional fixity—two topics of special interest to students of creativity. Individual differences in cognitive style and metacognition are then related to creative thinking, with problem solving and social cognition also briefly discussed.

With its applied emphasis, this chapter does not explore directions for future research. One section toward the end of the chapter is, however, devoted to unanswered questions. More important may be the section at the very end of the chapter, which is devoted to activities that demonstrate certain cognition tendencies. These activities, and in fact the entire chapter, were written specifically for nonspecialists and individuals who are interested in exploring how existing theories can be applied to the natural environment.

ATTENTION AND MEMORY

Attention is the process by which information is transferred from the sensory memory to the short term or working memory (see Fig. 3.1).[1] In a sense, information processing really begins in sensory memory, and by definition attention has not yet come into play at that point. However, the sensory memory has very little relevance to creativity. Information is raw (i.e., entirely based on data arriving from one of the five sensory modalities) and is not yet recognized or interpreted in the sensory store; it is merely detected. For our purposes, then, attention is the first concern. Attention is also a good starting point for this chapter because, in terms from literary criticism, it is a microcosm of the macrocosm. I say this because attention requires active participation by the individual. The same can be said of the other components of cognition, especially those that are relevant to creativity. (This is another difference between cognitive and operant approaches, or at least the operant approaches that focus on organisms as passive recipients of reinforcement and punishment.)

Humans do not passively respond to the environment, nor do they absorb information in a blind, unselective fashion. Rather, humans are highly selective, attending only to novel or otherwise salient stimuli. The model in Fig. 3.1 implies that humans only process and store (i.e.,

---

[1]There is some controversy about the distinctiveness of the memory stores. One alternative to the model in Figure 3.1 posits that human memory is continuous, with the depth of processing determining the effectiveness of the storage.

remember) those things that have earned their attention. Activity 1, at the end of this chapter, is intended to demonstrate the active involvement in information processing. Admittedly, some kinds of information may be nearly automatically processed. These require very little attention and effort. Activity 2 requires such *effortless processing*. But most cognition is effortful and requires the active participation of the individual. It is effortful in a literal sense. Certain resources, particularly attention, must be devoted to it.

Csikszentmihalyi (1988b) recognized the role of attention when he described what was needed in a theory of creativity: "First it must be explained why a person's psychic energy is attracted to the domain, i.e., why he or she is interested in it" (p. 166). The assumption here is that truly creative performance requires a large investment of time and energy. It is a matter of sustained effort, and that requires attention. Hayes (1985) and Simon and Chase (1973) similarly suggested that creative individuals only contribute to their field after they have mastered it. They specifically discussed the need for an individual to devote at least 10 years—or 10,000 hours—to his or her field in order to master it.

This notion of invested effort may appear straightforward, but not long ago creativity was viewed as independent of effort. As Albert (1975) described it, historically creative genius has been considered by some to be inborn, and insights in particular were defined as spontaneous and sudden. It was as if all at once the individual happened on a solution or idea. This view was consistent with many anecdotal reports of creativity (see Vernon, 1970) and compatible with the old presumption that all cognition was instantaneous (Radford & Burton, 1974). More recent explanations suggest that creative insights are only found if the individual is interested in and consciously attending to the problem and the possible solutions. These recent explanations do recognize the role of incubation and the possibility that an individual can work on a problem even though he or she is not conscious of the effort or of the options and ideational associations. Contemporary thought holds that the actual insight might come suddenly, but effort on some level of consciousness seems to be necessary. Even when incubation is involved, attention is required for the individual to notice a problem or area of interest and for him or her to assimilate the relevant information.[2]

Information processing is not entirely consciously directed. Anyone who has memorized something, stopped thinking about it, and

---

[2]Incidentally, incubation may seem like a good description of problem solving only because of the subjectivity involved in reports of insight (Gruber, 1988; Wallace, 1991). It may be that a great deal of effort is involved before an insight, but most of it is dismissed or forgotten when a creator tries to explain his or her efforts.

then retrieved it when it was needed has experienced the operation of long-term memory. In cognitive terms, the information is rehearsed, placed in long-term memory, and organized into some sort of cognitive structure. The organization often occurs without the individual being aware of it. In fact, the individual is typically only aware of a few "bits" of information at any one time. Activity 1 demonstrates the difficulties that arise when humans attempt to concentrate on too many pieces of information at any one time. The bits of information actually being used are in *working memory* (another label for short-term memory), but they are by no means the only data available. Information can be retrieved from long-term memory as needed.

There are individual differences in attention, and these are very important for an understanding of creativity. Wallach (1970) described these individual differences in terms of *attention deployment*. As he explained it, when attention is widely deployed, there is an increased probability of finding remote and original ideas. Wallach argued that the individual who is capable of wide attention deployment will have "a broader range of stimulus information . . . a broader range of memory traces . . . a greater sensitivity to the utilizing of incidental cues," with "more diffuse or extensive deployment of attention in the reception of information, in its retrieval, or both" (pp. 1248-1249). Wide attention deployment, then, allows an individual to consider possibilities that he or she might miss with narrow attention. Some of these possibilities are environmental and essentially *cues* to interesting problems or prospective solutions (Katz & Pestell, 1989; Mendelsohn, 1976; Mumford, Mobley, Uhlman, & Reiter-Palmon, 1991; Runco, Okuda, & Thurston, 1991; Wallach, 1970).

Martindale (1981) held a similar view, and suggested that creativity may be facilitated by *defocused attention*, a condition ostensibly occurring when an individual experiences low cortical arousal. Like wide attention deployment, defocused attention allows a large number of associative connections to be simultaneously activated. This in turn may allow more remote associations and easier analogical and creative thinking (see Kasof, in press; Martindale, 1981). Numerous theorists have tied analogical thinking to creative thinking (Gardner, 1982; Hofstadter, 1986; Kogan, 1989). Others have focused on associative processes (e.g., Mednick, 1962; Noppe, 1996).

Interestingly, attention may also help explain what Csikszentmihalyi (1988a) referred to as "the dangers of originality." Csikszentmihalyi suggested that the artwork of psychotic individuals is "obsessed with detailed repetitiveness [and] . . . redundant ornamentation" (p. 219). For Csikszentmihalyi, this obsession reflects *stimulus over-inclusion*, whereby individuals have difficulty selectively attending to the relevant features of the environment. He wrote that "by redrawing the same detail over and over, the patient gets visual confirmation that he can indeed control his attention and temporarily be a master of his own soul" (p. 222). The danger is that an individual can forget that there is a distinction between reality in the environment and reality in one's own thoughts.

Smith, Michael, and Hocevar (1990) also approached the relation between attention and creative thinking by considering what can go wrong.[3] They suggested that evaluation and pressure can cause anxiety and divide attention, and that this can detract from creative thinking because the individual directs his or her attention to the stressor rather than to the task itself. Simply put, anxiety will make concentration very difficult, if not impossible. Smith et al. specifically identified the encoding and rehearsal difficulties an anxious individual will experience. As suggested by Figure 3.1, this implies that the individual will not efficiently store or retain information. Kasof (in press), Martindale and Greenough (1973), Rawlings (1985), and Toplyn and Maquire (1991) presented data that are compatible with this view. Apparently, there is a threshold level of stress or pressure, below which there is no effect on creativity. Put differently, there may be an optimal level, with some challenge but not enough for stress per se (Runco & Radio Gaynor, 1993; Runco & Sakamoto, 1996).

There are fairly obvious practical implications of this theory of attention and anxiety. Parents and teachers, for example, might work to maintain a low level of stress and pressure for children and students. The children and students would thus be free to explore and consider alternatives, and they would in turn be expected to uncover creative associations. This view is entirely consistent with numerous descriptions of environments that are conducive to creativity (Harrington, Block, & Block, 1987; Rogers, 1980; Runco & Radio Gaynor, 1993). Of course, none of this intimates that children should never experience challenges. What children need is comfort and security for confidence and ease of associations, with occasional and personally meaningful challenges (Runco & Radio Gaynor, 1993).

INFORMATION AND KNOWLEDGE STRUCTURES

Surprisingly little research has been specifically directed at the role of memory in creative performances, although its functioning is implied by

---

[3]As a matter of fact, there is a long history of research focusing on behavior gone awry. Freud, for example, looked at developmental problems. In the cognitive research, Spoonerisms and "slips of the tongue" have been used as indicators of underlying processes (Motley, 1987), and illusions have been used to study normal perceptual processes (Gregory, 1978; Neisser, 1960).

the work cited previously on the need for sustained effort (Csikszentmihalyi, 1988b; Hayes, 1985; Simon & Chase, 1973). After all, what are the specific benefits of invested efforts? One is that the individual will collect a great deal of information in long-term memory. Usually the 10-year argument focuses on the individual's understanding of his or her field, and in particular knowledge of the assumptions and key issues. Understanding and knowledge are certainly dependent on memory.

As just noted, if attention is directed to some information, that information is maintained in working or short term memory (see Fig. 3.1). Information can be transferred to long-term memory if rehearsal or a mnemonic is used. If information is in long-term memory, it is relatively permanent, but it must be located and retrieved to be used. The information that is accessible in long-term memory defines an individual's knowledge base. It may be *declarative knowledge*, which describes the way things are, or *procedural knowledge,* which suggests how things should or can be done. Both kinds of knowledge reflect information that is organized and structured. Both can influence creative thinking.

This raises one of the pressing questions in the cognitive sciences, namely that of the organization of knowledge. Knowledge is undoubtedly organized or clustered in some sort of structures, but knowledge structures are not currently well defined. Many have been postulated, including what Piaget (1970) called *schema* and what Schank (1988) referred to as *thematic organization packets* (TOPs). The former are usually used when describing creativity in a literal sense—that is, the creation of something new regardless of its social value or aesthetic appeal. TOPs, on the other hand, are structures that allow individuals to find connections among remote events. Given that TOPs are abstract and general enough to allow disparate pieces of information to be connected, they may be critical for flexibility of thought, and thereby crucial for creativity (see Jausovec, 1994). Flexibility takes on great significance because some individuals develop expertise and large knowledge bases—and as a direct result become very rigid in their thinking (Rubenson & Runco, 1995). More often than not, creative thinking is most likely to occur when the individual is informed but flexible.

Clearly, creativity requires much more than the retrieval of information. Look back at the definition of creativity offered earlier, with its requirement of originality. That assumes a newness that memories can not satisfy. On the other hand, this assumes that memory is only reproductive. Memory that merely reproduces experience certainly could not satisfy the criterion of newness,[4] but just as different kinds of knowledge have been

---

[4]Of some relevance on this point is the operant view of the "integration of previously learned responses" (Epstein, in press). This integration occurs when an individual ties several responses together into a new response chain. Epstein's empiri-

identified, so too have different kinds of memory been defined. Some memories are very detailed and *episodic* (so named because they are based on one episode of experience). *Semantic memories,* on the other hand, involve only the gist or general meaning implied by experience. The latter are not simply recollections or duplicates of experience, but instead are reconstructions. These might be adapted and fresh and thus allow original thinking.

This view of memory was recognized by Vygotsky in a theory originally proposed in the 1930s. Vygotsky distinguished between memory as *reproductive imagination* and truly creative imagination (see Smolucha, 1992). In the reproductive process, an idea might arise through simple associative processes. Perhaps the individual will remember that tennis balls are round, drawing from some specific experience. That idea may appear to be original, at least when no one else thinks of it as a response to the frequently used divergent thinking test question, "name round things." However, for Vygotsky, truly creative ideas require *realistic thinking.* This refers to a critical process in which ideas are adapted and modified so they will fit a given problem or need. It is a kind of accommodation.

Memory functions are also implicit in most psychoanalytic theories of creativity (Abra, 1989; Gedo, 1997). This is evidenced by their use of concepts like *cathartic originality* (Csikszentmihalyi, 1988a; Runco, 1994b), wherein creative activity is an effort to release tension that originated in childhood trauma. Of course, such psychoanalytic views assume that critical memories are unconscious, but it is not too great a stretch to view long-term memory as a subconscious storage area. After all, information in long-term memory is not available to the individual until he or she brings it back into working memory.

Even in the strict cognitive approach, memory and knowledge are interdependent. Neither contributes much without the other. This is an important point because it highlights the fact that information is limited by memory. The degree to which individuals will benefit from experience is determined by their ability to encode, hold, and retrieve the information supplied by experience. This in turn suggests a rebuttal to the so-called

---

cal research has demonstrated how even four and five distinct responses—at least distinct initially—can be integrated or chained together (see Epstein, in press; Runco, 1992). The integrations may appear to be insightful—that is, appear to be sudden solutions to a problem. As Epstein described them, however, they are only new in their combination. The separate responses are a reflection of previous experience. The operant approach does not often use terms like *memory,* but surely some memory is needed for the storage of the previous experiences. Note that this is one of the few points of agreement between the cognitive and operant views of creativity: both rely on memory functions.

experiential bias of certain cognitive assessments. IQ tests, for example, have been criticized for having an experiential bias, the idea being that examinees cannot answer certain test questions unless they have the experience that provides them with the necessary information. Certainly, if asked about the distance between Los Angeles and Honolulu, an examinee who has traveled that route (or perhaps has friends or relatives who have) will have an advantage. But the theory of memory outlined here suggests that an individual needs both experience and ability to process and utilize the relevant information. This argument applies to tests of creative thinking—including the divergent thinking tests described here—as well as to IQ tests.

DIVERGENT THINKING

The question just presented about round things is typical of items on certain tests of creative thinking. These are tests of *divergent thinking* (Bachelor & Michael, 1997; Guilford, 1981; Runco, 1991a; Torrance, 1998; Wallach, 1970). Divergent thinking tests are unique in their containing only open-ended questions that allow a large number of diverse responses. They are unlike convergent thinking tests, including IQ and most academic tests, which typically have just one correct or acceptable answer (e.g., "In what direction does the sun rise?"). Several of the activities at the end of this chapter are intended to demonstrate divergent thinking.

Memory may be used when an individual is faced with divergent thinking test questions, like "name all of the things you can think of which are round" (also see Activity 3). To answer this question, the individual might inspect his or her immediate environment, searching for objects that fit the task demands—perhaps the top of a coffee mug, the tip of a pencil, and the zero on a word processor key). Alternatively, the individual could retrieve information from his or her long-term memory. (As I recall, baseballs, planets, and navels are each round.) In this sense, there are several strategies for responding to the task. Some strategies have a high likelihood of leading to original and even creative ideas.

Actually, memory must be used whenever an individual thinks divergently. The individual probably either draws ideas directly from memory or confirms that ideas are fitting by drawing knowledge about them from memory. This determination of the fit of ideas may be taken as a reminder about the role of judgment and selection. Empirical evidence for selections was presented in Runco (1991b); evidence for a relation between memory and divergent thinking was presented by Pollert, Feldhusen, Van Mondfrans, and Treffinger (1969) and Guilford (1981); and evidence for the relation between divergent thinking and actual creative achievement was presented in Runco (1991a, 1992). Although actual creative performance requires much more than the generation of ideas, divergent thinking seems to be quite important role in some creative performances.

Divergent thinking virtually always relies on memory and knowledge, but this claim should be qualified. This is because just as an individual can lack knowledge, so too can he or she have too much. When individuals have too much knowledge, they may focus on what is rather than what could be. Put differently, they think in a convergent manner rather than a divergent manner. In extreme cases they may even experience some form of *fixity*, which simply means that they only see one option and cannot see alternative interpretations and possibilities (Runco, 1985; Runco & Okuda, 1991). Educators should therefore be aware of the potential dangers of knowledge. It may be that they can present information—even so-called facts—in such a way as to leave them open to interpretation and modification (Runco & Okuda, in press). Information that is presented in too dogmatic a fashion may guarantee fixity and preclude creativity (Aviram & Milgram, 1977; Simonton, 1983).

An individual cannot experience fixity and simultaneously think divergently. The latter precludes the former. This is especially true when the thinking is divergent in a literal sense, and when ideas reflect *flexibility*. Operationally, flexibility is apparent when an individual gives a wide range of diverse responses. To do this, individuals probably look to diverse categories of ideas. When an individual defines categories (e.g., things that are round) in a flexible fashion, he or she will be more open to remote and original associates and ideas, and again will avoid fixity. Wallach (1970) suggested something similar, describing it as *category width*. More recently, McCarthy (1993) used quantum theory to describe how, "when attention is relaxed, memory capacity is increased and the boundaries between information are removed" (p. 32).

Flexibility is not all-important. Other divergent thinking indices include originality—the tendency to produce unique or highly unusual ideas—and fluency—the tendency to produce a large number of ideas. All three indices should be used to describe an individual's ideational profile. Some examinees are very fluent with ideas but relatively unoriginal or inflexible. Others are high in originality, flexibility, or both, but only moderately fluent. There are, then, important individual differences in divergent thinking profiles. There are also individual differences in cognitive style and metacognition.

COGNITIVE STYLE AND METACOGNITION

Individual differences in creative thinking are often explained in terms of ability or capacity (i.e., what an individual is capable of doing). However, many individual differences can be explained in terms of cognitive style and metacognition, and these are relatively independent of ability. *Cognitive style*, for example, is largely distinct from the individual's ability in that the former reflects what an individual prefers instead of what he or she is capable of doing. Individuals seem to vary along various style dimensions, including impulsivity-reflection, field dependence-independence, and assimilation-exploration, and several of these apparently facilitate creative thinking (Kogan, 1989; Martinsen & Kaufmann, 1999).

Metacognition allows individuals to think in a strategic fashion. Strategies are not necessarily used by those who are capable do using them, which is why they are defined as independent of other cognitive abilities and why they are described as metacognitive. As examples, consider Items 1 and 2 in Activity 3. As suggested earlier, individuals could answer these (or at least obtain hints) by searching their immediate environment. This strategy can be contrasted with the one that relies on a search of memory and existing knowledge. The strategic search of one's immediate environment is, of course, akin to what was described early in this chapter as cue usage (Freidman, Raymond, & Feldhusen, 1978; Runco, 1986; Runco & Okuda, 1988, 1991; Runco et al., 1991; Wallach, 1970; Ward, 1969).

In Runco et al. (1991) we investigated the cue usage of students while in a classroom. After presenting students with a variety of divergent thinking tests, teachers were asked to identify "environmentally cued" classroom objects in the responses. Comparisons indicated, somewhat surprisingly, that the students had not relied on cues when they were working on the divergent thinking tasks. Apparently these students—fourth, fifth, and sixth graders—more often used their memory and associative skills when generating ideas. This decision to ignore environmental cues when looking for ideas was probably a wise one. This is because the same environmental cues are available to everyone in each particular environment (e.g., the classroom), and ideas that are cued by the environment are therefore likely to be unoriginal. Other investigators have found fairly clear indications of cue usage (Friedman et al., 1978; Ward, 1969).

In Runco (1986; Runco & Okuda, 1988, 1991), I manipulated a second kind of strategy with explicit instructions. These directed examinees (a) to give as many ideas and solutions as possible, (b) to give only original ideas, or (c) to give as diverse a set of ideas as possible. Essentially, the explicit instructions supplied know-how, and therefore reflect a combination of declarative and procedural knowledge (see

Activity 4). When asked to give only original ideas, for example, students were told to "think of ideas that no one else will" and that "an original idea is one which will be thought of by no one else."

In Runco (1986), I found that the explicit instructions enhanced performance. Moreover, nongifted children benefited from explicit instructions more than gifted children, perhaps because the latter were already and spontaneously strategic in their ideation. In Runco and Okuda (1991), we found that the flexibility (or diversity) of ideas can also be manipulated with strategies and explicit instructions. Importantly, we found that when students gave the most diverse ideas, they did not necessarily find original ideas. The strategy that focuses on diversity thus may not help with originality. At least the metacognitive processes involved in finding diverse ideas seem to be distinct from those involved in finding original ideas. In the final investigation in this series (Chand & Runco, 1992), we also used explicit instructions to manipulate the use of strategies, but we compared the impact on three different kinds of problems. We found differential effects, with improvements most apparent in *problem generation* tasks and *presented problems* (see Activity 5).

Individual differences are both cognitive and metacognitive. Note also that the evidence for strategies and selections supports the argument presented earlier, namely that humans are actively involved in their information processing. The individual does not merely react to the environment, but selects those cues, bits of information, or strategies that are the most interesting or useful. Even when ideas are pulled from memory, this is not randomly accomplished, but instead is a selective process with an evaluation or valuation of the best ideas (Campbell, 1960; Runco, 1991b; Runco & Smith, 1992; Runco & Vega, 1990; Simonton, 1988). Attention, metacognition, and evaluation all show cognition to be an active, individualistic process.

PROBLEM SOLVING AND CREATIVITY

A great deal of what was proposed here implies that creative thinking is a kind of problem solving. In fact, a large portion of the research on creativity assumes that it is a special kind of problem solving (cf. Runco, 1994c). The actual interdependence of creativity on problem solving is, however, a matter of some debate.

In the theories of creativity that assume that creativity is a kind of problem solving, *problem solving* is defined in terms of progress toward some goal. Problems are defined very generally, with any situation containing an obstacle being problematic. Ironically, there are two significant problems with such a emphasis. The first is that many actual creative achievements seem to be independent of *a priori* obstacles and terminal goals. Art is, for example, often more than anything else an attempt at self-expression, and that is not really problem solving. The need to express oneself could be included in the definition of "a problem," but this may not be enough because it would have to include the desire to express one's self as well. That may differ from the *need* to express one's self. Along the same lines, creativity seems to be tied to psychological health and self-actualization (Maslow, 1971; Runco, Ebersole, & Mraz, 1991), and in this sense it is part of the actualizing process and not a reaction to obstacles or any external pressure. Granted, there is a semantic issue here, for an obstacle can be interpreted as fun or as a task where the means are more important than the ends. Such tasks are not literally or necessarily problematic, and yet they certainly can lead to creative activity.

The second difficulty with the problem-solving approach to creativity is that even when a problem is involved, it may require more than just solving.[5] Creativity may be dependent on skills that are distinct from problem-solving skills, including *problem-finding* abilities (see Activity 5). Furthermore, although there are cognitive facets of problem finding (Arlin, 1975; Chand & Runco, 1991; Mumford, Reiter-Palmon, & Redmond, 1994; Okuda, Runco, & Berger, 1991), these may be guided by affective and emotional tendencies. For instance, creative individuals are often characterized as having a high level of intrinsic motivation and a sensitivity to gaps (Runco, 1994b). Problems may thus be identified because the individual is especially sensitive, open to experience, or intrinsically motivated to investigate and consider a potentially problematic situation. The sensitivity of creative individuals has long been recognized (e.g., Greenacre, 1957; Richards, 1990), and there is a great deal of work on the relevance of intrinsic motivation (Amabile, in press; Hennessey, 1989; Hennessey & Zbikowski, 1993; MacKinnon, 1960/1983). More is said later about both sensitivity and intrinsic motivation. For now, the point is that conceptions of creativity as problem solving must take problem finding and affect into account. There are also several social considerations.

---

[5]Something should be said here about *artificial intelligence* (AI). This is a large area within the cognitive sciences, the focus being on computers and simulations of intelligence and creativity. I bring it up here because AI research typically assumes that creativity is a special kind of problem solving, rather than the other way around. AI research has uncovered a number of useful heuristics for innovative thinking (Simon, 1988), but most or even all of this work is limited by its assumption about the equivalence of creativity and problem solving (Csikszentmihalyi, 1988b).

SOCIAL COGNITION AND IMPLICIT THEORIES

Most of the material presented so far describes intrapersonal cognitive processes, such as attention and subsequent information processing, divergent thinking, or problem finding and problem solving. Educators will also be interested in *interpersonal* processes and social cognition.

There are at least two kinds of social cognition that are pertinent to creativity in the educational setting. One is related to the evaluations and selections of ideas, noted briefly earlier. For example, teachers may judge the ideas and divergent thinking of their students. The other kind of social cognition involves *implicit theories*. These reflect the opinions and ideas held by a particular group (e.g., parents or teachers). They can be contrasted with the explicit theories that are constructed and tested by social and behavioral scientists.

Interpersonal evaluations of ideas occur throughout childhood. Parents and teachers both react to the ideas given by children and students, for example, and these reactions have a significant impact, shaping the young individual's tendency to produce similar ideas in the future. Unfortunately, an adult cannot give an entirely objective evaluation of a child's ideas. This is because adults hold perspectives that differ from those of children. As Piaget (1970) and numerous other cognitive developmental theorists demonstrated, adults simply do not think like children. Elkind's (1981) description of children as *cognitive aliens* is an apt one, implying as it does that children reason about just about everything in their own unique way. How can an adult evaluate a child's idea if he or she does not understand why the idea was given?

This takes us back to the topic of attention, for all judgments reflect an individual's perspective, and this perspective is in turn determined by the direction of the individual's attention. Consider the differences found between interpersonal and intrapersonal judgments of ideas (Runco & Smith, 1992). When evaluating one's own work, an individual will tend to direct his or her attention to the context, setting, or problem rather than at his or her own efforts and ideas (Runco & Chand, 1994). Judges, on the other hand, be they colleagues, peers, critics, supervisors, parents, teachers, or some consumer, tend to direct their attention to the person or the product rather than the context, and they tend to judge the product based on its face value. These attentional tendencies are entirely consistent with attributional behaviors described in the social psychological literature (Nisbett & Ross, 1980), but the main point is that attention influences the judgments and evaluations that are necessary for the recognition of an idea or solution as creative.

Not only do different teachers and students have different perspectives; they also have different experiences and work with different information. Perhaps most importantly, an adult will lack information concerning other ideas that were considered by the child. This is important because the child may think that one idea is uncreative because he or she had other ideas that were similar. An adult may judge an idea as extremely creative because he or she does not know about those other similar ideas. A child may think of "Superman" as a solution to the problem, "Name Strong Things," but then disregard that idea because it is too obvious (at least to those individuals who read comic books or watch Saturday morning television) or because it is too similar to his or her other ideas (e.g., Spiderman, Superboy, Batman, and the Incredible Hulk). An adult may see Superman as both appropriate and original simply because he or she has not read the same comic books, watched the same television, or thought of Spiderman or Batman.

Given that intrapersonal judgments and interpersonal judgments tend to be quite discrepant (Runco & Smith, 1992; Simonton, 1988), we should not only expect judgments of adults and children to differ; we should also expect one adult's judgments to differ from those of another adult. Practically speaking, then, a parent may think that his or her child has a creative solution to a problem or for some school project, but the child's teacher may see the same idea or project as inappropriate, unoriginal, and uncreative. It might be inappropriate in the context of classroom objectives or the curriculum, or it might be unoriginal because other students gave the same idea. Again, different individuals have different perspectives, different experiences, and different available information.

Individuals also differ significantly in their expectations, and these most certainly influence judgments about ideas and potential solutions to problems, just as they influence judgments about behavioral acts and attitudes (Rosenthal & Jacobson, 1968). This is why implicit theories are so important to study. Implicit theories help individuals understand expectations for the simple reason that the latter are probably determined by the former. Implicit theories are relatively easy to examine, as demonstrated in the research with parents and teachers (Runco, 1984, 1989; Runco, Johnson, & Baer, 1992) and by Activity 6. Miller and Sawyers (1989) described the implicit theories children hold about creativity.

The implicit theories held by parents and teachers are particularly important to study because there is some indication that, although they respect creativity in general, they dislike the specific behavioral manifestations of it. Torrance (1963), Cropley (1992), and Raina and Raina (1971), for example, found that implicit theories of "an ideal child" were very different from actual descriptions of a creative child. The traits included in the former reflected some degree of conformity, compliance, politeness, and so on, but creative children seem to be moderately nonconforming, rebellious, and autonomous (Runco & Sakamoto, 1996). It is as if parents and teachers like creativity in the abstract but not in the concrete. Perhaps they value creative results, but do not appreciate the creative process. Of course, not all teachers and parents have problems with nonconformity, autonomy, and the like. Some are very supportive of whatever it takes to be creative (Albert & Runco, 1989; Runco & Albert, 1985; Runco, Johnson, & Bear, 1992).

CONCLUSIONS, QUALIFICATIONS, AND QUESTIONS

Cognitive research defines *creativity* as the production of original and adaptive ideas, solutions, and insights. Certain information processes contribute to such production, starting with a combination of focused and defocused attention. The former allows the individual to concentrate on a particular issue or problem, and the latter ensures that a variety of possibilities is considered. Defocused attention also precludes fixity and a reliance on simple reproductive memory. Information can be processed (e.g., divergently) in such a manner as to increase the likelihood of an original insight.

Active cognition was mentioned several times in this chapter, the argument being that it is especially vital for the study and description of creativity. Cognitive processes are selective; behavior is purposeful; and information is constructed rather than discovered (Mumford et al., 1994). Of course, this view of active processing should not be taken to the extreme. Surely we do not have complete control of all our reactions. Consider, for instance, the *reactive* information processing that occurs with some specific kinds of stimuli. The clearest example of this is in a contrast of verbal and nonverbal stimuli (Richardson, 1986; Runco, 1985; Runco & Albert, 1985). Verbal stimuli tend to elicit less original ideas and solutions than nonverbal stimuli. Runco and Albert (1985) suggested that this is because the nonverbal stimuli are less familiar to most persons. When faced with familiar stimuli—like "round things"—we tend to rely on rote associations. When faced with a less familiar stimulus—like those in Activity 7—we must put more effort into generating possibilities. With unfamiliar stimuli, we cannot rely on preconceived (and unoriginal) associations. Instead, we probably use what Mednick (1962) described as *serendipity* for ideational associations. Perhaps educators could use unfamiliar stimuli and tasks to facilitate serendipitous ideation.

It might be tempting to suggest that creativity is most likely if educators model and reinforce divergent thinking, nonconformity, autonomy, and even rebelliousness. After all, these are each associated with creative potential. However, they can all be exaggerated, the result being an inappropriately divergent, nonconforming, autonomous, and rebellious individual. Creative thinking requires the careful judgments of ideas; divergence alone is not sufficient for creative thinking. Some judgment must be made or the idea will not fit the task at hand (Kuhn, 1963; Runco, 2002). In Runco (1996), I pointed to *discretion,* the idea being that children and students should develop the potential to think divergently, but they should also know when it is appropriate to do so and when it is not appropriate.[6] Along the same lines, nonconformity only contributes to creativity up to a certain level. For both divergence and nonconformity, optimization is required (Runco & Radio Gaynor, 1993; Runco & Okuda, 1996).

Unanswered Questions. I opened this chapter with the claim that the attraction of cognitive studies in part reflects the abstraction and inference that are necessary for theory and research. This should be evident in the present chapter; think back about cognitive structures or memory stores. The existence and functioning of these and many other facets of cognition can only be inferred. This abstraction seems to intrigue cognitive scientists, but it also makes things difficult. For this reason, there are many unanswered questions in this area.

One unanswered question concerns the so-called *fourth-grade slump* (Torrance, 1968). This is a bit of a misnomer, for we now know that there are complicated developmental trends rather than just one slump (Runco & Charles, 1997; Urban, 1991). The real issue concerns the causes for the patterns of development. It may be that social pressure has a great impact on slumps in creativity, but maturational processes also contribute (Gardner, 1982). In fact, the maturational processes may have such a significant impact that environmental pressure—including that implied by the implicit theories of "the ideal child"—is secondary, acting only to determine the degree of the slump. We might think about this in the same manner that behavioral geneticists think of the combined effects of nature and nurture. In particular, geneticists use the concept *range of reaction,* with the range determined genetically and the reaction within the range determined environmentally. Slumps in creativity probably can be described a similar way, as a gene-environment interaction.

A second important unanswered question concerns *information integration.* Early work on this topic focused on such things as how children judge the area of a desirable cookie (Anderson, 1980). With their long-standing understanding that area can be calculated by multiplying

---

[6]My (Runco, 1996) definition of *creativity* was tripartite. It emphasized intentions and the ability to transform experience into meaningful and original interpretations, as well as discretion. The interpretive component was tied to assimilation and to evidence from Guilford (1983) and Bachelor and Michael (1991) that transformation plays a significant role in creative thinking.

height and width, adults tend to spontaneously integrate height and width information by multiplying the two pieces of information together. When estimating area (e.g., of a cookie), children merely add the two pieces of information together, and of course have quite idiosyncratic judgments as a result. Runco and Charles (1993) suggested that judgments of creativity also reflect information integration. They were particularly interested in judgments about creativity that were based on information about originality and appropriateness. Most contemporary theorists will agree that creativity is best defined in terms of both originality and adaptiveness or appropriateness (e.g., Rothenberg & Hausman, 1976). Originality may be the most important; however, by itself or taken to an extreme, it does not account for much. "Tangerine" may be a highly original idea when asked to "list square things," but surely it is not appropriate (and presumably should not be viewed as creative). Recall here what I said previously about optimal divergence and discretion.

How is information about originality and appropriateness integrated? In Runco and Charles (1993) we modified the original information integration techniques and asked subjects to rate various ideas for creativity, originality, and appropriateness (with distractor tasks between the assessments). Results suggested that appropriateness was not weighed very heavily when making judgments about creativity. In fact, there was an inverse relation between appropriateness and creativity (see Fig. 3.2). Given the multifaceted nature of creativity, much more could be done with information-integration techniques. Perhaps the various dimensions of teachers' implicit theories could be delineated, and their interactions uncovered, with information-integration methods.

There are several unanswered questions surrounding the judgmental interpretive tendencies of creative persons. Many judgmental tendencies have been identified, and interestingly, many of them are independent of traditional ability or logical skills. Apparently, most individuals often solve problems or deal with dilemmas using specific *heuristics,* even if they are capable of more accurately and algorithmically solving the problem. Heuristics seem to be very frequently used, perhaps because they require fewer cognitive resources than do time-consuming algorithms (see Activity 8). In Runco, Johnson, and Gaynor (1999) a large number of creative activities that may require judgmental skills were listed. Some activities related to education, but this was an exploratory analysis. One unanswered question is about the idiosyncratic judgmental tendencies of creative persons. A second is about the possibility that there are heuristics that are useful for particular creative efforts (Runco, 1994a; Runco et al., 1999).

The last unanswered question concerns cognitive-affect interactions. I already stated that cognition does not work in isolation (Isen,

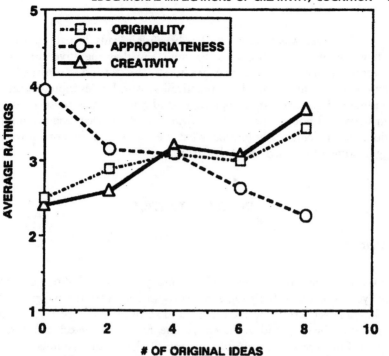

Figure 3.2. Results from Charles and Runco (in press) showing the relationship of judgments of original, appropriate, and creative ideas.

Daubman, & Nowicki, 1987; Lazarus, 1991; Runco, 1994b; Zajonc, 1980). Consider in this regard the concept of intrinsic motivation. Numerous studies have confirmed that creative effort is facilitated by intrinsic motivation (e.g., Amabile, in press; Hennessey, 1989; Hennessey & Zbikowski, 1993; MacKinnon, 1960/1983). There is, however, some controversy about how intrinsic motivation interacts with the cognitive components of creativity. On the one hand, it is easy to see that the knowledge that is necessary for creative insight may be dependent on intrinsic motivation, for an individual will probably not invest his or her time unless motivated to do so (Rubenson & Runco, 1992). But what is not clear is how intrinsic motivation works along with extrinsic motivation. Surely many creators (e.g., professional artists) are both intrinsically and extrinsically motivated (Dudek, Berneche, Berube, & Royer, 1991; Stohs, 1992). Moreover, it is not clear that knowledge is dependent on motivation. It may be the other way around! Individuals may not become interested or intrinsically motivated unless they understand the issue—that is, unless they first have a meaningful appraisal of the situation (Runco, 1993, 1994b).

This idea was reserved for last because it leads directly to my concluding statement. Recall once again my claim that cognitive approaches to creativity are intriguing and practical. The activities outlined here should demonstrate some of the practicality. And by describing what has been inferred about creative cognition—and a few of the questions as yet unanswered—I hope to have taken advantage of an affect-cognition interaction. In particular, I hope that what we know and do not know will suggest some of the intrigue of this area.

STUDY ACTIVITIES

Activity 1

What do you hear right now? Probably many things, including your heart beat, your breathing, the people in the room with you, the pages of your book, your feet scratching the carpet, and so on. If you direct your attention to your hearing and to the environment, you can detect many, many sounds. But here is the rub: How many of these same sounds had you noticed before I suggested that you listen? They were all available to you—the information was being detected by your sensory registers, and in your sensory memory—but it went unrecognized because your attention was directed elsewhere (presumably to the pages of this book). Attention is limited; at any one point in time we can only perceive so much.

Activity 2

Read the following passage.

> The night sky was pitch black. The moon was up, and very, very full. Most people would consider a night like this to be a beautiful one. The pitch black of the sky contrasted with the clarity of the stars. Of course, nights like this are full of activity. This particular one would make a good Halloween. It might also make for a romantic walk, or a appropriate time for blackmarket trading. As the song goes, "night time is the right time." The night was definitely pitch black.

Now think back: How many times was the phrase "pitch black" used? Most persons' estimates of such *frequency of occurrence* are relatively accurate because frequency of occurrence, like spatial position, is just about effortlessly processed. Most other kinds of information require attention and effort (Hasher & Zachs, 1970). If you want to feel effortful processing, which requires attention and energy, try thinking about two things at once. Who can multiply 31 x 31 while reciting the Pledge of Allegiance?

Activity 3

Answer the following questions:

1. Name all of the things you can think of that are strong.
2. List green, funny, liquid objects.
3. How are an apple and a mango alike?
4. List uses for a paper clip.

These are examples from divergent thinking tests. The first two exemplify an Instances test; the third exemplifies a Similarities test question; and the fourth exemplifies a Uses test question (Khandwalla, in press; Runco, 1991a; Wallach, 1970). Although there is some question about how to best administer divergent thinking tests (Runco, 1986, 1991a), with children it seems to help if the examiner describes them as "games" rather than tests, and allows as much time as examinees need to respond. Usually, responses are (a) counted, for an "ideational fluency" score; (b) compared to one another, with ideas from unique categories contributing to an "ideational flexibility" score; and (c) compared among subjects, with unique or unusual ideas contributing to an "ideational originality" score. As noted elsewhere in this chapter, nonverbal ("figural" or "visual") divergent thinking tests are also available (see Activity 7).

Activity 4

Try each of the following:

1. List all of the things you can think of that move on wheels. Give as many ideas as you can—the more the better. Spelling doesn't matter. The only important thing is quantity—the more ideas, the better.
2. List all of the things you can think of that are square. But focus on originality! Only consider ideas that no one else will think of.
3. List all of the things you can think of that are heavy. But focus on diversity! Try to list ideas from various categories. Consider this example: If you were asked to "name round things," you

might say "baseball, soccerball, tennis ball, and volleyball." But those are all in the same (athletic) category. What you should do here is to try to *use a variety* of categories. Again, be flexible (from Runco & Okuda, 1991).

Activity 5

Answer the following questions.

1. Your favorite television show, *Home Improvement,* was on last night. You had so much fun watching it that you forgot to do your homework. You are about to go to school this morning when you realize that your homework is due in your first class. Uh-oh . . . what are you going to do?

2. It's a great day for sailing, and your buddy, Chris, comes to your job and asks you if you want to go sailing. Unfortunately, you have a big project due tomorrow, and it requires a full day to complete. You would much rather be sailing. What are you going to do? Think of as many ideas as you can!

3. List different problems, issues, or difficulties in school that are important to you. You may write down problems about the campus itself, classes, professors, policies, classmates, or whatever. Try to be specific, give creative ideas (which no one else will think of), and take your time. Think of as many problems as you can!

4. Previously, you were asked to list problems that you may face at school. Now, I would like you to list problems, issues, or difficulties from work that are important to you. (These may reflect your current employment, or a past job.) You may write down any problems about your boss, co-workers, clients, policies, or whatever. Keep in mind that the more ideas, the better.

5. Go back to the school problems and choose the one problem which would allow the largest number of original solutions. Copy that problem here: _____. Now write as many original solutions as you can think of for the problem. And again, the more the better.

6. Go back to the work problems and choose the one problem that would allow the largest number of original solutions. Copy that problem here: _____. Now write as many original solutions as you can think of for the problem. And again, the more the better.

Like those given in Activity 3, these questions represent divergent thinking test questions. They are open-ended, and can be scored for fluency, flexibility, and originality. The questions here are different because they are real-world (or realistic) questions. In Okuda, Runco, and Berger (1991) and Chand and Runco (1992) it was suggested that these questions are better estimates of the potential for creative thinking because they are more similar to what is used in the natural environment. Note that the first two problems are presented problems, and the next two are problem-generation tasks. The skills required by the latter may differ from those involved in the former (Chand & Runco, 1992). The last two problems require both problem-generation skill—the selection of a workable problem—and problem-solving skill.

Activity 6

Place a "C" next to those characteristics in the following list that are indicative of children's creativity, or are commonly displayed by creative children. Then place a "U" next to the descriptors that are contraindicative of creativity, and characterize relatively uncreative children.

Lazy	Absent-Minded	Active
Curious	Cynical	Ambitious
Apathetic	Awkward	Clear-thinking
Bitter	Energetic	Inventive
Enterprising	Capable	Adaptable
Adventurous	Dull	Commonplace
Despondent	Alert	Impulsive
Daring	Aloof	Confident
Enthusiastic	Dreamy	Individualistic
Progressive	Self-confident	Artistic
Assertive	Industrious	Narrow interest
Imaginative	Intelligent	Wide interests

Each descriptor in the list was identified in Runco et al. (1992) in their work on parents' and teachers' views of children's creativity (also see Runco, 1984, 1989). In that research, the Lazy, Absent-minded, Cynical, Apathetic, Awkward, Dull, Commonplace, Despondent, Aloof, and Narrow Interests were contraindicative (negatively related to children's creativity), and all others were indicative. Importantly, that categorization of indicative versus contraindicative items reflects the implicit theories of one group. It is not necessarily a reflection of other implicit theories from other groups.

Activity 7

List all of the things the figures in Figure 3.3a and 3.3b could represent. If
you want a slightly more challenging task, first draw a figure, and then list
all of the things it could be. Wakefield (1985) asked subjects to draw their
own figure in his work comparing problem definition—the act of drawing—with problem solving—the listing of responses to a presented problem.

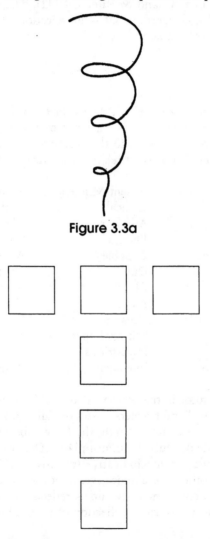

Figure 3.3a

**Figures 3.3a, b. Examples of figural (or visual) divergent thinking
test stimuli. Examinees are asked to name as many things as they
can that each figure might represent.**

Activity 8

Quickly jot down answers to these questions. How old are you? How do you travel from home to your closest supermarket? How tall are you? Most likely your answers to these questions are estimates. You could find exact answers using some sort of *algorithm,* but it would require more effort to produce the exact answers, and most of the time, estimates are sufficient. For this reason we often use estimates, finding them with *heuristics,* or shortcuts.

REFERENCES

Abra, J. (1989). Changes in creativity with age: Data, explanations, and further predictions. *International Journal of Aging and Human Development, 28,* 105-126.

Albert, R. S. (1975). Toward a behavioral definition of genius. *American Psychologist, 30,* 141-150.

Albert, R. S., & Runco, M. A. (1989). Independence and cognitive ability in gifted and exceptionally gifted boys. *Journal of Youth and Adolescence, 18,* 221-230.

Amabile, T. M. (in press). Within you, without you. In M. A. Runco & R. S. Albert (Eds.), *Theories of creativity* (rev. ed., pp. 61-91). Cresskill, NJ: Hampton Press.

Anderson, N. H. (1980). Information integration theory in developmental psychology. In F. Wilkening, J. Beden, & T. Trabasso (Eds.), *Information integration by children* (pp. 1-45). Hillsdale, NJ: Lawrence Erlbaum Associates.

Arlin, P. K. (1975). Cognitive development in adulthood: A fifth stage? *Developmental Psychology, 11,* 602-606.

Aviram, A., & Milgram, R. M. (1977). Dogmatism, locus of control, and creativity in children educated in the Soviet Union, the United States, and Israel. *Psychological Reports, 40,* 27-34.

Bachelor, P., & Michael, W. B. (1991). Higher-order factors of creativity within Guilford's structure-of-intellect model: A re-analysis of a 53 variable data base. *Creativity Research Journal, 4,* 157-175.

Bachelor, P., & Michael, W. (1997). The structure-of-intellect model revisited. In M. A. Runco (Ed.), *Creativity research handbook* (Vol. 1, pp. 155-182). Cresskill, NJ: Hampton Press.

Campbell, D. (1960). Blind variation and selective retention in creative thought as in other knowledge processes. *Psychological Review, 67,* 380-400.

Chand, I., & Runco, M. A. (1992). Problem finding skills as components in the creative process. *Personality and Individual Differences, 14,* 155-162.

Cropley, A. J. (1992). *More ways than one: Fostering creativity.* Norwood, NJ: Ablex.

Csikszentmihalyi, M. (1988a). The dangers of originality: Creativity and the artistic process. In M. M. Gedo (Ed.), *Psychoanalytic perspectives on art* (pp. 213-224). Hillsdale, NJ: The Analytic Press.

Csikszentmihalyi, M. (1988b). Motivation and creativity: Toward a synthesis of structural and energistic approaches to cognition. *New Ideas in Psychology, 6,* 159-176.

Dudek, S. Z., Berneche, R., Berube, H., & Royer, S. (1991). Personality determinants of the commitment to the profession of art. *Creativity Research Journal, 4,* 367-390.

Elkind, D. (1981). *Children and adolescence.* New York: Oxford University Press.

Epstein, R. (in press). Generativity theory and creativity. In M. A. Runco & R. S. Albert (Eds.), *Theories of creativity* (rev. ed., pp. 116-140). Cresskill, NJ: Hampton Press.

Freidman, F., Raymond, B. A., & Feldhusen, J. (1978). The effects of environmental scanning on creativity. *Gifted Child Quarterly, 22,* 248-251.

Gardner, H. (1982). *Art, mind, and brain.* New York: Basic Books.

Gedo, J. (1997). In M. A. Runco (Ed.), *Creativity research handbook* (Vol. 1, pp. 29-40). Cresskill, NJ: Hampton Press.

Gruber, H. E. (1988). The evolving systems approach to creative work. *Creativity Research Journal, 1,* 27-51.

Guilford, J. P. (1981). Higher order structure of intellect abilities. *Multivariate Behavioral Research, 16,* 411-435.

Guilford, J. P. (1983). Transformation abilities or functions. *Journal of Creative Behavior, 17,* 75-83.

Harrington, D. M., Block, J. H., & Block, J. (1987). Testing aspects of Carl Rogers' theory of creative environments: Child rearing antecedents of creative potential in young adolescents. *Journal of Personality and Social Psychology, 52,* 851-856.

Hayes, J. R. (1985). Three problems in teaching problem solving skills. In S. Chipman, J. W. Segal, & R. Glaser (Eds.), *Thinking and learning skills* (Vol. 2, pp. 391-406). Hillsdale, NJ: Lawrence Erlbaum Associates.

Hennessey, B. A. (1989). The effect of extrinsic constraint on children's creativity when using a computer. *Creativity Research Journal, 2,* 151-168.

Hennessey, B. A., & Zbikowski, S. M. (1993). Immunizing children against the negative effects of reward: A further examination of intrinsic motivation training techniques. *Creativity Research Journal,* *6,* 297-307.

Hofstadter, D. (1986). *Metamagical themas.* New York: Basic Books.

Isen, A. M., Daubman, K. A., & Nowicki, G. P. (1987). Positive affect facilitates creative problem solving. *Journal of Personality and Social Psychology, 52,* 1122-1131.

Jausovec, N. (1994). *Flexible thinking and individual differences in creative problem solving.* Cresskill, NJ: Hampton Press.

Kasof, J. (in press). Creativity and breadth of attention. *Creativity Research Journal.*

Katz, A. N., & Pestell, D. (1989). Attentional processes and the finding of remote associates. *Personality and Individual Differences, 10,* 1017-1025.

Khandwalla, P. N. (in press). An exploratory study of divergent thinking through protocol analysis. *Creativity Research Journal.*

Kogan, N. (1989). A stylistic perspective on metaphor and aesthetic sensitivity in children. In T. Globerson & T. Zelniker (Eds.), *Cognitive style and cognitive development* (pp. 192-213). Hillsdale, NJ: Lawrence Erlbaum Associates.

Kuhn, T. (1963). The essential tension: Traditional and innovation in scientific research. In C. W. Taylor & F. Barron (Eds.), *Scientific creativity: Its recognition and development* (pp. 341-354). New York: Wiley.

Lazarus, R. S. (1991). Cognition and motivation in emotion. *American Psychologist, 46,* 352-367.

MacKinnon, D. W. (1983). The highly effective individual. In R. S. Albert (Ed.), *Genius and eminence: The social psychology of creativity and exceptional achievement* (pp. 114-127). Oxford: Pergamon. (Original work published 1960)

Martindale, C. (1981). Creativity, unconsciousness, and cortical arousal. *Journal of Altered States of Consciousness, 3,* 69-87.

Martindale, C., & Greenough, J. (1973). The differential effect of increased arousal on creative and intellectual performance. *Journal of Genetic Psychology, 123,* 329-335.

Martinsen, O., & Kaufmann, G. (1999). Cognitive style and creativity. In M. A. Runco & S. Pritzker (Eds.), *Encyclopedia of creativity* (pp. 273-282). San Diego, CA: Academic Press.

Maslow, A. H. (1971). *The farther reaches of human nature.* New York: Viking Press.

McCarthy, K. A. (1993). Indeterminacy and consciousness in the creative process: What quantum physics has to offer. *Creativity Research Journal, 6,* 201-220.

Mednick, S. A. (1962). The associative basis for the creative process. *Psychological Review, 69,* 200-232.

Mendelsohn, G. A. (1976). Associative and attentional processes in creative performance. *Journal of Personality, 44,* 341-369.

Miller, H. B., & Sawyers, J. K. (1989). A comparison of self and teachers' ratings of creativity in fifth grade children. *Creative Child and Adult Quarterly, 14,* 179-185, 229-238.

Mumford, M. D., & Gustafson, S. B. (1988). Creativity syndrome: Integration, application, and innovation. *Psychological Bulletin, 103,* 27-43.

Mumford, M. D., Mobley, M. I., Uhlman, C. E., & Reiter-Palmon, R. (1991). Process analytic models of creative capacities. *Creativity Research Journal, 4,* 91-122.

Mumford, M. D., Reiter-Palmon, R., & Redmond, M. R. (1994). Problem construction and cognition: Applying problem representations in ill-defined domains. In M. A. Runco (Ed.), *Problem finding, problem solving, and creativity* (pp. 3-39). Norwood, NJ: Ablex.

Nisbett, R., & Ross, L. (1980). *Human inference: Strategies and shortcomings of social judgment.* Englewood Cliffs, NJ: Prentice Hall.

Noppe, L. D. (1996). Progression in the service of the ego, cognitive styles, and creative thinking. *Creativity Research Journal, 9,* 369-383.

Okuda, S. M., Runco, M. A., & Berger, D. E. (1991). Creativity and the finding and solving of real work problems. *Journal of Psychoeducational Assessment, 9,* 45-53.

Piaget, J. (1970). Piaget's theory. In P. Mussen (Ed.), *Carmichael's handbook of child psychology* (pp. 703-732). New York: Wiley.

Pollert, L. H., Feldhusen, J. F., Van Mondfrans, A. P., & Treffinger, D. J. (1969). Role of memory in divergent thinking. *Psychological Reports, 25,* 151-156.

Radford, J., & Burton, A. (1974). *Thinking: Its nature and development.* Chichester, England: John Wiley & Sons.

Raina, T. N., & Raina, M. K. (1971). Perception of teacher-educators in India about the ideal pupil. *Journal of Educational Research, 64,* 303-306.

Rawlings, D. (1985). Psychoticism, creativity and dichotic shadowing. *Personality and Individual Differences, 6,* 737-742.

Richards, R. (1990). Everyday creativity, eminent creativity, and health: Afterview for CRJ issues on creativity and health. *Creativity Research Journal, 3,* 300-326.

Richardson, A. G. (1986). Two factors of creativity. *Perceptual and Motor Skills, 63,* 379-384.

Rogers, C. R. (1980). *A way of being.* Boston: Houghton Mifflin.

Rosenthal, R., & Jacobson, L. (1968). *Pygmalion in the classroom.* New York: Holt, Rinehart & Winston.

Rothenberg, A., & Hausman, C. (1976). *The creativity question.* Durham, NC: Duke University Press.

Rubenson, D. L., & Runco, M. A. (1992). The psychoeconomic approach to creativity. *New Ideas in Psychology, 10,* 131-147.

Rubenson, D. L., & Runco, M. A. (1995). The psychoeconomic view of creative work in groups and organizations. *Creativity and Innovation Management, 4,* 232-241.

Runco, M. A. (1984). Teachers' judgments of creativity and social validation of divergent thinking tests. *Perceptual and Motor Skills, 59,* 711-717.

Runco, M. A. (1985). Reliability and convergent validity of ideational flexibility as a function of academic achievement. *Perceptual and Motor Skills, 61,* 1075-1081.

Runco, M. A. (1986). Maximal performance on divergent thinking tests by gifted, talented, and nongifted children. *Psychology in the Schools, 23,* 308-315.

Runco, M. A. (1989). Parents' and teachers' ratings of the creativity of children. *Journal of Social Behavior and Personality, 4,* 73-83.

Runco, M. A. (Ed.). (1991a). *Divergent thinking.* Norwood, NJ: Ablex.

Runco, M. A. (1991b). The evaluative, valuative, and divergent thinking of children. *Journal of Creative Behavior, 25,* 311-319.

Runco, M. A. (1992). Children's divergent thinking and creative ideation. *Developmental Review, 12,* 233-264.

Runco, M. A. (1993). Operant theories of insight, originality, and creativity. *American Behavioral Scientist, 37,* 59-74.

Runco, M. A. (1994a). Cognitive and psychometric issues in creativity research. In S. G. Isaksen, M. C. Murdock, R. L. Firestien, & D. J. Treffinger (Eds.), *Understanding and recognizing creativity* (pp. 331-368). Norwood, NJ: Ablex.

Runco, M. A. (1994b). Creativity and its discontents. In M. Shaw & M. A. Runco (Eds.), *Creativity and affect* (pp. 102-123). Norwood, NJ: Ablex.

Runco, M. A. (Ed.). (1994c). *Problem finding, problem solving, and creativity.* Norwood, NJ: Ablex.

Runco, M. A. (1996). Personal creativity: Definition and developmental issues. *New Directions for Child Development, 72,* 3-30.

Runco, M. A. (2002). *Critical creative processes.* Cresskill, NJ: Hampton Press.

Runco, M. A., & Albert, R. S. (1985). The reliability and validity of ideational originality in the divergent thinking of academically gifted and nongifted children. *Educational and Psychological Measurement, 45,* 483-501.

Runco, M. A., & Chand, I. (1994). Problem finding, evaluative thinking, and creativity. In M. A. Runco (Ed.), *Problem finding, problem solving, and creativity* (pp. 40-68). Norwood, NJ: Ablex.

Runco, M. A., & Charles, R. (1993). Judgments of originality and appropriateness as predictors of creativity. *Personality and Individual Differences, 15,* 537-546.

Runco, M. A., & Charles, R. (1997). Developmental trends in creativity. In M. A. Runco (Ed.), *Creativity research handbook* (Vol. 1, pp. 115-152). Cresskill, NJ: Hampton Press.

Runco, M. A., Ebersole, P., & Mraz, W. (1991). Self-actualization and creativity. *Journal of Social Behavior and Personality, 6,* 161-167.

Runco, M. A., Johnson, D., & Baer, P. (1992). Parents' and teachers' implicit theories of children's creativity. *Child Study Journal, 23,* 91-113.

Runco, M. A., Johnson, D., & Gaynor, J. R. (1999). The judgmental bases of creativity and implications for the study of gifted youth. In A. Fishkin, B. Cramond, & P. Olszewski-Kubilius (Eds.), *Investigating creativity in youth: Research and methods* pp. 115-143). Cresskill, NJ: Hampton Press.

Runco, M. A., & Okuda, S. M. (1988). Problem-discovery, divergent thinking, and the creative process. *Journal of Youth and Adolescence, 17,* 211-220.

Runco, M. A., & Okuda, S. M. (1991). The instructional enhancement of the ideational originality and flexibility scores of divergent thinking tests. *Applied Cognitive Psychology, 5,* 435-441.

Runco, M. A., & Okuda, S. M. (1996). Reaching creatively gifted children through their learning styles. In R. M. Milgram & R. Dunn (Eds.), *Teaching the gifted and talented through their learning styles.* New York: Praeger.

Runco, M. A., Okuda, S. M., & Thurston, B. J. (1991). Environmental cues and divergent thinking. In M. A. Runco (Ed.), *Divergent thinking* (pp. 91-97). Norwood, NJ: Ablex.

Runco, M. A., & Radio Gaynor, J. (1993). Creativity and optimal development. In J. Brzezinski, S. DiNuovo, T. Maek, & T. Maruszewski (Eds.), *Creativity and consciousness: Philosophical and psychological dimensions* (pp. 395-412). Amsterdam/Atlanta: Rodopi.

Runco, M. A., & Sakamoto, S. O. (1996). Optimization as a guiding principle in research on creative problem solving. In T. Helstrup, G. Kaufmann, & K. H. Teigen (Eds.), *Problem solving and cognitive processes: Essays in honor of Kjell Raaheim* (pp. 119-144). Bergen, Norway: Fagbokforlaget Vigmostad & Bjorke.

Runco, M. A., & Sakamoto, S. O. (in press). Experimental research on creativity. In R. S. Sternberg (Ed.), *Handbook of human creativity.* New York: Cambridge University Press.

Runco, M. A., & Smith, W. R. (1992). Interpersonal and intrapersonal evaluations of creative ideas. *Personality and Individual Differences, 13,* 295-302.

Runco, M. A., & Vega, L. (1990). Evaluating the creativity of children's ideas. *Journal of Social Behavior and Personality, 5,* 439-452.

Schank, R. (1988). *The creative attitude.* New York: Macmillan.

Simon, H. A. (1988). Creativity and motivation: A response to Csikszentmihalyi. *New Ideas in Psychology, 6,* 177-181.

Simon, H. A., & Chase, W. (1973). Skill in chess. *American Scientist, 61,* 394-403.

Simonton, D. K. (1983). Formal education, eminence, and dogmatism: The curvilinear relationship. *Journal of Creative Behavior, 17,* 149-162.

Simonton, D. K. (1988). *Scientific genius: A psychology of science.* New York: Cambridge University Press.

Smith, K. L. R., Michael, W. B., & Hocevar, D. (1990). Performance on creativity measures with examination-taking instructions intended to induce high or low levels of test anxiety. *Creativity Research Journal, 3,* 265-280.

Smolucha, F. (1992). The relevance of Vygotsky's theory for research on creativity and play. *Creativity Research Journal, 5,* 48-67.

Stohs, J. (1992). Intrinsic motivation and sustained art activity among male fine and applied artists. *Creativity Research Journal, 5,* 235-252.

Toplyn, G., & Maquire, W. (1991). The differential effect of noise on creative task performance. *Creativity Research Journal, 4,* 337-348.

Torrance, E. P. (1963). The creative personality and the ideal pupil. *Teachers College Record, 65,* 220-227.

Torrance, E. P. (1968). A longitudinal examination of the fourth-grade slump in creativity. *Gifted Child Quarterly, 12,* 195–199.

Torrance, E. P. (1998). Talent among children who are economically disadvantaged or culturally different. In J. Smutny (Ed.), *The young gifted child: Potential and promise* (pp. 95-118). Cresskill, NJ: Hampton Press.

Urban, K. (1991). On the development of creativity in children. *Creativity Research Journal, 4,* 177-191.

Vernon, P. E. (1970). *Creativity.* Middlesex, England: Penguin.

Wakefield, J. (1985). Towards creativity: Problem finding in a divergent-thinking exercise. *Child Study Journal, 15,* 265-270.

Wallace, D. B. (1991). The genesis of microgenesis of sudden insight in the creation of literature. *Creativity Research Journal, 4,* 41-50.

Wallach, M. A. (1970). Creativity. In P. Mussen (Ed.), *Carmichael's handbook of child psychology* (pp. 1211-1272). New York: Wiley.

Ward, W. C. (1969). Creativity and environmental cues in nursery school children. *Developmental Psychology, 1,* 543-547.

Zajonc, R. (1980). Feeling and thinking: Preferences need no inferences. *American Psychologist, 35,* 151-175.

Part III

Objective 2:
Recognizing Creativity

The second objective of an educational psychology of creativity is to help individuals recognize creativity in themselves and in others. Naturally, the ability to recognize creative processes and products derives from theoretical approaches. In the following chapters a number of the concepts previously described by Esquivel and Runco are revisited.

Two of the largest areas of creativity study have been research into the characteristics of creative persons and development of instruments or procedures to measure creative performance or products. As a way of organizing the two knowledge bases from personality and product research, it is helpful to think of the psychoanalytic-psychodynamic approach as motivating research on the affective, emotive aspects of creativity, leading to studies of the personality traits of creative persons. In contrast, the cognitive-constructivist approach may be thought of as stimulating the efforts to identify and describe cognitive problem-solving skills and strategies, thus leading to the development of various creativity tests and thinking skills training programs widely used in schools.

However, one should be reminded of the rationale for including the two theoretical approaches to creativity explanation in this book in the first place. Both approaches recognized the other's importance and contribution in the total picture. Thus, for the second objective of the educational psychology of creativity, an "either-or," personality versus product viewpoint will not do. An integrated, inclusive, complementary model is required.

In chapter 4, Treffinger has written about creativity and its measurement. He has been a long-time contributor to and advocate for the Creative Problem Solving (CPS) program, which is a comprehensive model and program for stimulating individuals' creative thinking skills and attitudes.

For this book, Treffinger first reviews the major themes of creativity measurement and several well-known instruments. But, he also challenges researchers to look beyond the idea of a single test or assessment instrument that will show who is or is not creative. Measurement of creativity and creative problem-solving skills is an important educational and, Treffinger asserts, achievable goal. But, "authentic" assessment of creative skills, processes, and outcomes requires a broad, inclusive model—a way of thinking about assessment that includes the person and the context in which creativity may occur. Authentic assessment refers to assessment of a person's accomplishments in meaningful and real-life relevant ways, with active participation by the individual in directing or otherwise managing his or her own learning. Treffinger offers just such a model (the COCO model) to guide instructional design, development, evaluation, and research efforts.

In chapter 5, Feldhusen and Westby clearly focus attention on the role of affect in the creative process. The knowledge base required for creative thought and the cognitive, creative thinking meta-skills that individuals develop to operate on the knowledge base are not enough to guarantee productive, creative solutions. Decades of research support the existence and importance of stable personality and style attributes in creative persons. We cannot recognize creativity in ourselves or others without an awareness of these characteristics and how they interact with the knowledge base and our cognitive operations.

In chapter 6, Lopez addresses the issue of the assessment and education of children from different language and cultural backgrounds. Because the most popular creativity tests are heavily dependent on language, the question is raised as to fairness of the tests to children of non-English, minority-culture backgrounds. Many of the personality instruments, too, rely on language and "majority-culture" tasks or procedures. Lopez discusses creativity in language-minority children. It appears from the general literature that minority children receive less attention in creativity programs. For example, they are underrepresented in enrollment in such programs. If educators are to achieve the second objective of the educational psychology of creativity, awareness of the special abilities and needs of minority, culturally different children must increase and proper assessment methods must be developed and used.

4

Assessment and Measurement in Creativity and Creative Problem Solving

Donald J. Treffinger
Center for Creative Learning

This chapter concerns the nature and role of assessment and measurement in the study and practice of creativity. In one way or another, at one time or another, every researcher and practitioner who is seriously interested in creativity will confront the issues of testing, assessment, measurement, or evaluation. Researchers are often concerned, for example, with translating theoretical constructs into operational variables to identify relationships or determine the effects of experimental programs. Practitioners will ask whether some people differ from others in their creative ability, and if so, in what ways, or under what conditions their performance or behaviors will differ. Teachers who attempt to foster creativity in their students will wonder whether, to what extent, or in what ways their efforts are successful. A company's management, or a school district's Board of Education, will examine a proposal for a new program or project to encourage creativity or innovation, and ask, "How will we know if it has been successful? How can we determine if our investment was wise and should be sustained?" In all of these ways, and in many others, it is necessary to deal with issues concerning testing, assessment, measurement, or evaluation of creativity.

This chapter summarizes several topics, although it addresses each of them only briefly, given the constraints of space within the broader overview of the intersection of educational psychology and creative studies. These topics include the rationale for the role of assessment and measurement in the study of creativity and problem solving; several basic principles of measurement, assessment, and evaluation that hold particular significance for creativity and problem solving; several practical resources for creativity assessment, and several important new or emerging issues and challenges for creativity assessment and measurement.

WHY MEASURE CREATIVITY?

Some people have conceived of creativity as a mysterious, esoteric, or elusive phenomenon that really cannot be studied scientifically. To the contrary, however, I begin with the proposition that creativity is an observable, and thus measurable, dimension of human behavior. There can be no doubt that creativity is complex and multidimensional, as theorists and researchers have long proposed (e.g., Rhodes, 1961; Treffinger, 1980, 1996b; Treffinger, Isaksen, & Firestien, 1983). Nonetheless, complexity does not render the construct impossible to assess. There are many valid and important reasons for being concerned with creativity measurement; for example, in Treffinger (1987) I identified eight general roles for creativity assessment. These included the following:

- Help to recognize and affirm the strengths and talents of individuals and enable people to know and understand themselves.
- Expand and enhance the understanding of the nature of human abilities and giftedness.
- Provide "baseline" data for assessing individuals or groups, guiding teachers in planning and conducting appropriate and challenging instruction.
- Provide pretest and posttest data for group comparisons for research or evaluation.
- Help instructors, counselors, or individuals discover unrecognized or untapped talent resources.
- Provide a common language for communication among professionals about the nature of creative abilities and skills.
- Help to remove creativity from the realm of mystery and superstition.
- Provide operational constructs to help advance theory and research on creativity.

ESSENTIAL DEFINITIONS

To provide a common foundational vocabulary, it is helpful to begin with a brief review of the definitions of several important terms. In informal conversation, many terms associated with measurement and creativity are often used casually and imprecisely. But, for professional communication, care in defining terms helps avoid confusion and misunderstandings.

Understanding Measurement and Assessment Terminology

The key terms include *qualitative and quantitative, measurement, assessment,* and *evaluation.*

Qualitative and Quantitative Data. In any assessment or evaluation task, some data will be gathered, analyzed, and interpreted. These data can be described as either *qualitative* or *quantitative.* Qualitative refers to information based on observation, biographical information, anecdotal records, or other similar efforts to view the subjects. Qualitative data include descriptions and anecdotal records, which provide a basis for in-depth analysis and discussion, including consideration of relevant context issues, possible biases, and values. Analyzing qualitative data is a process concerned more with discerning the meaning of information than with formulating and testing statistical hypotheses. When trying to answer questions such as *when or why* some behavior is occurring, qualitative data analysis can often yield important, valuable, and original insights. An observer's description and analysis of a child's curiosity and creativity, as expressed in spontaneous exploratory behavior in a typical school setting, is an example of the use of qualitative data concerning creativity. Data might be gathered in classrooms, in the lunchroom, and on the playground, involving many instances and examples of the student's curiosity and exploration, gathered over a period of several weeks.

Quantitative data analysis draws on resources that yield numerical scores or results, such as tests, rating scales, checklists, and self-report inventories. Quantitative procedures yield scores for variables based on clearly identified attributes, characteristics, or specific objectives; these specific scores or numerical data are used for statistical treatment. Thus, the results of quantitative data are expressed numerically (e.g., by using percentiles, averages, or means). For quantitative analysis, the items on instruments are intended to be free of judgments based on values, and efforts are made to eliminate error or bias or to control error by statistical procedures. Quantitative measures are best used to answer such questions as, "How much . . . or how many. . . ?" "What is the relationship between. . . . ?" "What are the effects of. . . . ?" or "What are differences between. . . . ?" for one or more operationally defined variables. The number of items generated by a participant in response to an open-ended question on a test of divergent thinking is an example of *quantitative data* on creativity assessment. After asking students, for example, to "List as many things as possible that you might see inside an elementary school," counting the total number of responses (a measure of ideational fluency) for each student involves using *quantitative* data.

No single instrument or analytical procedure can capture the complex and multidimensional nature of creativity effectively and comprehensively. Systematic efforts to understand creativity require a well-planned approach to studying individuals or groups, including both qualitative and quantitative data.

Measurement. The term *measurement* refers to the use of any instrument or testing procedure through which quantitative data can be obtained, and thus can be treated statistically.

Assessment. Assessment is a process of appraisal or taking stock of an individual (or a group) by drawing together information from a number of sources and attempting to organize and synthesize those data in a meaningful way in relation to a specific purpose, goal, or task. Assessment may involve qualitative or quantitative data, or a combination of both and frequently includes (but does not exclusively rely on) measurement sources. Assessment might be undertaken to identify and understand a person's (or a group's or team's) strengths and deficiencies in relation to the task or goal at hand, or for more specific diagnostic or prescriptive reasons, such as for instructional planning or for placement in a specific experimental treatment or program. Assessment is, therefore, a broader and more inclusive term than measurement.

Evaluation. Evaluation refers to a systematic process for decision making or determining the extent to which stated goals or objectives were achieved (Gronlund, 1981). For the purposes of this chapter, evaluation focuses on instructional or educational programs for which there are specific goals and objectives, accompanied by deliberate efforts to attain those goals. Evaluation may involve the use of qualitative or quantitative data, or both.

In both creativity assessment (recognizing creativity in individuals or groups) and evaluation (determining whether creativity objectives have been attained), measurement will often play an important role. Creativity assessment involves an attempt to recognize or identify creative characteristics or abilities among people, or to understand their creative strengths and potentials, in relation to goals or tasks that call for creative behavior, processes, or outcomes. Measurement might play a specific role in creativity assessment to the extent that specific tests, inventories, or rating scales provide evidence to help answer such questions. Educators are concerned with creativity assessment, for example, when posing such questions as those that follow:

- Who are the most (or least) creative students in this class?
- What characteristics suggest that a particular student is very creative?
- What are the creative strengths of the people in this group?
- How is creativity expressed differently among individuals of varying learning styles or preferences?
- How might we optimize a group's performance, or design the most effective training experience for a team or work group?

Measurement commonly plays an important role in evaluating instructional or training efforts related to creativity. If a special program for students purported to enhance or stimulate students' creative thinking skills, for example, pre- and posttests might be part of an evaluation design, posing such questions as the following:

- Was the program effective in enhancing students' creative thinking and problem solving skills?
- What impact did the program have on those who participated in it?
- Were participants better able to recognize problems, generate ideas, and plan for creative action after the training program than they were prior to it?
- Did participants in an experimental group demonstrate greater gains in creativity than students in a control group?

Understanding Creativity Terminology

Before reviewing specific creativity measurement instruments or resources, it is also important to clarify the definitions of creativity and problem solving. These terms are commonly used in a variety of ways in popular discussions as well as in the professional literature.

Creativity. Creativity has always been an elusive concept for which there is no single, universally accepted definition; indeed, more than 100 definitions of creativity or creative thinking can easily be documented (Treffinger, 1996a). The many and varied expressions of creativity in human behavior, and the variety of perspectives for studying complex dimensions of intellectual and personality constructs, make it improbable, and perhaps even unwise, to expect that there might be a single, universally accepted definition.

In previous work (Treffinger, 1988a, 1991, 1996b), I discussed several interrelated levels or dimensions for understanding creativity, proposing that four essential components of creative productivity can be identified. These can be organized using the COCO model, which is presented in Figure 4.1. In this view, creative productivity arises from one's characteristics, the operations one is able to use, the context within which one functions, and the nature of the intended or desired outcomes. These components identify aspects of creativity that can be defined, measured, and most importantly, nurtured.

The first component in the figure addresses the *characteristics* that people possess and use, including for example, their cognitive abilities, personal traits, intrinsic motivation, learning styles and psychological types, and creativity styles. The second component involves the *operations* or strategies and techniques people employ to generate and analyze ideas, solve problems, make decisions, and manage their thinking. Third, the model considers the *context* in which individuals or groups must function. Context includes the broad, stable influences often described as "culture," the more specific and immediate or situational dimensions suggested by "climate," the personal and interpersonal influences and skills involved in productivity (such as group dynamics, communication skills, and collaborative skills), and the physical setting or environmental resources or constraints in which people function. Finally, the fourth component involves the outcomes that result from peoples' efforts. Outcomes can be analyzed using a variety of specific criteria (e.g., Besemer & Treffinger, 1981).

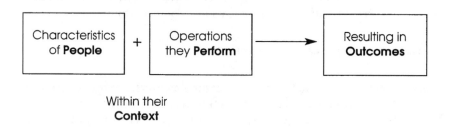

Figure 4.1. The COCO Model (Treffinger, 1988a, 1991, 1996b)

Researchers have defined creativity in even more specific or operational terms, focusing on the measurable variables in creative thinking. Torrance (1974/1987), for example, defined creativity as

> becoming sensitive to or aware of problems, deficiencies, gaps in knowledge, missing elements, disharmonies, and so on; bringing together available information; defining the difficulty of identifying the missing element; searching for solutions, making hypotheses, and modifying and retesting them; perfecting them; and finally communicating the results. (p. 22)

To translate the important elements of his definition into operational variables, Torrance focused initially on several specific verbal and figural divergent thinking variables, including *fluency* (the number or quantity of ideas produced), *flexibility* (the variety or number of different responses), *originality* (the uniqueness or statistical infrequency of ideas produced), and *elaboration* (refining or adding details to ideas to make them richer or more complete). Recent work by Torrance and his associates (e.g., Ball & Torrance, 1984) has led to the expansion and modification of the original categories, in an effort to take the richness and complexity of the construct of creativity more fully into account.

Creative Problem Solving. Problem solving, problem finding, and creative problem solving are also often defined in ways that are linked closely to creativity. Many different ways to describe or classify problem solving have also appeared in the literature. Getzels and Csikszentmihalyi (1976) offered a useful distinction among three classes of problem situations: presented problem situations, discovered problem situations, and created problem situations. Table 4.1 summarizes the definition of each category and describes the process involved in each resulting problem-solving situation. Isaksen (1995) distinguished Creative Problem Solving (CPS) from a more generic view of problem solving, referring to three important factors: problem or task definition, solution pathways or methods, and nature of the desired outcome. Problem solving often refers to well-defined, clearly structured tasks, with a relatively simple, predetermined solution that is generally readily available. By contrast, Isaksen proposed, linking "creativity" and "problem solving" involves working with tasks or problems that are ill-defined or ambiguous, for which the solution pathways or methods may be complex, not predetermined, or even unknown, and for which the desired outcomes must be produced or invented because they are not readily available for the problem solver(s).

CPS (Isaksen, Dorval, & Treffinger, 1994; Treffinger, Isaksen, & Dorval, 1994a, 1994b) represents a specific, structured approach to finding,

Table 4.1. Classifications of Problem Solving.

Type of Problem Situation	Process and Solution	Examples of Measures
Presented problem	Known problem Known procedure Known solution (by others)	Standardized test Fill-in-the-blank Multiple-choice Computation
Discovered problem	Known problem Known solution (by others)	Algorithmic Metacognitive Logical or analytical tests
Created problem	Unknown problem (all) Unknown process (all) Unknown solution (all)	Experimental creative problem solving assessments

Note: Adapted from Getzels and Csikszentmihalyi (1976, p. 80).

defining, and solving problems, and in particular, for working with problems that are ill-defined, complex, and for which new directions are required. (I use CPS to designate the specific framework, and creative problem solving to represent a general effort by anyone to solve problems creatively.) The CPS framework is comprised of three main components (Understanding the Problem, Generating Ideas, and Planning for Action) and six specific stages (Mess-Finding, Data-Finding, Problem-Finding, Idea-Finding, Solution-Finding, and Acceptance-Finding). Each of the six stages can involve both a generating phase (producing options) and a focusing phase (analyzing, refining, choosing, and developing options). The typology of problems proposed by Getzels and the stages of problem solving illustrated by the CPS model can contribute to an understanding of how creativity and problem solving are interrelated. When the parameters of the problem, the process for solving it, and the solution, are all ambiguous or unknown, there is clearly a greater challenge for creative thinking and imagination.

Some new problem-solving measures, such as those considered in this chapter, seek to go beyond the presented and discovered problem categories and to attend more toward those in the created problem category. Unfortunately, such measures are uncommon and still exist primarily in the form of preliminary or experimental measures for research use. Nonetheless, consideration of these issues is important, because they guide current efforts to identify some of the most significant and promising issues and future directions in the area of creativity and CPS measurement, assessment, and evaluation.

MEASUREMENT RESOURCES

This section describes and discusses several specific measurement resources commonly used in the areas of creativity and problem solving. The presentation of resources follows the componential structure of the COCO model (Fig. 4.1) to help organize or classify the major emphases of the instruments to be described. More comprehensive reviews and discussions of specific creativity assessment instruments and resources can be found in Cropley (1996), Hocevar (1981), Hocevar and Bachelor (1989), Isaksen, Firestien, Murdock, Puccio, and Treffinger (1994), or Puccio, Isaksen, Treffinger, and Murdock (in press).

Characteristics

Since the 1950s, much research has focused on the search for the traits, characteristics, and other personal attributes of creative people. I do not review at length these efforts to draw portraits of "the creative person" because they have been surveyed in detail elsewhere (e.g., Davis, 1986; MacKinnon, 1978; Torrance, 1979). By way of illustration only, then, the following list presents some of the characteristics most commonly presented as indicative of creativity, and thus most typically incorporated into creative characteristics checklists, self-report measures, rating scales, or observation instruments (e.g., Treffinger, 1996b). The characteristics commonly associated with creativity in individuals include the following:

- Fluency
- Flexibility
- Originality
- Elaboration
- Openness

- Risk-taking
- Curiosity
- Complexity
- Imagination
- Independence

- Tolerance of ambiguity
- Preference for complexity
- Rely on own judgments
- Playful with ideas
- Making connections between seemingly unconnected things

In the last decade, our perspective on characteristics of creativity has changed. Researchers today seek to consider *how people are creative* as well as *how creative people are.* "How creative people are" concerns one's degree or *level* of creativity, whereas "how people are creative" concerns one's *style* or preferred ways of expressing or using one's creativity. The area of learning style (or closely allied areas, such as personality types, cognitive styles, or creativity styles) has become an area of major attention and significance in research on creativity (e.g., Dunn, Dunn, & Treffinger, 1992; Isaksen, 1987; Kirton, 1976; Treffinger & Selby, 1993). The focus of research has expanded, from concern only with level or traits of creativity, toward inquiry into styles of creativity. This shift prompted researchers to frame questions regarding characteristics and their implications for creativity in new and different ways. Concern for level of creativity led researchers to focus on "how much" or "how little" creativity one might possess, or on whether or not a person shared the traits of highly creative producers. In contrast, a focus on style led researchers to highlight the importance of how people express or direct their creativity differently, in various settings or contexts, and how one's creativity might be optimized by knowing and building upon one's personal strengths. Knowledge of both level and style dimensions is important in creativity measurement (e.g., Isaksen & Kaufmann, 1991).

Several specific measurement resources can be identified for assessing characteristics associated with creativity. Some are primarily concerned with information about *level* of creativity (cognitive abilities and personality traits possessed to a greater or lesser degree by a person); others focus on *style* of creativity (identifying one's creative preferences or unique ways of functioning creatively).

Level: Cognitive Characteristics. Many creative thinking measures focus on divergent production or the generation of ideas or possibilities. Those representing cognitive characteristics, with an emphasis on level of creativity, include the *Torrance Tests of Creative Thinking* (TTCT; Torrance, 1974/1987); Guilford's (1967, 1977) measures of Divergent Production; and Wallach and Kogan's (1965) tasks. Mednick's (1962) *Remote Associates Test* (RAT) also measures creativity as a cognitive ability, although not in relation to divergent thinking.

The TTCT (Torrance, 1974/1987) measure fluency, flexibility, originality, and elaboration, which are divergent thinking (cognitive) skills. The TTCT include several verbal subtests (Asking Questions, Guessing Causes, Guessing Consequences, Product Improvement, Unusual Uses, and Just Suppose), and figural subtests as well (Picture Construction, Picture Completion, and Circles or Parallel Lines). More recent "streamlined scoring" efforts (Ball & Torrance, 1984) introduced additional criteria, and encouraged researchers and educators to look beyond strictly quantitative evaluation of test results, and to consider other scoring dimensions as well. Cramond (1992) described some useful guidelines for reviewing test responses to glean additional information about students' creative strengths. Although the TTCT are the most widely known and used instruments for assessing creative thinking (especially among children), the instruments have been criticized in relation to several psychometric and practical issues (e.g., Crockenberg, 1972; Wallach, 1988). Concerns have been expressed relating to the independence of scores on various subtests and scoring dimensions, the independence of creative thinking in relation to other cognitive variables, and the strength of the evidence regarding the long-term predictive validity, especially in relation to indicators of adult creative productivity. Additionally, concerns have been raised about the appropriateness of using scores from the TTCT to make global categorizations, such as labeling students as "creatively gifted or talented," or using scores to select individual children for (or to exclude individual students from) certain school programs.

Guilford and his associates developed a variety of instruments to assess specific dimensions of divergent thinking, both verbal and figural, based on the categories hypothesized in Guilford's (1967, 1977) Structure of Intellect (SOI) model. Specific tasks are used to represent a number of SOI factors (such as Divergent Production of Semantic Units, Divergent Production of Figural Units, Divergent Production of Semantic Systems, or others). In addition to divergent production operations, other SOI dimensions, such as transformations and implications outcomes, may also provide information relevant to creative behavior. Meeker's *SOI Learning Abilities Tests* (Meeker, 1979) also purport to assess creative thinking factors in structure-of-intellect terms, although the psychometric adequacy of these instruments has been seriously questioned in the literature (Clarizio & Mehrens, 1985).

Creativity tasks devised by Wallach and Kogan (1965) are also measures of ideational fluency and uniqueness, assessed through five tasks: Instances, Alternate Uses, Similarities, Pattern Meanings, and Line Meanings. These tasks have been used in a number of experimental studies, but have not been used extensively for assessing creativity in schools or other field settings.

The *Williams Creativity Assessment Packet* (Williams, 1980) also purports to assess several divergent thinking characteristics. The validity and reliability data concerning these instruments are very limited, however, and have been criticized strongly in the literature (e.g., Damarin, 1985; Rosen, 1985). Therefore, practitioners should be very cautious in considering their use in any field settings.

The RAT developed by Mednick (1962) also assesses cognitive skills purported to relate to creativity in verbal association. The RAT measures one's ability to make distant or "remote" connections among associatively linked words, when the basis for the common association is not common or obvious (based on free association word norms). Critics of the RAT question whether it is a measure of creative ability or more simply of vocabulary development or verbal proficiency. Its focus on a single, correct response also is considered antithetical to the very concept of creativity and problem solving by some reviewers (e.g., Milgram & Rabkin, 1980; Taft & Rossiter, 1966).

Most cognitive level instruments for assessing creativity have been the subject of considerable controversy among measurement specialists as well as creativity theorists and researchers. The skills they assess are considered by many to represent only one part of the larger universe of creative behavior. There is disagreement among researchers about the extent to which such variables as verbal fluency or originality, for example, truly represent valid indicators of real-life creative accomplishment. These concerns lead many to hold considerable reservations about the theoretical merits of using divergent thinking measures to represent the broader or more general construct of creativity. Torrance (1974/1987) contended quite specifically that these measures do represent a valid aspect of the construct, but that they did not purport to represent all important elements of that construct. It would not be wise to expect any single instrument to assess every aspect of a concept as complex as creativity. Measures of divergent thinking do provide information that serves an important and useful purpose in creativity assessment, but the test user should be aware of the limitations of the instruments and should exercise considerable caution in generalizing about the nature of the characteristics being measured. These cautions and limitations are especially important to keep in mind when attempting to understand the creative talents of individuals, or to compare and select individuals for specific programs. The tests should be used in conjunction with other data, and should be used in ways that place greater emphasis on finding a person's strengths than on attempting to make summary judgments or classifications of a person's creativity or lack thereof. Taken alone, cognitive-level measures do not provide a comprehensive description or assessment of a person's creative ability or potential. Under a definition of creativity including ideational productivity, however, they can and do provide relevant and useful information (Runco, 1990; Treffinger, 1985).

Level: Personality Characteristics. Efforts to assess personality characteristics associated with creativity have long played a prominent role in creativity measurement research. The work of several researchers at the Institute for Personality Assessment and Research at the University of California at Berkeley, especially during the 1960s and 1970s, provided many important contributions to the understanding of personal characteristics related to creativity. These researchers, including Barron (1969), MacKinnon (1978), Helson and Crutchfield (1970), and others, studied many creatively productive individuals, including architects, writers, scientists, managers, and mathematicians. Through intensive studies, involving extensive quantitative and qualitative assessment, they sought to identify characteristics or traits that consistently distinguished highly creative producers from their less creative peers. Some of the personality characteristics commonly identified, as summarized by MacKinnon (1978) included the following:

- Creative people are intelligent, although how they use their intelligence is more significant a factor in creative production than level of intelligence.
- Original.
- Independent in thought and action.
- Especially open to experience both of the inner self and outer world.
- Intuitive.
- Posses strong theoretical and aesthetic interests.
- Posses strong sense of destiny.

MacKinnon (1978) proposed that these were traits most generally indicative of creative persons. Although it is possible that at some point in any individual's lifetime, he or she might exhibit any one—or several—of these traits, those individuals who tend to be highly creatively productive more often exhibited these traits regularly and consistently, over sustained periods of time.

Davis and Rimm (1977) emphasized the usefulness of a characteristics approach for assessing creativity among elementary and secondary students. The characteristics they measured included psychological, personality, motivational, and biographical data. Some specific examples of personality characteristics assessed by Davis and Rimm include attitudes, motivations, interests, and values. The biographical reports include information such as past creative interests, habits, and activities. These researchers assumed that past creative interests, habits, and activities are very strong predictors of future behavior. Davis (1975) also proposed that most creative people are fully aware of their unique abilities and experiences. Thus, questions that ask the individual if he or she is creative, inventive, ingenious, or original may have a high degree of accuracy for prediction of future creative interests.

Many instruments have been used to assess personality characteristics associated with creativity. These include the *Alpha Biographical Inventory* (ABI; Taylor & Ellison, 1966); the *Adjective Checklist* (ACL; Gough, 1952); the *Biographical Inventory—Creativity* (BIC; Schaefer, 1970); the *Group Inventory for Finding Creative Talent* (GIFT; Rimm & Davis, 1980) and the *Khatena Torrance Creative Perception Inventory* (KTCPI; Khatena & Torrance, 1976).

Taylor's ABI (Taylor & Ellison, 1966) focuses on self-descriptions of behaviors or past and present activities in a number of areas of creative productivity. The BIC (Schaefer, 1970) asks the person to report past experiences regarding family history, educational history, hobbies, and other personal creative activities. Biographical inventories commonly build on the assumption that one's past and present activities will be the best predictors of one's future activities and accomplishments.

The ACL (Gough, 1952) asks respondents to read a list of 300 adjectives, checking the items they consider self-descriptive. Several clusters of items have been identified as the basis for subscales that can be used to predict various personality dimensions and behavioral traits among individuals; some of these have focused on sets of items correlated with creative productivity (e.g., Domino, 1970; Smith & Schaefer, 1969).

Davis and Rimm developed four inventories to assess personal characteristics related to creativity among children and adolescents. These are the GIFT (Rimm & Davis, 1976, 1980), two forms of the *Group Inventory For Finding Interests* (GIFFI I and II; Rimm & Davis, 1980), and the *Preschool Interest Descriptor* (PRIDE; Rimm 1983). The authors' stated intent for these instruments was to help to identify students for instructional opportunities, not to provide a basis for excluding students from programs. That is, high scores may help to confirm students' characteristics, but low scores should not be assumed to disconfirm creative characteristics in an individual. They also contended that the instruments should not be used as a single identification criterion for giftedness.

The KTCPI (Khatena & Torrance, 1976), is a self-description measure of personal creativity characteristics, including two scales (*What Kind of Person Are You* and *Something About Myself*). Each scale purports to yield information regarding several dimensions relevant to creative personality, including such variables as confidence, disciplined imagination, acceptance of authority, initiative, self-strength, individuality, and artistry.

These instruments have been used in research, and are supported (in varying degrees) by some evidence for their validity and reliability. The strength of the supporting evidence varies, however, among studies of subjects at different ages, and in relation to external criteria used. We cannot say with confidence that any of these measures gives a comprehensive assessment of all personal characteristics associated with creativity, in any setting or area of expression, or across all age levels. Thus, we conclude once again that, although the instruments in this category can be useful in obtaining information about students' personal creative characteristics, they (individually or as a group) do not provide a comprehensive assessment of creativity.

Style. Individual learning, personality, or creativity styles can play a powerful role in identifying and recognizing peoples' creative strengths and nurturing their creative productivity. When individuals are made aware of their creative strengths, they are better able to apply techniques for overcoming limitations and expanding their productivity. The benefits of obtaining information regarding both level and style are numerous—for individuals, teams, or groups. Individuals, for example, can use these data to enhance their awareness of their own strengths and potentials, to identify the kinds of problems or challenges they are most likely to define or encounter, or to recognize the methods and techniques best suited to their natural preferences and competencies. Level and style data can help the members of teams or groups to understand better each person's strengths, preferences, and potential limitations, to increase active participation, to improve communication, and to guide the group's activities.

The Kirton Adaptor-Innovator Inventory (KAI; Kirton, 1976, 1977, 1987) reflects Kirton's theory that people differ in predictable ways in how they define and solve problems. Some individuals prefer an "adaptive" approach, with an emphasis on working within existing systems or structures to improve them or make them better, gradually and systematically. People who are more adaptive are often seen as resourceful, efficient, thorough, enterprising, adaptable, methodical, organized, planful, precise, reliable, and dependable. Others prefer an "innovative" approach to change, which involves modifying or redefining existing paradigms, pressing for a high degree of originality, and less concern for efficiency, rule conformity, or "fitting in" with the present situation. People with more innovative preferences are usually viewed as ingenious, original, energetic, individualistic, independent, unconventional, spontaneous, insightful, and unique. Kirton holds that both adaptive and innovative preferences can lead to creativity, although their creativity will be expressed in different ways. Adaptors prefer to use their creativity to work within existing structures, whereas innovators seek new and different structures.

The *Myers Briggs Type Indicator* (MBTI; Myers & McCaulley, 1985) is a measure of psychological type, based on Jungian theory. It measures valuable and constructive differences among people along four principal dimensions: where they prefer to focus their attention (extroversion or introversion), the way they prefer to gather information (sensing and intuition), their primary focus in making decisions (thinking and feeling), and the way they prefer to deal with the outside world (judging or perceiving). The MBTI has been used widely in businesses, organizations, and a variety of counseling contexts. Information about MBTI preferences is important in becoming aware of and using to best advantage one's preferences in directing or focusing creative energies and resources, and thus in enhancing the possibility for creative accomplishment and productivity.

Learning styles involve the ways in which one prefers to organize and deal with various aspects of our physical, social, emotional, and perceptual environment. The *Learning Style Inventory* (LSI; Dunn, Dunn, & Price, 1975) was created for students in Grades 4-12, and the *Productivity Environmental Preference Survey* (PEPS; Dunn, Dunn, & Price, 1986) was developed for adults. These instruments measure 18 specific dimensions of learning styles. Environmental preferences include sound, light, temperature, and design. The emotional dimension includes motivation, persistence, responsibility, and structure. The sociological component includes one's preference for learning alone, in a pair, with peers, in a team, with a teacher or authority, or in varied ways. Finally, the physical component includes perceptual preferences (auditory, visual, tactile, or kinesthetic), intake, time of day, and mobility. Learning style measures have been the focus of considerable research and practical applications (e.g., Dunn & Dunn, 1978), and have also been related to strategies for enhancing creative productivity and giftedness in school or at home (Dunn et al., 1992).

Summary: Measures of Characteristics. Systematic efforts to understand and assess cognitive and personality characteristics associated with creativity will help researchers and educators to expand and improve their efforts to nurture creative productivity among many people. Assessing these characteristics is a complex challenge. We should not expect to find a single test or measurement instrument that will provide all the information that is necessary to recognize and nurture any person's creative talent.

The shift from a focus only on one's level of creativity to an emphasis on understanding *both* level and style has been a major recent advance in research and practice relating to the assessment of creativity characteristics. Contemporary views recognize that the potential for creative productivity exists in all people, and that assessment can be used more powerfully to find, clarify, and guide the realization of those potentials. These efforts have challenged us to look beyond searching only for scores by which people can be categorized as creative or not creative, or by which people can be sorted and labeled on creative ability (such as "high" or "low" creative). The importance of assessing creativity characteristics is derived from our ability to use those data to nurture creativity more effectively among all people.

Operations

The operations component of the COCO model includes the strategies and techniques people use to generate and analyze ideas, make decisions, and solve problems, and to monitor and manage their own cognitive efforts. Operations represent deliberate mental or intellectual activities that all people can learn and apply to be productive thinkers. The operations involved in productive thinking have been classified in a variety of ways. Guilford (1967, 1977) described them as specific intellectual abilities or factors. They have also been described as multiple talents (e.g., Schlichter, 1986; Taylor, 1986), multiple intelligences (e.g., Gardner, 1983), or as a sequence of increasingly complex and interrelated learning outcomes (e.g., Feldhusen, 1995b; Treffinger, 1988b; Treffinger, Feldhusen, & Isaksen, 1990, 1996). Creative productivity requires people to know, apply, deliberately and actively select, monitor, and modify a variety of techniques, strategies, methods, or techniques. Feldhusen (1993, 1995a) proposed that creative cognition—cognitive activity that leads to products that are perceived as new and useful—can be linked in important and powerful ways to talent; it involves the integration and use of a number of specific cognitive and metacognitive skills, motivations and dispositions, and an extensive, well-organized, and accessible knowledge base.

Thus, assessing and measuring productive thinking is clearly a complex challenge; there is no single measure that encompasses one's proficiency in all relevant operations. The specific variables to be assessed will depend on the particular framework or model used to define and describe the operations. Because there are several levels or categories in most operational models, many of which may then be further subdivided, several different instruments or tasks may be needed to provide an accurate representation.

Fundamental operations related to creative thinking can be assessed using the same instruments described in the previous section under "cognitive characteristics," such as measures of divergent thinking. One's ability to generate ideas can be represented as a characteristic (i.e., we can assess whether some individuals are naturally strong in generating many, varied, or unusual ideas). Because people can learn strategies for increasing production of a number of ideas (fluency), greater variety of ideas (flexibility), and increased novelty of ideas (originality), these variables can also be used to describe basic operations or skills related to creativity.

At the present time, there appear to be few (if any) instruments to measure metacognitive skills, or to measure the more complex operations involved in creativity or problem solving. Measures of complex creative problem-solving skills (particularly in relation to open-ended, real-life problems) are generally still in highly experimental stages of development, if they are available at all. For the CPS approach (Isaksen, Dorval, & Treffinger, 1994; Treffinger et al., 1994a), several instruments, rating scales, checklists, and inventories have been developed for experimental and research use (e.g., Treffinger, 1994a). Table 4.2 illustrates directions for assessing operations at three different levels of complexity of instruction in creative learning (Treffinger, 1995).

Context

A person's context—the situation, setting, or environment in which one functions—plays an important role in stimulating or inhibiting creative productivity. A challenging, motivating, dynamic setting might bring out an individual's best, for example, whereas conflict, constant criticism, and pressure may stifle productivity. The organizational or team climate may include both individual or personal and group or interpersonal dimensions. Numerous elements in either dimension can serve as "gates" for creativity. When the gates are open, creative potential is enhanced, but when they are closed or blocked, imagination and creativity wither. Jones (1984) identified four factors that frequently serve as "barriers" or contextual influences of creativity; these are *strategic, perceptual, values,* and *self-image* barriers. Jones developed an experimental measure for individuals to assess the relative extent to which each of these four blocks to creativity influence their behavior. Evidence for the validity and reliability of the instrument is quite preliminary, and the measure is not widely available for use outside the research setting.

At the group or interpersonal level, the organizational climate for creativity has been investigated by Amabile (1989) in relation to children, and by Ekvall (1983) and others with adults. Ekvall identified 10 factors contributing to a creative climate, which are challenge, freedom,

Table 4.2. Measures of Operations at Three Levels of Complexity in Instruction.

Level of Complexity	Instructional Focus	Assessment or Measurement Resources
Level 1: Basic Tools (e.g., Creative and critical thinking tools; Metacognitive skills).	Direct Instruction; Teacher presents and manages activities or exercises, directs students in applying them and in monitoring their efforts.	Measures of divergent thinking, basic critical thinking skills; checklists, rating scales
Level 2: Learning and Practicing a Structured Approach to Problem Solving (e.g., Applying the CPS process to realistic tasks).	Appropriate leadership; use of realistic (but contrived or teacher-presented) tasks and problems; collaborative or cooperative small groups, role playing, and simulations.	CPS Skills Inventory, CPS Information Quiz, CPS Attitude Inventories (Treffinger, 1994a); computer-based simulations; interactive videodisc tasks; checklists to assess: competence, confidence, commitment; performance demonstration
Level 3: Real Problems (e.g., Applying CPS methods to problems and challenges for which there is personal ownership and commitment to action).	Effective facilitation; focus on challenges for which problem solvers have personal ownership.	Portfolio Assessment and documentation: —Product samples —Video/Audio —Prototypes —Creative Behavior —Checklists —Testimonials or letters

dynamism and liveliness, trust and openness, idea time, playfulness and humor, conflict, idea support, debate, and risk-taking. *Ekvall's Creativity Climate Questionnaire* (CCQ) instrument is primarily an experimental measure, used mostly for research purposes and in some training programs. Ekvall's original measure has been reanalyzed extensively, and formulated into a nine dimension framework and assessment tool, the *Situational Outlook Questionnaire* (SOQ; Isaksen, Lauer, Murdock, Dorval, & Puccio, 1995; Treffinger, Isaksen, & Dorval, 1996). The SOQ yields data regarding the degree to which group members perceive their organization's climate and situation as supportive of creativity, innovation, and change, with specific scores for each of the nine dimensions. Treffinger et al. (1996) used the climate dimensions, as formulated by Ekvall and revised in the SOQ, to describe several important factors contributing to a supportive climate for creativity and innovation in educational settings (for adults as well as in classroom settings).

Prior to the development of these resources, there were relatively few instruments that were well validated for use in assessing specific factors contributing to the environment or context for creativity. As a result, practitioners have long relied on informal lists of blocks or barriers to creativity (which are presented in many popular texts on creativity). Even though much more research and development is needed to enable practitioners to assess the context dimension more effectively across many groups and settings, it seems wise nonetheless for practitioners to refrain from making judgments about a particular person's creative ability as if it depended only on traits within that person. The importance of context should not be overlooked or disregarded simply because it cannot be assessed easily, and the effects of many complex situational variables cannot be dismissed in favor of superficial generalizations about any person's "creative ability" or aptitude.

Outcomes

Outcomes refer to the results or products that come from the efforts of individuals or groups. Measurement of outcomes or creative products assesses the extent or degree to which specific criteria of creativity are present or absent.

Measures of creative products are also in a relatively early or preliminary stage of development. A model of Creative Product Assessment developed by Besemer and O'Quin (1987), based on extensive research and development to test and extend the model proposed originally by Besemer and Treffinger (1981), is a specific example of a quantitative instrument intended to assess creativity criteria in various products. This approach involves consideration of 14 criteria, organized into three major dimensions: novelty, resolution, and elaboration–synthesis. These criteria have been used experimentally by judges or evaluators to assess creativity criteria in a variety of different artistic, scientific, educational, and consumer products. The criteria have also been adapted into rating scales to assess creative product dimensions of student inventions (Treffinger, 1988c). In Puccio, Treffinger, and Talbot (1995), we also demonstrated that there are interactions between style dimensions and assessments of creative products. In evaluating new product ideas, adaptors and innovators weighed specific criteria of creativity in significantly different ways. The more adaptive evaluators sought products that were described as adequate, logical, well-crafted, and useful, whereas the more innovative evaluators emphasized criteria such as original, attractive, transformational, and expressive.

THE STATUS OF CREATIVITY MEASUREMENT IN EDUCATION

Although there has been growing emphasis on the importance of creativity and "thinking skills" in education, it does not seem that commensurate attention has been given to systematic efforts to measure creativity and problem solving, either in relation to assessment of students' characteristics and needs or to evaluation of instructional or programmatic outcomes.

Our overview of measurement resources in the four components of creative productivity (characteristics, operations, context, and outcomes) may inform us, at least in part, regarding the reasons for the present status. There is no single instrument that might be used to assess creativity or problem solving. Within each of the four dimensions, there are several instruments, but they are not equally appropriate or useful at all ages or across all settings. In many cases, the evidence for validity and reliability is incomplete or not fully satisfactory. As we proceed from the dimensions that have been recognized for longer periods of time (such as assessment of personal characteristics and styles or creative thinking measures), into more complex areas such as problem-solving context, or outcomes, the challenges are even more complex. At best, it would be necessary to develop a complex composite of several instruments for any particular assessment or evaluation context, and even then, results must be qualified and generalizations made with great caution. As Cropley (1996) proposed, "measurement of creativity probably requires new procedures that cross conventional test boundaries" (p. 203). Similarly, Feldhusen and Goh (1995) concluded that "assessment of such a multidimensional construct as creativity requires multiple channels of measurement . . ." (p. 240). Measuring creativity is not an easy task, then, and those who seek simple, all-purpose resources will surely be dissatisfied.

Tests, when used, are not always employed appropriately or wisely (see, e.g., Alvino, McDonnell, & Richert 1981; Hunsaker & Callahan, 1995). Hunsaker and Callahan reported that, although many schools have adopted definitions of giftedness that include creativity, they have seldom offered definitions of creativity, or if they have, it has often been a narrow or limited conception of creativity (very often overlooking the product and context dimensions). Consequently, Hunsaker and Callahan argued, there have also been numerous operational problems. The common problems they noted include mismatches between definitions and instruments, reliance on a single instrument, and insufficient attention to the adequacy and usefulness of the instrument(s) selected. Creativity measures are often administered inappropriately in school settings, used to assess skills or abilities they were not intended to measure, or interpreted inappropriately. Table 4.3 summarizes several potential "uses" and parallel "common abuses" of creativity tests in educational settings.

To be sure, then, the challenge of measuring creativity and problem solving in educational settings is still elusive and fraught with peril. Cropley (1996) argued that creativity tests should be considered most useful as indicators of potential, inasmuch as children may seldom create products that attain wide acclaim. He proposed that although a number of instruments exist, their success in reliably measuring real life creativity is open to doubt. Hunsaker and Callahan (1995) summarized the status of creativity measurement in education and outlined several important steps that are still needed:

> In summary, many issues in creativity assessment raised over a decade ago continue to prove worrisome even after years of effort. Concerted efforts in . . . creativity assessment . . . will be needed to address these problems successfully. . . . Unfortunately, the data from this study indicate that we have a great distance to go both as researchers and practitioners. . . (p. 114)

The complex challenges in this area of research are certainly not unimportant, then, and they should not be considered insurmountable. Despite reservations about existing instruments and current practices, there are many new and promising directions in creativity measurement (cf. Houtz & Krug, 1995). I consider these in the closing section of this chapter.

Table 4.3. Common Uses and Abuses of Creativity Tests.

Potential Uses	Common Abuses
Comparing group performances	Cutoff scores for individual students Unethical competition among teams or individuals
Enhance comprehensive understanding of abilities, through a profile	Seeking a CQ (Creativity Quotient) in place of IQ (substituting a misuse of one test for a misuse of another)
Assessing mastery of basic divergent thinking skills to prepare more complex thinking skills or processes	"Divergent busywork" (assigning more divergent thinking exercises to students already strong in those skills)
	Training people in a variety of skills without techniques for transfer to actual workplace tasks
Assess individuals' growth in creative abilities over time	One-shot judgments
Assist teachers and managers in understanding and identifying dimensions of creativity that are relevant to instruction	Requesting global nominations, without training or experience, to seek ways to sort or label individuals
Develop a database for prediction of individuals' academic and creative accomplishments	Short-term assessment, relying only on external norms
Increase effectiveness for recognizing and responding to individuals' strengths	Searching for "weaknesses" to remediate
Complex data used as part of our effort to obtain a richer, more comprehensive understanding of the individuals' characteristics and needs	"Quick and dirty" quantification to justify inclusion or exclusion decisions

FUTURE DIRECTIONS FOR CREATIVITY MEASUREMENT

What are some of the most promising or intriguing future directions for creativity measurement? Several new avenues of research and development are important for today's educators.

Learning Styles

Research on learning styles has already suggested many new pathways for understanding, identifying, and nurturing creativity (e.g., Isaksen & Kaufmann, 1991; Kirton, 1977, 1987). Continuing research in this area will be particularly significant in helping educators and trainers maximize the effectiveness of programs intended to enhance creative productivity at various age levels. Promising research directions in this area include comparisons of the stylistic demands of one's task or work with one's personal and ideal preferences, or clarification of the specific effects of style preferences on selection and use of various creative thinking, critical thinking, and creative problem-solving strategies.

Assessing Metacognitive Skills

We need studies of more or less successful efforts by people to monitor, manage, and modify their own creative thinking and CPS efforts. These include, for example, efforts to clarify how individuals can best monitor their own efforts to generate many, varied, or unusual ideas in different individual or group contexts; ways to help people choose and apply different strategies in different settings or for different purposes; investigations of guidelines for applying strategies appropriately within or across varied task or content situations; and, development of guidelines for individuals and groups to follow in modifying their efforts and choices when they are not as productive as desired.

Authentic Assessment

The introduction of *authentic assessment* is one of the most widely discussed and potentially important new developments in the area of assessment in education (e.g., Hart, 1994; Perrone, 1991; Wiggins, 1993). It is relevant to creativity assessment in many situations within and beyond education. Authentic assessment refers to any effort to assess a person's learning or accomplishments—the attainment of important or valued outcomes—in ways that relate meaningfully to the uses or applications of that learning in real-life situations or under conditions that approximate real situations. It also emphasizes an active, self-directed role for the learner in monitoring and managing her or his own learning experiences.

As the pressures for authentic assessment have grown larger on the horizon of education and training, the topic has become the focus for many responses—from enthusiastic to fearful. Authenticity (dealing with matters that are real and have significant consequences) presents complex challenges and issues. These concern the overall *process* of designing, implementing, monitoring, and evaluating authentic assessment. They refer to the *what* and *how* of authentic assessment; these are the issues about which there is the greatest variety of approaches and diversity of interpretations, questions, and concerns. Some of the major questions in relation to the overall process of authentic assessment are presented here. In stating these as challenges or opportunities for creative thinking, I have worded them as problem statements, in the form, "In what ways might we. . . ?" "How might we. . . ?" or "How to. . . ."

- How might educators differentiate among profiles, portfolios, and the final products, in terms of the purposes and uses of each?
- How might we minimize the start-up or front-load time required for teachers and students to initiate authentic assessment?
- Who "owns" the profile, or the portfolio, and who should be involved in the creation and use of each?
- How might the responsibility for learning and keeping the portfolio be shifted from the teacher to the student?

In Treffinger (1994b) and Treffinger and Cross (1994) we proposed that the overall process of authentic assessment might be divided into four broad categories or stages: *preparation, instruction, achievement,* and *documentation.* In relation to creativity assessment, the four components of the COCO model (Fig. 4.1) should be taken into account in each of these four stages. Profiling can be particularly valuable in identifying creative strengths, for example, but it is very important for profiling efforts to incorporate data from all four components of the COCO framework, not just from the "characteristics" section. Instructional tasks should be designed that take into account learning style differences and an appropriate environment for creative productivity (context). The achievements of various students may differ in relation to the way the students develop projects and express themselves (characteristics), and in relation to the aspects of creativity they emphasize in their products (outcomes in the COCO model). One's portfolio or documentation will also incorporate the COCO components. Differences in style, environmental influences, strategies used, and various product goals will all be reflected in many ways in the structure and contents of one's portfolio.

I explain each of the four stages in authentic assessment briefly, and identify some of the major emerging questions and issues within each area.

Preparation: The Profile. Preparation is the stage of authentic assessment concerned with diagnosis or planning for educational programming. It involves creating a *profile,* which is a planning document about a person, for a purpose (Isaksen, Puccio, & Treffinger, 1993). In relation to creativity, a profile should be considered the starting point or the initial entry-level assessment of the student's creative talents (strengths and needs) for a particular set of tasks or outcomes. It should serve as a benchmark, a reference at one point in time and effort, to which the student's future efforts can be compared as a gauge of progress or change. The profile can be a diagnostic resource to assist those who are responsible for planning appropriate instructional opportunities and experiences, for selecting necessary resources, and for providing the required services. The profile may include *static* data (e.g., test scores and previous grades or recommendations that reflected the student's knowledge or characteristics in a certain context and at a particular time). These data provide baseline data in relation to personal characteristics, thinking skills, or knowledge within a certain task domain. The profile may also include more dynamic data, in the form of all or part of a student's prior or present portfolio. One's present activities and accomplishments can help to define the path for future experiences and challenges.

It is also important to approach it as a profile for a purpose, not an overall characterization of one's creative ability, and to establish and maintain a specific task or goal on which the profile focuses. My creative strengths profile is about "me," but I am constantly changing and growing. The me I really need to know also depends on many factors around me: where I am, what I am attempting to do, with whom I am working, when I am doing it (and how much time I have), the other things on my mind—and more. Therefore, "my profile" must be a moving image of me, not a still photograph. I am always in the process of becoming!

Illustrative Profile Questions. Some of the major questions in relation to understanding and using profiles in authentic assessment are as follows:

- In what ways might we select or modify existing instruments or sources of data to assist with the development of the profile?
- How might the information contained within the profile be interpreted and used as benchmarks and as diagnostic tools for

programming and developing an individual educational plan for students?

- How might profiles be viewed more as dynamic assessments of a learner's strengths and needs, in relation to a particular task or setting, than as static, "all-purpose" characterizations of a learner? This question calls for a more ecological view of profiling, as proposed by Isaksen and Puccio (1992) and Isaksen et al. (1993).
- How to deal with the issues of privacy or confidentiality in students' personal or reflective journals?
- How to use exemplary work of others to help students set challenging goals, while neither intimidating the students ("the awe of masterpieces") nor suggesting that their goal is simply to reproduce or copy the ideas or products of others?

Instruction: The Tasks. This dimension holds that significant and powerful learning experiences involve valued tasks: experiences that are perceived by the student and by others as important and valuable in real life. If assessment is to be authentic, there must also be a foundation of "authentic instruction," or of doing more than completing activities or exercises because they meet a requirement and prepare one for the next assignment. Authentic tasks call for deliberate selection and active monitoring of resources and strategies, active involvement of individuals and groups, use of productive thinking, and modifying one's own actions as necessary.

Illustrative Instruction Questions. Some of the major questions in relation to the instruction component are as follows:

- How to assist teachers and students with the metacognitive and reflective dimensions of authentic assessment?
- How to develop an appropriate scope and sequence for instruction, based on the unique strengths, talents, and sustained interests of students as revealed through authentic assessment? (How to ensure that the instruction is as authentic as the assessment?)
- How to identify and teach strategies students must know to create, maintain, and present a portfolio? How to support the idea that teaching how to keep a portfolio is worthwhile instruction in itself?

Achievement: The Outcomes. The terms *achievement* and *outcomes* can be defined in many ways, but in relation to authentic assessment I refer to a result of learning that is important and valuable. The achievement may involve mastery, exemplary activity, products, or experiences. The final product may take many different forms (e.g., tangible products created, a performance or presentation for an actual audience, processes that are shared or applied to real situations).

Illustrative Outcomes Questions. Some of the major questions in relation to the outcomes or results component are as follow:

- How to determine what skills and strategies students will need (and hence, should be considered authentic outcomes) for life and work in our world of rapid change, or for an uncertain and changing future?
- In what ways might we create appropriate mastery activities and experiences for students to demonstrate proficiency of process and in-depth understanding and application of content?
- How to ensure that those who review or critique the portfolio do not arbitrarily assign grades to the content? How to provide appropriate and meaningful criteria for review and critique?
- How to provide time and opportunity for appropriate critiquing, debriefing, and revision of products or outcomes?
- How to identify outside agencies or experts to assist with the evaluation of student products and performances?

Documentation: The Portfolio. Authentic assessment challenges educators to document students' growth, learning, and achievement in new ways. A *portfolio* is an ongoing collection or sample of products and assignments that the student has identified as exemplary of his or her present level of accomplishment, or her or his growth. (The portfolio should not necessarily be thought of only as a collection of the student's "best" work.) The contents of a portfolio typically provide evidence of one's ability to use or apply what one has learned, not merely to verify what or how much was learned.

One kind of portfolio focuses on growth and change over time, and might contain examples of initial or early efforts as well as those selected by the student to document progress. Viewed this way, the portfolio does not just contain those works which show the student's best efforts, but those that illustrate changing performances. Reflection concerning the metacognitive component of instruction is also important. This can be accomplished by having the student keep a journal, for example, detailing the processes or strategies attempted, the thinking tools used, the problems encountered (and how they were solved), and one's perceived changes in thought, feelings, and actions during the period.

There may be other purposes or circumstances when a different kind of portfolio will be created, in which one seeks to present a representative sampling of one's best work and most significant achievements. The metacognitive dimensions of this kind of portfolio might include the student's reasons for her or his choices, and explanations of the most successful elements of the portfolio as perceived by the student. The contents of the portfolio create a new benchmark for future goals and efforts.

Illustrative Portfolio Questions. Some of the major questions in relation to developing and using portfolios in authentic assessment include the following:

- How to maintain an appropriate balance between *traditional test (static)* data and *performance (dynamic)* data when documenting mastery (attainment of outcomes)?
- How to help parents, community members, employers, and higher education institutions interpret and use the information contained in portfolios, in place of or in conjunction with grades and test results?
- How to determine which formats should be used to assemble portfolios for different goals and purposes, and to demonstrate one's creative ideas and actions effectively for different audiences?
- How to assure that one's portfolio includes and documents the person's *understanding of process* as well as content achievements?

Many unresolved questions and challenges surround authentic assessment, especially in relation to outcomes as complex and varied as creativity and problem solving. In education and training today, there are significant pressures to reduce reliance on oversimplified and low-level performance objectives and tests. These pressures will become increasingly important in the coming decade. The challenge of assessing creativity characteristics, operations, context, and outcomes extends far beyond selecting a single instrument, or even combining scores from several instruments. The challenge of creativity assessment for tomorrow, and for the 21st century, is to begin to learn how to assess many dimensions of creative productivity, under unique circumstances, and with important and realistic outcomes clearly in view. The challenge is to ask, and to begin to be able to answer, "what works best for whom, for what purposes, and under what conditions?"

REFERENCES

Alvino, J., McDonnell, R., & Richert, S. (1981). National survey of identification practices in gifted and talented education. *Exceptional Children, 48,* 124-132.

Amabile, T. M. (1989). *Growing up creative.* New York: Crown Books.

Ball, O. E., & Torrance, E. P. (1984). *Streamlined scoring workbook: Figural A, TTCT.* Bensenville, IL: Scholastic Testing Service.

Barron, F. (1969). *Creative person and creative process.* New York: Holt, Rinehart & Winston.

Besemer, S. P., & O'Quin, K. (1987). Creative product analysis: Testing a model by developing a judging instrument. In S. G. Isaksen (Ed.), *Frontiers of creativity research: Beyond the basics* (pp. 341-357). Buffalo, NY: Bearly Limited.

Besemer, S. P., & Treffinger, D. J. (1981). Analysis of creative products. *Journal of Creative Behavior, 15*(3), 158-178.

Clarizio, H. F., & Mehrens, W. A. (1985). Psychometric limitations of Guilford's Structure of Intellect model for identification and programming of the gifted. *Gifted Child Quarterly, 29*(3), 113-120.

Cramond, B. (1992). *The Torrance Tests of Creative Thinking: Going beyond the scores.* Paper presented at the annual convention of the National Association for Gifted Children, Los Angeles, CA.

Crockenberg, S. (1972). Creativity tests: Boon or boondoggle? *Review of Educational Research, 42,* 27-45.

Cropley, A. J. (1996). Recognizing creative potential: An evaluation of the usefulness of creativity tests. *High Ability Studies, 7*(2), 203-219.

Damarin, F. (1985). Review of the Williams Creativity Assessment Packet. In J. Mitchell (Ed.), *Ninth mental measurements yearbook* (pp. 410-411). Lincoln, NE: Buros Institute of Mental Measurement.

Davis, G. A. (1975). In frumious pursuit of the creative person. *Journal of Creative Behavior, 9*(2), 75-87.

Davis, G. A. (1986). *Creativity is forever.* Dubuque, IA: Kendall-Hunt.

Davis, G. A., & Rimm, S. (1977). Characteristics of creatively gifted children. *Gifted Child Quarterly, 21*(4), 546-551.

Domino, G. (1970). Identification of potentially creative personalities from the Adjective Check List. *Journal of Consulting and Clinical Psychology, 35,* 48-51.

Dunn, R., & Dunn, K. (1978). *Teaching students through their individual learning styles.* Reston, VA: Reston Publishers.

Dunn, R., Dunn, K., & Price, G. E. (1986). *Productivity environmental preference survey.* Lawrence, KS: Price Systems.

Dunn, R., Dunn, K., & Price, G. E. (1975). *Learning style inventory.* Lawrence, KS: Price Systems.

Dunn, R., Dunn, K., & Treffinger, D. J. (1992). *Bringing out the gifted-ness in your child.* New York: Wiley.

Ekvall, G. (1983). *Climate, structure and innovativeness of organizations: A theoretical framework and an experiment.* Stockholm, Sweden: FA Radet.

Feldhusen, J. F. (1993). A conception of creative thinking and creativity training. In S. G. Isaksen, M. C. Murdock, R. L. Firestien, & D. J. Treffinger (Eds.), *Nurturing and developing creativity: The emergence of a discipline* (pp. 31-50). Norwood, NJ: Ablex.

Feldhusen, J. F. (1995a). Creativity: A knowledge base, metacognitive skills, and personality factors. *Journal of Creative Behavior, 29,* 255-268.

Feldhusen, J. F. (1995b). Creativity: Teaching and assessing. In L. W. Anderson (Ed.), *International encyclopedia of teaching and teacher education* (pp. 476-481). New York: Pergamon.

Feldhusen, J. F., & Goh, B. E. (1995). Assessing and accessing creativity: An integrative review of theory, research, and development. *Creativity Research Journal, 8,* 231-247.

Gardner, H. (1983). *Frames of mind.* New York: Basic Books.

Getzels, J. W., & Csikszentmihalyi, M. (1976). *The creative vision.* New York: Wiley.

Gough, H. G. (1952). *The adjective checklist.* Palo Alto, CA: Consulting Psychologists Press.

Gronlund, N. E. (1981). *Measurement and evaluation in teaching.* New York: Macmillan.

Guilford, J. P. (1967). *The nature of human intelligence.* New York: McGraw-Hill.

Guilford, J. P. (1977). *Way beyond the IQ.* Buffalo, NY: Bearly Limited.

Hart, D. (1994). *Authentic assessment: A handbook for educators.* Reading, MA: Addison-Wesley/Innovative Learning.

Helson, R., & Crutchfield, R. S. (1970). Creative types in mathematics. *Journal of Personality, 38,* 177-197.

Hocevar, D. (1981). Measurement of creativity: Review and critique. *Journal of Personality Assessment, 45,* 450-464.

Hocevar, D., & Bachelor, P. (1989). A taxonomy and critique of measurements used in the study of creativity. In J. A. Glover, R. Ronning, & C. Reynolds (Eds.), *Handbook of creativity* (pp. 53-75). New York: Plenum.

Houtz, J. C., & Krug, D. (1995). Assessment of creativity: Resolving a mid-life crisis. *Educational Psychology Review, 7,* 269-300.

Hunsaker, S. L., & Callahan, C. M. (1995). Creativity and giftedness: Published instrument uses and abuses. *Gifted Child Quarterly, 39,* 110-114.

Isaksen, S. G. (1995). Linking creativity and problem solving. In G. Kaufmann, T. Helstrup, & K. H. Teigen (Eds.), *Problem solving and cognitive processes.* Bergen, Norway: Fagbokforlaget.

Isaksen, S. G., Dorval, K. B., & Treffinger, D. J. (1994). *Creative approaches to problem solving.* Dubuque, IA: Kendall/Hunt.

Isaksen, S. G., Firestien, R. L., Murdock, M. C., Puccio, G. J., & Treffinger, D. J. (1994). *The assessment of creativity: An occasional paper from the Creativity Based Information Resources Project.* Buffalo, NY: Center for Studies in Creativity.

Isaksen, S. G., & Kaufmann, G. (1991). Adaptors and innovators: Different perceptions of the psychological climate for creativity. In T. Rickards, P. Colemont, P. Grøholt, M. Parker, & H. Smeekes (Eds.), *Creativity and innovation: Learning from practice* (pp. 47-54). Delft, The Netherlands: Innovation Consulting Group TNO.

Isaksen, S. G., Lauer, K. J., Murdock, M. C., Dorval, K. B., & Puccio, G. J. (1995). *Manual for the Situational Outlook Questionnaire.* Williamsville, NY: Creative Problem Solving Group-Buffalo.

Isaksen, S. G., & Puccio, G. J. (1992). *Profiling for creative problem solving.* Paper presented at the sixth International Creativity Networking Research Conference, Greensboro, NC.

Isaksen, S. G., Puccio, G. J. & Treffinger, D. J. (1993). An ecological approach to creativity research: Profiling for creative problem solving. *Journal of Creative Behavior, 27*(3), 149-170.

Jones, L. (1984, April/June). Barriers to effective problem solving. *Creativity and Innovation Network,* pp. 71-74.

Khatena, J., & Torrance, E. P. (1976). *Khatena Torrance Creative Perception Inventory.* Chicago: Stoelting Company.

Kirton, M. J. (1976). Adaptors and innovators: A description and measure. *Journal of Applied Psychology, 61,* 622-629.

Kirton, M. J. (1977). *Manual for the Kirton Adaption-innovation Inventory.* London: National Foundation for Educational Research.

Kirton, M. J. (1987). Cognitive style and personality. In S. G. Isaksen (Ed.), *Frontiers of creativity research: Beyond the basics* (pp. 282-304). Buffalo, NY: Bearly Limited.

MacKinnon, D. W. (1978). *In search of human effectiveness: Identifying and developing creativity.* Buffalo, NY: Bearly Limited.

Mednick, S. A. (1962). The associative basis of the creative process. *Psychological Review, 69,* 220-232.

Meeker, M. (1979). *Manual for the use of the SOI Learning Abilities Test.* El Segundo, CA: SOI Institute.

Milgram, R., & Rabkin, L. (1980). Developmental test of Mednick's associative hierarchy of original thinking. *Developmental Psychology, 16*(2), 157-158.

Myers, I. B., & McCaulley, M. (1985). *Manual: Guide to the development and use of The Myers Briggs Type Indicator*. Palo Alto, CA: Consulting Psychologists Press.

Perrone, V. (Ed.). (1991). *Expanding student assessment*. Alexandria, VA: Association for Supervision and Curriculum Development.

Puccio, G. J., Isaksen, S. G., Treffinger, D. J., & Murdock, M. C. (Eds.). (in press). *Handbook of creativity assessment*. Buffalo, NY: Creative Education Foundation.

Puccio, G. J., Treffinger, D. J., & Talbot, R. J. (1995). Exploratory examination of relationships between creativity styles and creative products. *Creativity Research Journal, 8,* 157-172.

Rhodes, M. (1961). An analysis of creativity. *Phi Delta Kappan, 42,* 305-310.

Rimm, S. (1983). *PRIDE: Preschool and Kindergarten Interest Descriptor*. Watertown, WI: Educational Assessment Service.

Rimm, S., & Davis, G. A. (1976). GIFT: An instrument for the identification and measurement of creativity. *Journal of Creative Behavior, 10*(3), 178-182.

Rimm, S., & Davis, G. A. (1980). *GIFFI: Group inventory for finding interests*. Watertown, WI: Educational Assessment Service.

Rosen, C. L. (1985). Review of the Williams Creativity Assessment Packet. In J. Mitchell (Ed.), *Ninth mental measurements yearbook* (pp. 411-412). Lincoln, NE: Buros Institute of Mental Measurement.

Runco, M. A. (1990, July/August). The divergent thinking of young children: Implications of the research. *G/C/T Magazine*, pp. 37-39.

Schaefer, C. E. (1970). *Biographical inventory-creativity*. San Diego, CA: Educational and Industrial Testing.

Schlichter, C. (1986). The Talents Unlimited model. In J. S. Renzulli (Ed.), *Systems and models for developing programs for the gifted and talented*. Mansfield Center, CT: Creative Learning Press.

Smith, J. M., & Schaefer, C. E. (1969). Development of a creativity scale for the Adjective Check List. *Psychological Reports, 29,* pp. 87-92.

Taft, R., & Rossiter, J. R. (1966). The Remote Associates Test: Divergent or convergent thinking. *Psychological Reports, 19,* 1313-1314.

Taylor, C. W. (1986). The multiple talents approach. In J. S. Renzulli (Ed.), *Systems and models for developing programs for the gifted and talented*. Mansfield Center, CT: Creative Learning Press.

Taylor, C., & Ellison, R. (1966). *Alpha Biographical Inventory*. Salt Lake City, UT: Institute for Behavioral Research in Creativity.

Torrance, E. P. (1979). *The search for satori and creativity*. Buffalo, NY: Bearly Limited.

Torrance, E. P. (1987). *The Torrance Tests of Creative Thinking.* Bensenville, IL: Scholastic Testing Press. (Original work published 1974)

Treffinger, D. J. (1980). The progress and potential of identifying creative talent among gifted and talented students. *Journal of Creative Behavior, 14*(1), 20-34.

Treffinger, D. J. (1985). Review of the Torrance Tests of Creative Thinking. In J. Mitchell (Ed.), *Ninth mental measurements yearbook* (pp. 1633-1634). Lincoln, NE: Buros Institute of Mental Measurement.

Treffinger, D. J. (1987). Research on creativity assessment. In S. G. Isaksen (Ed.), *Frontiers of creativity research* (pp. 103-119). Buffalo, NY: Bearly Limited.

Treffinger, D. J. (1988a). Components of creativity: Another look. *Creative Learning Today, 2*(5), 1, 4.

Treffinger, D. J. (1988b). A model for creative learning. *Creative Learning Today, 2(3)*, 4-6.

Treffinger, D. J. (1988c). *Student invention evaluation kit.* Honeoye, NY: Center for Creative Learning.

Treffinger, D. J. (1991). Creative productivity: Understanding its sources and nurture. *Illinois Council for the Gifted Journal, 10*, 6-8.

Treffinger, D. J. (1994a). *Assessing CPS performance.* Sarasota, FL: Center for Creative Learning.

Treffinger, D. J. (1994b). Productive thinking: Toward authentic instruction and assessment. *Journal of Secondary Gifted Education, 6*(1), 30-36.

Treffinger, D. J. (1995). Assessing creativity: A creative challenge. *Think Magazine, 5*(4), 18-22.

Treffinger, D. J. (1996a). *Creativity, creative thinking, and critical thinking: In search of definitions.* Sarasota, FL: Center for Creative Learning.

Treffinger D. J. (1996b). *Dimensions of creativity.* Sarasota, FL: Center for Creative Learning.

Treffinger, D. J., & Cross, Jr., A. (1994). *Professional development module: Authentic assessment of productive thinking* (Field test ed.). Sarasota, FL: Center for Creative Learning.

Treffinger, D. J., Feldhusen, J. F., & Isaksen, S. G. (1990). The organization and structure of productive thinking. *Creative Learning Today, 4*(2), 6-8.

Treffinger, D. J., Feldhusen, J. F., & Isaksen, S. G. (1996). *Guidelines for selecting and developing productive thinking materials.* Sarasota, FL: Center for Creative Learning.

Treffinger, D. J., Isaksen, S. G., & Dorval, K. B. (1994a). *Creative problem solving: An introduction* (rev. ed.). Sarasota, FL: Center for Creative Learning.

Treffinger, D. J., Isaksen, S. G., & Dorval, K. B. (1994b). Creative problem solving: An overview. In M. A. Runco (Ed.), *Problem finding, problem solving, and creativity* (pp. 223-236). Norwood, NJ: Ablex.

Treffinger, D. J., Isaksen, S. G., & Dorval, K. B. (1996). *Climate for creativity and innovation: Educational implications.* Sarasota, FL: Center for Creative Learning.

Treffinger, D. J., Isaksen, S. G., & Firestien, R. L. (1983). Theoretical perspectives on CPS and its facilitation. *Journal of Creative Behavior, 17,* 9-17.

Treffinger, D. J., & Selby, E. C. (1993). Giftedness, creativity, and learning style: Exploring the connections. In R. Dunn & R. Milgram (Eds.), *Teaching and counseling gifted adolescents through their learning styles: An international perspective* (pp. 87-102). New York: Praeger.

Wallach, M. A. (1988). Testing for creativity and giftedness. In F. D. Horowitz & M. O'Brien (Eds.), *The gifted and talented: Developmental perspectives* (pp. 99-123). Washington, DC: American Psychological Association.

Wallach, M. A., & Kogan, N. (1965). *Modes of thinking in young children.* New York: Holt, Rinehart & Winston.

Wiggins, G. (1993, November). Assessment: Authenticity, context, and validity. *Phi Delta Kappan, 75,* 200-214.

Williams, F. E. (1980). *Creativity assessment packet.* Buffalo, NY: DOK.

5

Creative and Affective Behavior: Cognition, Personality, and Motivation

John F. Feldhusen
Erik L. Westby
Purdue University

Creativity is the production of ideas, problem solutions, plans, works of art, musical compositions, sculptures, dance routines, poems, novels, essays, designs, theories, or devices that at the lowest level are new and of value to the creator and at the highest level are recognized, embraced, honored, or valued by all or large segments of society. Between the lowest and highest levels is a continuum of more or less recognized and useful creative productions, but always the production is new, novel, or unique relative to some definable context. Vulgar limericks may represent low-level creative productions for a small ephemeral, limited audience, whereas the sonnets of Shakespeare are known to and have been loved by millions of people for hundreds of years.

What conditions in the environment and what characteristics in humans give rise to creativity? It is first and always in the mind that problems, blockages, shortcomings, dangers, and so on, are perceived in the physical world around us, or potential for new plans, new theories, new art, new devices are envisioned, but our perceptions depend on or derive from our experiences with a real world around us. So there is an interplay or interaction between the minds of the creators and the world around them that gives rise to the act or cognition of creativity.

The minds of creators are not tabla rasa. At any age they are already loaded with information, and the knowledge base continues to grow, and it is from the knowledge base as a source of current perceptions and conceptions that problems, shortcomings, and potentials arise (Feldhusen, 1993). One form of intelligence (convergent) strives mainly to understand and control the world as given while another form (divergent) searches for problems, shortcomings, solutions, and potentials. Some minds seem to function best as convergent processors, others more as divergent processors. There is a continuum for each dimension with a possibility of high levels in both in one individual and medium or low levels in another.

The creating individual uses the knowledge base as information to be manipulated or processed, a set or combination of cognitive processes drives the creative process, and personal traits or characteristics of the individual motivate and control creative processing (Feldhusen, 1993). All three domains—the knowledge base, cognitive processes, and personal motivators—function interactively in creative thinking.

THE KNOWLEDGE BASE

Previously, we (Feldhusen, 1993; Feldhusen, 1995a, 1995b; Feldhusen & Goh, 1995) argued that the knowledge base is the fundamental information source for creative thinking and problem solving. The knowledge base may consist of at least 100,000 units of information, concepts, definitions, and may take 10 or more years to learn or acquire. In the mind of the creative thinker, information is well articulated, highly and selectively retrievable, and procedural knowledge is fluent and efficient. The latter, procedural knowledge, is really commensurate with what we otherwise call the cognitive and metacognitive processes of creative thinking and production.

We use both terms, *creative thinking* and *productivity* to emphasize the critical and necessary roles of both the cognitive ideation and the results thereof. The latter is inventions, theories, works of art, and so forth. The knowledge base is analogous or comparable to data or information in computer operations, but in reality it is much more dynamic or interactive than computer data. The knowledge base serves as the template for perceptions and interpretations of the phenomena encountered in the world. We understand or find meaning when we set new perceptions against existing schemas, ideas, beliefs, conceptions, values, all of which are a part of the knowledge base. But in the act of creation, we may reinterpret new phenomena, see objects from a different point of view, reconceptualize an existing theory, or transform an idea. Thus, the knowledge base is, in a sense, a dynamic springboard to the new creation.

The knowledge base is not a dead set of information. It is like working memory in that it is functional and supportive of creative thinking. Some proponents of creation have argued that the knowledge base simply represents rote, memorized facts and that one may think creatively without a store of information. Fluency or brainstorming is, however, one of the clearest areas for evidence of the role of the knowledge base. Pollert, Feldhusen, Von Mondfrans, and Treffinger (1969) showed that available information determines success in production of ideas in fluency tasks. Creative production of ideas may seem to yield new ideas or conceptions, but it always builds on or grows out of existing information or knowledge.

The knowledge base is the sum of declarative and procedural information possessed by an individual, and it tends to be large and dynamically useful in the cognition of creative thinkers. It is acquired through a variety of experiences and thrives on use or active retrieval and participation in new cognitive activity.

PROCESSES IN CREATIVE THINKING AND PRODUCTION

Sternberg and Davidson's (1983) "creative insights" offers an excellent starting point for conceptualizing the creative processes. Beginning with the assumption of a knowledge base, there is selective encoding of information entering the knowledge base. That is, new information is selected, categorized, classified, and labeled in ways that enhance later retrievability. It is related to and integrated into the existing network of cognitive structures. In the highly creative mind, the network is extensive and linkages will be made that are not detected by less creative minds.

More directly related to creativity is Sternberg and Davidson's "selective retrieval." Given a problem, need, shortcoming, or potential perceived by the creative individual, there is efficient retrieval from memory of relevant information that may prove useful or connected to the newly encountered situation. This phase is analogous to fluency or traditional brainstorming, both being essentially memory processes from well-encoded knowledge bases. There is, in a sense, a parade of information passing by awareness into short-term and working memory.

Sternberg and Davidson's model proposes "selective combination," putting pieces or units of information together to "create" new conceptions, insights, plans, inventions, poems, sonatas, dance routines, or designs (Perkins, 1986). If the selective combination is a response to a problem, it can be called a creative problem solution. At an earlier time the selective combination might have been called a "gestalt" (Lewin, 1954).

The selective combination, the creative insight, the new design, next faces the world of judgment or evaluation. Does the individual self see merit or value in the idea or creation? Is it a solution to his or her problem? Does he or she see it as having potential for evaluation by others and being judged a good and unique idea or plan? Will some larger world embrace it as a feat of creative genius? At several levels of audience there is the judgment (Csikszentmihalyi, 1990; Feldhusen, 1993). For example, only a handful of people recognize and find merit in the new conception of gifted education focusing on talents and talent development and promulgated by Gagne (1985, 1993) and Feldhusen (1985a, 1985b). Perhaps it will never be accepted in the field of gifted education. Conversely, Csikszentmihalyi's (1990) conception of the "flow" experience is now widely accepted in psychology. It took Darwin nearly a lifetime to gain wide-scale recognition of his evolutionary theory, and there was general dismissal and opposition to it for many years. So, the self and societal processes of evaluation of new ideas or new productions may come slowly or in other cases quickly.

From the Guilford (1967, 1977) structure of intellect, we may finally borrow two concepts—*divergent thinking* and *transformations*—to enhance our understanding of creative thinking processes, but both may be related to Sternberg and Davidson's creative insights. Divergent thinking, in the Guilford model, is fluent, open to multiple directions and lines of thought, and above all open to diverse associations that might result in selective combinations. It is not convergent in seeking one and only one solution or idea. Transformations as products imply that information, retrieved selectively from the knowledge base, has also undergone a process of change that may render it more effective, aesthetically pleasing, useful and/or a unique solution to a problem.

Imagination and visualization are also cognitive processes that operate within the creativity network. Imagination is a projective process in which things not present are conjectured. It gives rise to selective combination as in the weird characters of Dr. Seuss or the pronouncements of futurist Toffler. Visualization is an extension of imagination that produces imagery in the mind and the images reflected in poetry, sculpture, film, inventions, dances, and music. Both imagination and visualization are fundamental cognitive operations in creative thinking.

PERSONALITY

A number of researchers have focused on the personality and motivational characteristics of creative thinkers (Rhodes, 1961). The set of personality characteristics that seem to be associated with creativity differ from individual to individual within a field and differ as well normatively across fields of human endeavor. However, there is considerable generality to these characteristics across individuals and fields (Shaw & Runco, 1994).

Torrance (1963) reported that highly creative people are often obnoxious, discourteous, negative, critical of others, and unwilling to yield or take no for an answer. On the other hand, Torrance and other researchers have pointed out many positive characteristics. MacKinnon (1963), for example, using case study methodology, found that highly creative architects were individualistic, determined, inventive, independent, enthusiastic, industrious, appreciative, and progressive. Some of these characteristics could become negative in some social situations, but predominantly they are viewed as positive personal characteristics.

In a comprehensive effort to synthesize research in this area, Barron and Harrington (1981) reviewed 15 years of research on personality characteristics of creative individuals and concluded that a fairly stable set of core characteristics (e.g., high valuation of esthetic qualities in experience, broad interests, attraction to complexity, high energy, independence of judgment, autonomy, intuition, self-confidence, ability to resolve or accommodate apparently opposite or conflicting traits in one's self-concept, and finally, a firm sense of self as "creative") continued to emerge as correlates of creative achievement and activity in many domains.

Although there is commonality among these sets of personal characteristics of highly creative individuals, the personality of the creative individual operates within contexts that facilitate or impede creative thinking and productivity. The creative individual is typically pressed to live within the confines of behaviors, values, and beliefs that are accepted by society. Cropley (1992) described the creative individual as existing in a shadow area of undesirable, ill-mannered, or even proscribed behavior. He suggested that creative people go beyond the limits of societal norms of behavior, to the point where social nonconformity is often their most visible social characteristic. Crutchfield (1962) and Rodgers (1954) argued that creativity is facilitated by environments that are free from external pressure or control and are warm and supportive. Thus, a conflict emerges between societal pressures on the one hand, and the personal characteristics of the would-be creative individual and the conflict may indeed both inhibit and serve as impetus to the potentially creative individual. It seems that the circumstances in which a person is working are integral personal components of creative functioning. They may be overwhelmingly negative and inhibit creative functioning, or they may be open, neutral, positive, or facilitating and enhance the processes.

The personal characteristics reviewed so far and the environment surrounding the individual give rise to the motivation that drives creative thinking and productivity. Societal needs and problems evoke selective encoding of relevant information and provide motivation stimulation for the creative individual. Although environmental pressures may often seem to be negative regarding creative production, creative individuals can turn or transform them into positive and facilitating conditions.

Among all the personal and socially interactive characteristics that may be involved in or related to creative thinking productivity, five are salient: curiosity, openness to experience, imagination, visualization, and persistence. They pave the way or evoke the motivational states that generate creative thinking and productivity.

Curiosity provokes exploration in both a physical and cognitive sense. Confronted by new experiences, it guides our selective retrieval of related information from the knowledge base. If the new experience is unique or singular, it may also evoke selective encoding or classified placement in the knowledge base. Finally, it stimulates selective combination in that the individual may combine currently perceived information with stored information in the knowledge base to create new solutions, procedures, performances, or products. These various process are all involved in fluent thinking, in original production, and in elaboration.

Openness or receptiveness to new experiences is a facilitation condition. It implies that the creative person is open to, interfaces with, or deals well with troubling or conflicting information in cognitive processing. The open person is also devoid or free from selection biases, thereby opening the door to fluent evocation of a greater range of ideas, selective retrieval of more relevant information, and finally selective combinations that might otherwise be untenable. As the counterpart of openness, flexibility implies a capacity for selective combination that rigid or less flexible individuals would not be able to admit to working memory.

Imagination and visualization are affective processes that work in combination with the cognitive processes of selective combination, fluency, and elaboration to create images of products and performances that may turn out to be more adaptive or creative than other products and performances. Imagination can be chiefly abstract without actual images or icons of reality as in mental rehearsal of a logic problem or a problem-solving sequence. It is visual when the individual actually constructs or creates mental representations of objects or performances. The objects or behavioral sequences are seen as real phenomenon.

Persistence is the cognitive process and physical energy that drives creativity and allows the cognitive processes to move through obstacles, lethargy, and discouragement to successful production of creativity. It is a dynamic facilitation process that combines with all the cognitive processes. In a sense it is also energy that keeps the individual functioning cognitively.

MOTIVATION

People are more or less motivated to create. In a case study approach, Feldhusen (1986) studied the lives of 20 creatively productive people and found that very early in their lives all had high energy levels, intense devotion to work or study, a strong sense of independence and individualism, an internal locus of control, and heightened sensitivity to details. The best motivation for creative production is intrinsic in nature. Deci and Ryan (1985) argued that intrinsically motivated behavior is innate and results in creativity, flexibility, and spontaneity, whereas extrinsically motivated actions are characterized by pressure and tension and result in low self-esteem and anxiety. Amabile (1990) presented abundant research evidence for the efficacy of intrinsic motivation in creative activity. But, is extrinsic motivation the enemy of creativity? Perhaps, as Hennesey and Amabile (1988) stated, "under certain circumstances or with certain individuals, intrinsic and extrinsic forces combine in an additive fashion" (p. 310). Thus, extrinsic motivation from rewards and competitions may also drive the creative process and not necessarily be a deterrent to creative production.

In a discussion of affect and creativity, Runco (1994) pointed to emotional involvement and Basadur's (1994) problem ownership as illustrations of real-world intrinsic motivation to create and/or solve problems. The response internally is a sense that something must be done, must be created. Runco concluded that "emotions direct lines of thought and are responsible for the motivation and effort needed . . . [to create]" (p. 278).

Halpern (1996) argued that creative thinking and production arise chiefly from self-motivation. She urged that teachers, mentors, and parents cultivate a love of learning and that would-be creators generate their own rewards out of the self-satisfaction that comes from producing ideas, works of art, performances, and so on. At the same time, she cautioned that there must be the maturation to work hard intellectually and to self-monitor one's own creative efforts. Self-motivation and self-monitoring are enhanced by the affective characteristics of willingness to take risks, tolerance of ambiguity, and nonconformity.

Gardner (1993) studied the lives of seven highly creative people—Freud, Einstein, Picasso, Stravinsky, Eliot, Graham, and Gandhi—who represented diverse academic, artistic, and political occupations. He found that their motivation to create seemed to derive from such personality characteristics as self-confidence, alertness, being unconventional, hard-working, and deep commitment to the field of their work. They were all highly self-absorbed, somewhat asocial, and motivated to pursue their work and projects, often disregarding the needs, feelings, or interests of others. All were also motivated to promote self, to bring their work to the attention of others, and to gain recognition for themselves and their creative production, often even at the expense of others. They were also all relentlessly committed to their work on a daily basis, persistently, day in and day out, creatively producing and then promoting their work.

Perhaps the near ultimate drive or motivation to create derives from what White (1959) called "competence motivation" or "effectance motivation." This is a need to feel competent and effective in one's life experiences and activities. People want to be more or less creative and productive in life's daily tasks and especially in one's work, occupation, art, business, or profession. We strive for mastery in our fields of endeavor well as in avocational activities.

Harter (1990) extended the concept of competence and effectance motivation to a need to master cognitive, social, and physical activities and challenges in our lives. Thus, the creative individual goes beyond routine or normal achievements and strives for mastery, expertise, and new conceptions of phenomena. Harter also argued for the role of self-perception of competence and extends it to include self-reward systems and the seeking of optimal challenges.

Much of the motivation to create may also derive from observation of models, mentors, and heroes (Pleiss & Feldhusen, 1995). Schunk (1996), a preeminent modeling researcher, suggested that models influence and motivate observers in four ways: First, they display competence, superior performance, or creativity. Second, they are perceived by the observer as similar generally to self and appropriately emulatable. Third, the effective model appears credible or believable to the observer. Credibility derives from consistency and plausibility of model behavior. Fourth, effective models display infectious enthusiasm and hence evoke motivation in observers to emulate or duplicate observed behavior. Overall then, creative behavior can be motivated through observation of powerful models who display creative thinking and productivity (Pintrich & Schunk, 1996).

Perhaps the most powerful motivational force in human behavior and creative thinking and production is the flow phenomenon as posited by Csikszentmihalyi (1990). Flow is utterly embracing absorption psychologically in one's work or creative activity to the point where time is forgotten and contact with the mundane exigencies of daily life become irrelevant. It is deep intrinsic motivation leading to total involvement in one's creative endeavor. There is no concern about payoffs or rewards. Flow is also associated with freedom to explore, examine, express and hence perpetuates curiosity and flexibility of cognition leading to both playfulness and productivity.

CONCLUSION

In conclusion, it is clear that there is a set of personal characteristics, emotional manifestations, and affective behaviors that underlie and give rise to motivation to create, and that, in concert with a generative knowledge base and mastery of a set of cognitive processes, empowers the potentially creative individual to produce new ideas, theories, conceptions, inventions, works of art, performances, or products that the culture will come to see as useful, aesthetically stimulating, or enhancing of understanding of the world around us.

STUDY ACTIVITIES

1. Describe the knowledge base. What does it include?
2. What are three salient personal characteristics of highly creative people?
3. Who is the most creative person you have ever known? What are some of his or her personal characteristics?
4. How important is intelligence in creative thinking?
5. Does chance play a role in creative thinking?
6. What is meant by affect in creativity?
7. How do you motivate people to be creative?

REFERENCES

Amabile, T. M. (1990). Within you, without you: The social psychology of creativity and beyond. In M. A. Runco & R. S. Albert (Eds.), *Theories of creativity* (pp. 61-91). Newbury Park, CA: Sage.

Barron, F., & Harrington, D. M. (1981). Creativity, intelligence, and personality. *Annual Review of Psychology, 32*, 439-476.

Basadur, M. (1994). Managing the creative process in organizations. In M. A. Runco (Ed.), *Problem finding, problem solving, and creativity* (pp. 237-268). Norwood, NJ: Ablex

Cropley, A. J. (1992). *More ways than one: Fostering creativity.* Norwood, NJ: Ablex.

Crutchfield, R. S. (1962). Conformity and creative thinking. In H. E. Gruber, J. Terrell, & M. Wertheimer (Eds.), *Contemporary approaches to creative thinking* (pp. 120-140). New York: Atherton Press.

Csikszentmihalyi, M. (1990). The domain of creativity. In M. A. Runco & R. S. Albert (Eds.), *Theories of creativity* (pp. 190-212). Newbury Park, CA: Sage.

Deci, E. L., & Ryan, R. M. (1985). *Intrinsic motivation and self-determination in human behavior.* New York: Plenum.

Feldhusen, J. F. (1985a). The teacher of gifted students. *Gifted Education International, 3*(2), 87-93.

Feldhusen, J. F. (1985b). *Toward excellence in gifted education.* Denver, CO: Love Publishing.

Feldhusen, J. F. (1986). A conception of giftedness. In R. J. Sternberg & J. E. Davidson (Eds.), *Conceptions of giftedness* (pp. 112-127). New York: Cambridge University Press.

Feldhusen, J. F. (1993). A conception of creative thinking and creativity training. In S. G. Isaksen, M. C. Murdock, R. L. Firestein, & D. J. Treffinger (Eds.), *Understanding and recognizing creativity: The emergence of a discipline* (pp. 31-50). Norwood, NJ: Ablex.

Feldhusen, J. F. (1995a) Talent development vs. gifted education. *The Educational Forum, 59,* 346-349.

Feldhusen, J. F. (1995b). *Talent identification and development in education (TIDE)* (2nd ed.). Sarasota, FL: Center for Creative Learning.

Feldhusen, J. F., & Goh, B. E. (1995). Assessing and accessing creativity: An integrative review of theory, research, and development. *Creativity Research Journal, 8,* 231-247.

Gagne, F. (1985). Giftedness and talent: Reexamining the definition. *Gifted Child Quarterly, 29*(3), 103-112.

Gagne, F. (1993). Constructs and models pertaining to exceptional human abilities. In K. A. Heller, F. J. Monks, & A. H. Passow (Eds.), *International handbook of research and development of giftedness and talent* (pp. 69-87). New York: Pergamon.

Gardner, H. (1993). *Creating minds: An anatomy of creativity seen through the lives of Freud, Einstein, Picasso, Stravinsky, Eliot, Graham, and Gandhi.* New York: Basic Books.

Guilford, J. P. (1967). *The nature of human intelligence.* New York: McGraw-Hill.

Guilford, J. P. (1977). *Way beyond the IQ.* Buffalo, NY: Creative Education Foundation.

Halpern, D. F. (1996). *Thought and knowledge: An introduction to critical thinking* (3rd ed.). Mahwah, NJ: Lawrence Erlbaum Associates.

Harter, S. (1990). Issues in the assessment of self-concept of children and adolescents. In A. M. LaGreca (Ed.), *Through the eyes of the child:*

Obtaining self-reports from children and adolescents (pp. 292-325). Boston: Allyn & Bacon.

Hennesey, B. A., & Amabile, T. M. (1988). The conditions of creativity. In R. J. Sternberg (Ed.), *The nature of creativity: Contemporary psychological perspectives* (pp. 11-38). New York: Cambridge University Press.

Lewin, K. (1954). Behavior and development as a function of the total situation. In L. Carmichael (Ed.), *Manual of child psychology* (pp. 918-970). New York: Wiley.

MacKinnon, D. W. (1963). *The study of lives.* New York: Atherton Press.

Perkins, D. N. (1986). *Knowledge as design.* Hillsdale, NJ: Lawrence Erlbaum Associates.

Pintrich, P. R., & Schunk, D. H. (1996). *Motivation in education.* Englewood Cliffs, NJ: Prentice-Hall.

Pleiss, M. K., & Feldhusen, J. F. (1995). Mentors, role models, and heroes in the lives of gifted children. *Educational Psychologist, 30,* 159-169.

Pollert, L. H., Feldhusen, J. F., Van Mondfrans, A. P., & Treffinger, D. J. (1969). Role of memory in divergent thinking. *Psychological Reports, 25,* 151-156.

Rhodes, M. (1961). An analysis of creativity. *Phi Delta Kappan, 42,* 305-310.

Rodgers, C. (1954). Towards a theory of creativity. *ECT.: A Review of General Semantics, 11,* 249-260.

Runco, M. A. (Ed.). (1994). *Problem finding, problem solving and creativity.* Norwood, NJ: Ablex.

Schunk, D. H. (1996). *Learning theories: An educational perspective* (2nd ed.). Englewood Cliffs, NJ: Merrill.

Shaw, M. P., & Runco, M. A. (Eds.). (1994). *Creativity and affect.* Norwood, NJ: Ablex.

Sternberg, R. J., & Davidson, J. E. (1983). Insight in the gifted. *Educational Psychologist, 18,* 51-57.

Torrance, E. P. (1963). The creative personality and the ideal pupil. *Teachers College Record, 65,* 220-226.

White, R. W. (1959). Motivation reconsidered: The concept of competence. *Psychological Review, 66*(5), 297-333.

6

Creativity Issues Concerning Linguistically and Culturally Diverse Children

Emilia C. Lopez
Queens College, City University of New York

The goal of this chapter is to review the research on the creative abilities of linguistically and culturally diverse (LCD) children. LCD children are defined as children who reside in bilingual households where English and a second language are used for communication, monolingual homes where a language other than English is spoken, or English-speaking homes where a dialect (e.g., black English dialect) is spoken. The definition applies to children whose cultural backgrounds differ from the mainstream of American society.

The chapter begins with a historical overview of the cross-cultural creativity research. The data discussed are most relevant to the creativity skills of African American, Native American, and Hispanic children living in the United States. Cross-cultural creativity studies are included because of their significant contribution to the creativity literature. The problems encountered when identifying creative LCD children are examined. Recommendations are made to enhance assessment procedures and research methods.

AN HISTORICAL OVERVIEW

The Early Research: 1950s to 1970s

In the 1950s, Guilford (1956, 1959) challenged researchers and practitioners to recognize creativity as an important variable in the identification of gifted and talented individuals. Early studies attributed individual differences in creative performance to genetic factors. However, subsequent research showed that the development of creative abilities was largely related to experience (Pezzullo, Thorsen, & Madaus, 1972; Torrance, 1978). During the 1960s and 1970s, Torrance (1978) and Renzulli (1973) were among the first psychologists to encourage educators to develop the untapped creative potential of LCD children. The 1960s and 1970s were productive years in terms of the number of empirical investigations and discussion papers that addressed issues concerning the creativity skills of LCD children. The most important issues addressed during this period included: (a) the creative strengths of LCD children, (b) the relationship between bilingualism and creativity, (c) the influence of cultural factors on creativity development, and (d) the assessment of creativity.

The Creative Strengths of LCD Children. Based on his research and practical experience with LCD children, Torrance (1969) identified a set of creative characteristics (Table 6.1) which he described as follows:

> I believe I have identified a set of characteristics that helps guide the search for the strengths of culturally different students and for giftedness among such students. I have called these characteristics creative positives. I must first caution the reader that not all members of culturally different groups are gifted in all of these positives. I do contend that these creative positives occur to a high degree among culturally different groups generally and that more gifted youngsters will be found among them on this basis than if the search is confined to traditional areas. (Torrance, 1977, p. 25)

Taken singly, these characteristics did not add significantly to the prediction of creativity in LCD children (Haensly & Torrance, 1990; Torrance, 1969), and Torrance warned educators of the dangers of overgeneralization. Torrance's work is notable for its efforts to operationalize the creative strengths that LCD children brought to learning situations. These creative positives emphasized that it is possible to conceive of creative behavior through more ordinary means and as individuals attempt to solve everyday real-life problems (Ripple, 1989). The identification of

Table 6.1. Creative Positives of Disadvantaged Students as Identified by Torrance (1969, 1977).

1. Ability to express feelings and emotions.
2. Ability to improvise with commonplace materials and objects.
3. Articulateness in role playing, sociodrama, and story telling.
4. Enjoyment of and ability in visual arts, such as drawing, painting, and sculpture.
5. Enjoyment of and ability in creative movement, dance, dramatics, and so forth.
6. Enjoyment of and ability in music, rhythm, and so forth.
7. Use of expressive speech.
8. Fluency and flexibility in figural media.
9. Enjoyment of and skills in group activities, problem solving, and so forth.
10. Responsiveness to the concrete.
11. Responsiveness to the kinesthetic.
12. Expressiveness of gestures, body language, and so forth, and ability to interpret body language.
13. Humor.
14. Richness of imagery in informal language.
15. Originality of ideas in problem solving.
16. Problem centeredness or persistence in problem solving.
17. Emotional responsiveness.
18. Quickness of warm-up.

these creative positives also highlighted that LCD children demonstrated creativity skills in ways that were different from the more traditional definitions of creativity that emphasized the genius perspective.

Other empirical studies during this period attempted to identify creativity strengths by comparing LCD children's scores on creativity tests with the scores of nonminority children (DeVito, 1975; Gezi, 1969; Richmond, 1968; Torrance, 1967, 1971, 1977). Torrance (1977) reviewed 20 studies designed to investigate the effects of race and socioeconomic status on creativity and reported that in 86% of the comparisons, the finding was either no difference between the LCD and nonminority children or differences in favor of the LCD groups. Torrance found that LCD students tended to perform higher on figural measures of creativity than on verbal measures of creativity. A few studies reported that LCD children performed poorly in all areas of creativity when compared to nonminority children (DeVito, 1975; Richmond, 1968).

Relationship Between Bilingualism and Creativity. An issue that generated much debate during the 1960s and 1970s was the relationship between bilingualism and cognitive ability. Many investigators reported that speaking two languages resulted in greater cognitive flexibility (i.e., Duncan & DeAvila, 1979). However, the outcomes of these investigations were often contradictory and inconclusive (Diaz, 1983). For example, several studies reported that bilinguals demonstrated better developed skills than monolinguals in such cognitive skills as semantic development, abstract levels of thinking, awareness of grammatical errors, concept formation, ability to compare words on the basis of semantic dimension, ability to analyze linguistic output objectively, and ability to perceive two languages as independent and different language systems (Lambert, Tucker, & d'Anglejan, 1973; Peal & Lambert, 1962; Riegel, Ramsey, & Riegel, 1967). Other studies reported that bilinguals had advantages over monolinguals in some areas but not in others (Peal & Lambert, 1962). Still other investigations claimed that bilinguals had no advantages over monolinguals in many of the cognitive areas investigated (Cummins, 1977; Diaz, 1983).

Diaz (1983) noted that the results of many of those early studies did not apply to the creativity literature because the definitions for the construct of *cognitive flexibility* varied from study to study. To illustrate, Peal and Lambert (1962) used the term *cognitive flexibility* to describe performance on tests of general cognitive reasoning, whereas Landry (1974) used it to describe divergent thinking skills measured by tests of creativity.

A review of studies that defined creativity as divergent thinking indicates that their findings were also inconclusive. Many studies reported that bilinguals demonstrated greater creative flexibility than monolinguals (Carringer, 1974; Jacobs & Pierce, 1966; Landry, 1974), whereas others reported no differences between the two groups (Janssen, 1969), or differences in other areas of creativity (Cummins & Gulutsan, 1974; Landry, 1973). Cummins (1977) attributed these inconclusive findings to a failure to control for levels of language proficiency. He found that the majority of the studies exploring creativity with bilingual populations failed to measure the children's language proficiency skills. Thus, the samples included children at various stages of second language acquisition, with some at the very early stages and others at more advanced levels of bilingualism. Many studies included children who had poor language skills in both their first and second languages. The samples were often chosen based on their predetermined placement in bilingual and monolingual classrooms with no objective measures of language competence.

The assessment of language proficiency should explore many factors that include: (a) levels of expressive/receptive language, (b) levels of cognitive language skills, (c) instructional background, (d) contexts in which each of the languages is spoken, and (e) history of language acquisition and second language learning (Cummins, 1977, 1981, 1984; Dulay, Burt, & Krashen; 1982, Esquivel, 1985; Hamayan, Kwiat, & Perlman, 1985; Mattes & Omark, 1991). Failure to assess language proficiency in a comprehensive manner can result in inadequate interpretations of creativity and other test data and in inconclusive research results confounded by language variables.

Influence of Cultural Factors on Creativity Development. The early cross-cultural research has supported the hypotheses that cultural factors strongly influence the course of creativity development, the level of creative functioning, and the type of creativity that flourishes most. The results of numerous investigations (e.g., Getzels, 1975; Meeker, 1969; Mistry & Rogoff, 1985) suggest that differences in cultural backgrounds influence individuals' cognitive styles (i.e., defined as individual style in perceiving, thinking, and problem solving; Diaz, 1983). Differences were reported, for example, on the cognitive styles of Mexican American and African American children with both groups functioning as more field dependent in comparison to nonminority groups who tended to function as more field independent (Buriel, 1975; Ramirez, 1973; Sanders, Scholz & Kagan, 1976).

Torrance (1963, 1967) conducted a series of cross-cultural studies designed to investigate creative development in children between the grades one and six in Western Samoa, New Delhi, India, Singapore, Germany, Norway, and Australia. He also included a United States sample of African American children from low socioeconomic backgrounds and a sample of mostly white children from middle class backgrounds. The investigators used native examiners in all the different cultures, and the assessments were conducted in the children's native languages. Torrance found that the development of creativity skills varied from culture to culture, with each culture demonstrating its own pattern of creativity growth and discontinuities or periods of creativity decline. Differences in creative functioning were also noted in verbal versus figural domains, with a tendency for members of some cultures to perform at higher levels on figural or verbal tests. For example, German, Norwegian, Australian, and Indian groups performed somewhat better on verbal measures of creativity, whereas Samoan and African American children performed higher on figural measures.

Bernal and Reyna (1974) contributed to the cross-cultural research via an investigation that examined the behaviors valued by Mexican American individuals. Their research found that Mexican Americans placed high value on cognitive and linguistic abilities, pragmatic alertness, sensitivity to others, leadership ability, interpersonal skills, and bilingual fluency. Bernal and Reyna's research established that the behaviors and products considered valuable and creative can vary across cultural groups. Thus, there is a need to define creativity within individuals' cultural context.

   Assessment of Creativity in LCD Students. The Torrance Test of Creative Thinking (TTCT) (Torrance, 1974) was the first creativity test validated and normed with a wide range of LCD children in the United States. The TTCT was translated for use in more than 32 languages (Haensly & Torrance, 1990), and a considerable number of studies have attested to its validity with several groups of LCD children in the United States (Torrance, 1972). During the 1960s and 1970s, researchers and educators also encouraged the use of such informal measures as observations and biographical data to identify gifted and creative LCD children. Emphasis was placed on assessment and identification practices that were sensitive to LCD children's linguistic and cultural backgrounds.

   Summary of Early Research. Many issues related to the creativity skills of LCD children were first addressed during the 1960s and 1970s. Among the issues explored during this period were the creative strengths of LCD children, the relationship between bilingualism and creativity, the influence of cultural factors on creativity development, and the assessment of creativity in LCD children. Although these early studies yielded inconclusive results due to methodological flaws, they laid the groundwork for the cross-cultural creativity research and generated interest in exploring the creative abilities of LCD children.

The Current Research

The 1980s were characterized by continued interest in the creativity skills of LCD children (Heath, 1987; Kessler & Quinn, 1987; Robles, 1988), and the literature produced thus far in the 1990s seems to follow this course (Lopez, Esquivel, & Houtz, 1992; Martorell, 1991). Research continues to be directed toward examining the creative strengths of LCD children with the TTCT as the preferred measure of creativity. Less effort appears to be focused toward research that investigates the effects of cultural factors on the creative abilities of LCD children and examines creativity within the context of homogeneous cultural groups. Thus, LCD children from different cultural backgrounds (e.g., Puerto Rican, Colombian, American Indians) are still clustered as one group, with little consideration given to major linguistic and cultural differences between the groups.

Recent empirical investigations addressing the nature of the relationship between bilingualism and creativity have continued to yield contradicting results (Diaz, 1983; Ricciardelli, 1992). However, more investigators are now attempting to measure language proficiency by using a number of different measures (e.g., language samples, normed instruments, observations) to explore the many dimensions of language proficiency (Diaz, 1983). An investigation conducted by Lemmon and Goggin (1989) demonstrated the significance of controlling for language variables. This study examined the creativity strengths of bilingual and monolingual students and initially found that monolinguals performed better than bilinguals. Upon further analyses of the data, the investigators found that monolinguals demonstrated higher creativity strengths only when compared to bilingual subjects with less competent bilingual skills (Ricciardelli, 1992).

PROBLEMS IN THE IDENTIFICATION OF CREATIVE LCD CHILDREN

Despite the interest in the identification of creative LCD children, this population continues to be underrepresented in programs for the gifted and talented (Mitchell, 1988; Richert, 1987; Smith, LeRose, & Clasen, 1991). Richert reported that African Americans, Hispanics, and Native Americans were underrepresented by 30% to 70% in gifted and talented programs. A number of barriers contribute to the status of underrepresentation.

The first major concern is that programs continue to emphasize definitions of giftedness that rely on the identification of children who score significantly above average on cognitive and academic measures (Adderholdt-Elliot, Algozzine, Algozzine, & Haney, 1991; Melesky, 1984; Richert, 1985). Adderholdt-Elliot et al. (1991) reported that only 5% of the directors of programs for the gifted and talented they surveyed across the country indicated using a more expansive definition of giftedness and talented that indicated creative or productive thinking, leadership ability, visual and performing arts, and psychomotor ability, as well as intellectual ability and academic aptitude (Marland, 1972). Despite the fact that those programs claimed to use the more expansive definition, they continued to limit themselves to the use of academic achievement and IQ tests when identifying gifted and talented children. Hunsaker's (1994) survey of school districts also indicated that children with special talents are often not included in programs for the gifted.

Given many statistics pointing to the great number of LCD children who fail academically and ultimately drop out of school, educators may feel that there is a need to stress the academic needs of these students

(Renzulli, 1973; Torrance, 1984). However, the overemphasis on cognitive and academic skills places LCD children at a disadvantage because they tend to score poorly on academic and cognitive tests that are insensitive to their linguistic and cultural backgrounds (Richert, 1987). If skills such as creativity are assigned second priority, the search for the brightest will not necessarily mean that the most creative LCD children will be identified, as the research has clearly shown that the most intelligent children are not necessarily the most creative or talented (Guilford, 1967; Rampaul, Singh, & Didyk, 1984; Torrance, 1965; Toth & Baker, 1990).

A second concern is the shortage of normed measures appropriate for the identification of creative LCD children. This scarcity of normed measures is a major drawback in an educational system in which there is tremendous emphasis on hard data and scores for the purposes of labeling and program placement (Barkaa & Bernal, 1991). Despite the fact that there are over 225 different creativity tests measuring such areas as divergent thinking, attitudes and interests, personality variables, verbal and figural skills, math/science, movement/dance, dramatics, artistic abilities, and musical strengths, only 16% of those 225 tests have been the subject of known research and validation studies with the general population, and even fewer have been validated with LCD populations (Haensly & Torrance, 1990).

Only two tests are recommended due to the existence of validity data available with LCD children. The TTCT appears to be the most frequently recommended creativity test with LCD children (Davis, 1989) and the most widely validated with this population (Torrance, 1972). Haensly and Torrance (1990) also recommend the Group Inventory for Finding Talent (GIFT), a personality/attitude measure that has been validated with African American and Hispanic children (Rimm, 1976).

Mistry and Rogoff (1985) recommend the use of informal creativity measures as an additional source of assessment data with LCD students. Informal methods of creativity assessment can include divergent thinking tasks, as well as inventories, biographical data, nominations (e.g., teacher, peer, and/or parent), judgments of products, questionnaires, rating scales, and observations (Davis, 1989; Haensly & Torrance, 1990; Hocevar, 1981; Michael & Wright, 1989). In practice, informal measures are not as frequently used as normed tests (Hunsaker, 1994; Patton, Prillaman, & Van Tassel-Baska, 1990) because of difficulties in interpreting qualitative data that does not yield a score (Davis, 1989) or judging qualitative products based on poorly operationalized constructs (Hocevar, 1981; Reis & Renzulli, 1991). Evaluation scales designed to judge students' creative products may provide more objective and standardized alternatives (Reis & Renzulli, 1991), but their utility remains to be established for products created by LCD children.

The use of multiple sources of information can also be complex because it is difficult to decide what data to use when performance is high on one measure and low on others (Adderholdt-Elliot et al., 1991). Evaluation systems such as Baldwin's Identification Matrix (Baldwin, 1985) can be instrumental when using multiple criteria to determine program eligibility.

A third concern is the shortage of validated measures in languages other than English. Translated versions of some of the creativity tests are available in languages other than English. The TTCT, for example, has been translated in over 32 languages. The process of test translation is questionable because of a number of difficulties encountered when translating test items (Cummins, 1984). The developmental level of a word or concept may change from one language to the other, and some words cannot be translated because there are no equivalent concepts in the language of interest. The process of translation can also significantly change the content and validity of tests, as the translated items may not reflect the constructs that the tests were originally intended to measure. For this reason, educators and psychologists should restrain from translating creativity tests during bilingual evaluations. The preferred alternative is to use translated versions of tests that have been validated with the specific language and cultural groups of interest (Geisinger, 1994).

A fourth concern is that creative LCD children are not being identified because the instruments and procedures used to measure their creativity skills have the same biases associated with the assessment of achievement and cognitive skills of LCD children. Historically, the process of assessing LCD children has been criticized for using such biased procedures as testing children in their non-native language, ignoring the effects of a second language and cultural differences on test scores, and disregarding sources of linguistic and cultural biases in tests (Figueroa, 1990).

Limited English Proficient (LEP) children who are tested in their non-native language typically score poorly on tests that require receptive and expressive English language skills. According to Cummins (1981, 1984), children exposed to a second language are able to establish basic social types of communication exchanges within two years after exposure to the second language, but the cognitive linguistic skills that are required in academic, cognitive, and language tests may take up to 5 to 7 years to develop proficiently in the second language. Thus, second language learners tend to score lower in language-based tests despite having been exposed to English for over two years.

Although some may argue that creativity tests are not achievement or intelligence tests and that speakers of English as a second language should not encounter the same difficulties in creativity tests, there are research data supporting the view that these measures are all somewhat interrelated. Several correlational studies have shown that creativity measures correlate moderately with measures of cognition and achievement (Ausubel, 1978; Esquivel & Lopez, 1988; Getzels & Jackson, 1962; Guilford, 1967; Mednick, 1962; Rampaul, Singh, & Didyk, 1984; Yamamoto, 1964). Torrance (1974) reported a median correlation of .06 between figural creativity and intelligence and a median correlation of .21 between verbal creativity and intelligence. Rampaul, Singh, and Didyk (1984) reported correlations between creativity and achievement ranging from .08 to .19 using a sample of Native American children, whereas and Esquivel and Lopez (1988) found correlations ranging from .21 to .40 between creativity and achievement scores with a sample of heterogeneous LCD children.

Overall, these results suggest that measures of intelligence, achievement, and creativity may be measuring, to some extent, children's language skills. In light of this information, it is then reasonable to hypothesize that speakers of English as a second language may do poorly on verbally loaded creativity tests. It certainly seems clear that further research is needed to explore this relationship with LCD children.

A lack of sensitivity to the individual's cultural values can also be a source of bias that may be present in the identification of creative LCD children. Taylor (1975) argued that what is regarded as creative in one culture may not be creative in another. Because individuals develop behaviors and skills supported by their surrounding environment (Sternberg, 1988), their creative abilities may be expressed within the context of what is valued within their own cultural group (Torrance, 1969). As such, LCD children may express their creative abilities in ways that deviate from the traditional standards of creative behavior (Baldwin, 1985; Gardner, 1983; Maker, Nielson, & Rogers, 1994). Native Americans, for example, nurture values related to interdependence, collective decision making, and group cohesiveness (Florey & Tafoya, 1988). These are values that are not typically emphasized in current assessment procedures in which individual performance and competition are encouraged and expected.

Traditionally, evaluators also expect and assume that most children are familiar with test-taking procedures. LCD children who have never been exposed to typical testing procedures can demonstrate difficulties in exhibiting the appropriate test-taking behaviors. Subsequently, they may demonstrate deficits in some testing tasks despite being able to solve similar tasks in everyday types of situations (Mistry & Rogoff, 1985). It is important in these situations to understand that LCD children's lack of demonstrated abilities does not necessarily imply an inherent lack of ability or a lack of potential to demonstrate creative abilities. Assessment climates or learning environments that allow children to demonstrate their knowledge and skills within natural settings (e.g., classrooms, creative activities) while incorporating their cultural backgrounds and past experiences are most relevant in these situations.

IMPLICATIONS FOR PRACTICE AND RESEARCH

Implications for Practice

As the number of LCD children increase in school settings, there is a pressing need to develop assessment tools that are sensitive to the strengths of particular cultural groups and that identify the creative behaviors that are valued most by those groups (Renzulli, 1973). According to Haensly and Torrance (1990), the collection of assessment data for the purpose of identifying creative children and adolescents should help to accomplish four major goals. First, the data should help school professionals become more aware of the creative skills that should be developed and practiced, as well as the personality characteristics, attitudes, and values that support creative responsiveness. Second, the information collected should highlight individual students' strengths and deficits for creative learning and problem solving. Third, the strengths and deficits identified should directly translate into learning activities, instructional planning, and educational opportunities. Fourth, the assessment data should generate evaluation procedures to assess educational outcomes and objectives. Table 6.2 includes a list of practical recommendations designed to improve assessment practices with LCD creative children.

Educational programs also need to be implemented for LCD children with special talents and creative skills. The Schoolwide Enrichment Triad Model (SEM) is an example of a comprehensive educational program designed to support talent development. The model provides instructional procedures and programming alternatives with a broad range of advanced-level enrichment experiences for all students (Renzulli, 1994). A Total Talent Portfolio is used to identify students' special abilities and talents. The portfolio can include scores from traditional standardized tests as well as more informal products (e.g., teacher ratings, product evaluations for musical abilities). Students are encouraged to become involved in enrichment clusters that nurture special interests and lead to the completion of unique projects in such areas as fine arts, drama, athletics, and photography. A recent review of the literature indicates that the SEM has been utilized in a variety of schools that serve diverse ethnic populations. Results of preliminary investigations suggest that the model encourages creativity in targeted students (Renzulli & Reis, 1994).

Table 6.2. Practical Recommendations for the Assessment of Creative LCD Children.

1. Use a broader definition of creativity that acknowledges the creative potential of all children and recognizes the type of ordinary creativity involved in solving everyday real-life situations.

2. Use a variety of tests, including formal as well as informal measures in the form of observation scales, checklists, inventories, nominations, product judgment, interviews and biographical data.

3. Review test items before assessment sessions to determine their appropriateness for the children's specific linguistic and cultural backgrounds.

4. Evaluate the standardization and norming procedures for normed creativity tests and consider their appropriateness for LCD children's specific linguistic and cultural background, socioeconomic status, and prior education.

5. Assess limited English proficient (LEP) and bilingual children's language proficiency in English and the second language to identify strengths and weaknesses and to determine what language(s) to use when evaluating creative abilities. Assess language proficiency within a multidimensional model while examining variables such as the developmental progression of the children's first and second languages, the length of exposure to the second language, the children's instructional history, the context in which each of the languages are experienced, and the quality of the language used in social as well as academic situations.

6. Conduct assessment sessions in the native language of the children, preferably through the use of bilingual evaluators.

7. Avoid using interpreters to assess bilingual children. Use interpreters only when other alternatives are unavailable. Interpreters should demonstrate adequate bilingual proficiency, prior training as interpreters, and knowledge of the children's cultural backgrounds. If an untrained interpreter is the only alternative, training should be provided in the process of translating for assessment procedures.

8. Alter assessment procedures to meet the needs of the children by, for example, accepting oral responses to written measures and by changing time limits.

9. Include nonverbal measures of creativity with LEP and bilingual students to decrease the effects of language variables throughout the assessment process.

10. Use tasks that assess the kinds of creative behaviors that are valued by the children's particular cultural backgrounds.

Table 6.2. Practical Recommendations for the Assessment of Creative LCD Children (con't).

11. Interpret testing results within the context of the children's specific linguistic and cultural backgrounds.
12. Focus on identifying LCD children who have well-developed talents as well as those who demonstrate potential talents.
13. Use assessment personnel who are trained to assess LCD children and are sensitive to linguistic and cultural differences.
14. Train assessment personnel to use and interpret informal and nonverbal creativity measures.
15. Implement education programs that address the needs of LCD children and nurture their creative potential.
16. Educate classroom and assessment personnel to recognize creative positives and to refer creative LCD children for gifted and talented programs.
17. Develop a collaborative relationship between the school and the home to encourage parents to identify and nurture the creative abilities of their children.

Implications for Research

The creativity skills of LCD children continue to be of interest to researchers as well as practitioners because of the numerous issues that remain open to exploration. Future studies with bilingual populations should control for language proficiency. Efforts need to be directed toward exploring the creative strengths of LCD children through homogeneous samples that examine the relationship between the children's creativity skills and their specific language and cultural backgrounds. The nature of the relationship between bilingualism and creativity also needs to be examined further through comparison of homogeneous samples of LCD children at various stages of second language acquisition and at different levels of language proficiency. Diaz (1983, 1985) recommends the use of longitudinal studies as a medium by which to evaluate cause-effect relationships between bilingualism and creativity.

An area of research that needs exploration with samples of LCD children is the relationship between the development of creativity and classroom variables. There is literature available indicating a relationship between instructional variables and students' creative abilities (Houtz, 1990). This type of research has been slow to accumulate with LCD samples of children. Torrance's (1967) cross-cultural studies indicated that teachers can influence the type of creativity behaviors that children develop within classroom situations. Esquivel (1985) found that gifted classroom placement leads to an increase in the creativity skills of economically disadvantaged culturally different children. Lopez et al. (1993) conducted classroom observations of LCD children in a gifted program and found that the students' creativity scores were significantly related to instructional environments that were characterized by self-initiated activities, self-evaluation experiences, opportunities to manipulate materials, and open discussions. These findings appear to support the hypothesis that specific environmental variables can enhance the creativity skills of LCD children. However, more research is needed to help establish clear cause-and-effect connections.

SUMMARY AND REVIEW

The early research on creativity development indicated that environmental factors had a direct effect on children's creative abilities. During the 1960s and 1970s, empirical studies were designed to investigate the effect of linguistic and cultural factors on the creativity skills of LCD youngsters. Research efforts were also directed toward examining the creative strengths of these children and developing assessment instruments for identification purposes. The results of those early empirical investigations were questioned because of failure to control for the confounding effects of such variables as language proficiency and cultural background.

Current research efforts continue to be directed toward examining the creative strengths of LCD children and the relationship between bilingualism and creativity. However, little research has been conducted examining the development of creativity within specific cultural groups. Furthermore, recent empirical investigations continue to be criticized for failing to control confounding variables (e.g., language proficiency) that render the results inconclusive.

In terms of the identification of LCD children, recent data indicate that LCD children continue to be underrepresented in programs for the gifted and talented. The problems leading to the underrepresentation of LCD children include (a) an overemphasis on cognitive and achievement tests with little emphasis on the identification of creative abilities, (b) a shortage of creativity measures sensitive to the backgrounds of LCD children, and (c) the use of biased measures and procedures in creativity assessment (e.g., children not being tested in their native language, failure to consider the effects of linguistic and cultural factors on test performance).

Overall, there is a need to implement assessment practices that will provide children with the opportunity to demonstrate their creative abilities. LCD children also need opportunities to demonstrate their creative strengths within the context of their own linguistic and cultural backgrounds. A number of best recommendations were made with the goal of improving the assessment procedures to be followed when identifying creative LCD children.

Future empirical studies need to continue to expand and build on the literature through carefully designed studies with well-defined samples of LCD children and controls for language proficiency and cultural background. There is also a need to develop creativity instruments that assess children's strengths in the context of their own linguistic and cultural backgrounds. Finally, research efforts should be directed toward examining the instructional variables that influence the development of LCD children's creativity skills.

STUDY ACTIVITIES

1. Examine a verbal and a figural test of creativity. Identify the strengths and the weaknesses of each measure in terms of its utility for linguistically and culturally different children.
2. Identify the creative strengths of some of the linguistically and culturally different children in your classroom or school. Identify and describe creativity measures that could be used to identify their creative strengths.
3. Interview several individuals from varied linguistic and cultural backgrounds and ask, How do they define creative behavior? What occupations do they consider to be creative? How would they describe a creative child? Compare and contrast their responses, taking into consideration their linguistic and cultural backgrounds.

REFERENCES

Adderholdt-Elliot, M., Algozzine, K., Algozzine, B., & Haney, K. (1991). Current state practices in educating students who are gifted and talented. *Roeper Review, 14,* 20-23.

Ausubel, D. P. (1978). The nature and measurement of creativity. *Psychologia, 21,* 179-191.

Baldwin, A. Y. (1985). Programs for the gifted and talented: Issues concerning minority populations. In F. D. Horowitz & M. O'Brien (Eds.), *The gifted and talented: Developmental perspectives* (pp. 223-249). Washington, DC: American Psychological Association.

Barkaa, J. H., & Bernal, E. M. (1991). Gifted education for bilingual and limited English proficient students. *Gifted Child Quarterly, 35,* 144-147.

Bernal, E., & Reyna, J. (1974). *Analysis of giftedness in Mexican-American children and design of a prototype identification instrument: Final report* (Report No. OEC-47-062-113-307). Austin, TX: Southwest Educational Development Laboratory.

Buriel, R. (1975). Cognitive styles among three generations of Mexican-American children. *Journal of Cross-Cultural Psychology, 6,* 417-429.

Carringer, D. C. (1974). Creative thinking abilities of Mexican youth: The relationship of bilingualism. *Journal of Cross-Cultural Psychology, 5,* 492-504.

Cummins, J. (1977). Cognitive factors associated with the attainment of intermediate levels of bilingual skills. *Modern Language Journal, 61,* 3-11.

Cummins, J. (1981). Four misconceptions about language proficiency in bilingual education. *NABE Journal, 5,* 31-44.

Cummins, J. (1984). *Bilingualism and special education: Issues in assessment and pedagogy.* San Diego, CA: College-Hill.

Cummins, J., & Gulutsan, M. (1974). Bilingual education and cognition. *Alberta Journal of Education Research, 20,* 259-269.

Davis, G. A. (1989). Testing for creative potential. *Contemporary Educational Psychology, 14,* 257-274.

DeVito, P. J. (1975). An analysis of selected behavioral characteristics of disadvantaged students. *Journal of Educational Research, 68,* 178-181.

Diaz, R. M. (1983). Thought and two languages: The impact of bilingualism on cognitive development. In E. W. Gordon (Ed.), *Review of research in education* (Vol. 10, pp. 23-54). Washington, DC: American Educational Research Association.

Diaz, R. M. (1985). Bilingual cognitive development: Addressing three groups in current research. *Child Development, 56,* 1376-1388.

Dulay, H., Burt, M., & Krashen, S. (1982). *Language two.* New York: Oxford University Press.

Duncan, S. E., & DeAvila, E. A. (1979). Bilingualism and cognition: Some recent findings. *NABE Journal, 4,* 15-50.

Esquivel, G. B. (1985). The effects of special classroom placement on the creativity, self-concept, and academic achievement of culturally different gifted children. *SABE Journal, 1,* 18-25.

Esquivel, G. B., & Lopez, E. C. (1988). Correlations among measures of cognitive ability, creativity, and academic achievement for gifted minority children. *Perceptual and Motor Skills, 67,* 395-398.

Figueroa, R. A. (1990). Assessment of linguistic minority group children. In C. R. Reynolds & R. W. Kamphaus (Eds.), *Handbook of psychological and educational assessment of children: Intelligence and achievement* (pp. 671-696). New York: Guilford.

Florey, J., & Tafoya, N. (1988). *Identifying gifted and talented American Indian students: An overview.* Washington, DC: Office of Educational Research and Improvement. (ERIC Document Reproduction Service No. ED 296 810)

Gardner, H. (1983). *Frames of mind: The theory of multiple intelligences.* New York: Basic Books.

Geisinger, K. F. (1994). Cross-cultural normative assessment: Translation and adaptation issues influencing the normative interpretation of assessment instruments. *Psychological Assessment, 6,* 304-312.

Getzels, J. W. (1975). Creativity: Prospects and issues. In I. A. Taylor & J. W. Getzels (Eds.), *Perspectives in creativity* (pp. 326-344). Chicago: Chicago Aldine.

Getzels, J. W., & Jackson, P. W. (1962). *Creativity and intelligence: Exploration with gifted students.* New York: Wiley.

Gezi, K. I. (1969, March). *Analyses of certain measures of creativity and self-concept and their relationships to social class.* Paper presented at the meeting of the California Educational Research Association, Los Angeles, CA. (ERIC Document Reproduction No. ED 031 533)

Guilford, J. P. (1956). The structure of the intellect. *Psychological Bulletin, 53,* 267-293.

Guilford, J. P. (1959). Three faces of intellect. *American Psychologist, 14,* 469-479.

Guilford, J. P. (1967). *The nature of human intelligence.* New York: McGraw-Hill.

Haensly, P. A., & Torrance, E. P. (1990). Assessment of creativity in children and adolescents. In C. R. Reynolds & R. W. Kamphaus (Eds.), *Handbook of psychological and educational assessment of children: Intelligence and achievement* (pp. 697-722). New York: Guilford.

Hamayan, E., Kwiat, J., & Perlman, R. (1985). *The identification and assessment of language minority children.* Arlington Heights: Illinois Resource Center.

Heath, I. A. (1987). Investigating the relationship between creativity and communicative competence strategies among bilingual and bidialectical adolescents (Doctoral dissertation, Florida State University). *Dissertation Abstracts International, 48,* 12A.

Hocevar, D. (1981). Measurement of creativity: Review and critique. *Journal of Personality Assessment, 45,* 450-464.

Houtz, J. C. (1990). Environments that support creative thinking. In C. Hedley, J. Houtz, & A. Baratta (Eds.), *Cognition, curriculum, and literacy* (pp. 61-76). Norwood, NJ: Ablex.

Hunsaker, S. L. (1994). Adjustments to traditional procedures for identifying underserved students: Successes and failures. *Exceptional Children, 61,* 72-76.

Jacobs, J. F., & Pierce, M. L. (1966). Bilingualism and creativity. *Journal of Elementary English, 43,* 499-503.

Janssen, C. (1969). *A study of bilingualism and creativity: Final report.* Paper presented at the meeting of the American Personnel and Guidance Association Convention, Las Vegas, Nevada. (ERIC Document Reproduction No. ED 034 269)

Kessler, C., & Quinn, M. E. (1987). Language minority children's linguistic and cognitive creativity. *Journal of Multilingual and Multicultural Development, 8,* 173-186.

Lambert, W. E., Tucker, G. R., & d'Anglejan, A. (1973). Cognitive and attitudinal consequences of bilingual schooling: The St. Lambert project through grade five. *Journal of Educational Psychology, 65,* 141-159.

Landry, R. G. (1973). The relationship of second language learning and verbal creativity. *Modern Language Journal, 57,* 110-113.

Landry, R. G. (1974). A comparison of second language learners and monolinguals on divergent thinking tasks at the elementary school level. *Modern Language Journal, 58,* 10-15.

Lemmon, C. R., & Goggin, J. P. (1989). The measurement of bilingualism and its relationship to cognitive ability. *Applied Psycholinguistics, 10,* 144-155.

Lopez, E. C., Esquivel, G. B., & Houtz, J. C. (1993). The creative skills of culturally and linguistically diverse gifted students. *Creativity Research Journal, 6,* 401-412.

Maker, C. J., Nielson, A. B., & Rogers, J. A. (1994). Giftedness, diversity, and problem solving. *Teaching Exceptional Children, 27,* 4-18.

Marland, S. P., Jr. (1972). *Education of the gifted and talented.* Washington, DC: U.S. Government Printing Office.

Martorell, M. (1991). Language proficiency, creativity, and locus of control among Hispanic bilingual gifted children (Doctoral dissertation, Fordham University). *Dissertation Abstracts International, 52,* 3226A.

Mattes, L. J., & Omark, D. R. (1991). *Speech and language assessment for the bilingual handicapped* (2nd ed.). San Diego, CA: Academic Communication Associates.

Mednick, S. A. (1962). The associative basis of the creative process. *Psychological Review, 69,* 220-232.

Meeker, M. (1969). *The structure of the intellect: Its interpretation and uses.* Columbus, OH: Charles E. Merrill.

Melesky, T. J. (1984). Identifying and providing for the Hispanic gifted child. *NABE Journal, 9,* 43-57

Michael, W. B., & Wright, C. R. (1989). Psychometric issues in the assessment of creativity. In J. A. Glover, R. R. Ronning, & C. R. Reynolds (Eds.), *Handbook of creativity* (pp. 33-55). New York: Plenum.

Mistry, J., & Rogoff, B. (1985). A cultural perspective on the development of talent. In F. D. Horowitz & M. O'Brien (Eds.), *The gifted and talented: Developmental perspectives* (pp. 125-144). Washington, DC: APA

Mitchell, B. M. (1988). A strategy for the identification of the culturally different gifted talented child. *Roeper Review, 10,* 163-165.

Patton, J. M., Prillaman, D., & Van Tassel-Baska, J. (1990). The nature and extent of programs for the disadvantaged gifted in the United States and territories. *Gifted Child Quarterly, 24,* 94-96.

Peal, E., & Lambert, W. (1962). The relation of bilingualism to intelligence. *Psychological Monographs, 76,* 1-23

Pezzullo, T. R., Thorsen, E. E, & Madaus, G. F. (1972). The heritability of Jensen's level I and II and divergent thinking. *American Educational Research Journal, 9,* 539-546.

Ramirez, M. (1973). Cognitive styles and cultural democracy in education. *Social Science Quarterly, 53,* 895-904.

Rampaul, W. E., Singh, M., & Didyk, J. (1984). The relationship between academic achievement, self-concept, creativity, and teacher expectations among Native children in a Northern Manitoba school. *Alberta Journal of Educational Research, 30,* 213-225.

Reis, S. M., & Renzulli, J. S. (1991). The assessment of creative products in programs for gifted and talented students. *Gifted Child Quarterly, 35,* 128-134.

Renzulli, J. S. (1973). Talent potential in minority group students. *Exceptional Children, 39,* 437-444.

Renzulli, J. S. (1994). Teachers as talent scouts. *Educational Leadership, 52,* 75-81.

Renzulli, J. S., & Reis, S. M. (1994). Research related to the Schoolwide Enrichment Triad Model. *Gifted Child Quarterly, 38,* 7-20.

Ricciardelli, L. A. (1992). Creativity and bilingualism. *Journal of Creative Behavior, 26,* 242-252.

Richert, E. S. (1985). Identification of gifted students: An update. *Roeper Review, 8,* 68-72.

Richert, E. S. (1987). Rampant problems and promising practices in the identification of disadvantaged gifted students. *Gifted Child Quarterly, 31,* 149-154.

Richmond, B. O. (1968). *Creative and cognitive abilities of white and negro children.* Athens, GA: University of Georgia. (ERIC Document Reproduction No. ED 030 922)

Riegel, K. E., Ramsey, R. M., & Riegel, R. M. (1967). A comparison of the first and second languages of American and Spanish students. *Journal of Verbal Behavior, 6,* 536-544.

Rimm, S. (1976). *Group inventory for finding talent.* Watertown, WI: Educational Assessment Service.

Ripple, R. E. (1989). Ordinary creativity. *Contemporary Educational Psychology, 14,* 189-202.

Robles, R. T. (1988). The relationship between creativity and self-esteem in Puerto Rican kindergarten children (Doctoral dissertation, Pennsylvania State University). *Dissertation Abstracts International, 49,* 09A.

Sanders, M., Scholz, J. P., & Kagan, S. (1976). Three social motives and field independence-dependence in Anglo American and Mexican American children. *Journal of Cross-Cultural Psychology, 7,* 451-462.

Smith, J., LeRose, B., & Clasen, R. E. (1991). Underrepresentation of minority students in gifted programs: Yes! It matters! *Gifted Child Quarterly, 35,* 81-83.

Sternberg, R. J. (1988). *A three-fact model of creativity.* In R. Sternberg (Ed.), *The nature of creativity* (pp. 125-147). Cambridge, England: Cambridge University Press.

Taylor, I. A. (1975). A retrospective view of creativity investigation. In I. A. Taylor & J. W. Getzels (Eds.), *Perspectives in creativity* (pp. 1-36). Chicago: Chicago Aldine.

Torrance, E. P. (1963). *Education and the creative potential.* Minneapolis: University of Minnesota.

Torrance, E. P. (1965). *Rewarding creative behavior.* Englewood Cliffs, NJ: Prentice-Hall.

Torrance, E. P. (1967). *Understanding the 4th grade slump in creative thinking: Final report.* Athens, GA: University of Georgia . (ERIC Document Reproduction No. ED 081 273)

Torrance, E. P. (1969). Creative positives of disadvantaged children and youth. *Gifted Child Quarterly, 13,* 71-81.

Torrance, E. P. (1971). Are the Torrance Tests of Creative Thinking biased against or in favor of "disadvantaged" groups? *Gifted Child Quarterly, 15,* 75-80.

Torrance, E. P. (1972). Predictive validity of the Torrance Tests of Creative Thinking. *The Journal of Creative Behavior, 6,* 236-252.

Torrance, E. P. (1974). *Torrance Tests of Creative Thinking: Norms technical manual.* Princeton, NJ: Personnel Press.

Torrance, E. P. (1977). *Discovery and nurturance of giftedness in the culturally different.* Reston, VA: Council for Exceptional Children.

Torrance, E. P. (1978). Dare we hope again? *Gifted Child Quarterly, 22,* 292-312.

Torrance, E. P. (1984). The role of creativity in the identification of the gifted and talented. *Gifted Child Quarterly, 28,* 153-156.

Toth, L. S., & Baker, S. R. (1990). The relationship of creativity and instructional style preferences to overachievement and underachievement in a sample of public school children. *Journal of Creative Behavior, 24,* 190-198.

Yamamoto, K. A. (1964). Threshold of intelligence in academic achievement of highly creative students. *Journal of Experimental Education, 32,* 401-405.

Part IV

Objective 3:
Fostering Creativity

The third goal of the educational psychology of creativity is to help educators help themselves and their pupils foster and sustain environments in schools that encourage creativity, creative thinking, and creative problem solving. As might have been guessed, this goal is as broad as the goals of explaining and recognizing creativity. The territory of theory, research, and educational practice applicable to school structure, operation, and change to which educational psychology contributes and from which it draws is enormous.

To be helpful, however, it is possible to identify a number of different categories of research and practice concerned with fostering creative development. These include teacher education, school organization, curriculum development, and teacher-pupil classroom interaction. Within these four major categories, there are subcategories of interest as well. For example, a consideration of teacher-education practices that foster creativity may include also discussion of the preparation of other school personnel besides teachers, such as administrators, psychologists, and counselors.

In the area of curriculum development, we can consider the development of specific instructional packages that might be designed to train various thinking skills. We might consider also the use of particular teaching methods, teaching techniques, or the availability of certain teaching resources. Or, we can consider the provision of various "extracurricular" services, such as assessment, counseling, parent education, and so on, which may support the development of creative skills and attitudes. And we can consider the impact of technology, specifically computers, on our ability to improve productivity and human thinking skills.

In the category of teacher-pupil interaction, we can discuss many factors: the general learning climate that the teacher fosters in the classroom, the type of expectations communicated to students by the teacher, the specific classroom management or discipline techniques used, the teacher's use of rewards and reinforcements for creative thinking, or the frequency and level of questions teachers ask during lessons, for example. We also can look at student factors, such as their preparation and backgrounds, developmental level and motivation, or learning and behavior styles, for example. The chapters that follow touch on many of these issues. Nevertheless, the reader is encouraged to think about the breadth of issues raised (sensitivity to problems), peruse a variety of resources (divergency), and then select some works to follow-up on in depth (understanding, reorganization, insight).

Esquivel and Hodes (chap. 7), review a number of issues and research themes concerning the natural development of creativity across the life span. *Natural* distinguishes the issues that are of particular concern to these authors. As opposed to deliberate efforts to improve creativity, through environmental interventions, specific teaching methods, or other artificial means, Esquivel and Hodes are concerned with traditional developmental trends in creativity. These authors are interested in what factors influence the normal growth of creative thinking skills or attitudes. What have researchers observed about the normal growth of creative abilities in early childhood, for example? What home and family background factors influence the development of creativity? Are growth patterns steady or do they fluctuate through school years? Does creativity decline with age? Esquivel and Hodes point to the foundational influences of a number of theorists and writers in analytic and humanistic psychology. A central theme of this literature is that creativity is a natural life force. The source of creative development lies within the individual. It is human nature to create—to solve problems. These authors argue persuasively that many factors in the external environment operate to inhibit, curtail, repress, or otherwise ignore creative effort. Nevertheless, creative expression is a healthy force for which well-adjusted, growing children, adolescents, and adults strive.

In chapter 8, Michael, a student and colleague of J. P. Guilford with a long record of research and writing about creativity and problem solving, reviews the history and development of Guilford's structure of intellect and the consequent model of human problem solving. Michael's chapter serves the third purpose of educational psychology, not because of Guilford's measurement contributions, which are without parallel, but because of the problem-solving model itself. How can Purpose 3 be realized, how can educators design and deliver instruction, without a model of the overall thinking and creating process?

The structure-of-intellect problem-solving (SIPS) model provides a picture for designers to use to construct, organize, and sequence learning materials and activities to build creative thinking skills and attitudes. What is so special about SIPS? The reader is reminded of the theme established in the first of the educational psychology of creativity's purposes—the interaction of both affective and cognitive components. This theme is repeated in the three chapters presented to address the second purpose—recognizing creativity. Process and product research must be integrated together to yield the knowledge and procedures necessary to effectively recognize creativity in ourselves and others. The SIPS model, from its inception more than 40 years ago, to the present day, is interactive and integrative. All of Guilford's contents, operations, and products are projected to interact together in the creative problem-solving process. Instructional activities based on this model can be distinguished by this integration.

In chapter 10, Tighe, Piccariello, and Amabile continue the discussion of creativity in the classroom by writing about the role of intrinsic motivation in creative development and the environmental conditions that foster this type of motivation in learners. These authors focus attention on the classroom environment created and maintained largely by the teacher and other school personnel. Well-designed curriculum materials and instructional activities are not enough for they, too, are delivered in a larger context for learning. The larger context must be examined as well. (Other sources containing a description of Amabile's general theory of creativity include Amabile, 1983, 1990.)

This concept of intrinsic motivation (Deci, 1975), that individuals will perform a task for the joy or delight in the actual work, is critical to the growth of creativity. Tighe, Picariello, and Amabile make a strong case that learning environments that attempt to promote creative thinking should be characterized by intrinsic motivational structures and that there are many things teachers can do to help develop this motivation among their pupils.

Environments that are supportive of creative thinking have been extensively studied. Interestingly, much of the research comes from workplace studies in real-life occupations and organizations. There is little disagreement that the results of many studies suggest the important influences on creativity for a large number of workplace and classroom conditions (see Houtz, 1990; Kuhn & Kaplan, 1959; Lasswell, 1959; MacKinnon, 1962; McPherson, 1964; Pelz, 1976; Proshansky, 1976). The following list contains a number of often cited environmental conditions that appear to aid or hinder creativity. Some are obvious. Others may require a bit of thinking to see how they exert an influence, either positive or negative.

Aid

Freedom from criticism and time constraints
Adequate resources
Praise for innovative work
Direct encouragement for new ideas, flexible thinking
Opportunity for reflection
Opportunity to share ideas with colleagues
Opportunity to work independently
Opportunity to experiment
Opportunity to see things through
Encouragement to tackle complex problems
Encouragement to think holistically
Encouragement of self-evaluation
Encouragement of question asking
Tolerance of ambiguity
Individualized, student-focused instruction
Democratic classroom processes
Integrated curriculum
Positive discipline techniques
Willingness to play
Humor
Balance of cooperative and competitive activities

Hinder

Over focus on specific goals
Fixation on one or a few ideas
Pressure to conform, to "go along"
Limited resources
Requirements for speed and high productivity
Emphasis on repetitive, mundane tasks
Rigid adherence to time schedules
Premature evaluation
Overbearing supervision, micromanagement
Use of punishment
Fear of failure
Personal attacks, ridicule
Cultural stereotyping
Teacher-focused instruction
Authoritarian classroom management
Insensitivity to individual differences

Secrecy
Overprotectiveness
Too much competition
Politeness (unwillingness to confront or challenge)
Overgeneralizing

In chapter 11, Shaw discusses a specific curriculum approach to language arts teaching termed *whole language*. Shaw has found, in his research and teaching, that whole language embodies many of the principles of creative learning that exist in the broader creativity, creative thinking, and problem-solving literatures. From his experience as a teacher-trainer and curriculum designer, Shaw argues that the whole-language method is exceptionally well suited to developing creativity in students and its general principles and methods are extremely adaptable to teaching in other subject matter domains.

A substantial debate continues in education and psychology regarding the transfer of generic creative problem-solving skills across knowledge domains. Many of the available training programs and teaching techniques are based on generic skills, such as problem definition, divergent thinking, asking questions, hypothesis testing, and so on. If whole language, as a method-grown-into-a-philosophy, as Shaw explains, is truly applicable to learning in other disciplines, it may become an effective way for educators to address the "transferability" problem.

REFERENCES

Amabile, T. M. (1983). *The social psychology of creativity.* New York: Springer-Verlag.

Amabile, T. M. (1990). Within you, without you: The social psychology of creativity, and beyond. In M. A. Runco & R. S. Albert (Eds.), *Theories of creativity* (pp. 61-91). Newbury Park, CA: Sage.

Deci, E. (1975). *Intrinsic motivation.* New York: Plenum.

Houtz, J. C. (1990). Environments that support creative thinking. In C. Hedley, J. Houtz, & A. Baratta (Eds.), *Cognition, curriculum, and literacy* (pp. 61-76). Norwood, NJ: Ablex.

Kuhn, T. S., & Kaplan, N. (1959). Environmental conditions affecting creativity. In C. W. Taylor (Ed.), *The third annual University of Utah research conference on the identification of scientific talent* (pp. 313-316). Salt Lake City: University of Utah.

Lasswell, H. D. (1959). The social setting of creativity. In H. H. Anderson (Ed.), *Creativity and its cultivation* (pp. 203-221). New York: Harper & Row.

MacKinnon, D. W. (1962). The nature and nurture of creative talent. *American Psychologist, 17,* 484-495.

McPherson, J. H. (1964). Environment and training for creativity. In C. W. Taylor (Ed.), *Creativity: Progress and potential* (pp. 129-153). New York: McGraw-Hill.

Pelz, D. C. (1976). Environments for creative performance within universities. In S. Messick & Associates (Eds.), *Individuality in learning* (pp. 229-247). San Francisco, CA: Jossey-Bass.

Proshansky, A. M. (1976). Interpersonal climate of creative research training. In S. Messick & Associates (Eds.), *Individuality and learning* (pp. 225-264). San Francisco: CA: Jossey-Bass.

7

Creativity, Development, and Personality

Giselle B. Esquivel
Traci G. Hodes
Fordham University

In this chapter we examine the literature regarding the influence of developmental factors and personality on creativity within the individual. What does the term *development* mean with respect to creativity? Is one born creative? What are the factors that either enhance or serve as potential blocks to the development of creativity? How does creative output change across an individual's lifetime? Is the development of creativity different for females than for males? These are the types of questions the first part of this chapter attempts to answer.

The second half of the chapter examines the history of the relation between personality research and creativity. What is the construct of personality and how has this construct been linked to the phenomenon of creativity? Is there a creative personality? How are intellective and nonintellective (that is, socioemotional) factors related to creativity? Are creative individuals well adjusted? Are they mentally ill? Finally, what can be done in educational settings to enhance the positive characteristics of students for creativity?

DEVELOPMENTAL FACTORS AND CREATIVITY

First, we examine the literature on the life-span development of creativity. Next, we explore the ways in which creativity changes in old age. Many researchers have looked at the role environment plays in the development of creativity, but more specifically, we give emphasis to family and school influences. Then, creative development and the similarities and differences exhibited in males and females are examined. The issue of what research questions still need to be explored in the field of the development of creativity also are posed.

Before going any further, it is necessary to define what is meant by *creative development* as it is discussed in the following pages. In addition, how is creativity distinguished from giftedness and how are the two terms similar? The term *creativity*, according to Vernon (1989), refers to a "person's capacity to produce new or original ideas, insights, restructurings, inventions, or artistic objects, which are accepted by experts as being of scientific, aesthetic, social, or technological value" (p. 94). However, Maslow (1958), in his study of creative development, concluded that:

> a fair proportion of my subjects, though healthy and creative in a special sense . . . were not productive in the ordinary sense, nor did they have great talent or genius, nor were they poets, composers, inventors, artists or creative intellectuals . . . I learned that a first-rate soup is more creative than a second-rate painting, and that, generally, cooking or parenthood or making a home could be creative while poetry need not be: it could be uncreative. (p. 53)

Creative development is affected by environment and upbringing as well as one's genes. Certain personality factors are also related to creative development. The term *giftedness* refers to any individual who is much above average ability. This term usually refers to persons who are high in general intelligence or ability. Gowan (cited in Wallace, 1985) stated, "giftedness represents only potentiality, the major variable is creativity" (p. 21).

The term *gifted* is usually applied to children, while in contrast, from a developmental perspective, the term *creative* is usually applied to adults. "Being gifted implies that a person has been 'given' a gift, rather than the person developing or producing something through his or her own effort. Creative refers to sustained, purposeful action" (Wallace, 1985, p. 362). Moustakas (1977) stated that "Creativity is a turning point awakened in times of challenge or crisis, involving an unknown and unpredictable path, in which there is a particular focus, concentration, exertion, or unfolding as the individual shapes new ways of being and becoming, as the individual engages in new actions and creates new life" (p. 25). For the creative adult, his/her abilities have become a means, an integrated, seasoned instrument, for organizing and living a purposeful creative life. For the child, the gift in question is still to be developed and its formal structures mastered.

LIFE SPAN DEVELOPMENT

Lehman's (1953) "definitive study of *Age and Achievement* represents the beginning of life span research specific to creativity development" (Kogan, 1973, p. 146). As Kogan stated, this landmark study represents the major effort in the field. The majority of research looking at life-span creative development occurred from the time of Lehman's (1953) definitive work through the early 1970s (Dennis, 1968; Dudek, 1974; Gowan, 1972; Kogan, 1973; Lehman 1968).

From a life-span perspective, creativity develops in stage spurts, and begins during the initiative-intuitive period of a child's development (Gowan, 1972). Gowan stated that the child in this period responds to the warm affection of the opposite sexed parent by enlarging the bridge between fantasy and the real world. His studies found that boys who are affectionately close to their mothers and girls who are close to their fathers during the 4 to 7 age period tend to become more creative than others of similar ability. Additionally, the individual who gains mental health as he or she goes through the developmental process exhibits increasing creativeness. Conversely, an individual who experiences strain and anxiety as a result of lack of warmth with either parent evidences diminished creativity (Gowan, 1972).

The process of creative development is not a continuously smooth one. In fact, the shift and reorganization of concepts required as the child shifts from one cognitive level to another may demand energy or impose strain that temporarily diminishes creative performance (Gowan, 1972). Torrance (1975a) stated that there are discontinuities within the overall development of creativity, and that these occur within a culture whenever children in that culture are confronted with new stresses and demands. Cultural factors strongly influence the course of creative development, the level of creative functioning, and the type of creative functioning that flourishes most. Thus, there are discontinuities of some kind in almost all cultures (Torrance, 1975a).

Within our own culture, the so-called fourth-grade slump is commonly associated with the discontinuity of creative development. This slump is characterized by a decrease in originality, concurrent with an increase toward conformity of thought. At this age (9-10), artistic expression may be viewed as having lost its freedom and spontaneity (Dudek, 1974). From

Torrance's (1975a) point of view, this slump is culture-made, not genetically determined, and was not evident in other cultures that he studied. Dudek summarized the reason for the fourth grade slump in another way. As viewed from a developmental perspective, it is not a slump in creativity, but rather a change in the quality of expressiveness. At this age, the child sees and integrates reality in a differentiated as opposed to a global way. The child, expressing a new visual realism, can now express new cognitive mastery in more realistic drawings and paintings. Dudek viewed this subtle expression of thought as indicating more, not less, imagination and creativity.

The next reported drop in creativity occurs around the seventh grade (age 12-13). Again, the child is in the process of shifting from one cognitive level to another—from concrete to formal operations (Dudek, 1974). What one researcher might see as a slump, another might view as simply reorganization. As a result of the latest development, the adolescent can hypothesize, predict, perform combinatorial analyses, imagine, and so on. However, it is also at this stage that the child needs support and encouragement to continue using his or her imagination because of the strong social pressures to conform (Dudek, 1974).

Beginning in secondary school and proceeding through college, meaningful external criteria of creativity become available. For example, individuals have the opportunities to involve themselves in many activities not directly related to their classes or grades. Examples are clubs for science, writing, painting, acting, and various leadership roles (Kogan, 1973). However, does evidence of creativity in secondary school predict future creativity in adulthood? Dudek (1974) found that creativity measures taken in the first grade correlated poorly with measures of creativity taken in later years. However, creative thinking becomes more crystallized with age, so that after age 10 there is a reasonable stability in its expression (Dudek, 1974).

Kogan (1973) brought up the issue of depth versus breadth. Secondary school students may try a number or activities or they may focus in on one. Are we able to predict which students are going to continue to be creative into adulthood? Kogan asserted that because our way of measuring creativity in adulthood is directly tied to one's output in his or her career, predictability of future creativity may be best when a student focuses in on one activity. It is with this fact that we discuss the work of Dennis (1968) and Lehman (1968).

The approach of Lehman and Dennis in their respective studies of life-span creativity can be called product-centered (Kogan, 1973). In his work, *Age and Achievement*, Lehman (1953) sought a sound method for the study of the correlation between age and achievement. He canvassed authoritative histories of science, noting dates on which important discoveries had either been made or first reported, and then ascertained the ages of the various scientists when they first announced their outstanding work. Lehman also examined the ages at which people occupied their prominent posts. These posts included statesmen, college presidents, heads of large corporations, and judges on the U.S. Supreme Court. He also studied the ages at which businessmen, actors and actresses, and movie directors were near the top of their earning power. For his 1968 study, Lehman used Wehr and Richards' (1960) *Physics of the Atom* as a reference guide, and found that 134 scientists made 154 outstanding contributions to the field of science. Lehman then plotted the ages (25 to 64) at which these scientists made their respective contributions. His results showed that the people studied exhibited noticeable and consistent decreases at the uppermost age levels, indicating that contributors became progressively less productive at those ages. The graph in Figure 7.1 represents only production rates that have been realized at successive age levels and not potential production rates. They do not imply that there is a decrease in the potential of these gifted individuals with age. Lehman stated that the age factor cannot be regarded as causing the decreases in creative productivity. Rather, it is the concomitants of advancing age that need to be studied. Lehman summarized his results in the following manner:

> With the advance in chronological age beyond the early twenties there is likely to be found: a decrement in physical vigor and sensory capacity, more illness, glandular changes, more preoccupation with practical concerns, less favorable conditions for concentration, weakened intellectual curiosity, more mental disorders, and an accumulation of unfavorable habits. (p. 103)

The work of Dennis, which was originally published in the *Journal of Gerontology* in 1966, had a different focus from that of Lehman (1968). Dennis examined the productivity of three groups of subjects from the ages of 20 to 80. He studied scholars, scientists, and artists. Obviously, the subjects were not uniform with regard to their degree of eminence. In addition, some sources from which the subjects were gathered were highly selective, whereas others included every person within the specific field who had ever produced a creative product. Dennis noted that although the productivity among the three groups was unequal, at no time did he directly compare these unlike data.

Dennis found characteristic curves among and between the three groups he chose to study. For example, output during the 20s was a considerably small part of total output; as low as 2% in some groups. For almost all groups, the period between ages 40 and 49 was either the most productive or just slightly below their peak. For scholars, the 70s were as productive as the 40s. However, scientists showed a significant decline

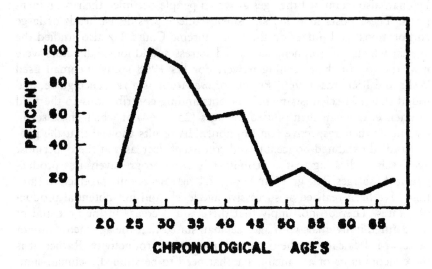

Figure 7.1. Age versus percentage of contributions to progress in
atomic physics, representing 154 superior contributions by 138
"still living" contributors (1.12 works each)

during this time period. The decline by the artists was even greater than
that evidenced by the scientists. Dennis hypothesized that the results
occurred in this manner because there are contrasting ways in which productivity is achieved in the three fields of endeavor. In some fields it is
proper for people to collaborate and have assistants. This is common
among scholars who publish. In other fields, the contributions are mainly
individual. This would be more characteristic of artists creating new
works. In some kinds of work, data and information must be collected,
stored, and classified. In some fields, contributors receive credit for modifying or amplifying previous views. In others, this is not possible.

Kogan (1973) presented a precise summarization of the work of
both Lehman (1968) and Dennis (1968). Lehman's principle finding was
that major creative achievements occur relatively early in one's career--
usually between the ages of 20 and 40. Although the incidences of
achievement may continue at a high level before declining with advancing
age, later achievements are less outstanding and significant than earlier
produced work. Dennis, however, showed that maximal output occurs at
ages greater than that indicated for the highest quality achievement found
in Lehman's work.

DECLINE IN OLD AGE?

Given both Lehman's and Dennis' research, how can one explain what appears at first to be a decline in creativity as one grows older? Kogan (1973) raised the question of whether at some point in the life span a switch in emphasis from depth to breadth must occur in order to account for creativity in old age. This stands in contrast to the traditional view of creativity in which activities and products are assessed. Is "the elderly individual to be considered as still manifesting creativity only to the extent that s/he continues to engage in such activities and to turn out such products?" (Kogan, 1973, p. 157). If creative output is looked at from this perspective, then creativity and retirement are incompatible. However, if one views the existence of creativity in the elderly from a different vantage point taking into consideration how an individual's life changes as he or she grows older, there is the possibility of equating creativity with aging. In Kogan's view, it is premature to speak of declines of creativity given the present methods of measuring its existence.

There are other ways of studying the supposed decline in creativity in old age. Gowan (1972) asserted that those individuals who continue to be creative preserve their creative drives by a search for greater amounts of mental health and for environments that stimulate and enhance creative response. Lehman (1968) said that some elderly people are set in their ways, which is a poor condition for bold discovery. Additionally, the individual who already has achieved prestige and recognition may try less hard thereafter to achieve further success. Physical changes can also account for decreases in creativity. "Arthritic hands, declining stamina and failing eyesight, for example, may impede an older painter's productivity, but have no effect on the artist's capacity to conceptualize unique relationships in the world" (Romaniuk & Romaniuk, 1981, p. 368). Welford (1958) stated that elderly subjects react poorly to tests involving time pressures and evaluation. Reactions to these tests may include symptoms of withdrawal from the assessment procedures. At this point, there are many questions left unanswered, and research is needed in order to find the "best" definition of creativity in old age and the methods to appropriately measure its existence.

ENVIRONMENTAL FACTORS

Guilford (1962) aptly stated the debate that exists when discussing the role environment plays in the development of creativity:

On the one hand, there are those who will tell you that a creative genius is entirely due to a lucky accident of a certain unique combination of genes. At the other extreme, there are those who say that the primary abilities are generalized, learned habits or skills, produced by certain kinds of practice. (p. 164)

Researchers began studying creative development in the early 1960s and have continued their investigation into the 1990s. One emphasis during this stretch of time has focused on what aids or hinders the development of creativity. Two environmental areas that have been investigated have been the child's home environment and the school environment.

MacKinnon (1962, 1965) based his studies of creative individuals on Rank's (1932) earlier conceptualization of the three stages or phases in one's winning of his or her own individuality and realization of creative potential. In the first stage of development, "will" is experienced as "counterwill"; a resistance to the demands and restraints of one's parents because of one's own dependency on them. The child then feels guilt because of this. If the parents accept the child as an individual, giving the child autonomy and opportunities to assert his or her will, the child achieves a secure sense of self. This leads to the second phase of development, in which the individual strikes out on his or her own, attempting to form goals, ideals, and moral and ethical standards other than those socially sanctioned. If the individual is successful with this, there is movement to the final stage of development. This stage is characterized by the unified working together of the three fully developed powers of the will, counterwill, and the ideal formation born from the conflict between them. This last stage, itself, becomes a goal-setting, goal-seeking force.

How was MacKinnon able to connect Rank's theory to his own research? He found when looking at the environments in which creative architects were raised that there were similarities between his subjects' experiences and the processes Rank described. For example, parents of these future architects had respect for their children and confidence in their ability to do what was appropriate. Parents gave children freedom in their exploration of the environment. There was an emphasis on the development of personal ethical codes of conduct. These various factors led to the child achieving a sense of personal autonomy. In a more recent study, Monks and Van Boxtel (1985) found that families of gifted children tend to show strong family ties and warm relationships between their members. Parents were found to give their children more freedom and to be more involved with their gifted children than parents of nongifted children. Reasonably high expectations, combined with involvement, seemed to represent the optimal family backgrounds for highly achieving gifted children. Additionally, the authors found that families with gifted adolescents saw themselves as more independent, permissive, intellectual, unstructured, and harmonious in their interactions.

Creativity, however, may be tolerated differently depending on the culture or socioeconomic status of the family. Monks and Van Boxtel (1985) stated there is evidence that in lower class families, outstanding performances are often regarded as nonconformist behavior, and that such behavior is not positively reinforced.

Children's creative development is influenced not only by their home environment, but also by their school environment. MacKinnon (1962) noted the importance of "discussing with our students as well as with our children, at least upon occasion, the most fantastic of ideas and possibilities" (p. 493). Guilford (1962), in discussing the influence of the school, stated the need for an awareness that each individual has a unique personality, and that in our respect for the individual we should tolerate his or her right to be different, within the limits of personal safety and welfare. Goodale (1970) stated that studies on personality correlates of creative people suggest that a major step in encouraging creativity in the classroom is the support of activities that increase students' self-confidence and persistence, and a tolerance on the part of teachers for student behaviors typically seen as "unpleasant." It is important that the child not be penalized for being different or for exhibiting his or her independence and curiosity. Along the same lines, Dirkes (1978) stated that students need to be taught how to brainstorm in order to encourage creative thinking, generate possibilities, examine given information carefully, compare responses, formulate generalizations, and problem solve. The critical aspect of brainstorming is that ideas produced are done so without judgment. In her study, Dirkes found that when students were unfamiliar with the concept of brainstorming, they often were reluctant to express original ideas on subject matter. She hypothesized that "most students probably do not believe that the production of trial-and-error and of related ideas are helpful or else they do not think that teachers are interested in their thinking" (p. 816).

Carlson (1964) pointed out the importance of the teacher-student bond. She stated that the greatest qualitative products develop through mutual relationships such as that between the learner and teacher. She characterized these relationships as a dialogue between two people having original ideas and mutual trust, including treating students' questions and ideas with respect, showing students that their ideas have value, and having students do things for practice without evaluation and consequences. Goodale (1970) added that when a child shows signs that personal interests are not being satisfied by proposed assignments, the teacher can then modify assignments enough to include the child's interests.

These can be difficult tasks for a teacher, however. Having to manage 25 unique individuals within one room is a tall order. Guilford (1962) found that teachers generally preferred students with high IQs who conformed to the usual standards, rather than the more creative students who tended to be "irritating at times" (p. 165). Guilford stated teachers naturally stress conventional answers to problems, which can limit the development of creativity. Monks and Van Boxtel (1985) noted that most school systems are oriented toward the middle area of the normal distribution of ability, so young gifted children may find the work too easy and may become lazy or even disruptive.

Torrance (1962), in his examination of creative development, discussed both the family and the school environments. Beginning at 2 to 3 years of age, children experience a spurt in language development and are constantly attempting to discover more about their environment by asking questions. However, if children are brought up without books or pictures, for example, and are not allowed to ask questions, they will find it difficult to read or interpret pictures. Torrance believes that creativity must be nurtured. For example, children need guidance in learning how to ask questions, especially if they have not received such guidance at home. Basic to the development of better questioning skills is the teacher's ability to be respectful of children's questions and to help them gain the skills for finding the answers. Without this critical guidance from the teacher, most children will cease to develop after a certain stage and will become discouraged.

Teachers also play a role in the development of task commitment in their students (Monks & Van Boxtel, 1985). Monks and Van Boxtel noted that educational curricula are commonly aimed toward teaching the average student. Students who work above this average, who require flexibility in the curriculum, or are simply not engaged by the activities, are less likely to develop the task commitment it takes to work in a creative manner, and more likely to sit idle and frustrated in the classroom. Related to the concept of task commitment is that of discipline and self-control (MacKinnon, 1962). MacKinnon stated that these skills must be learned, and then used flexibly. Students need to be guided as to when in the creative process these skills are required. For example, if one has too much self-control early in the creative process and prejudges an experience, that individual is excluding from perception large areas of experience. Carlson (1964) stated that tactless criticism can wilt the creative process, and that a lack of assistance on ways to improve the creative product can stunt the creator, causing a plateau in creative development rather than movement toward a peak.

Because Torrance (1975b) emphasized the nurturing aspect of creativity, it is only natural that he developed suggestions borne from his observations for the nurturance of creativity. Although the following recommendations by Torrance for the encouragement of creativity in the classroom were first issued in the mid-1970s, they are pertinent and timely today:

1. Give students opportunities to use what they learn as tools in their thinking and problem solving.
2. Give students a chance to communicate what they learn.
3. Show interest in what students have learned, rather than in their grades.
4. Provide learning tasks of appropriate difficulty.
5. Permit students to learn in their preferred ways.
6. Recognize and acknowledge many different kinds of excelling.
7. Give genuine purpose and meaning to learning experiences (Torrance, 1975b).

GENDER DIFFERENCES IN THE DEVELOPMENT OF CREATIVITY

Reflection on the research reviewed so far shows that the majority of it has referred to males. One exception to the lack of data of female development is with Terman (Eccles, 1985). In 1921, Terman began a longitudinal study of approximately 831 gifted boys and 613 gifted girls ages 7 to 15. Researchers have been able to locate 80% of the original sample at each new round of data collection (Burks, Jensen, & Terman, 1930; Cox, 1926; Terman, 1925/1926; Terman & Oden, 1947). Thus, this makes the Terman study the most complete set of data available on the life-span development of gifted males and females. However, creativity and giftedness are not necessarily the same. As stated in the beginning of the chapter, giftedness in children refers more to having possession of a gift, whereas creativity is related to a purposeful action leading to a product (Wallace, 1985). Although Terman's sample was made up of individuals with high IQs, Wallace stated that Terman's longitudinal sample "has not produced a single truly illustrious individual" (p. 362). In other words, these individuals were extraordinary in terms of their intellectual abilities, yet they were unable to produce works of novelty, originality, and usefulness.

In order to understand why creativity might develop differently among males and females, it is useful to examine how young children develop their gender identity. Freud's psychosexual theory stresses that the basic patterning of sexual attitudes is instinctual, but that these patterns are eventually channeled, distorted, or influenced by cultural forces. The social learning theory sees the patterning of sexual attitudes stemming from the culture, and does not place any emphasis on the instinctual patterns that Freud mentioned. The cognitive-developmental theory asserts that gender-role concepts are the result of the child's active structuring of his or her own experience; they are not passive products of social training (Kohlberg, 1966).

Although each of these theories has a different emphasis, the child's external world or culture is mentioned in all as having some sort of influence on the development of gender-role identity. What kind of signals does society send to youngsters? From an early age, boys are given different toys than are girls (Vernon, 1989). Additionally, boys are expected to be aggressive and to participate in physical activities, whereas girls are expected to be quieter, more conformist, and to express themselves in a verbal rather than physical manner (Vernon, 1989). Lewis and Houtz (1986), in their study exploring divergent thinking processes with 5- and 6-year-old children, found that boys produced a greater number of mechanical, scientific, and sportslike games, whereas girls outperformed the boys in categories dealing with life and domestic ideas. However, the authors also found that with training, both boys and girls were able to move past gender-specific stereotypes, and think of activities to pursue traditionally associated with the opposite gender. Simply stated, the authors asserted that "when boys and girls experience equal rules for expressing their ideas, they perform equally. When the rules are unequal, as in real life, girls may be able to adapt more easily" (p. 1032).

Not only do children receive messages from home concerning their gender-role identity, but the classroom is also a potent environment for messages to be sent and received. For example, teachers may deter girls from taking advanced science and mathematics courses, while encouraging them to explore the arts and humanities. Terman and Oden's (1947) follow-up study of gifted girls found that girls tended to become underachievers in high school, while up to that time they may have been the opposite. The hypothesis is that achievement drop off is linked to female adult gender-role identity. Furthermore, Maccoby (1966) stated that girls appear to be more afraid of and disorganized by failure than boys. When girls were given an intelligence test and experienced difficulty with the tasks, they became passive, whereas the boys became more active (Murphy, cited in Maccoby, 1966). Interestingly, one educational environment in which girls do not experience competition with boys is in single-gender schools. These schools tend to produce more scientists than mixed-gender schools, perhaps because of the absence of competition with their male counterparts (Vernon, 1989).

Despite the role that culture plays in the formation of gender-role identity, and the effect that has on creative development, Maccoby and

Jacklin (1974) showed that many of the widely accepted beliefs about the abilities and personalities of the genders are traditional stereotypes that are not confirmed by controlled investigations. Vernon (1989) noted, however, that it is possible to make a case for certain biological gender differences, particularly those that are responsible for aggression, exploration, and initiative in males, and nurturance in females. For example, there are biological differences in physical musculature and hormones that produce greater strength and suitability for fighting in males. Vernon stated, therefore, that it is likely that males are, for the most part, more aggressive and dominant, whereas females are more submissive and concerned with child nurture and domestic activities. Vernon also stated that these biological differences may underlie spatial, mechanical, and technological talents, even predisposing scientific inclination in males, and verbal and domestic inclinations in females.

Schwartz (1977) stated that there are traditional inhibitors to creative development in females in addition to the more commonly found barriers in all humans. One of the principal inhibitors of creative production is the nonrecognition of creativity. Generations of women have been taught that creativity is a rare, nondomestic, male characteristic. Schaefer (1980), in his study of 10 highly creative adolescent girls, suggested that their need for autonomy and achievement conflicted with their need for parental and peer group acceptance, which required being feminine and socially acceptable. In school, girls may hold themselves back in order to receive acceptance from their female peers and to avoid the discomfort that acting against the feminine role may entail. It is suggested that these stereotypes also exist in the peer culture, in which creativity, the need for achievement, and the taking of intellectual risks are discouraged. Vernon (1989) stated that there are large numbers of girls who reject the stereotypes and aim to achieve high-level scientific or business careers. However, in the process, they may encounter considerable emotional stress as a result of their decision.

CREATIVITY AND PERSONALITY

Personality may be defined as the dynamic organization of distinct psychological characteristics of an individual that determines his or her adjustment to the environment (Allport, 1937). Although these characteristics are primarily of a motivational, temperamental, and social affective basis, they are closely associated with other functions of a more intellective or cognitive nature such as creativity. Moreover, the creative process may be strongly influenced by personality factors and embedded into affective experiences at different points in time. Based on this assumption, it became important to study the relation between creativity and personality. From a theoretical perspective, creativity has been studied as it relates to the underlying personality structures that give consistency to surface creative behaviors, as reflected in the psychodynamic perspective. However, from an empirical basis, creativity has been studied as it relates to a set of personality traits or patterns that help distinguish creative individuals. This approach places emphasis on the study of individual differences (Cattell, 1968). Consequently, although the creative process has been examined in its own terms, it is intrinsically linked to the study of individual differences. In fact, creativity became an object of scientific study primarily because of the general interest in individual differences (Guilford, 1968).

Galton (1869) was one of the first scientists to explore distinct characteristics among individuals of genius. However, his studies were based on the notion that creativity and intelligence are fairly indistinguishable from each other and determined primarily by hereditary factors. Similarly, Terman (1925) studied longitudinally the personality characteristics of children identified as gifted on the basis of their intellectual ability. Contrary to popular belief, he found that these children possessed many positive personality characteristics, including curiosity, motivation, and a positive self-image. Although Terman's study contributed to a better understanding of gifted children, it failed to recognize creativity as distinct in its relation to personality. These traditional views set a precedent for defining creativity as an inborn special gift, unique to some individuals, who were usually of high intelligence.

As the study of intelligence and giftedness expanded, the idea of creativity as a distinct aspect of personality became recognized. Thurstone (1938) introduced the concept of multiple abilities and nonintellective factors affecting giftedness and creative performance, such as persistence and motivation. He observed (Thurstone, 1952) that university students with high intelligence were not necessarily the most original in idea production. Similarly, other investigations during the 1950s (e.g. Getzels & Jackson, 1962; Taylor, 1965) began to examine creativity as a distinct construct. Guilford's (1967a, 1967b) theory of intelligence, however, may have provided a turning point for understanding the nature of creativity. In his structure of intellect (SOI) model, Guilford identified abilities most relevant for creative thinking in two categories: (a) "divergent production" abilities, characterized by fluency, flexibility, and elaboration, and (b) the process of transformation, pertaining to revising what one experiences or knows, thereby producing new forms and original patterns. Furthermore, Guilford (1967a, 1967b) not only defined *creativity* as a distinct construct involving originality and divergent thinking, but also as a mental process that may be influenced by personality factors such as motivation, needs, interests, attitudes, and emotions.

Torrance was another major contributor to the paradigm shift that occurred in the study and understanding of creativity. It became apparent that creativity is not only a distinct process but that it is influenced by environmental, personality, and cultural factors. In essence, everyone may have the potential to exhibit some degree of creativity. However, highly creative individuals possess certain characteristics that set them apart. Torrance's numerous studies (e.g., Torrance, 1960, 1965, 1969) explored the nature of creativity and its relation to culturally based personality characteristics. According to Torrance, sociocultural values have a strong influence on personality and, consequently, on the way in which creativity is developed and expressed. Some positive creative characteristics found among disadvantaged minority children are, for example, the ability to improvise with commonplace materials, articulateness in role-playing and storytelling, richness of imagery in language, responsiveness to the kinesthetic, and humor and emotional expressiveness.

In summary, the relevance of these historical developments in the area of creativity as it relates to personality is that creativity came to be perceived as a distinct process or the result of a combination of abilities that are present to some degree in all individuals and, therefore, can be developed. Furthermore, there are distinct personality characteristics that may be attributed to creative individuals as well as varied ways in which creativity is manifested.

METHODS OF PERSONALITY RESEARCH

Methods for studying personality aspects of creativity have been tied to how creativity is defined. When creativity was viewed as a unique characteristic of some individuals, an "ideographic" approach, describing the individual in his or her uniqueness was emphasized. Based on a traditional view that emphasized creativity as being an innate gift possessed by unique individuals, original studies of personality characteristics were restricted to a very small number of scientists or artists. Initially, many of these studies used anecdotal reports and descriptive observations of the characteristics of mostly eminent individuals from creative occupational groups (Hadamard, 1945; Wallas, 1945).

More empirically based approaches began in the 1950s. For example, Roe (1952) studied scientists recognized by some outstanding product or performance. These creative individuals were selected by panels of experts in each field and were administered personal interviews and intelligence and projective tests. In general, the natural scientists were found to be lonely and shy as children, satisfied with and devoted to their vocation, and restricted in their social activities. The social scientists were very concerned with personal relationships and had greater involvement in social activities. They all had in common a strong drive and absorption in their work (Roe, 1952). Similarly, Taylor (1965) studied nonintellective characteristics of scientists employing correlational techniques and using biographical inventories that were cross-validated on several samples. He found that intelligence accounted for only a minor portion of the variation in creative performance and that many characteristics are usually involved in creativity. In general, some motivational characteristics suggested by his studies include great dedication to one's work, intellectual persistence, liking to think, liking to toy with ideas, need for recognition, need for variety, tolerance of ambiguity, and a high energy level.

MacKinnon (1978) studied outstanding writers, architects, and mathematicians at the Institute for Personality Assessment and Research at the University of California in Berkeley. The methodology employed in his studies involved, initially, the nomination of highly creative individuals in a profession by a panel of experts, such as university professors, working independently. The participants were then chosen on the basis of the panel's mean rating of creativity for each person nominated. A wider sample of persons in that field was also selected from such sources as a professional directory, in order to ensure that the traits found to characterize the highly creative were related to their creativity rather than to characteristics typical of all members of that profession. The comparison sample was matched to the group being studied with respect to age and geographic location, but had lower mean creativity ratings. The subjects were then assessed with various personality scales. The data were examined by computing the correlations between the external creativity ratings and individuals' scores on personality traits and by comparing differences of mean scores between groups on the assessed variables.

An important aspect of MacKinnon's studies is that they had a theoretical basis, more specifically, Rank's (1976) psychoanalytic personality theory, which emphasizes motivational and temperamental characteristics and their influence on the creative personality type. According to Rank, there are three types of personality labeled as the *adapted type*, the *neurotic type*, and the *creative type*. MacKinnon found correspondence between three samples of architects varying in degrees of creativity and these personality types. The creative sample of architects was more independent, flexible, intuitively alert, open to feelings, perceptive, curious, theoretical, and esthetic. Although, like the neurotic type, they experienced significant tension, conflict, and anxiety, they were able to handle problems and showed ego strength and self-assertiveness. They strove toward an inner artistic standard of excellence. The adapted type sample of architects showed greater social adjustment and concern with meeting professional standards.

Findings based on these methods of study suggested that creativity involves many personality characteristics and abilities. As mentioned earlier, creativity is not a single dimension of personality nor confined to a small number of individuals, but rather it is distributed to different degrees throughout the population. This "nomothetic" approach entails looking at common traits or factors and comparing individuals in terms of hypothesized dimensions of personality (Cattell & Butcher, 1968). This approach led to the application of multivariate methods of factor analysis for studying creative personality attributes, used most extensively by Guilford (1968) in his Aptitude Research Project at the University of Southern California.

CREATIVE PERSONALITY CHARACTERISTICS

Creative personality characteristics, found through factor-analytic methods of study, may be described either in terms of cognitive related attributes that have a more direct effect on problem solving and divergent thinking or as affective and motivational traits which influence the creative process and a creative orientation to life in general. Table 7.1 contains descriptions of major creative traits as presented by various theorists.

In their review of creative personality research, Dellas and Gaier (1970) discussed the traits of creative persons from both the cognitive and personological view. These authors stated, however, that creative persons are distinguished more by their interests, attitudes, and drives, than by intellectual abilities.

Dacey's (1989) eight essential personal qualities of the creative mind follow:

1. *Tolerance of ambiguity*: The ability to remain open-minded in the face of ambiguity and to postpone the need for closure, a major trait vital to creativity and to the seven following traits.
2. *Stimulus freedom*: The ability to break free from assumptions about a situation and to disengage from a particular mind set, involves the ability to bend rules and to cross the boundaries of structure without anxiety or fear of being wrong.
3. *Functional freedom*: The ability to seek alternate patterns and to use different approaches for defining and solving problems. The opposite, *functional fixity*, is a rigid way of seeking solutions that interferes with creative problem solving.
4. *Flexibility*: The ability to see the entire aspects of a situation or to view problems holistically and from different perspectives.

Table 7.1. Creative Characteristics.

From Dellas and Gaier (1970): Cognitive and Personality Characteristics of Creative Persons

Cognitive:

- Above average intelligence
- Ability to produce unusual and appropriate ideas
- Exceptional retention & more ready availability of life experiences
- Ideational fluency & cognitive flexibility

Personality:

- Absence of impulse and imagery control by means of repression
- An openness to internal and external stimuli
- Intuitiveness
- Independence in attitudes and social behavior
- Strong, intrinsic motivation

From Dacey (1989): The Eight Essential Personal Qualities of the Creative Mind

- tolerance of ambiguity
- stimulus freedom
- functional freedom
- flexibility
- risk-taking
- preference for disorder
- delay of gratification
- androgyny

- Able to be playful and childlike
- Interested in engaging more frequently in solitary activities
- More unconventional
- Less afraid of their feelings and emotions
- More independent in thinking and judgment

Table 7.1. Creative Characteristics (con't).

From Davis and Rimm (1977): Characteristics of Creatively Gifted Children

- High in self-confidence and willing to take risks
- Quite conscious of own tendencies toward nonconformity and creativeness
- High in energy level, spontaneous, adventurous, sensation seeking
- Eager to try new activities and to have creative hobbies
- Preferring complexity, attracted to the mysterious, having stronger beliefs than normal population in spirits, supernatural phenomena
- Possessing childlike playfulness and a sense of humor
- Idealistic, reflective, inquisitive about the universe and significance of his or her being
- Showing some amount of artistic, musical or dramatic experience

From Maslow (1976): Essential Aspects of Self-Actualizing Creativeness

- A special kind of perceptiveness
- Being attuned to the real world of nature rather than to the verbalized world of concepts
- Openness to experience
- Greater spontaneity and expressiveness
- Attraction to the unknown and the mysterious
- Better integration in terms of feelings and thinking
- Possessing childlike qualities
- Being more self-accepting and aware

5. *Risk Taking*: The ability to take moderate risks as opposed to limited or miscalculated huge risks, highly correlated to tolerance of ambiguity.
6. *Preference for disorder*: The ability to tolerate disorder and complexity and to find it more interesting and a challenge to be able to bring personal order out of disorder.
7. *Delay of gratification*: The ability to persist and to postpone satisfaction with the purpose of reaching a higher level objective.
8. *Androgyny*: The ability to integrate both feminine and masculine aspects of personality, without being bound by gender-role stereotypes. This higher level of gender-role identity has been linked to creativity.

Maslow (1976) provided, from a humanistic perspective, a more personalized description of the creative personality. According to Maslow, creativity is found in everyone, but it is most significantly developed in the self-actualized personality. The self-actualized person has attained the highest degree of psychological development. Creativity is not viewed as a special talent, but an inherent aspect of personality that can show itself even in the ordinary affairs of life. For Maslow (1976), the expressive quality of self-actualizing creativeness is that it is "emitted" or radiated, and hits all of life, regardless of problems. According to Moustakas (1977), creativity is the essence of psychological health.

CREATIVITY AND SOCIAL EMOTIONAL ADJUSTMENT

The socioemotional adjustment of creative individuals has been an issue of critical concern throughout history and across cultures. Prentky (1980) provided a survey of how creativity has been associated with psychopathology. Based on clinical observations of biographical data, writers, artists, and poets have been generally described as possessing negative social characteristics and poor emotional adjustment. The lives of Edgar Allan Poe or Vincent Van Gogh are often cited as classical examples of the apparent link between pathology and creativity. The stereotype of the "mad" scientist is one that continues to permeate popular thinking. Theoretically, this outlook has been given some validity by early psychoanalytic writers, or by interpretation of their writings, as suggesting an association between neurotic conflict and the creative process.

This controversy continues to affect the study of creativity and personality, but it is currently viewed from a broader perspective. Indeed, many studies during the 1960s suggested that creative individuals tend to have characteristics that society views as negative, such as introversion, interpersonal difficulties, and a higher incidence of manic-depressive disorders (Schubert & Biondi, 1977).

At the same time, other studies have demonstrated that creativity correlates positively with social maturity, assertiveness, a positive self-image, and developmental status (Foster, 1968). This discrepancy has been explained by the multifaceted nature of creativity and the fact that a set prototype of the creative personality does not exist but that various configurations of creative personality characteristics may be possible, or that creative individuals may exhibit paradoxical extremes of both positive and negative qualities (McMullan, 1976).

Furthermore, the very fact that the discrepancy exists leads one to look at other possible factors that may have an impact on the adjustment of creative individuals. A set of factors may be related to general biological predispositions or temperamental characteristics, such as emotional sensitivity, which are shared by or can coexist in terms of both pathological and creative processes (Martindale, 1989). Another set of factors includes the many extraneous environmental influences that impact on the direction taken by these personality traits, such as the receptivity of significant others and the context in which personality traits manifest themselves. For example, a creative child's questioning attitude, unconventional thinking, or emotional expressiveness may come into conflict with parental or teacher expectancies of appropriate behavior or with adults' limited tolerance for such behaviors. This reaction may, in turn, lead to personality clashes or to the actual development of poor adjustment patterns by the child. In a study comparing creative children in a regular classroom to creative children in a gifted program, a significant positive correlation was found between self-esteem and creativity for children in the gifted classroom, where creativity was rewarded, whereas the reverse was true for creative children in the regular classroom. The more creative children had the lower self-esteem within the regular classroom situation, where creativity was less acceptable or even discouraged (Esquivel, 1985). Therefore, it is important to view the relation between creativity and personality within a broader ecological context.

EDUCATIONAL IMPLICATIONS OF PERSONALITY RESEARCH

The preceding sections have examined the nature of creativity as it relates to personality, described the methods of study and the characteristics that may be attributed to highly creative individuals, and suggested the importance of environmental factors that impact on the development and adjustment of the creative personality. Based on an understanding of these concepts, we now address the role that educators play in recognizing creative characteristics in students and in creating a learning environment that is conducive to creative learning for all students.

A major task for teachers and other educators is to recognize the unique cognitive and affective characteristics of students in order to be able to influence their growth and facilitate their learning. Teachers can play a significant role in identifying those students who exhibit gifted potential, particularly those with high intellectual ability, academic aptitude, or specific talents. However, it is more difficult to identify students with creative ability. To facilitate identification of creative students several methods are recommended. Observational checklists, personality and biographical inventories, and creativity tests are available (Gowan, Khatena, & Torrance, 1981; Renzulli, Hartman, & Callahan, 1975).

More importantly, however, creative students need also to experience acceptance and validation of their unique qualities within the classroom environment. It is critical, therefore, that teachers foster the creative learning characteristics of all students. Teachers can accomplish this by providing a receptive environment, designing goals geared toward creative development; and implementing teaching techniques, instructional methods, and class management styles that are conducive to creative learning. Additionally, teachers can make use of evaluation and feedback methods that reinforce and encourage the development of higher level thinking and creative attitudes.

Torrance (1981b) suggested that educators who place less emphasis on the strict accumulation of knowledge and greater emphasis on developing a creative attitude toward learning will, in turn, motivate students to acquire and use information in more original and meaningful ways. On the affective level, less stress needs to be given to conformity and obedience, as signs of adjustment, and more to the expression of courage, independence in judgment, critical thinking, and high moral values. Moreover, excessive emphasis on gender-role differences may lead to the stifling of creative feminine qualities in male students, such as emotional sensitivity, and of creative characteristics associated with masculinity in female students, such as assertiveness, self-confidence, and impulsivity.

Creative teaching techniques include the use of brainstorming, open-ended questions, problem-solving, and imaginative activities that enrich visual, language, and kinesthetic imagery. Creative teaching minimizes correction and criticism and allows for greater communication among students, encourages divergent ideas and self-directed learning (Renzulli & Callahan, 1981, Torrance, 1981; Treffinger, 1981a). Creative teaching results not only in creativity but enhances academic learning, socioemotional adjustment, and the positive development of the creative personality.

UNANSWERED QUESTIONS AND SUMMARY

This chapter has explored various aspects of the development of creativity and the creative personality. In doing so, it becomes apparent that there are various questions with which future research should be concerned. Thus far, the most glaring gap in creative development research is evident in the literature on creative females. This includes the lack of a coherent theoretical framework (Eccles, 1985). There is a need for comprehensive, longitudinal studies of the processes that shape the educational and vocational choices of both creative males and females. Eccles noted that without appropriate longitudinal studies, it cannot be known whether a particular variable mediates gender differences in achievement-related choices and behaviors or not. As of yet, we still remain unclear as to what are the best predictors of future creativity. There are tests that measure creativity in children, but these do not necessarily predict creative output in adulthood.

In addition to longitudinal data, Wallace (1985) encouraged the use of the evolving systems approach when measuring creativity across the life span. This approach is guided by three ideas: the creative individual is unique, developmental change is multidirectional, and the creative person is an evolving system. The evolving systems approach states there are many alternative pathways possible in development, and that development of the creative person is multicausal, unpredictable, and irreversible. This approach recommends the use of studying how someone does something at which he or she is extraordinarily good. It would seem that using this method and longitudinal data would be beneficial to studying the development of creativity within individuals.

Another area in need of further study is the existence of creativity across the life span, especially when one reaches old age. It is unclear as to what is creativity in old age, and how we should account for the change in lifestyle once a person retires. Is creativity "dead" at this point, or is there a need to view creativity from a different developmental perspective? Following this, how do we reliably measure creativity in older persons? Until we decide what creativity is at this point in the life span, it will be difficult to measure its existence.

There is need for further research concerning the environmental factors that influence the development of creativity. What are the best ways to educate and encourage parents regarding the importance of providing an environment that will stimulate and encourage creativity? It is important to learn more about how creativity is viewed within cultures other than middle-class America, and how this relates to the development of creativity. Within the classroom, how can we best prepare teachers to promote creative thinking in students? This includes encouraging diversity of beliefs and approaches toward problem solving, so that students find out what works best for them, rather than learning "one way." How can administration support teachers to move past the curriculum and encourage exploration? Who is best prepared to give this support, and what are the most useful techniques?

As for personality research, the construct of creativity in its relation to personality evolved conceptually as a distinct process that is shared in various degrees by everyone and manifested in diverse ways as a result of sociocultural and developmental influences. Various methods of study employed in understanding creative individuals have suggested a relation between high creative ability and personality factors. In general, creativity has become associated with characteristics such as curiosity, flexibility, playfulness, tolerance for ambiguity, androgyny, risk-taking, and independence.

Controversy exists, however, between the idea that creative individuals are poorly adjusted and the view of creativity as a sign of mental health. Attempts at exploring these discrepancies include the idea that creativity is multifaceted, that the creative individual exhibits paradoxical extremes, that certain predispositions may be shared by both pathological and creative processes, and that environmental influence may affect the manner in which creative potential is expressed.

Regardless of this debate, it is accepted that educators play a significant role in recognizing the unique cognitive and affective characteristics of creative students and in facilitating their learning, as well as in creating a classroom environment that fosters creative development in all children. Research argues for specific instructional policies and methods that will compliment and enhance the development of positive creative personality characteristics and attitudes.

STUDY ACTIVITIES

1. Talk with several people who are beyond retirement age. Do these people still work in their chosen professions? What are their reasons for continuing or ceasing their work activity? How do these people define creativity? What do they currently do now that they consider to be creative? What interferes with and what enhances their creativity? What childhood family and school factors do they attribute as having stimulated their creative development and interests? Share these ideas with others and attempt to develop a definition for creativity for the people interviewed.

2. Speak with a teacher of any level (e.g., elementary, secondary, university). How does the teacher account for the differences in learning style within the classroom? What types of students does this teacher like best and what types cause this teacher the most "heartache"? How would this

teacher teach in an ideal situation? How does the teacher attempt to connect the reality of day-to-day teaching with the ideal?

3. Observe children across three age groups or grade levels. How is creativity exhibited throughout the age groups? Are there differences? Similarities? Are there students who exhibit giftedness, but lack creativity? What types of risks do girls take as opposed to boys? Do you see different expectancies from the teacher for girls and boys? What do you witness as creative behaviors? What would you say is characteristic of the creative child?

4. Interview two adults—one in a scientific field, and one in an artistic field. What does their work entail? How do they define creativity in terms of their work? What types of situations encourage and hinder their creativity? If possible, find out the type of environment in which they were raised—was it one that promoted creativity? Compare and contrast your findings across the two fields.

5. Study the biography of at least two recognized individuals from separate creative fields (e.g., arts, music, mathematics, literature, science). Note their salient personality characteristics. Are you able to recognize characteristics common to creative individuals? Are there distinct similarities or differences between these individuals? Is there a relation between their distinct creative personality traits and their specific fields? Have a discussion focused on these issues.

6. Observe the behavior of students in a classroom. Look for creative behaviors. Identify those students who most exhibit creative characteristics and behaviors. What are the students like in terms of their achievement, participation, interpersonal relationships, and socioemotional adjustment? Compare these students with those students of high intellectual ability and achievement.

7. Reflect on your own creative tendencies or characteristics. Are these characteristics in keeping with your personality? As an educator, do you encourage creativity in the classroom? How comfortable did you feel attempting the creative tasks and teaching strategies suggested here? Would you describe yourself as a "sage on the stage" or as a "guide on the side" in terms of your instructional methods? What are the merits of either approach?

8. The following personality test is an example of an instrument that measures gender-role identification and was included in Dacey's (1989) text, *Fundamentals of Creative Thinking*. Take the test and see how you score. Keep in mind that the test was devised many years ago (J. S. Dacey, personal communication, December 8, 1992), and several of the questions may be considered out of date. As you complete the test, think of how you would modify the questions in order to bring them more up to date:

Sex Role Identification Questionnaire

Directions: If you agree with a statement, put a letter A on the line in front of the statement and a letter B on the line in front of a statement with which you disagree:

_____ 1. If I get too much change in a store, I always give it back.
_____ 2. I think I would like the work of an interior decorator.
_____ 3. I am somewhat afraid of the dark.
_____ 4. I become irritated when I see someone spit on the sidewalk.
_____ 5. In school, I was sometimes sent to the principal for bad behavior.
_____ 6. I like to hunt.
_____ 7. A windstorm usually scares me.
_____ 8. I prefer a shower to a bath.
_____ 9. I always tried to get the best grades I could.
_____ 10. I think I would enjoy the work of a building contractor.
_____ 11. I like to boast about my achievements now and then.
_____ 12. I would never feel right if I thought I was not doing my share of the work of any group to which I belonged.
_____ 13. I get excited rather easy.
_____ 14. I am apt to hide my feelings about some things to the point that people may hurt me without knowing it.
_____ 15. When someone talks against certain nationalities, I usually speak against such talk even if it makes me unpopular.
_____ 16. I think I would like racing a car.
_____ 17. The thought of being in an automobile accident is very frightening to me.
_____ 18. I must admit I feel sort of scared when I go to a strange place.
_____ 19. I think I would enjoy being a nurse.
_____ 20. Sometimes I just feel like picking a fight with someone.
_____ 21. I believe I have a certain talent for understanding other people, and for sympathizing with their problems.
_____ 22. I prefer adventure stories to romantic stories.
_____ 23. I like to look at "men's" magazines.
_____ 24. I think I would enjoy being a dress designer.

THE SEX-ROLE IDENTIFICATION SCALE

Sex-role identification has been associated with creativity. Those persons who are androgynous have a higher level of sex-role identification that surpasses the more traditional standards and tend to be more creative.

Scoring: If you are a female add (1) point for each answer below that is the same as yours. If you are a male, add (1) point for every answer that is the same as yours.

1. A	7. A	13. A	19. A
2. A	8. B	14. A	20. B
3. A	9. A	15. B	21. A
4. A	10. B	16. B	22. B
5. B	11. B	17. A	23. B
6. B	12. A	18. A	24. A

Scores: 1 2 3 4 5 6 7 8 9 10 11 12 13 14 15 16 17 18 19 20 21 22 23 24

	Creative	Creative
T	Man	Woman
Y		
P		
E		
	Average Score	

Source: Dacey, J. S. (1989). *Fundamentals of creative thinking.* Lexington, MA: Lexington Books.

REFERENCES

Allport, G. W. (1937). *Personality: A psychological interpretation.* New York: Holt.

Burks, B., Jensen, D. W., & Terman, L. M. (1930). *The promise of youth: Follow-up studies of a thousand gifted children. Volume III: Genetic studies of genius.* Stanford, CA: Stanford University Press.

Carlson, R. K. (1964). Developing an original person. *Elementary English, 41,* 268-278.

Cattell, R. B. (1968). *The prediction of achievement and creativity: Measuring the main dimensions of personality.* New York: Bobbs-Merrill.

Cattell, R. B., & Butcher, H. J. (1968). *The prediction of achievement and creativity.* New York: Bobbs-Merrill.

Cox, C. (1926). *The early mental traits of three hundred geniuses. Volume II: Genetic studies of genius.* Stanford, CA: Stanford University Press.

Dacey, J. S. (1989). *Fundamentals of creative thinking.* Lexington, MA: Lexington Books.

Davis, G. A., & Rimm, S. (1977). Characteristics of creatively gifted children. *Gifted Child Quarterly, 521,* 46-551.

Dellas, M., & Gaier, E. L. (1970). Identification of creativity—The individual. *Psychological Bulletin, 73,* 55-73.

Dennis, W. (1968). Creative productivity between the ages of 20 and 80 years. In B. L. Neugarten (Ed.), *Middle age and aging: A reader in social psychology* (pp. 106-114). Chicago: University of Chicago Press.

Dirkes, M. A. (1978). The role of divergent production in the learning process. *American Psychologist, 33,* 815-820.

Dudek, S. Z. (1974). Creativity in young children—attitude or ability? *Journal of Creative Behavior, 8,* 282-292.

Eccles, J. S. (1985). Why doesn't Jane run? Sex differences in educational and occupational patterns. In F. D. Horowitz & M. O'Brien (Eds.), *The gifted and talented: Developmental perspectives* (pp. 251-300). Washington, DC: American Psychological Association.

Esquivel, G. B. (1985). The effects of special classroom placement on the creativity, self concept and academic achievement of culturally different children. *SABE Journal, 1,* 18-25.

Foster, F. P. (1968). The human relationships of creative individuals. *Journal of Creative Behavior, 2,* 111-118.

Galton, F. (1869). *Hereditary genius.* New York: Appleton.

Getzels, J. W., & Jackson, P. W. (1962). *Creativity and intelligence: Explorations with gifted students.* New York: Wiley.

Gilligan, C. (1982). *In a different voice: Psychological theory and women's development.* Cambridge, MA: Harvard University Press.

Goodale, R. A. (1970). Methods for encouraging creativity in the classroom. *Journal of Creative Behavior, 4,* 91-102.

Gowan, J. C. (1972). *Development of the creative individual.* San Diego, CA: Knapp.

Gowan, J. C., Khatena, J., & Torrance, E. P. (1981). *Creativity: Its educational implications.* Dubuque, IA: Kendall/Hunt.

Guilford, J. P. (1962). Creativity: Its measurement and development. In S. J. Parnes & H. F. Harding (Eds.), *A sourcebook for creative thinking* (pp. 164-168). New York: Charles Scribner's Sons.

Guilford, J. P. (1967a). Creativity: Yesterday, today, and tomorrow. *Journal of Creative Behavior, 1,* 3-14.

Guilford, J. P. (1967b). *The nature of intelligence.* New York: McGraw-Hill.

Guilford, J. P. (1968). *Intelligence, creativity and the educational implications.* San Diego, CA: Knapp.

Hadamard, J. S. (1945). *An essay on the psychology of invention in the mathematical field.* Princeton, NJ: Princeton University Press.

Kogan, N. (1973). Creativity and cognitive style: A life-span perspective. In P. B. Baltes & K. W. Schaie (Eds.), *Life-span developmental psychology: Personality and socialization* (pp. 145-160). New York: Academic Press.

Kohlberg, L. (1966). A cognitive-developmental analysis of children's sex-role concepts and attitudes. In E. E. Maccoby (Ed.), *The development of sex differences* (pp. 82-172). Stanford, CA: Stanford University Press.

Lehman, H. C. (1953). *Age and achievement.* Princeton, NJ: Princeton University Press.

Lehman, H. C. (1968). The creative production rates of present versus past generations of scientists. In B. L. Neugarten (Ed.), *Middle age and aging: A reader in social psychology* (pp. 99-105). Chicago: University of Chicago Press.

Lewis, C. D., & Houtz, J. C. (1986). Sex-role stereotyping and young children's divergent thinking. *Psychological Reports, 59,* 1027-1033.

Maccoby, E. E. (1966). Sex differences in intellectual functioning. In E. E. Maccoby (Ed.), *The development of sex differences* (pp. 25-55). Stanford, CA: Stanford University Press.

Maccoby, E. E., & Jacklin, C. N. (1974). *The psychology of sex differences.* Stanford, CA: Stanford University Press.

MacKinnon, D. W. (1962). The nature and nurture of creative talent. *American Psychologist, 17,* 484-495.

MacKinnon, D. W. (1965). Personality and the realization of creative potential. *American Psychologist, 20,* 273-281.

MacKinnon, D. W. (1978). *In search of human effectiveness: Identifying and developing creativity.* Buffalo, NY: Creative Education Foundation.

Martindale, C. (1989). Personality, situation, and creativity. In J. A. Glover, R. R. Ronning, & C. R. Reynolds (Eds.), *Handbook of creativity* (pp. 211-232). New York Plenum Press.

Maslow, A. H. (1958). Emotional blocks to creativity. *Journal of Individual Psychology, 14,* 51-56.

Maslow, A. (1976). Creativity in self actualizing people. In A. Rothenberg & C. R. Hausman (Eds.), *The creativity question* (pp. 86-92). Durham, NC: Duke University Press.

McMullan, W. E. (1976). Creative individuals: Paradoxical personages. *Journal of Creative Behavior, 10, 265-275.*

Monks, F. J., & Van Boxtel, H. W. (1985). Gifted adolescents: A developmental perspective. In J. Freeman (Ed.), *The psychology of gifted children* (pp. 275-295). New York: Wiley.

Moustakas, C. E. (1977). *Creative life.* New York: D. Van Nostrand.

Prentky, R. A. (1980). *Creativity and psychopathology: A neurocognitive perspective.* New York: Praeger.

Rank, O. (1932). *Art and artist: Creative urge and personality development.* New York: Knopf.

Rank, O. (1976). Life and creation. In A. Rothenberg & C. R. Hausman (Eds.), *The creativity question* (pp. 114-120). Durham, NC: Duke University Press.

Renzulli, J. S., & Callahan, C. M. (1981). Developing creativity training activities. In J. C. Gowan, J. Khatena, & E. P. Torrance (Eds.), *Creativity: Its educational implications* (pp. 119-124). Dubuque, IA: Kendall/Hunt.

Renzulli, J. S., Hartman, R. K., & Callahan, C. M. (1975). Scale for rating the behavioral characteristics of superior students. In W. B. Barbe & J. S. Renzulli (Eds.), *Psychology and education of the gifted* (2nd ed., pp. 264-273). New York: Irvington.

Roe, A. (1952). *The making of a scientist.* New York: Dodd, Mead.

Romaniuk, J. G., & Romaniuk, M. (1981). Creativity across the life span: A measurement perspective. *Human Development, 24,* 366-381.

Schaefer, C. E. (1980). A psychological study of 10 exceptionally creative adolescent girls. In J. S. Renzulli & E. P. Stoddard (Eds.), *Gifted and talented education in perspective* (pp. 44-54). Reston, VA: Council for Exceptional Children.

Schubert, D. S., & Biondi, A. M. (1977). Creativity and mental health: Part III: Creativity and adjustment. *Journal of Creative Behavior, 11,* 186-197.

Schwartz, L. L. (1977). Can we stimulate creativity in women? *Journal of Creative Behavior, 11,* 264-270.

Taylor, C. W. (1965). Who are the exceptionally creative? In J. J. Gallagher (Ed.), *Teaching gifted students: A book of readings* (pp. 51-64). Boston, MA: Allyn & Bacon.

Terman, L. M. (1925/1926). *Mental and physical traits of a thousand gifted children: Genetic studies of genius: Volume 1.* Stanford, CA: Stanford University Press.

Terman, L. M., & Oden, M. H. (1947). *The gifted child grows up. Twenty-five years' follow-up of a superior group: Volume IV: Genetic studies of genius.* Stanford, CA: Stanford University Press.

Thurstone, L. L. (1938). Primary mental abilities. *Psychometric Monographs, 1.*

Thurstone, L. L. (1952). Creative talent. In L. L. Thurstone (Ed.), *Applications of psychology* (pp. 18-37). New York: Harper.

Torrance, E. P. (1960). Explorations in creative thinking. *Education, 81,* 216-220.

Torrance, E. P. (1962). *Guiding creative talent.* Englewood Cliffs, NJ: Prentice-Hall.

Torrance, E. P. (1965). *Rewarding creative behavior.* Englewood Cliffs, NJ: Prentice-Hall.

Torrance, E. P. (1969). Creative positives of disadvantaged children and youth. *Gifted Child Quarterly, 13,* 71-81.

Torrance, E. P. (1975a). Discontinuities in creative development. In E. P. Torrance & W. F. White (Eds.), *Issues and advances in educational psychology* (pp. 204-217). Itasca, IL: F. E. Peacock.

Torrance, E. P. (1975b). Motivation and creativity. In E. P. Torrance & W. F. White (Eds.), *Issues and advances in educational psychology* (pp. 280-292). Itasca, IL: F. E. Peacock.

Torrance, E. P. (1981a). Creative teaching makes a difference. In J. C. Gowan, J. Khatena, & E. P. Torrance (Eds.), *Creativity: Its educational implications* (pp. 99-108). Dubuque, IA: Kendall/Hunt.

Torrance, E. P. (1981b). Toward the more humane education of gifted children. In J. C. Gowan, J. Khatena, & E. P. Torrance (Eds.), *Creativity: Its educational implications* (pp. 6-18). Dubuque, IA: Kendall/Hunt.

Treffinger, J. (1981). Teaching for self-directed learning: A priority for the gifted and talented. In J. C. Gowan, J. Khatena, & E. P. Torrance (Eds.), *Creativity: Its educational implications* (pp. 109-118). Dubuque, IA: Kendall/Hunt.

Vernon, P. E. (1989). The nature-nurture problem in creativity. In J. A. Glover, R. R. Ronning, & C. R. Reynolds (Eds.), *Handbook of creativity* (pp. 93-110). New York: Plenum Press.

Wallace, D. B. (1985). Giftedness and the construction of a creative life. In F. D. Horowitz & M. O'Brien (Eds.), *The gifted and talented: Developmental perspectives* (pp. 361-385). Washington, DC: American Psychological Association.

Wallas, G. (1945). *The art of thought.* London: C. A. Watts.

Wehr, M. R., & Richards, J. A. (1960). *Physics of the atom.* Reading, MA: Addison-Wesley.

Welford, A. T. (1958). *Ageing and human skill.* London: Oxford University Press.

8

Guilford's Structure-of-Intellect and Structure-of-Intellect Problem-Solving Models

William B. Michael
University of Southern California

BACKGROUND AND CHAPTER OUTLINE

One of the most insightful and renown contributors to a cognitive theory of intelligence and problem solving has been the late J. P. Guilford (1897-1987). In his comprehensive structure-of-intellect (SOI) model and in his subsequent structure-of-intellect problem-solving (SIPS) model, Guilford gave considerable emphasis to the place of creativity. His two models have provided a framework within which programmatic research has been carried out over a 30-year period to provide empirical support for the constructs involved. His two models have also had important implications for test construction, identification of high-level personnel, and the teaching-learning process.

In this chapter, both models are described along with an identification of those SOI abilities in creative problem solving that have received empirical support. The SIPS model is then systematically related to each of the seven steps in Rossman's (1931) paradigm for invention, a form of creative problem solving. Implications of the SIPS model in teaching for creative endeavor are pointed out in the hope that teachers may be able to apply in a classroom setting key concepts of this model, particularly in mathematics and science instruction. Next, unanswered questions and unresolved issues associated with the two models are detailed. Following a brief summary and review of this chapter are suggested problem exercises, a set of references, and a brief list of selected readings.

THEORY, EMPIRICAL RESEARCH, AND APPLICATIONS OF THE SOI MODEL

Historical Antecedents

The publication of Thurstone's (1935) *Vectors of Mind* and his subsequent work on primary mental abilities (Thurstone, 1938) afforded Guilford a factor-analytic methodology that he needed to analyze correlational data in his studies of personality and aptitudes. This methodology (Thurstone, 1947) permits one to take a matrix of many intercorrelated variables such as psychological tests and to find a relatively small number of statistically derived dimensions (factors) to account for the covariation among the test variables. A factor analysis isolates particular groupings or clusters of intercorrelated test variables that display certain common observable characteristics. These intercorrelated variables, each of which may show a relatively low degree of relationship with the measures in other clusters, are expected to exhibit moderate to substantial correlations with (i.e., factor loadings on) a mathematically derived dimension.

In the instance of ability or personality tests, an examination is made of the extent to which content is comparable across tests within a given cluster as well as the psychological processes or activities that appear to be required to respond to the items within these tests. An inference is then made concerning what each group of test variables that are correlated with a statistically derived dimension appears to reflect in psychological terms. This inference is also facilitated by contrasting the contents and processes associated with a given group of tests that are correlated highly with a particular factor with the contents and processes of other sets of tests that are weighted substantially on other factors but not on this particular factor. In a highly interpretable analysis, the variables in each of the sets of tests weighted on a given factor will show substantial factor loadings just on that factor, but negligible loadings on all other factors—a property referred to as *simple structure*.

During World War II, Guilford made use of this methodology in the study of mental abilities for which psychological tests were developed for selection of pilots, bombardiers, and navigators. By the end of World War II, approximately 25 psychologically interpretable factors related to mental ability had been identified and found to be useful in predicting pilot success as indicated by a marked reduction in the failure rate of military personnel in pilot training. During the early 1950s, Guilford developed a model within the categories of which nearly 40 mental abilities that had been empirically identified through the use factor-analytic techniques could be placed. At an international conference on factor analysis held in Paris in 1955, Guilford (1956, 1959) presented his first version of the now well-known SOI model that, in its framework, is somewhat akin to the periodic table of chemical elements.

Up to 1955, the direction of his approach to the identification of mental abilities had been primarily inductive. The SOI model afforded a hypothetico-deductive orientation in that hypotheses could be derived from the model, or theory, concerning the nature of those abilities that had not been previously verified. For each of these hypothesized abilities, a set of experimental tests was devised and factor-analyzed along with anchor tests of known factorial content to ascertain whether the experimental tests hypothesized to represent a given SOI ability were weighted primarily on one factor that could be interpreted as corresponding to the hypothesized ability. If this same set of tests failed to show, for the most part, any substantial loadings on any other factor a sufficient but not necessary condition existed for inferring that the construct validity of the hypothesized ability had received empirical support. In his many studies carried out before 1980, Guilford conceptualized the SOI abilities to be relatively independent or uncorrelated with one another—a circumstance in the factor-analytic procedures known as orthogonality of factors.

From 1955 to 1969, this heuristic SOI model constituted the theoretical framework within which Guilford and his many graduate students in the University of Southern California Aptitudes Research Project carried out programmatic research in a series of funded investigations, the results of which led to what they considered empirical verification of nearly 60 additional abilities hypothesized within the model. Thus by 1970, approximately 100 of the 120 originally hypothesized mental abilities were judged to have been established. This heuristic model may well have generated more dissertations and publications than any other one proposed in the 1950s or 1960s. As is to be indicated in a subsequent section, two significant modifications in the SOI model were made that augmented the number of factors: the first to include 150 hypothesized abilities (Guilford, 1985) and the second to comprise 180 hypothesized abilities (Guilford, 1988).

Characteristics of the Original SOI Model

In the original model of 120 hypothesized abilities, for which Guilford (1967; Guilford & Hoepfner, 1971) provided detailed descriptions and summaries of numerous data-based studies, there was postulated the existence of (a) four kinds of content (stimulus material or input information)—figural (F), semantic (M), symbolic (S), and behavioral (B); (b) five types of operations portraying psychological processes—cognition (C), convergent production (N), divergent production (D), memory (M), and evaluation (E); and (c) six forms of products (responses or output reflecting newly generated information)—units (U), classes (C), relations (R), systems (S), transformations (T), and implications (I). Within this framework, a first-order ability was defined by Guilford (1985) as being represented by one type of psychological operation processing one kind of content (input) to generate one form of product (output).

For example, in a familiar standardized test of vocabulary involving the citation of a given word in an item stem and the enumeration of four or five alternative potential synonym responses of which only one is correct, the ability factor would be identified as the cognition of semantic units. This first-order ability would be represented by the trigram CMU. A second example of a first-order ability involving the writing of a short paragraph, poem, or speech on an assigned topic would involve an ability called divergent production of semantic systems (DMS)—an ability requiring an open-ended and fairly unrestrained creation (divergent production) of interrelated meaningful sentences constituting a semantic system.

Figure 8.1 shows a geometric representation of the SOI model. The three dimensions of contents, operations, and products contain four, five, and six elements, respectively—each element representing a distinct characteristic of that dimension. Along each of the three axes portraying the three dimensions, equal spaces have been drawn to represent the elements. Connections of the lines setting off these elements serve to generate 120 cubes (4 contents x 5 operations x 6 products), with each cube representing one of the 120 hypothesized abilities. As mentioned previously, the resulting abilities portrayed were hypothesized to be relatively independent of one another. Below the large cube within which 120 cubes are placed in Figure 8.1, is a brief description of what each one of the elements within each dimension signifies. Although its actual date of origin and the name of the contributor cannot be specifically identified, this figure has been widely distributed and reproduced in one form or another in numerous publications. See also Table 8.1.

Modifications in the Original SOI Model

Two major alterations were incorporated within the original SOI model of 120 hypothesized abilities. Guilford (1985) reported that the figural part of the contents dimension could be separated into a visual and auditory component, as a considerable portion of an individual's sensory input is

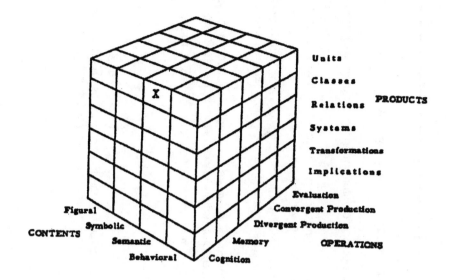

Figure 8.1. The original structure-of-intellect model

auditory. Previously, in most of Guilford's psychological tests, items had been presented in a printed manner requiring use of sight. This addition of a new element of content resulted in a model with 150 different abilities (5 contents x 5 operations x 6 products).

Only 5 or 6 weeks before his death, Guilford (1988) submitted to *Educational and Psychological Measurement* an expanded version of this 150 variable model, in which he separated memory into two components. Thus, a 180-ability model was generated (5 contents x 6 operations x 6 products). The operations factor of memory was separated into memory retention (long term) and memory recording (short term). This most recent model is presented in Figure 8.2.

SOI Abilities Associated With Creativity

Many research bulletins and publications concerned with creativity that were prepared by Guilford and his students have been summarized in the two volumes by Guilford (1967) and Guilford and Hoepfner (1971) and in a short book by Guilford (1968). Altogether about a dozen factors of

Table 8.1. Definitions of the Structure-of-Intellect Categories.

Operations

Major kinds of intellectual activities or processes; things that the organism does with the raw materials of information, information being defined as "that which the organism discriminates."

C— *Cognition.* Immediate discovery, awareness, rediscovery, or recognition of information in various forms; comprehension or understanding.

M— *Memory.* Retention or storage, with some degree of availability, of information in the same form it was committed to storage and in response to the same cues in connection with which it was learned.

D— *Divergent production.* Generation of information from given information, where the emphasis is on variety and quantity of output from the same source. Likely to involve what has been called transfer. This operation is most clearly involved in aptitudes of creative potential.

N— *Convergent Production.* Generation of information from given information, where the emphasis is upon achieving conventionally accepted best outcomes. It is likely the given (cue) information fully determines the response.

E— *Evaluation.* Reaching decisions or making judgments concerning criterion satisfaction (correctness, suitability, adequacy, desirability, etc.) of information.

Contents

Broad classes or types of information discriminable by the organism.

F— *Figural.* Information in concrete form, as perceived or as recalled possibly in the form of images. The term figural minimally implies figure-ground perceptual organization. Visual spatial information is figural. Different sense modalities may be involved (e.g., visual kinesthetic).

Table 8.1. Definitions of the Structure-of-Intellect Categories (con't).

S— *Symbolic.* Information in the form of denotative signs having no significance in and of themselves, such as letters, numbers, musical notations, codes, and words, when meanings and form are not considered.

M— *Semantic.* Information in the form of meanings to which words commonly become attached, hence most notable in verbal thinking and in verbal communication but not identical with words. Meaningful pictures also often convey semantic information.

B— *Behavioral.* Information, essentially nonverbal, involved in human interactions where the attitudes, needs, desires, moods, intentions, perceptions, thoughts, and so on, of other people and of ourselves are involved.

Products

Forms that information takes in the organism's processing of it.

U— *Units.* Relatively segregated or circumscribed items of information having "thing" character. May be close to Gestalt psychology's "figure on a ground."

C— *Classes.* Conceptions underlying sets of items of information grouped by virtue of their common properties.

R— *Relations.* Connections between items of information based on variables or points of contact that apply to them. Relational connections are more meaningful and definable than implications.

S— *Systems.* Organized or structured aggregates of items of information; complexes of interrelated or interacting parts.

T— *Transformations.* Changes of various kinds (redefinition, shifts, or modification) of existing information or in its function.

I— *Implications.* Extrapolations of information, in the form of expectancies, predictions, known or suspected antecedents, concomitants, or consequences. The connection between the given information and that extrapolated is more general and less definable than a relational connection.

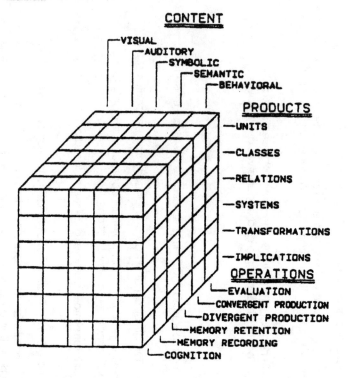

CONTENT
—VISUAL
  —AUDITORY
    —SYMBOLIC
      —SEMANTIC
        —BEHAVIORAL
PRODUCTS
—UNITS
—CLASSES
—RELATIONS
—SYSTEMS
—TRANSFORMATIONS
—IMPLICATIONS
OPERATIONS
—EVALUATION
—CONVERGENT PRODUCTION
—DIVERGENT PRODUCTION
—MEMORY RETENTION
—MEMORY RECORDING
—COGNITION

Figure 8.2. Revised structure-of-intellect model

creativity have been identified fairly consistently in a number of studies. Divergent production in relation to different kinds of content and forms of products has predominated as the major psychological operation involved in creativity, particularly in the context of several fluency and flexibility factors. Divergent production appears to be highly important in creative writing, public speaking, and artistic endeavors such as composition and performance in music, acting, painting, sculpture, ceramics, and various forms of design. It should be made clear, however, that there are indeed other psychological operations involved in creativity, such as convergent production and evaluation. For example, in mathematics, science, engineering, and invention, a unique solution or answer (product) is required—a product often reflecting ingenuity, novelty, cleverness, and elegance. This form of creativity often requires convergent production (focusing on a single end result within the context of many imposed constraints) with the outcome customarily representing a transformation of the input information, as might occur in the product of a novel invention or a new medical discovery (e.g., a vaccine for a serious disease).

Commonly Identified Fluency Factors. Following are the three commonly identified fluency factors:

1. *Ideational fluency* involves the listing of as many items within a given classification as one can produce, such as citing as many things as possible that are commonly *white, soft,* and *edible.* This ability would be considered to represent the divergent production of semantic units (DMU). An alternative name for this factor involving semantic material would be *verbal fluency.* This factor also could be supplemented by related factors representing divergent production of symbols, figures, or social behaviors that would be designated as DSU, DFU, and DBU, respectively. All four factors would be considered as the manifestation of creativity at a relatively low level of quality.

2. *Associational fluency* requires the citing of as many items as possible that would have comparable properties and referred to as the divergent production of semantic relations (DMR). An example would be to list as many words as possible that mean nearly the same as the word *hard.* This factor could be supplemented with other factors involving symbolic, figural, or behavioral elements that would be designated as DSR, DFR, and DBR, respectively.

3. *Expressional fluency* necessitates the divergent production within the context of a system of interrelated stimuli, such as being given the initial letters of four words and being asked to use each word only once to create as many sentences as possible. This activity would be defined as the divergent production of semantic systems (DMS). Specifically, if given the letters E, c, f, s, one could write the sentence "Eagles can fly silently." Expressional fluency could also be studied in the context of trying to restate a given sentence in a number of different ways. This factor also could be supplemented with other expressional fluency factors representing different kinds of content that would be respectively designated as DSS, DFS, and DBS.

Commonly Identified Flexibility Factors. Flexibility factors typically involve a substantial change in mental set with the result that transformations frequently occur in the form of the product representing a striking contrast to the kind of content or input information given the individual. Either divergent production or convergent production may be required depending, respectively, on whether multiple outcomes or responses are expected or whether a single optimal solution or answer is required. In the instance of divergent production, Guilford differentiated between *spontaneous flexibility* in which a task appears to be relatively

simple and results frequently in products that can be interpreted as constituting the element of a class and *adaptive flexibility,* or *redefinition,* in
which more difficult tasks require an altered product constituting a transformation.

Three flexibility tasks involving *divergent production* that were
commonly identified include the following:

1. *Spontaneous flexibility* requires an individual to cite as many common
alternative uses as possible for a very familiar object such as a tin can.
This ability would be classified as the divergent production of semantic
classes (DMC), although this designation has been somewhat controversial, in terms of whether the product is a *class* or a *transformation.*

2. *Adaptive flexibility* (verbal) necessitates the individual to come up with
several clever, novel, or rare responses as in suggesting a "catchy title" or
slogan for an anecdote or short story—an originality factor that would be
categorized as the divergent production of semantic transformations
(DMT).

3. *Adaptive flexibility* (figural) can be found in many puzzles or games in
which one has to generate as many solutions as possible in manipulating
concrete objects. An example would be to take away in as many different
ways as possible as many match sticks as one wishes from an array of
many squares formed by matches in order to leave three complete squares.
This factor would be designated as the divergent production of figural
transformation (DFT).

Flexibility factors necessitating use of *convergent production* are
associated with tasks that often involve a more general ability of differen-
tiating figure from ground—a Gestaltlike perceptual phenomenon in
which one must achieve a unique solution involving a finite number of
responses. This task requires convergent production of a given kind of
content resulting in a transformation. Three of the most commonly identified flexibility of closure factors include the following:

1. *Flexibility of closure* (figural) represents an ability in which an individual endeavors to locate one or more concealed figures or stimuli of a given
type (either visual or auditory) embedded within a highly complex set of
stimuli as in finding all the squares in an intricate geometric design or as
in identifying in a pictorial representation of a garden all the hidden ani-
mals or toys—a gamelike task often occurring in a supplementary section
of a Sunday newspaper. This ability would be defined as the convergent
production of figural transformations (NFT).

2. *Flexibility of closure* (symbolic) requires an individual to find within a field of complex stimuli such as sentences, musical notes, or mathematical formulas all possible sets of stimuli that meet carefully stated criteria, even though the product may constitute an entity cutting across several classes or units within the field of stimuli. For example, an examinee could be asked to form all four-letter words dealing with a sport or game that can be constructed from adjacent letters within the same word or across two or more words within a series of sentences or to find all possible two-digit prime numbers that can be located among the elements of two number series each consisting of 10 two-digit numbers. This ability would be referred to as the convergent production of symbolic transformations (NST).

3. *Flexibility of closure* (semantic) constitutes an ability to identify or to select which one of several available (listed) stimuli or procedures can be adapted to achieve a specified outcome or solution to a problem—especially in mathematics, science, engineering, invention, or household repair. An example would be to choose which one of five given stimuli (e.g., guitar, hammer, shoestring, thermos bottle, or wrist watch) could be best adapted to slicing a brick of cheese. This ability requires an individual to process one kind of given information into a form of product constituting new information (a unique solution)—a process having necessitated a transformation from an existing mental set in a familiar context to a substantially altered product in a foreign context. The ability just described would be defined as the convergent production of semantic transformations (NMT).

Three remaining frequently identified creative abilities involve a product of implications, one requiring cognition and the other two divergent production.

1. *Sensitivity to problems* is concerned with being able to identify defects, deficiencies, or needs in a complex problem situation or to anticipate difficulties that one may encounter in facing a complex task or situation. For example, one might need to identify shortcomings in the floor plan of a house, or one might need to anticipate and plan for difficulties that might be encountered in traveling in a highly underdeveloped country. Within the SOI model this ability would be referred to as the cognition of semantic implications (CMI).

2. *Elaboration* (verbal) pertains to generating as many extrapolations, inferences, or hypotheses as possible from a set of complex stimuli reflecting semantic content. For example, given a symbol such as a bell, one

might be asked to name as many occupations or groups of individuals as one could that are suggested by the symbol. Another illustration would be to cite as many consequences as one can suggest regarding what might result from a major environmental disaster such as a gigantic earthquake in California or a nuclear accident in a power plant. This ability would be classified as the divergent production of semantic implications (DMI).

3. *Elaboration* (figural) refers to an ability to construct or derive as many concrete objects as possible from a given set of several objects. For example, given four straight lines, two squares, two rectangles, and three triangles, an examinee might be asked to form as many geometric figures (configurations of stimuli) as possible without constraint. Such an ability would be categorized as the divergent production of figural implications (DFI). This ability could be supplemented by a corresponding one involving the processing of symbolic content (DSI).

Higher Order Creative Abilities

Until 1981, Guilford tended to stress the importance of first-order SOI abilities that were relatively independent of one another including those within the domain of creativity. Breaking his long-held stand of thinking intelligence to consist of several score independent abilities represented by orthogonal factors, Guilford (1981) urged the study of higher order abilities and introduced a method of mathematically determining higher order factors that could be interpreted as reflecting higher order abilities. Higher order abilities represent composites of first-order abilities that are at least moderately correlated with one another. Restating Guilford's (1985) conceptualization of higher-order abilities in the SOI model, Michael and Bachelor (1990) wrote the following:

> Whereas the trigram DMU for [a] test of ideational fluency signifies a first-order factor, in Guilford's (1985) conceptualization, a second-order factor is one in which a specification of an element in each of two of the three dimensions [in the SOI model] is given or fixed but in which the elements in the third dimension are free to vary (a dot [or bullet] being used in the trigram to indicate the dimensions for which the elements can change). For instance, the second-order factor DM· would be interpreted as the divergent production of semantic products with at least two forms of products being represented. A third-order factor is defined as one in which one element in a dimension is fixed but in which at least two elements in the remaining two dimensions are free to vary. Thus, the trigram DM·· would indicate the divergent production of at least two forms of products (last dot) from at least two kinds of content (first dot shown and placed in the middle of the

trigram). Additional information regarding this formulation . . . may be found in Khattab et al. (1982). (p. 60)

Within the SOI model framework, five papers have been published, in which confirmatory maximum likelihood factor analyses (Jòreskog & Sòrbom, 1984, 1986) have been carried out to evaluate the tenability of alternative hypotheses regarding the presence of higher order factors of creativity in correlational data bases derived from the University of Southern California Aptitudes Research Project directed by Guilford. Khattab, Michael, and Hocevar (1982) obtained evidence of the existence of higher order product factors of transformations requiring the processing of both symbolic and semantic content in measures associated with flexibility of closure, originality, and ingenuity in answering problem-oriented items. Subsequently, Michael and Bachelor (1990) found support for both first-order and higher order factors of divergent production. In a third analysis in which 53 SOI test variables were included, Bachelor and Michael (1991) isolated a factor representing a generalized divergent production of semantic content cutting across several products as well as a factor portraying a generalized convergent production ability that could not be considered to reflect creativity with the possible exception of two or three measures involving transformations. Concentrating on a re-analysis of intercorrelations of scores in 21 divergent production measures of figural and symbolic content, Bachelor, Michael, and Kim (1994) identified higher order creativity-oriented factors involving divergent production of transformations and implications. Finally, Chen and Michael (1993) obtained evidence for the presence of first-order and higher order dimensions of social intelligence indicative of creative behaviors in social interactions.

In all five studies, moderate to high correlations were noted among the higher order factors that were interpreted as indicative of creative activities. In all studies, the results suggested that creativity may be considered as multidimensional and that the tests defining any higher order factor were at least moderately intercorrelated. Thus, it would appear that creativity can be conceptualized somewhat more parsimoniously within the context of higher order or general factors, although first-order factors frequently can be identified as being viable concepts for both the understanding and measurement of creative endeavors.

THE SIPS MODEL: A CONCEPTUALIZATION OF THE PROBLEM-SOLVING PROCESS

In his conceptualization of creative thinking as a form of problem solving, Guilford (1964, 1965, 1967, 1968; Guilford & Hoepfner, 1971; Guilford & Tenopyr, 1968) proposed a variation of the SOI model, which he referred to as the SIPS model. As revealed in Figure 8.3, this information-processing model postulates the same psychological operations or processes as those in the SOI model, although convergent production and divergent production have been placed in one category of production.

At the bottom of the figure is a box labeled *memory storage,* in which various forms of SOI products have been illustrated adjacent to four kinds of designated content just below the box. Within this dynamic information-processing model, the several arrows indicate the direction of information flow that, although mostly forward, can be backward (as revealed by feedback loops at the many points of interchange of data) in problem-solving endeavors.

In a simplistic manner, what occurs in the SIPS model is that the individual recognizes a problem situation and gives it an initial structure after some preliminary filtering of information that arouses attention and directs future efforts. Then, the problem solver establishes what can be referred to as a search model or strategy. This search model, which may undergo many modifications in the process of problem solving, contains one or more items of information (cues) that resemble in their distinct characteristics the form of one or more of the products in memory storage. As the initial efforts of problem solving take place, the search model may acquire additional new unique characteristics from both the external (frequently additional information) and internal (often motivational or affective) environment as well as from the memory storage with continuous ongoing evaluation of all resulting information that will facilitate the direction of subsequent problem-solving activities. Next, the individual, through a trial-and-error self-regulatory process, produces one or more tentative solutions or answers to the problem that in turn are evaluated.

Within this self-regulating process involving much filtering, the interplay of cognition, memory, evaluation, and production is revealed in Figure 8.3 in terms of the many two-way arrows. The process so far described may repeat itself many times with the production of tentative or refined solutions or answers subject to ongoing evaluation as additional information is generated from the memory storage and new information is filtered from the external and internal environment—an activity resulting in altered cognitions, still more evaluation, and production of alternative or new solutions. These repetitive cycles often constitute successive approximations to the solution of a problem or may lead to a sudden insight of a

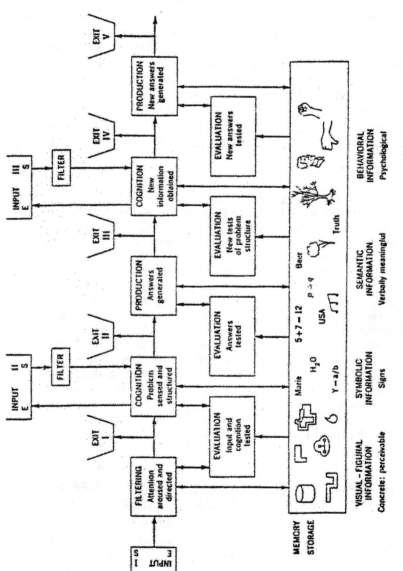

Figure 8.3. J. P. Guilford's original model of the problem-solving process

solution that is judged to be satisfactory to the problem solver or to a significant other. One may exit at any time if the effort is judged to be either too demanding or nonproductive, if other priorities supersede the immediate problem-solving endeavor, or if the solution is perceived as satisfactory.

In passing, it may be of interest to note that the SIPS model is quite similar to a computerized cybernetics model. Moreover, in its emphasis on evaluation, there is a close resemblance to the model proposed by Miller, Galanter, and Pribram (1960), which they entitled Test, Operate, Test, and Exit. One key concept in creativity in the problem-solving context, especially in mathematics, science, engineering, and invention, is the construct of *transfer recall* (Guilford & Tenopyr, 1968), which can be illustrated by finding new uses for a familiar object such as a brick or glass bottle—a process resulting in a transformed product. As Michael (1977) stated:

> Viewed somewhat negatively, transfer recall is retrieval of information instigated by cues in relation to which the information had not been committed previously to memory storage or had not been assimilated as part of those cues. Viewed positively, transfer recall is the retrieving of information from a partial set of cues in the memory storage and the using of this information in a new context and in novel ways. This transformed use of retrieved information is effected largely by flexibly reclassifying, reinterpreting, or redefining well-organized information within the memory storage in relation to the demands of a clearly defined problem. In contrast to *replicative recall* in an associational learning context that necessitates the retrieval of previously stored information in its original or essentially original form, as in recalling the capitals of states as the states are enumerated in alphabetical order, transfer recall in a cognitivist learning context embodies and requires active use of a search model scanning the realm of a rich memory storage to select the kinds of information necessary to fit the requirements of a carefully defined problem. (p. 159)

RELATION OF THE SEVEN STEPS IN ROSSMAN'S PARADIGM TO THE SEVERAL COMPONENTS OF THE SIPS MODEL

This section constitutes an adaptation of earlier work by Michael (1977) as well as of more recent contributions (Michael, 1984, 1990) regarding the SIPS model. The 1984 paper was given at the University of Houston, Clear Lake at a conference entitled "Heuristics in Mathematics and Science Education." This paper was subsequently translated into Chinese and published in a professional journal in the People's Republic of China (Michael, 1990).

Detailed steps central to the SIPS model are set forth with respect to each of the seven stages in Rossman's (1931) paradigm for invention, which reflects a significant form of creative problem-solving activities. Rossman's model, which is more or less linear in its portrayal of problem solving, contains steps that closely parallel the five proposed by Dewey (1910) for problem solving and the four suggested by Wallas (1926) in the act of creative production. In the writer's opinion, Rossman's seven steps, in contrast to Dewey's five or Wallas' four, represent a significant improvement in the conceptualization of the problem-solving process. Moreover, Rossman's conceptualization exhibits a surprisingly close fit to the key concepts set forth in the SIPS model.

In Table 8.2, the pertinent developmental processes of the SIPS model are described along with their correspondence to Rossman's (1931) formulation. This table highlights virtually all the principal activities that were hypothesized by Guilford (1968; Guilford & Tenopyr, 1968) to describe the characteristics of problem solving within the framework of the constructs taken from the SOI model. To comprehend the interaction of the five psycho-logical operations central to problem solving as well as the iterative properties of the SIPS model, the relatively detailed presentation in Table 8.2 is informative. It is helpful to consult Figure 8.3 as each step of Table 8.2 is reviewed.

IMPLICATIONS OF THE SIPS MODEL IN TEACHING FOR CREATIVE ENDEAVOR

In this section, each of the five SOI psychological operations of cognition, memory, convergent production, divergent production, and evaluation is related to how the teaching process can be developed to facilitate the manifestation of creative endeavor on the part of students, especially those in mathematics and science courses. Initially, it may be advisable to assess the standing of students on each of the SOI abilities that have been associated with creative thinking. Standardized tests are available (Meeker & Meeker, 1975-1992; Meeker, Meeker, & Roid, 1985). Baseline data presented as profiles will afford teachers some indication of the relevant strengths and weaknesses of students in each of several SOI abilities thought to be significant in creative problem-solving endeavors. If one may assume that adequate time can be devoted to encourage the development of creative behaviors described within the framework of relevant SOI abilities and that a learning atmosphere conducive to the reward and reinforcement of creative behaviors can be provided, suggestions for the viable use of each of the five previously cited SOI psychological operations in the teaching-learning process aimed at the realization of creative prob-

Table 8.2. Correspondence of Rossman's Seven Steps in Problem Solving (Invention) to Activities in Guilford's SIPS Model.

Step 1 (Rossman): Observation of a need or felt difficulty (initial comprehension of a problem situation or area of concern).

Guilford's SPS Activities: Accompanying the sensing or perception of a problem situation, sensory inputs (Input I) from the external environment (E) and from the internal environment or soma (S)—the emotional, temperamental, and/or motivating dimensions needed to energize the organism—are filtered in a manner to arouse and to direct attention to retrieving selectively and simultaneously figural, symbolic, semantic, and/or behavioral content (old information) from the memory storage that is evaluated in combination with sensory inputs (new information). Both new and old information are integrated to afford an *initial cognition* of a possible problem situation. If the problem is evaluated as trivial or inappropriate for further consideration, additional activity would be terminated by one's making an exit (Exit I) from the problem-solving endeavor

Step 2 (Rossman): Analysis of need; formulation and definition of the problem.

Guilford's SPS Activities: Additional refinements in cognition occur through further use of memory and evaluation operations involving filtering of new sensory inputs (Input II) with a possible exit (Exit II) if the individual becomes distracted, disinterested, or disinclined to work further. Otherwise, continuing activity occurs to structure and to define the parameters and characteristics of the problem and thus to enhance the level of cognition (understanding) of the problem.

Step 3 (Rossman): Survey of all available information or data that appear relevant. Preliminary or rudimentary incubation (unconscious effort) possible, depending on complexity or difficulty level of problem.

Guilford's SPS Activities: Associated with a systematic survey of all available information is the development of a search model (strategy for identifying cues in new information being filtered from both the external and internal environment and in old information being retrieved from the memory storage—information that can be matched with the requirements of the problem. Considerable evaluation occurs at this stage concerning the relevance of accumulating knowledge and data to fulfilling the demands of the problem. Still further refinements in cognition have occurred concerning problem definition and constraints.

Table 8.2. Correspondence of Rossman's Seven Steps in Problem Solving (Invention) to Activities in Guilford's SIPS Model (con't).

Step 4 (Rossman): Formulation of numerous possible (objective) solutions, often highly tentative.

Guilford's SPS Activities: The activities of the third step just described blend almost imperceptibly with those of the fourth step in which the applications of the search model lead to formulations of many tentative solutions (answers) that are derived from use of convergent production (a process intended to yield an unique answer) and/or divergent production (a process often associated with the generation of numerous hypotheses subsequently to be evaluated or verified). These two production operations are subjected to ongoing evaluation. Crucial to this fourth step is *transfer recall*, a process primarily involving in creative endeavor (a) the selective retrieval of old information from a partial set of cues in memory storage and (b) the subsequent transformed use of this information in a new context as well as in novel or original ways. Transformations in creative problem solving are represented by flexibly redefining, restructuring, or reinterpreting well-organized knowledge within the memory storage to meet well defined problem requirements in a new setting. A decision regarding the attainment of a satisfactory answer to the problem is accomplished through evaluation activities with implicit or explicit criteria. The achievement of a satisfying early solution to a problem (a circumstance most likely to arise in the instance of a relatively simple problem quickly solved) or the presence of distraction or discouragement on the part of the individual may lead to termination of problem-solving efforts (Exit III). This fourth step serves to conclude what might be viewed as the first of several cycles or iterations of problem solving, especially in the instance of a very difficult task or challenge.

Step 5 (Rossman): Examination, critical analysis, and evaluation of these tentative solutions for their strong points and weak points as well as for a possible need to refocus the problem itself. Persistent and ongoing incubation (unconscious work) probable, particularly for difficult or complex problems.

Guilford's SPS Activities: Beginning with Step 5 and continuing through Step 7, a reiteration of the process encountered in the first four steps (particularly Steps 2, 3, and 4) takes place with feedback loops permitting an interchange of information gained from any previous step to occur. In problems of great complexity, substantial evaluation is evident at the fifth step regarding the appropriateness of several tentative alternative solutions, of modes of achieving these solutions (as in evaluating relative merits of two or more mathematical proofs of the same problem), and of the impact of the solutions

Table 8.2. Correspondence of Rossman's Seven Steps in Problem Solving (Invention) to Activities in Guilford's SIPS Model (con't).

on a possible redefinition or restructuring of the problem itself. If these alternative solutions are judged unsatisfactory, then a second segment of cognition of new sources of external data or internal information (Input III) arises. These new data are filtered and evaluated in conjunction with old information from the memory storage to afford a restructuring, reinterpretation, or reconceptualization of the former problem situation prior to the occurrence of the sixth step involving the production of new answers. At or close to the conclusion of the fifth step it may be advantageous to take a hiatus from the evaluative activities (which may have created mental blocks, rigidity, or interferences) so that during a period of rest *incubation* can result—a period of delay in conscious endeavor during which unconscious activity involving transfer recall may lead to a sudden (insightful) solution in Step 6. An individual who has tired of the problem or who has exhausted immediately available time in light of the priorities of other events may elect to terminate activity, at least temporarily (Exit IV).

Step 6 (Rossman): Generation and formulation of new ideas, hypotheses, or solutions to the problem that itself may possibly have been reformulated.

Guilford's SPS Activities: In light of refinements in the cognition of the problem and its possible new focus as a consequence of extensive evaluation of tentative prior solutions (Step 5), the production of a new solution (sometimes sudden; sometimes incremental and painstaking) takes place—an outcome quite analogous to what has occurred at a relatively simple level in Step 4 for a comparatively elementary problem.

Step 7 (Rossman): Testing and evaluating more promising solutions followed by possible acceptance of one solution as being satisfactory, although additional refinements may be anticipated or required.

Guilford's SPS Activities: The unique solution or the most promising ones reached in the previous step (Step 6) are subjected to intensive evaluation and testing and may be related to and compared with the initial solution at Step 4. If the one or more solutions surviving the second iteration (cycle) found in Steps 5 to 7 (somewhat parallel to the process followed during the first iteration primarily represented by Steps 2 to 4), then the individual terminates work and leaves the creative problem-solving endeavor (Exit V). If the results obtained are evaluated as being still unacceptable, a third iteration, or

Table 8.2. Correspondence of Rossman's Seven Steps in Problem Solving (Invention) to Activities in Guilford's SIPS Model (con't).

cycle, comprising Steps 8, 9, and 10 (paralleling Steps 4, 5, and 6 of the previous iteration) is initiated. Still further iterations may continue indefinitely with feedback from previous cycles being incorporated in the continuing operations of cognition, memory, evaluation, and production (convergent or divergent) to achieve what is finally judged to be a truly creative and aesthetically satisfying, if not cost effective, solution.

Note: The contents of this table with some slight modifications have been taken from Michael (1984, 1990). To some extent, ideas in Michael (1977) were also incorporated within this table. The reader is urged to consult the diagram in Figure 8.3 that illustrates the dynamic nature of the SIPS model. A careful study of this diagram in conjunction with the text of this table should permit one to understand how the SIPS model can serve to explicate in a step-by-step manner the process of creative problem solving (invention) proposed by Rossman (1931).

lem solving are proposed. Paraphrased almost verbatim with some modifications and minor additions from the paper by Michael (1984) and its published version (Michael, 1990), the following suggestions occur.

Cognition

For each instructional experience, a teacher may give an overview involving use of advance organizers to orient the learner to the goals and objectives of the unit of instruction in which creative outcomes are anticipated. Student understandings need to be developed within the framework of organizing units of information into classes (concepts) by demonstrating both similarities and differences in units as well as both positive and negative instances of membership of these units in classes. The role and function of units in classes within knowledge systems need to be illustrated, especially in defining the structural bases of instructional topics having hierarchical characteristics as in logic and higher mathematics. Moreover, efforts should be expended toward (a) a clear definition of problems with emphasis on what information is relevant or irrelevant, (b) appropriate sequencing of instructional materials (e.g., ordering of problem sets in mathematics for difficulty level or complexity) particularly with respect to complexity and logical inter-relationships, and (c) the acquisition of sensitivity to the kinds of information that may be required to be selected from memory storage (previously assimilated knowledge).

Memory

A highly organized memory storage is essential for creative activities, as problem solving cannot occur in a vacuum. A teacher can facilitate the improvement of many abilities by ordering and organizing content in instructional units in such a manner as to reduce interference (negative transfer) by affording students sufficient practice to internalize both the content and process characteristics that are common to a given classification of problem-solving experiences. Although overlearning in terms of frequent practice can help to minimize interference among somewhat similar instructional units, caution must be exercised that overlearning with its associated completeness and specification of cues in the recently acquired information does not generate a mental set or rigidity in thinking (often referred to as functional fixedness) that in a foreign context or in an unfamiliar problem situation will work against the reinterpretation or the redefinition of the overlearned information or other well-established knowledge or habits.

A comparable statement can be made with reference to recency of exposure to new information as potentially introducing interference for recalling other kinds of knowledge that may be required in solving a novel problem. Often, in such occasions of overlearning or of recency of exposure, a period of relaxation can provide an opportunity for differential forgetting of interfering responses to occur or for incubation (unconscious thought) to take place followed by sudden and selective application of transfer recall, especially if some subsidence of overly critical self-evaluation can be allowed.

Convergent Production

The facilitation of maximal use of cognitive and memory abilities is generally prerequisite to instruction for convergent production. Supplementing the use of models, algorithms, and numerous illustrative examples to direct problem-solving activities aimed at realizing a unique solution, a carefully designed search model can provide guidelines for selective retrieval of pertinent and promising material from the memory storage. Such information can be combined with external inputs to afford the student an opportunity for self-discovery of the processes required to achieve what is typically the unique answer to a mathematics or science problem. Care must be exercised that simple rules or algorithms in problem solving do not generate a mental block against which original and novel ways of effecting the solution can be achieved.

Divergent Production

Although highly relevant to artistic endeavors, creative writing, and public speaking, divergent production customarily assumes a secondary role to convergent production in many problem-solving activities, such as those in mathematics, science, engineering, and invention. As stated earlier, divergent production tends to emphasize fluency of responses in open-ended situations rather than a focus on the achievement of a single answer or response. Divergent production would seem to afford its greatest contribution in scientific thinking to the generation of numerous hypotheses in the early stages of problem solving that are subsequently tested and evaluated for relevance and workability. In the teaching-learning situation, training models can be established for hypothesis formulation as in (a) asking students to suggest consequences or implications of some highly improbable events such as those associated with an environmental disaster or scientific breakthrough, or (b) scheduling brainstorming sessions in a nonevaluative, permissive atmosphere that encourage one to suggest possible transformations of information as in offering new or unusual uses of familiar objects.

Evaluation

As the evaluation process takes place at nearly all steps of problem-solving and creative activities in which cognition, memory, convergent production, and divergent production take place, it is important that students become familiar with how criteria for judging the worth and relevance of outcomes at each step of the problem-solving process can be established. Particular emphasis should be placed on having students not only consider within a problem statement information that is either relevant or irrelevant to reaching a solution but also develop an awareness of constraints that have been placed on the formulated problem task. The use of test questions that require a complete problem solution or minimally an outline of the steps followed (often referred to as *open assessment*) is probably superior to the use of multiple-choice items in assisting a teacher to determine in a course assignment or examination the logical consistency as well as the ingenuity of the process employed in solving one or more assigned problems, especially in mathematics, science, or engineering.

An instructor must also take into account in a realistic manner the maturity level of students so that a reasonable expectation or norm of both the degree and quality of creative behaviors and resulting products can be approximated. Consideration also may be given to the sensitivity and originality with which students, particularly those in college offerings, could identify problem areas and formulate hypotheses in both laboratory and theory courses. Sometimes, highly creative students can suggest insightful hypotheses as a consequence of an amazing sensitivity to implications of existing theories and empirical findings but cannot easily solve the problems evolving from these hypotheses. In both examinations and class assignments including field work and laboratory, it is important that evaluative feedback from the instructor be furnished in a prompt and tactful way so that in association with self-evaluations made by students, appropriate and reasonable direction can be given to guide them in creative problem solving and to prevent them from repeating the same kinds of previously made errors in future learning.

Finally, the creation and employment of training models, especially on the part of elementary school and secondary school science and mathematics educators, for evaluation on a step-by-step basis of creative problem-solving activities can help both teachers and students (when provided with immediate and relevant feedback) to explore alternative strategies. Such strategies can minimize the commission of nonproductive errors and encourage the substitution of new and novel approaches, notwithstanding the risk-taking that may be involved.

Conclusion

Creative problem solving, especially in mathematics, science, engineering, and invention is a complex process requiring use of abilities of cognition, memory, convergent production, and evaluation with secondary emphasis upon divergent production for hypothesis generation. The SIPS model of information processing with its external and internal outputs accompanied by numerous feedback loops to permit the interchange of data from one step of problem solving to another shows at least modest promise in providing a conceptual framework within which creative problem solving and the products that it generates can be comprehended. The model also affords a heuristic means for the potential improvement of methods employed by teachers to facilitate the manifestation of creative endeavor on the part of their students.

UNANSWERED QUESTIONS AND UNRESOLVED ISSUES

Although the SOI model as well as the SIPS model has provided a helpful framework for understanding the nature of human intelligence, it has been subject to a number of criticisms primarily with reference to the empirical support that it has received rather than in terms of its usefulness and heuristic value as a theory. In fact, most of the criticisms have been concerned with methodology, including the questionable reliability of many of the measures hypothesized to represent the underlying constructs of the SOI theory. Specifically, eight concerns have been expressed.

Subjectivity of the Statistical Procedures. In the exploratory factor-analytic procedures that Guilford followed involving the rotation of factor axes (mathematically derived dimensions) to prescribed positions to yield psychological meaningfulness, the charge has been made that the process followed could be adapted or forced in such a way as to meet the investigator's expectations of obtaining support for the existence of a factor and for the consequent conclusion that this mathematically interpretable factor had led to support for the existence of a hypothesized SOI first-order ability. Recently developed confirmatory factor-analytic techniques have provided a more objective basis for evaluating the tenability of a number of alternative hypotheses concerning the existence of first-order as well as of higher-order factors within which many of the first-order factors may be subsumed.

Lack of Clarity in Factor Structures. In many instances, it has been observed that the magnitudes of intercorrelations among tests serving to describe one factor have not been substantially different from the magnitudes of correlations of these same tests with other tests defining different factors. This observation has been supported by more recent findings of the presence of broad general factors that appear to include sets of tests that seem to define different first-order factors. In part, this lack of clarity may be a function of the fact that elements within a given dimension may not be clearly differentiable, as in the instance of semantic and symbolic content, operations of cognition and convergent production, and products of classes, relations, and systems. Moreover, many of the SOI tests intended to represent only one factor (supposedly pure or univocal tests) actually show substantial weights on two or three factors (factorially complex tests). This circumstance may reflect to some extent the inability of those constructing psychological tests to separate at times two or more elements within any one of the three dimensions of the SOI model.

Lack of Replicability of Factor Structures. In his many research studies, Guilford was not able to show convincingly that the empirical outcomes intended to verify the presence of many first-order factors could be replicated across samples from different populations, as the sets of tests employed frequently differed rather substantially from sample to sample. To some extent, this difficulty was overcome through the use of anchor or marker test variables that had been demonstrated in many previous analyses to define the same factor. Unfortunately, many of the experimental tests hypothesized to represent several first-order abilities and shown statistically to define first-order factors in a given study were not used in subsequent analyses involving new samples.

High Degree of Specificity of SOI First-Order Factors. It would appear that the scope of many of the SOI factors was so narrow and specific that their usefulness in day-to-day intellectual activities would be hard to demonstrate. It is for this reason that higher order factors that represent a constellation of many first-order factors working together in a complementary fashion would seem to be more readily interpretable and useful in understanding the characteristics of intellectual functioning than are first-order factors.

Minimizing the Importance of Correlation Among First-Order Factors. Consistent with the position that higher-order factors appear to be more realistic and interpretable in the realm of mental activity is the concern that many factor analysts expressed regarding Guilford's adherence until 1981 to the position that first-order factors could be conceptualized as being relatively independent. It would appear that in creative problem solving that an individual uses many abilities simultaneously in varying combinations with the result that correlations among them would appear to be inevitable. In fact, a hierarchical ordering of first-, second-, and even third-order abilities would seem to be required in a dynamic ongoing process resembling in many ways the previously described operations in the SIPS model.

Limited Reliability of Many SOI Tests. The relatively low reliability of scores on several of the SOI tests (frequently below .60) would tend to make difficult the accurate identification of a factor and could lead to the potential generation of an error factor (an artifact).

Level of Confidence Concerning Whether SOI Tests Intended to Represent Creativity Duplicate Creative Abilities in Real Life Situations. There has been a long-standing need to do additional research concerning whether the abilities in the SOI model interpreted to portray creative activities actually parallel the processes in creative endeavor in school-centered learning and in subsequent occupational and recreational pursuits. Research directed toward finding such a correspondence is very much needed, although the implementation of such research poses a number of practical difficulties in terms of cooperation and commitment from individuals in the relevant agencies or institutions.

Need to Relate SOI Abilities to Motivational and Affective Characteristics of Creative Endeavor. A marked tendency has existed for several decades to treat cognitive and affective components of creativity in a rather discrete way, almost as if intellectual and affective indicators were independent of one another. It seems obvious that these two broad dimensions of behavior interact and reinforce one another in the creative process. Systematic research needs to be done to understand better how these two key aspects of human behavior can mutually enhance and contribute to the act of creation.

SUMMARY AND REVIEW

In this chapter, the major features of two important models associated with intellectual functioning and creative problem solving have been described. First, the SOI model developed by Guilford (1956, 1959, 1967) was presented along with the identification of 12 empirically verified creative abilities associated with this model: ideational fluency, often referred to as verbal fluency, associational fluency, expressional fluency, spontaneous flexibility, adaptive flexibility (verbal), adaptive flexibility (figural), flexibility of closure (figural), flexibility of closure (symbolic), flexibility of closure (semantic), sensitivity to problems, elaboration (verbal), and elaboration (figural). An important distinction was made between the role of divergent production frequently involved in open-ended tasks, such as writing, speaking, and artistic performance, and that of convergent production requiring the transformation of a given kind of information or content into a new product form constituting a single outcome or unique and possibly ingenious solution as found in invention, mathematics, science, or engineering problem-solving activities.

Within the context of the SOI model higher order factors representing selected combinations of correlated first-order factors were described. Three empirical studies lending support to higher order constructs of creativity derived from the SOI model were briefly reviewed.

The second model given detailed consideration was called the SIPS model. Within this model the dynamic functioning of the intellectual operations of cognition, convergent and divergent production, memory, and evaluation were described in relation to the seven steps of the Rossman model of invention (a problem-solving process). Next, implications of the SIPS model in teaching for creative endeavor were developed.

Finally, unanswered questions and unresolved issues were detailed pertaining largely to methodoglical and statistical issues employed in the verification of the constructs within the two models. In addition to several concerns that were expressed, suggestions for needed research particularly in terms of linking intellectual functioning and motivational characteristics of behavior in creative problem solving were made.

STUDY ACTIVITIES

Try out your creative capabilities in responding to the following tasks.

1. Construct two or three test items that you think would correspond to 4 or 5 of the 12 previously identified SOI creative abilities.
2. Give three examples of those tasks in which transformations would be required in problem-solving endeavors.
3. Plan two instructional units appropriate to either an elementary or secondary school setting. In one, emphasize divergent production and in the other stress convergent production involving transformations.
4. How might college or university professors with whom you have studied or with whom you are currently studying modify their instructional practices to facilitate your manifestation of creative endeavor?

5. How might teachers in either an elementary or secondary school setting carry out instruction in a subject matter area of interest to you so as to enhance creativity among students?

6. Speculate on how motivational procedures can be combined with sound intellectual approaches to the teaching of subject matter so as to augment creative performance. Try to be specific.

7. In testing and evaluation activities in the classroom, how can teachers be more creative in the ways in which they assess the ability of students to apply new knowledge?

REFERENCES

Bachelor, P. A., Michael, W. B., & Kim, S. (1994). First-order and higher-order symbolic and figural factors in structure-of-intellect divergent production measures. *Educational and Psychological Measurement, 54,* 608-619.

Bachelor, P. A., & Michael, W. B. (1991). Higher-order factors of creativity within Guilford's structure-of-intellect model: A re-analysis of a fifty-three variable data base. *Creativity Research Journal, 4,* 157-175.

Chen, S. A., & Michael, W. B. (1993). First-order and higher-order factors of creative social intelligence within Guilford's structure-of-intellect model: A re-analysis of a Guilford data base. *Educational and Psychological Measurement, 53,* 619-641.

Dewey, J. (1910). *How we think.* Boston, MA: D. C. Heath.

Guilford, J. P. (1956). Les dimensions de l'intellect. In H. Laugier (Ed.), *L'analyse factorielle et ses applications* (pp. 53-74). Paris: Centre National de la Recherche Scientifique.

Guilford, J. P. (1959). Three faces of intellect. *American Psychologist, 14,* 469-479.

Guilford, J. P. (1964). *Basic problems in teaching for creativity.* Paper presented at the Conference on Creativity and Teaching Media, La Jolla, CA.

Guilford, J. P. (1965, September). *Intelligence—1965 model.* Paper presented at the annual meeting of the American Psychological Association, Chicago.

Guilford, J. P. (1967). *The nature of human intelligence.* New York: McGraw-Hill.

Guilford, J. P. (1968). *Intelligence, creativity, and their educational implications.* San Diego, CA: Knapp.

Guilford, J. P. (1981). Higher-order structure-of-intellect abilities. *Multivariate Behavioral Research, 16,* 411-435.

Guilford, J. P. (1985). The structure-of-intellect model. In B. B. Wolman (Ed.), *Handbook of intelligence* (pp. 225-266). New York: Wiley.

Guilford, J. P. (1988). Some changes in the structure-of-intellect model. *Educational and Psychological Measurement, 48,* 1-4.

Guilford, J. P., & Hoepfner, R. (1971). *The analysis of intelligence.* New York: McGraw-Hill.

Guilford, J. P., & Tenopyr, M. L. (1968). Implications of the structure-of-intellect model for high school and college students. In W. B. Michael (Ed.), *Teaching for creative endeavor* (pp. 25-45). Bloomington: Indiana University Press.

Jòreskog, K. G., & Sòrbom, D. (1984). *LISREL VI: Analysis of linear structural relationships by maximum likelihood, instrumental variables, and least squares.* Mooreville, IN: Scientific Software, Inc.

Jòreskog, K. G., & Sòrbom, D. (1986). *LISREL VI: Analysis of linear structural relationships by maximum likelihood, instrumental variables, and least squares methods: User's guide* (4th ed.). Uppsala, Sweden: University of Uppsala.

Khattab, A-M., Michael, W. B., & Hocevar, D. (1982). The construct validity of higher order structure-of-intellect abilities in a battery of tests emphasizing the product of transformations: A confirmatory maximum likelihood factor analysis. *Educational and Psychological Measurement, 42,* 1090-1105.

Meeker, M., & Meeker, R. (1975-1992). *Structure-of-Intellect Learning Abilities Test.* Los Angeles: Western Psychological Services.

Meeker, M., Meeker, R., & Roid, G. (1985). *Manual: Structure-of-Intellect Learning Abilities Test.* Los Angeles: Western Psychological Services.

Michael, W. B. (1977). Cognitive and affective components of creativity in mathematics and the physical sciences. In J. C. Stanley, W. C. George, & C. H. Solano (Eds.), *The gifted and the creative: A fifty-year perspective* (pp. 142-172). Baltimore, MD: Johns Hopkins University Press.

Michael, W. B. (1984, July). *Application of Guilford's structure-of-intellect problem-solving (SIPS) model to teaching for creative endeavor in mathematics and science.* Paper presented at the first annual conference of the Institute for Logic and Cognitive Studies: Heuristics in Mathematics and Science Education, University of Houston, Clear Lake, TX.

Michael, W. B. (1990). Application of Guilford's structure-of-intellect problem-solving (SIPS) to teaching for creative endeavor in mathematics and science. *Journal of East China Normal University (ECNU): Educational Science Edition, 27,* 9-19.

Michael, W. B., & Bachelor, P. (1990). Higher-order structure-of-intellect creativity factors in divergent production tests: A re-analysis of a Guilford data base. *Creativity Research Journal, 3,* 58-74.

Miller, G. A., Galanter, E. H., & Pribram, K. H. (1960). *Plans and the structure of behavior.* New York: Holt, Rinehart & Winston.

Rossman, J. (1931). *The psychology of the inventor: A study of the patentee.* Washington, DC: Inventors Publishing Co.

Thurstone, L. L. (1935). *Vectors of mind.* Chicago: University of Chicago Press.

Thurstone, L. L. (1938). Primary mental abilities. *Psychometric Monographs, 1.*

Thurstone, L. L. (1947). *Multiple-factor analysis.* Chicago: University of Chicago Press.

Wallas, G. (1926). *The art of thought.* New York: Harcourt, Brace.

SELECTED READINGS

The following suggested references tend, for the most part, to be written for the individual who is looking for a general orientation to the area of creativity, although several are oriented to the SOI framework.

Barron, F. (1963). *Creativity and psychological health.* Princeton, NJ: D. Van Nostrand.

Barron, F., & Harrington, D. M. (1981). Creativity, intelligence, and personality. *Annual Review of Psychology, 32,* 439-476.

Butcher, H. J. (1973). Intelligence and creativity. In P. Kline (Ed.), *New approaches in psychological measurement.* New York: Wiley.

Getzels, J. W., & Jackson, P. W. (1962). *Creativity and intelligence.* New York: Wiley.

Glover, J. A., Ronning, R. R., & Reynolds, C. R. (Eds.). (1989). *Handbook of creativity.* New York: Plenum Press.

Guilford, J. P. (1967). *The nature of human intelligence.* New York: McGraw-Hill.

Guilford, J. P. (1968). *Intelligence, creativity, and their educational implications.* San Diego, CA: Knapp.

Guilford, J. P., & Hoepfner, R. (1971). *The analysis of intelligence.* New York: McGraw-Hill.

Guilford, J. P., & Tenopyr, M. L. (1968). Implications of the structure-of-intellect model for high school and college students. In W. B. Michael (Ed.), *Teaching for creative endeavor* (pp. 25-45). Bloomington: Indiana University Press.

Michael, W. B. (Ed.). (1968). *Teaching for creative endeavor.* Bloomington: Indiana University Press.

Stanley, J. C., George, W. C, & Solano, C. H. (Eds.). (1977). *The gifted and the creative: A fifty-year perspective 1925-1975.* Baltimore, MD: Johns Hopkins University Press.

Torrance, E. P. (1962). *Guiding creative talent.* Englewood Cliffs, NJ: Prentice-Hall.

9

Environmental Influences on Motivation and Creativity in the Classroom

Elizabeth Tighe
Brandeis University

Martha L. Picariello
Chicago, IL

Teresa M. Amabile
Harvard University Graduate School of Business Administration

In the early 1930s, at the request of many teachers and superintendents concerned about the development of teaching curricula in English, the National Council of Teachers of English created a Curriculum Commission to build a course of study from kindergarten through graduate school. Excerpts from a section of the report on "The Nature and Management of Creative Expression" appear here. These excerpts are followed by an analysis of research on environment, intrinsic motivation, and creativity—research that in many ways upholds the insights proffered by educators more than 60 years ago.

[Creativity] occurs when a person recognizes the dignity of his own experience, and when he imposes upon his experience the discipline of expression in an effort to share it with others. . . . In creative expression the reason for transferring the experience lies not in some material benefit to be attained by the writer or the speaker, but in his pleasure and interest in the experience itself. . . . The most dangerous fallacy in the teaching of creative expression lies in the assumption that it is of importance only to the "gifted" child. . . . The real object is the development of the pupils' capacity to value experience for its own sake and not for some utilitarian end or practical consideration. His pleasure in the experience is increased and deepened through the increased grasp of the experience developed by the effort to transfer it.

This intrinsic reward of the creative process must be carefully differentiated, especially under usual classroom conditions, from the external motive of social advantage which may accrue in composition . . . external and utilitarian considerations, such as prizes, grades, or credits to be earned, are wholly alien to the genuine creative impulse. They can be justified only as a means of breaking down inhibiting and conditioning forces which might otherwise prevent the appearance of creative composition at all. When these material and utilitarian motives become paramount, the work ceases to be creative. (Hatfield, 1935, pp. 110-112)

The report was based on insights from teachers of English, not on empirical investigation. Interestingly, however, the report emphasized a basic phenomenon that has received much empirical support—the difference between intrinsic and extrinsic motivation in their influence on creativity. Much research has demonstrated, as the 1935 report suggested, that creativity is more likely to flourish when one is intrinsically motivated than when one is extrinsically motivated. In other words, motivation arising from interest in the task itself is more conducive to creativity than motivation arising from certain external goals. Although this distinction might sound simple, the more than 60 years since the publication of this report have seen a continuing concern about the destruction of creativity in the classroom. This suggests either that past reports have fallen on deaf ears, or that utilizing this "simple" distinction in the methods of the classroom is not, in fact, a simple task.

THE BASIC MODEL OF CREATIVITY: A SOCIAL-PSYCHOLOGICAL PERSPECTIVE

The social psychological perspective focuses on creativity—the production of novel, appropriate ideas—as an individual behavior influenced by the behaviors and characteristics of others. Much research has examined how others, in the context of a social situation, can affect creative performance by affecting motivation. In the componential model of creativity (Amabile, 1983a, 1983b, 1996), task motivation is one of the three major components of creativity, along with domain-relevant skills and creativity-relevant processes.

Basic Premises of the Componential Model

Creativity in any domain depends on the interplay of domain-relevant skills, creativity-relevant processes, and task motivation (Amabile, 1983a, 1983b, 1996). The presence of each of these on any given task is necessary in order for any level of creativity to be achieved on that task. Domain-relevant skills consist of knowledge and technical skills within the domain. Acquisition of such skills depends on both formal and informal education. Although some might argue that too much knowledge or technical skill can lead to the routine use of algorithms that limit one's ability to generate creative responses, even novices who successfully break new ground in a field must have some understanding of the domain in which the task falls if they are to generate appropriate solutions (cf. Kuhn, 1970; Simonton, 1977, 1988).

Knowledge of the domain is not enough for creativity. The solution must not only be appropriate, it must also be original. Creativity-relevant processes, which are not specific to any one domain, lead to novel responses. These processes describe the cognitive styles and work styles of the individual, which can depend on both training and specific personality characteristics. Thinking styles conducive to creativity include breaking set (Duncker, 1945; Newell, Shaw, & Simon, 1962), keeping one's options open, and general heuristics, such as "When all else fails, try something counterintuitive" (Newell et al., 1962). In addition, work styles such as long attention span, high energy level, and persistence on difficult tasks are also conducive to creativity.

The final component, task motivation, is comprised of the individual's attitude toward the task and perceptions of the reasons for engaging in the task. These attitudes and perceptions are dependent on one's initial intrinsic motivation, the salience of extrinsic constraints, and one's ability to minimize the salience of extrinsic constraints. In the componential model, one's initial motivation toward the task affects both whether or not one engages in the task, and the level of creativity of the task once it is undertaken. The intrinsic motivation principle of creativity (Amabile, 1996) states that intrinsic motivation is conducive to creativity and extrinsic motivation can be detrimental, primarily when the extrinsic incentive is experienced as controlling.

Intrinsic and Extrinsic Motivation Defined

> Every art and every inquiry, and similarly every action and pursuit, is thought to aim at some good. . . . If then there is some end of the things we do, which we desire for its own sake (everything else being desired for the sake of this), and if we do not choose everything for the sake of something else (for at that rate the process would go on to infinity, so that our desire would be empty and vain), clearly this must be the good and the chief good. (Aristotle, Ethics Book I.2)

In Aristotle's words, "which we desire for its own sake" is what social psychologists commonly refer to as an intrinsically motivated activity. Choosing "for the sake of something else" is what is referred to as an extrinsically motivated activity. That is, intrinsically motivated activities are performed primarily for the satisfaction they yield rather than the attainment of some external goal.

Most modern intrinsic motivation theorists have adopted an organismic approach to the study of intrinsic and extrinsic motives. These theorists view individuals as active—initiating behaviors rather than simply responding to environmental stimuli. White (1959) and Harter (1978) defined intrinsic motivation in terms of individuals' innate needs to be effective in their interactions with the environment. Feelings of effectance are achieved through experiences of competence. DeCharms (1968), based on Heider's (1958) concept of perceived locus of causality, proposed that intrinsic motivation results from the individual's desire to be the primary locus of causality of his or her own behavior. Deci and Ryan (1985) characterized an intrinsically motivated state as oriented toward seeking and conquering optimal challenges. In their conceptualization, intrinsic motivation results from both the need for competence and the need for self-determination.

It has been proposed that individuals are intrinsically motivated when they seek enjoyment, interest, satisfaction of curiosity, self-expression, or personal challenge in their work (Amabile, 1993). Each of these qualities, however, can co-occur with an extrinsically motivated state. That is, an individual can engage in a task for external reward but still experience enjoyment, curiosity, self-expression, or personal challenge. The only way to clearly distinguish an intrinsically motivated state from an extrinsically motivated state is to observe whether the behavior occurs when there are no external incentives. Intrinsic motivation, therefore, is often operationally defined as engaging in an activity in the apparent absence of extrinsic incentives. Jackson (1968) contrasted intrinsic and extrinsic motivation in terms of the school environment as follows:

> This is the distinction between "extrinsic" motivation (doing school work for the rewards it will bring in the form of good grades and teacher approval) on the one hand, and "intrinsic" motivation (doing school work for the pleasure that comes from the task itself) on the other. (p. 28)

The principles of intrinsic motivation can be very useful for understanding classroom interaction and the nurturance of creativity in the classroom. Much of the research on intrinsic motivation illuminates the ways in which motivation and creativity can be influenced by seemingly subtle factors in the social, or classroom, environment.

Social Influences on Intrinsic Motivation

The underlying theme in much of the intrinsic motivation literature is a counterpoint to traditional learning theory. Learning theory proposed that rewards enhance behavior (Skinner, 1938). Give an animal a treat, and it can be trained to roll over, jump through hoops, and balance a ball on its nose; give the child a gold star for spelling a word correctly and the child will, similarly, be trained to master the task. In recent years, researchers have provided evidence that this relation is not guaranteed, especially when the behavior involved is intrinsically motivated at the start. If one initially engages in a behavior for the pleasure it yields rather than for a payoff, then extrinsic rewards for engaging in the behavior actually tend to decrease the likelihood that the task will be enjoyed for its own sake in the future (Lepper & Greene, 1978).

Self-Perception Theory (Bem, 1972) proposed that individuals who are rewarded for an intrinsically motivated activity will—on observing their own behavior—conclude that they must have engaged in the activity partly to achieve the external reward. Therefore, they perceive their own intrinsic motivation toward the activity as lower than it was prior to engaging in the activity for external reward. This phenomenon has been termed the *overjustification effect.*

As a test of the overjustification effect, Lepper, Greene, and Nisbett (1973) demonstrated that rewarding nursery school children for an activity toward which they were initially intrinsically motivated (drawing with magic markers) resulted in decreased intrinsic motivation. In this study, some of the children expected to receive a reward for drawing with the markers, whereas a second group received the markers as an unexpected reward after task engagement. A third group of children received no reward for drawing with the markers. Two weeks later, the children were observed during a free-play period in which they had an opportunity to play with many different activities. Those children who earlier had been given the expected reward now played with the markers significantly less than the children in the other groups. This finding suggests that the mere act of receiving a reward does not undermine intrinsic motivation, but that, as self-perception theory would suggest, perceiving the reward as the reason for task engagement causes the undermining of intrinsic motivation. Similarly, cognitive evaluation theory (Deci & Ryan, 1985), which emphasizes individuals' innate desires for competence and self-determination, predicts that reward might shift one's causality orientation from internal to external, thereby decreasing one's self-determination and subsequent intrinsic motivation. This theory, however, also predicts that if a reward provides information regarding one's competence, then subsequent intrinsic motivation should increase.

Ross (1975) further demonstrated that the negative effect of external rewards on intrinsic motivation depends not merely on their existence or expected attainment, but more importantly on their relative salience. Children in this study were led to expect a reward, an attractive toy, for engaging in an activity in which they had previously shown interest. For some of the children, the toy was placed directly in front of them as they worked on the task. For others, it was set off to the side. During subsequent free-play periods, those children for whom the reward was made salient exhibited significantly less interest in the task than did the other children.

In a study complementary to Ross' (1975) demonstration of the negative effect of salient rewards, Fazio (1981) demonstrated the beneficial effect of making salient one's initial interest. Children in this study worked on a previously intrinsically motivated activity for a salient or nonsalient reward as in the Ross (1975) study. In addition, their initial interest in the activity was made either salient or not salient. This was done by having each child identify a photograph of him or herself engaging in the activity. This photograph was taken during an initial free-play period. The photograph, like the reward (Hershey Kisses), was then either placed directly in front of the child or off to the side. Those children who worked with the photo directly in front of them were significantly more interested in the activity on subsequent free-play measures than were those children for whom the photo was not salient. This was true even when the reward was salient. This study suggests that salient external rewards do not reduce interest in enjoyable tasks when the individual's initial interest is made salient.

Deci and Ryan (1985) emphasized that the effects on intrinsic motivation are not so much determined by the salience of the reward itself, but instead by the salience of either the informational, controlling, or amotivational aspects of the reward. For example, positive feedback tends to make salient the informational aspect, which signifies a person's competence at the task. Research has shown that if the informational aspect of the extrinsic motive is most salient, intrinsic motivation will be maintained or enhanced (Deci, 1971; Zuckerman, Porac, Latin, Smith, & Deci, 1978). In some instances, however, positive feedback can make salient the controlling aspect, especially when the feedback makes reference to the individual doing well in terms of what is expected by the experimenter (Pittman, Davey, Alafat, Wetherill, & Kramer, 1980; Ryan, 1982). The controlling aspect of an extrinsic reward signifies that the reward is an attempt to control the individual's behavior. When this aspect is most salient, intrinsic motivation will decrease. Rewards, deadlines, and surveillance also tend to make the controlling aspect of the social environment most salient, as each tends to pressure the individual to think, feel, and act in a prescribed manner (Amabile, DeJong, & Lepper, 1976; Deci, 1972; Lepper & Greene, 1975). Negative feedback, on the other hand, will often make the amotivating aspect of the event most salient. This aspect of an extrinsic reward signifies to the individual that effectance simply cannot be attained. If the amotivating aspect is most salient, the individual is likely to experience feelings of incompetence, and intrinsic motivation will decrease (Deci, Cascio, & Krussell, 1973). Deci and Ryan (1985) also emphasized that in the context of an autonomous causality orientation (i.e., if the person already feels self-determined and competent at the task), negative feedback will not necessarily make the amotivating aspect most salient. If the negative feedback is interpreted as an indication of how to improve performance and facilitate future competence, intrinsic motivation will not decrease.

To summarize the social influences on intrinsic motivation: Rewards do not always enhance behavior or performance. If rewards are seen as an effort to control one's behavior, intrinsic motivation will decrease, as will the likelihood that the task will be done freely in the future. It should be noted that tangible rewards such as money, toys, food, or gold stars are not the only forms of extrinsic motives that may undermine intrinsic motivation. Factors such as surveillance (Lepper & Greene, 1975), time pressure (Amabile et al., 1976), and expectation of evaluation (Amabile, 1979) also have been shown to undermine intrinsic motivation. Many of these contingencies are endemic to the typical classroom.

The Influence of Intrinsic Motivation on Creativity

Research also has demonstrated that salient, controlling extrinsic incentives inhibit not only intrinsic motivation, but also creativity. The effect of evaluation, or the expectation of evaluation, although conducive to creativity on algorithmic tasks (where the path to the solution is clearly predefined), consistently appears to hinder creativity on heuristic tasks (where the path to the solution is not clearly predefined). In a study that examined the effects of evaluation expectation and task type on the creativity of undergraduates' artwork, evidence was provided for the detrimental effects of evaluation expectation (Amabile, 1979). Half of the individuals who participated were told that expert artists would be evaluating their work; the other half did not expect to be evaluated. For evaluation-expectation subjects, one group was given a technical focus which either included explicit instructions that their collages would be rated on neatness, balance of design, planning, organization, recognizability, and expressiveness or did not include detailed instructions. A second group of evaluation-expectation subjects was given a creativity focus: half were told that their collages would be rated on novelty of ideas as well as use of shapes, variation of shapes, asymmetry, amount of detail, complexity, and effort evident, whereas others were not provided with this specific detail. A third group was not told to focus on any particular aspects. In most cases, those individuals not expecting any evaluation made collages that were consistently rated as more creative than did those expecting evaluation. Interestingly, the evaluation subjects who were told explicitly how to "be creative" produced collages rated significantly more creative than any other group. Thus, it appears that expectation of evaluation can have positive effects when specific instructions on how to produce "creative" works are given. Considering that these individuals were given an algorithm for generating solutions that would be rated high in creativity, however, their artwork cannot be considered creative in the same sense as it would have been if they had arrived at the finished product on their own, without explicit instructions from the experimenter. The detrimental effect of the expectation of evaluation on creativity has been replicated in several additional studies (Amabile, Goldfarb, & Brackfield, 1990; Hennessey, 1989) and has been shown to be related to personal attributes such as shyness (Cheek & Stahl, 1986) and skill level (Conti & Amabile, 1995; Conti, Amabile, & Pollack, 1995; Hill, Amabile, Coon, & Whitney, 1994; Pollak, 1992).

Another study (Berglas, Amabile, & Handel, 1981) used children's artwork to examine the effects of actual, rather than expected, evaluation on creativity. All children produced two designs. After the first design, children received either task-based praise regarding the qualities of the work, person-based praise in which the child was praised as a good artist, or no praise. In addition, children were either led to believe that the experimenter's opportunity for another job depended on the child's performance (interdependence), or, that the experimenter was gaining experience before assuming a position at another school (independence), or children were given no information regarding the experimenter. Although person-based praise and beliefs of interdependence appeared to decrease creativity, the group that received neither evaluation on their first artwork nor any information about the experimenter was more creative on the second design than all other groups.

The results of these two studies indicate that both expectation of evaluation and actual evaluation can hinder creativity. It is important to note, however, that actual evaluation in the second study might in fact be conceptually indistinct from evaluation expectation. Because children received evaluation on their first design, it would be natural for them to expect evaluation on their second. It should also be noted that the negative effects of evaluation do not apply when the evaluation is noncontrolling, that is, when it is informational (providing competence feedback) or when it conveys positive recognition of creative work (Amabile & Gryskiewicz, 1987, 1989).

Other extrinsic constraints have also been found to hinder creativity. For example, in a study in which the effects of contracting for a reward was examined, children were allowed to use a Polaroid camera as a reward for a storytelling task (Amabile, Hennessey, & Grossman, 1986). They were told either that in order to use a camera they must promise to later tell a story, or simply that they would do two tasks—first use a camera and then tell a story. As expected, those who were made to feel the contingency between telling the story and receiving the reward were less creative in their stories than those who were not.

Additionally, two studies involving competition—which effectively combines evaluation with reward—suggest that those who believe they are competing with others on a task perform less creatively than those who do not believe they are competing (Amabile, 1982, 1987). In the first study (Amabile, 1982), one group of children made collages as part of an art activity. Children in the other group were told that their collages would be judged by three adults who would award prizes to the three best. Those in the competitive group made collages that were rated as less creative than those in the noncompetitive group. In the second study, 49 corporate executives, managers, educators, and researchers solved Luchins' (1942) water jar problems. These problems require a set pattern of solutions for several problems and then require a different solution pattern for the last problem. Half of the subjects were given competitive instructions telling them that a winner would be chosen based on the number of problems correct and the time to solve the problems. A greater number of individuals in the noncompetitive group were able to break set and solve all the problems correctly.

Overall, these studies support the hypothesis that intrinsic motivation fosters creativity, but controlling extrinsic motivation inhibits creativity. All of the reviewed studies, however, examined social influences that raise extrinsic motivation and result in lower levels of creativity presumably because they lower intrinsic motivation. None actually examined direct effects of intrinsic motivation on creativity.

In a study in which an attempt was made to examine the direct effects of intrinsic motivation on creativity (unmediated by extrinsic motivation), individuals who identified themselves as actively involved in creative writing were brought into the laboratory to write haiku-style poems (Amabile, 1985). Before writing the poems, they were asked to rank-order, according to personal importance, seven reasons for writing. Some of the subjects ranked seven intrinsic reasons, such as "You feel relaxed when writing" and "You achieve new insights through writing." Others ranked seven extrinsic reasons for writing, such as "You enjoy public recognition of your work" and "You have heard of cases where one best selling novel or collection of poems has made the author financially secure." Others were not asked to consider their reasons for writing at all. As demonstrated in previous studies, those who were asked to consider extrinsic reasons for writing wrote poems that were rated as significantly less creative than poems written by the other subjects. This finding suggests that simply thinking of external constraints can undermine creativity. Those who focused on intrinsic reasons, however, were not significantly more creative than those in the control condition. Although this finding might appear problematic, it is likely that—in the choice to select as subjects of this study individuals who were already highly engaged in poetry writing—a ceiling effect was observed: subjects' intrinsic motivation was so high at the outset that there was not much margin for it to be increased. Thus, the detrimental effects of salient extrinsic incentives is again observed, but no direct evidence is provided for the beneficial effects of intrinsic motivation.

Up to this point the research that has been reviewed has focused on how controlling extrinsic constraints—such as reward and evaluation expectation—lower intrinsic motivation and, subsequently, creativity. Intrinsic motivation and creativity are presumably decreased because the task is no longer perceived as an end in and of itself, but rather as a means to an end. Deci and Ryan (Deci, 1975; Deci & Ryan, 1980, 1985) noted that intrinsic motivation is characterized by feelings of competence and self-determination. Their cognitive evaluation theory (Deci & Ryan, 1985) proposes that choice enhances a sense of self-determination by creating an internal locus of causality. When self-determination is manipulated through the perceived presence or absence of choice, intrinsic motivation also increases or decreases, respectively (Swann & Pittman, 1977; Zuckerman et al., 1978).

Amabile and Gitomer (1984) tested the application of this idea to creativity in a study of children's artwork. In this study, some children were given choice over what materials to use in an art project, whereas others were given the same materials that were selected by children in the choice condition but were not allowed to choose the materials themselves. Those children given choice made collages that were rated significantly more creative than those who used the same materials but had not been given choice of which materials to use. Presumably the children given choice felt more self-determined than those not given choice. Hence, they were more intrinsically motivated, and, consequently, more creative.

In summary, much research provides support for the proposition that intrinsic motivation is conducive to creativity and controlling extrinsic constraints—such as rewards and competition—can be detrimental to creativity. Other situational factors, however, can be conducive to creativity. These include choice that enhances self-determination and informational feedback that can enhance the attainment of competence. Taken together, these studies show a strong link between intrinsic motivation and creative performance.

Intrinsic Motivation in the Classroom

Researchers studying classroom climate have emphasized the importance of intrinsic motivation in fostering children's positive attitudes toward school (Anderson & Walberg, 1974; Ellett & Walberg, 1979; Epstein & McPartland, 1976; Williams & Batten, 1981). These researchers have suggested that student satisfaction measures are related to a positive school climate. In particular, Epstein and McPartland identified three factors associated with a positive school climate. The first factor, satisfaction, measured students' general reactions to school. The second factor, commitment to classwork, measured the level of student interest in work. The third factor was comprised of students' reactions to the teacher. It is likely that, in the school context, satisfaction corresponds to the fulfillment of the competence and self-determination needs suggested by Deci and Ryan (1985). Students who feel as though they have some control over their participation and performance and who receive adequate information regarding their abilities are likely to feel satisfied in the school context. These same factors that have been identified as affecting school climate might affect both the students' satisfaction with the school atmosphere and the quality of the work they do—including their creativity.

In an in-depth examination of children's perceptions of their classroom climate, DeCharms and his co-workers (1976) found that children who perceived themselves as "origins" of their own classroom behavior (i.e., self-reliant, autonomous, responsible) were more intrinsically motivated toward school than were children who perceived themselves as "pawns" (i.e., under the control and direction of those in authority). Moreover, children with an origin orientation performed better on several measures of academic achievement. Ryan and Grolnick (1986) conceptualized origin orientation as the degree to which children perceived their classroom environment as supportive of their self-determination. These researchers found that children with a high origin orientation wrote more creative short stories on a school-related theme than did children with a low origin orientation. Extending this research, Picariello (1991) found that children with a high origin orientation were more intrinsically motivated and more creative on poetry and short-story activities. These studies of children's perceptions of their classroom climate indicate strong links between children's origin orientation, self-determination, intrinsic motivation, and creative performance.

Although much research has identified extrinsic factors that undermine intrinsic motivation, there is some research with children that suggests that emphasizing intrinsic motives can shield one from the negative influences of extrinsic constraint. In a study done with third- and fourth-grade school children (Hennessey, Amabile, & Martinage, 1989), children in the intrinsic motivation training group watched a videotape of other children expressing intrinsic interest in school. The training tape focused on two factors. The first factor was the emphasis on the enjoyable aspects of learning. For example, one child described social studies as his most preferred activity out of all activities assigned by the teacher. He then explained why he enjoyed social studies. The second factor was an emphasis on the practice of cognitively distancing oneself from socially imposed constraints. For example, the adult in the tape asked the children if they think much about getting good grades and rewards from parents. The children on the tape then noted that it was, indeed, nice to get good grades, but that it was more important to learn for the sake of learning. Children in this study's control group watched a videotape of the same two children discussing their favorite foods, rock groups, and other nonacademic pursuits. Two days after the training, all children took Harter's (1981) assessment of intrinsic motivation. In addition, some children were offered a reward to engage in a storytelling activity and others engaged in the activity without reward. The intrinsic motivation training children were significantly more creative on the storytelling task and more intrinsically motivated on Harter's measure than those children who did not view this tape. Moreover, the trained children appeared to be immunized against the negative effects of constraint. Although children in the control group exhibited decreased creativity under expected reward, there was no such decrement in the trained children. In fact, their creativity was higher in the reward condition—a complete reversal of the usual undermining effect.

On the possibility that the results from this study might have been skewed by the fact that the tapes in the control condition were more enjoyable or "fun" than those in the intrinsic motivation training condition, a conceptual replication was done (Hennessey & Zbikowski, 1993). Once again, there was a main effect of training, with children exposed to the intrinsic motivation training and offered a reward producing the most creative stories. Their creativity, however, was only significantly different from the no training/reward group. Although no support was provided for the additive effect of reward and training, the results from both of these studies provide clear evidence that without training, salient external reward can undermine creativity.

IMPLICATIONS FOR CREATIVITY IN THE CLASSROOM

The discussion of implications for the classroom begins with an anecdote that raises important issues concerning motivation in the school setting. It begins with a simple complaint:

> "Why is everything we read in school so boring?" a young student asked her father.
>
> "What do you mean, boring?" he replied. "What do you read that is so boring? Everything that you read in school," he commented, "people have been reading those works for centuries. Do you really think they would last that long if they were boring?"
>
> The student nodded "yes," but then was left with a puzzle. Why would the works of Shakespeare, Chaucer, and others have lasted centuries if they were boring? What made the literature read in school different from that read for pleasure? Then the student recalled what her father had said several years prior when a grade school teacher called to inform her parents the student was reading Richard Wright's autobiography, Black Boy, during a free-reading period: "Well I don't think it's right for someone your age to be reading this," the father responded. "but I can't tell you what you can and cannot read; nobody can do that."
>
> But isn't that precisely what happens in school. . . . They tell one what one has to read? Could it be that simple, that merely the fact of having to read as an assignment made it so difficult to enjoy what was read?
>
> To find out, that summer the student obtained a list of all the books to be read the following year in her English class and decided to read them during the summer at leisure rather than as an assignment. The student found enjoyable all of the works that older students had warned her were tedious and boring. Her father was right. These were not boring books. She also realized that these books and others were assigned not so that the teacher could fulfill his or her role as teacher by assigning the standard reading lists, but instead because

they were books the teachers likely thought were interesting and wanted to share with the students. The books and short stories read in subsequent years were no longer assignments, but instead opportunities to read what was of interest to her teachers and an opportunity to try to figure out why the teacher found such books and short stories interesting. She also realized that it is true, nobody can tell you what to read. They can make suggestions, but the decision to read or not to read still remains with the individual.

This example illustrates not that there was something special about the school this student attended that resulted in positive attitudes toward school, nor that teachers gave the student total choice of what to read and when to read it. Instead, this example illustrates that this student was fortunate to develop, with the help of parents, a tool for learning in any educational system. That tool is the ability to find and emphasize the intrinsic reasons for learning.

Although psychological constructs such as the salience of rewards, the controlling nature of rewards, or the informational nature of rewards, appear clear in their effects on intrinsic motivation and creativity, their application to the classroom is not entirely clear. Although many researchers in education identify factors such as control (Mitchell, 1968), competition (Anderson & Walberg, 1974; Ellett & Walberg, 1979), and evaluations and expectations (Brookover & Lezotte, 1979) as negatively affecting school climate, only recently has there been a move toward considering these factors within the framework of effects on children's intrinsic motivation (e.g., Middleton, 1995).

Much evidence has accumulated regarding the multitude of factors that undermine intrinsic motivation and creativity. Such evidence should help in understanding how to avoid these negative consequences. Certainly, no one at this point in time is capable of controlling all factors so that only those conducive to intrinsic motivation are allowed to operate. Given all of the described negative effects of controlling extrinsic motivation, how does one enhance intrinsic motivation and nurture creativity in the classroom?

Some researchers have examined the elements of the school setting that should enhance intrinsic motivation in the classroom. This research is not framed directly in terms of the social psychological research on intrinsic motivation; but, the concepts examined are similar. Much of this research focuses on relieving the student of externally imposed constraints, something that was a primary aim of open classrooms in the 1960s (Silberman, 1970). Although some have suggested that the distinction between the effects of open and traditional classrooms is not clear (Horwitz, 1979; Ramey & Piper, 1974), there is empirical evidence that students in open classrooms tend to score higher on standard tests of creativity (e.g., Goyal, 1973; Haddon & Lytton, 1968, 1971; Sullivan, 1974). Considering that open classrooms were designed to decrease the salience of teacher-initiated constraints on performance, such as grading or authoritative teaching, and emphasized individualized performance on tasks, it follows that intrinsic motivation should have been enhanced. It is, therefore, possible that increased intrinsic motivation in the open classroom might account for the better performance on creativity tests of students in the open classroom as compared to students in traditional classrooms. Another possible explanation for better creative performance of students in open classrooms is that more of the activities in an open classroom, such as creative writing, are similar to those used on standard tests of creativity (Amabile, 1983a).

The success of the open classroom was encouraging. One must, however, recognize that instructors entering into an open classroom situation likely viewed the program as directly opposed to the traditional classroom: instructors were likely to believe that the traditional classroom constrains the student and inhibits the development of intrinsic pursuits, whereas the new program would succeed in nurturing the development of interest in learning. This is likely also true of novel educational programs today, such as charter schools. Perhaps it was not the simple removal of extrinsic constraints that increased intrinsic motivation in the open classroom, but instead the presence of teachers entering the classroom with the specific desire to recognize and nurture intrinsic interests. It is possible that, were this desire fostered in all teachers, regardless of the ecological structure of the classroom, less of a gap between traditional and open (or other novel) classrooms would be observed.

Teacher Effects on Intrinsic Motivation and Creativity

> Just so the muse. She first makes man inspired, and then through these inspired ones others share in the enthusiasm, and a chain is formed, for the epic poets, all the good ones, have their excellence, not from art, but are inspired, possessed, and thus they utter all these admirable poems. So is it also with the good lyric poets. (Plato, The Ion)

Here, Plato suggests that creative writing in poetry evolves from listening to, being inspired by other creative poets. Can teachers provide such inspiration to their students?

There is evidence that teachers' attitudes, perceptions, beliefs, and behaviors can have an important impact on children's intrinsic motivation and creativity. The teacher can serve as an important model of intrinsic motivation. The students of teachers who believe in the importance of student autonomy tend to be curious, prefer challenging work, and desire to master work independently (Deci, Nezlek, & Sheinman, 1981). When children perceive that their teachers are intrinsically motivated toward work, the children themselves are more intrinsically motivated and perceive themselves as more competent (Deci et al., 1981). In addition, children who perceive greater warmth in their teachers appear to be more intrinsically motivated and more creative than children who do not perceive their teachers to be very warm (Picariello, 1992; Ryan & Grolnik, 1986). In a field study that examined the effects of controlling teaching strategies on children's learning (Flink, Boggiano, & Barrett, 1990), some elementary school teachers were pressured to optimize their students' performance on puzzle tasks (an induced extrinsic motivational orientation), and other teachers were oriented toward helping their students learn how to solve the puzzles (an induced intrinsic motivational orientation). When the children were tested on the tasks, the children who had been taught by the nonpressured teachers significantly outperformed the children taught by the pressured teachers. In addition, research has uncovered several personality traits of teachers whose students showed the greatest increases in creativity: likable, interested in children, satisfied, enthusiastic, courteous, and professional (Rosenthal, Baratz, & Hall, 1974). In essence, the teacher is the link to the muse's chain. Teachers not only impart knowledge, but also, through their own abilities and beliefs, can inspire others.

The stereotype of the traditional classroom includes several teacher induced constraints on performance. The teacher's evaluation might appear as all important in achieving grades. The teacher might appear to restrict the choice of material to be studied. The teacher might even appear to control whether or not the students are allowed to verbally express their inspirations while in the classroom. Notice, however, that these constraints are not the result of the structure of the classroom, but rather, a result of the perceived attitudes and practices of the teacher as head of the classroom. The transformation of many classrooms in the 1970s from traditional to open was an attempt to minimize the salience of extrinsic constraints on learning. The nurturance of intrinsic motivation, however, involves not just the minimization of extrinsic constraints by removing them from the school context, but more so, the development of intrinsic role models such as teachers with the desire to inspire—teachers who themselves are intrinsically motivated and who recognize how to maintain intrinsic motivation.

> Teaching is not like inducing a chemical reaction; it is much more like painting a picture or making a piece of music, or on a lower level like planting a garden or writing a friendly letter. You must throw your heart into it, you must realize that it cannot all be done by formulas, or you will spoil your work, and your pupils, and yourself. (Highet, 1958, p. viii)

Highet described four qualities of good teachers—teachers who inspire. First and foremost, they must know and like the subject. They must know the subject beyond what is in the textbook and what will appear on the final exam; they must constantly keep up on the field through a love of the subject. Second, they must like the students. Third, they "should know much else" (p. 43); good teachers show that interest and knowledge in the subject has not blinded awareness of other areas of study or aspects of the world, but instead has increased interest in other domains. And, finally, they must have a sense of humor that links them to the student through enjoyment. Research on the possibilities of modeling effects on creativity suggests that teachers must enjoy their work if creativity is to be nurtured in the classroom. Unfortunately, the current environment in which many teachers train and work too often appears to undermine their intrinsic motivation.

To better understand the relation of intrinsic motivation to aspects of classroom interaction, several steps must be taken. First, researchers must analyze the classroom in terms of the incentives for both social and academic behavior. Jackson's (1968) statement that the inducements employed in the classroom are complex is likely true. However, this should present a challenge rather than a blockade to those interested in understanding the role of intrinsic motivation in the classroom. As intrinsic motivation research has demonstrated, incentives other than tangible prizes have been shown to undermine intrinsic motivation. Researchers in education also need to consider the extent to which factors such as surveillance, time pressure, competition, and evaluation affect intrinsic motivation in the classroom.

Once the types of incentives occurring in the classroom have been identified, researchers must then examine the meanings teachers and students attach to various forms of inducements. Only by identifying the intrinsic and extrinsic repertoires of the teacher, the student, and the classroom in general, can problems be rectified. For example, it is likely that grades the teacher gives in an effort to provide information regarding a student's competence are perceived by many students as an attempt to control their behavior. By identifying such discrepancies, teachers might better emphasize the true nature of grades in terms of their informational aspect rather than the controlling aspect, instead of presuming that students understand the informational aspects of grades.

Finally, researchers should also search for patterns of inducements given in the classroom and how these patterns relate to developmental changes in intrinsic and extrinsic motivation. For example, nearly all first graders appear to be intrinsically motivated. Why do they change? By identifying the patterns of inducements used in the classroom, their meanings, and their effects on intrinsic motivation, a developmental sequence of school motivation might be proposed. A first stage, evident in most first graders, might be intrinsic motivation, characterized by happiness, curiosity, and interest in learning. A second stage in the development of school motivation might consist of becoming increasingly aware of the rules of the classroom situation. It is likely that during this second stage a conflict might arise between pursuing one's own interests in learning and understanding and obeying the rules that govern this pursuit. A third stage might be characterized by the resolution of the conflict presented at the second stage. The conflict might be resolved with either a predominantly proschool or predominantly antischool sentiment. It is likely that for many children as they enter the second stage the classroom rules are novel, and, therefore, relatively salient. This would result in many perceiving the rules that govern the pursuit of knowledge as controlling and as undermining their intrinsic interest. As suggested by Fazio (1981) and Hennessey et al. (1989), it is possible that if intrinsic interest is emphasized above rule awareness—while the importance of the rules to one's pursuit of knowledge is minimized—the negative outcomes of the third stage could be avoided, thus fostering a predominantly proschool sentiment.

Perhaps some children are able to cognitively distance themselves from constraints on learning by maintaining a personal emphasis on intrinsic interests. However, given that the majority of students appear to exhibit undermined intrinsic interest, it is likely that few children are equipped with this tool. It is necessary, therefore, that teachers recognize the possible undermining influences of the extrinsic motives they introduce to the learning situation. As suggested by the intrinsic motivation training study (Hennessey et al., 1989), teachers might boost intrinsic motivation and creativity by emphasizing learning for enjoyment despite the rules that govern the process, rather than by removing all rules that govern the process.

The evidence suggests a strong link between the salience of constraints in the classroom and subsequent interest and performance in school. Although it is recognized that individual differences might mediate the effects of situational constraints on intrinsic motivation, all of the effects discussed here occurred despite individual differences. It is also recognized that some tasks, by nature, simply might not be enjoyable. The suggestion is not that all tasks can be made enjoyable through an emphasis on intrinsic motivation. What is of importance in terms of learning, based on the arguments presented here, is that individuals involved in the classroom should be aware of the undermining influences of situational constraints on activities that are initially intrinsically motivated. There are few things more unfortunate than a child initially interested in learning who turns away from the joy of learning because of salient constraints in the classroom.

Given this, there are two possible solutions to the problem of how to maintain intrinsic motivation and creativity in the classroom. One can attempt to reduce the constraints in the school environment, as was done in open classroom situations, and hope that children's interests can withstand the constraints of the rest of society. Or, one can teach children to deal effectively with the constraints as they exist, emphasizing the maintenance of intrinsic motivation in spite of the external constraints that abound.

To exhibit the need for understanding the factors associated with intrinsic motivation and creativity in the classroom, the discussion of implications for the classroom will end as it began, with a personal anecdote:

While teaching math in a local high school, I overheard a teacher comment on a recent award she had received for excellence in teaching. The award was prescribed by the superintendent of schools as a way to motivate teachers, rewarding good performance and providing a role model for other teachers. This reward recipient was enraged at having received the award and intended to write a letter to the superintendent to inform him of her fury. She noted to her lunchroom colleagues that not only did the award set her on a pedestal where she did not belong—since all other teachers in the school system are equally qualified and motivated—but also it suggested that she teaches for the purposes of receiving external rewards. She adamantly professed that she taught for the pleasure she received and not for such external rewards. It sounded as though she felt the award might undermine teachers' intrinsic motivation to teach. I was impressed.

Several days after I overheard this conversation, I approached her regarding a student in her special needs program who was in the computer class I was teaching. I had taken over the course mid-way through the year and this student was already failing at this point. The student refused to participate in any of the class activities. I asked this teacher about this student's disability and what could be done to eradicate his habit of literally doing nothing during class. She reported that his disability was simply that he was disruptive and further commented, "It is a little unrealistic of you to expect him to do anything in class. He's failing so badly that no matter what he does in your class he still will not be able to pass!"

This teacher whom I thought understood the negative effects associated with the perception of one's work as motivated by an external reward, appeared to allow such an instrumentality to govern the work of her students. Unenthusiastic about the prospect of having "dead-weight" in my class, I explained to the student that although it was unlikely he would be able to pass the course after his poor showing in the first half of the semester, there was nothing to stop him from taking the opportunity to learn as much as he could from me simply for the sake of knowing about computers. He participated from that day on.

REFERENCES

Amabile, T. M. (1979). Effects of external evaluation on artistic creativity. *Journal of Personality and Social Psychology, 37*, 221-233.

Amabile, T. M. (1982). Children's artistic creativity: Detrimental effects of competition in a field setting. *Personality and Social Psychology Bulletin, 8*, 573-578.

Amabile, T. M. (1983a). *The social psychology of creativity.* New York: Springer-Verlag.

Amabile, T. M. (1983b). The social psychology of creativity: A componential conceptualization. *Journal of Personality and Social Psychology, 45*, 357-376.

Amabile, T. M. (1985). Motivation and creativity: Effects of motivational orientation on creative writers. *Journal of Personality and Social Psychology, 48*, 393-399.

Amabile, T. M. (1987). The motivation to be creative. In S. Isaksen (Ed.), *Frontiers in creativity research: Beyond the basics* (pp. 223-254). Buffalo, NY: Bearly Limited.

Amabile, T. M. (1993). Motivational synergy: Toward new conceptualizations of intrinsic and extrinsic motivation in the workplace. *Human Resource Management Review, 3*, 185-201.

Amabile, T. M. (1996). *Creativity in context.* Boulder, CO: Westview Press.

Amabile, T. M., DeJong, W., & Lepper, M. R. (1976). Effects of externally imposed deadlines on subsequent intrinsic motivation. *Journal of Personality and Social Psychology, 34*, 92-98.

Amabile, T. M., & Gitomer, J. (1984). Children's artistic creativity: Effects of choice in task materials. *Personality and Social Psychology Bulletin, 10*, 209-215.

Amabile, T. M., Goldfarb, P., & Brackfield, S. C. (1990). Social influences on creativity: Evaluation, coaction, and surveillance. *Creativity Research Journal, 3*, 6-21.

Amabile, T. M., & Gryskiewicz, N. (1989). The creative environment scales: The work environment inventory. *Creativity Research Journal, 2*, 231-254.

Amabile, T. M., & Gryskiewicz, S. S. (1987). *Creativity in the R & D laboratory* (Tech. Rep. No. 30). Greensboro, NC: Center for Creative Leadership.

Amabile, T. M., Hennessey, B. A., & Grossman, B. S. (1986). Social influences on creativity: The effects of contracted-for reward. *Journal of Personality and Social Psychology, 50*, 14-23.

Anderson, G. J., & Walberg, H. J. (1974). Learning environments. In H. J. Walberg (Ed.), *Evaluating educational performance* (pp. 81-99). Berkeley, CA: McCutchan.

Bem, D. J. (1972). Self-perception theory. In L. Berkowitz (Ed.), *Advances in experimental social psychology* (Vol. 6, pp. 2-62). New York: Academic Press.

Berglas, S., Amabile, T. M., & Handel, M. (1981). *Effects of evaluation on children's artistic creativity.* Unpublished manuscript, Brandeis University, Waltham, MA.

Brookover, W. B., & Lezotte, L. W. (1979, May). *Changes in school characteristics coincident with changes in student achievement* (Occasional Paper No. 17). Michigan State University, Institute for Research on Teaching, East Lansing, MI.

Cheek, J. M., & Stahl, S. (1986). Shyness and verbal creativity. *Journal of Research in Personality, 20,* 51-61.

Conti, R., & Amabile, T. M. (1995, May). *Problem solving among computer science students: The effects of skill, evaluation expectation, and personality on solution quality.* Paper presented at the annual meeting of the Eastern Psychological Association, Boston, MA.

Conti, R., Amabile, T. M., & Pollack, S. (1995). The positive impact of creative activity: Effects of creative task engagement and motivational focus on college students' learning. *Personality and Social Psychology Bulletin, 21,* 1107-1116.

DeCharms, R. (1968). *Personal causation: The internal affective determinants of behavior.* New York: Academic Press.

DeCharms, R. (1976). *Enhancing motivation: Change in the classroom.* New York: Irvington.

Deci, E. L. (1971). Effects of externally mediated rewards on intrinsic motivation. *Journal of Personality and Social Psychology, 18,* 105-115.

Deci, E. L. (1972). Effects of contingent and non-contingent rewards and controls on intrinsic motivation. *Organizational Behavior and Human Performance, 8,* 217-229.

Deci, E. L. (1975). *Intrinsic motivation.* New York: Plenum.

Deci, E. L., Cascio, W.F., & Krussell, J. (1973, May). *Sex differences, verbal reinforcement, and intrinsic motivation.* Paper presented at the meeting of the Eastern Psychological Association, Washington, DC.

Deci, E. L., Nezlek, J., & Sheinman, L. (1981). Characteristics of the rewarder and intrinsic motivation of the rewardee. *Journal of Personality and Social Psychology, 40,* 1-10.

Deci, E. L., & Ryan, R. M. (1980). The empirical exploration of intrinsic motivational processes. In L. Berkowitz (Ed.), *Advances in experimental social psychology* (pp. 40-80). New York: Academic Press.

Deci, E. L., & Ryan, R. M. (1985). *Intrinsic motivation and self-determination in human behavior.* New York: Plenum Press.

Duncker, K. (1945). On problem solving. *Psychological Monographs, 58*(270).

Ellett, C. D., & Walberg, H. J. (1979). Principals' competency, environment, and outcomes. In H. J. Walberg (Ed.), *Educational environments and effects* (pp. 140-164). Berkeley, CA: McCutchan.

Epstein, J. L., & McPartland, J. M. (1976). The concept and measurement of the quality of school life. *American Educational Research Journal, 13,* 15-30.

Fazio, R. H. (1981). On the self-perception explanation of the overjustification effect: The role of the salience of initial attitude. *Journal of Experimental Social Psychology, 17,* 417-426.

Flink, C., Boggiano, A. K., & Barrett, M. (1990). Controlling teaching strategies: Undermining children's self-determination and performance. *Journal of Personality and Social Psychology, 59,* 916-924.

Goyal, R. P. (1973). Creativity and school climate: An exploratory study. *Journal of Psychological Researches, 17,* 77-80.

Haddon, F. A., & Lytton, H. (1968). Teaching approach and the development of divergent thinking abilities in primary schools. *British Journal of Educational Psychology, 38,* 171-180.

Haddon, F. A., & Lytton, H. (1971). Primary education and divergent thinking abilities: Four years on. *British Journal of Educational Psychology, 41,* 136-147.

Harter, S. (1978). Effectance motivation reconsidered: Toward a developmental model. *Human Development, 21,* 34-64.

Harter, S. (1981). A new self-report scale of intrinsic versus extrinsic orientation in the classroom: Motivational and informational components. *Developmental Psychology, 17,* 300-312.

Hatfield, W. W. (Chairman). (1935). *An experience curriculum in English: A report of the curriculum commission of the National Council of Teachers of English* (English Monograph No. 4). New York: D. Appleton-Century.

Heider, F. (1958). *The psychology of interpersonal relations.* New York: Wiley.

Hennessey, B. A. (1989). The effect of extrinsic constraints on children's creativity while using a computer. *Creativity Research Journal, 2,* 151-168.

Hennessey, B. A., & Zbikowski, S. (1993). Immunizing children against the negative effects of reward: A further examination of intrinsic motivation training techniques. *Creativity Research Journal, 6,* 297-308.

Hennessey, B. A., Amabile, T. M., & Martinage, M. (1989). Immunizing children against the negative effects of reward. *Contemporary Educational Psychology, 14,* 212-227.

Highet, G. (1958). *The art of teaching.* New York: Vintage Books.

Hill, K. G., Amabile, T. M., Coon, H. M., & Whitney, D. (1994). *Testing the componential model of creativity.* Unpublished manuscript, Brandeis University, Waltham, MA.

Horwitz, R. A. (1979). Psychological effects of the open classroom. *Review of Educational Research, 49,* 71-85.

Jackson, P. W. (1968). *Life in classrooms.* New York: Holt, Rinehart & Winston.

Kuhn, T. S. (1970). *The structure of scientific revolutions.* Chicago: University of Chicago Press.

Lepper, M. R., & Greene, D. (1975). Turning play into work: Effects of adult surveillance and extrinsic rewards on children's intrinsic motivation. *Journal of Personality and Social Psychology, 31,* 479-486.

Lepper, M. R., & Greene, D. (1978). Overjustification research and beyond: Toward a means-end analysis of intrinsic and extrinsic motivation. In M. Lepper & D. Greene (Eds.), *The hidden costs of reward* (pp. 109-148). Hillsdale, NJ: Lawrence Erlbaum Associates.

Lepper, M. R., Greene, D., & Nisbett, R. E. (1973). Undermining children's intrinsic interest with extrinsic rewards: A test of the "overjustification" hypothesis. *Journal of Personality and Social Psychology, 23,* 129-137.

Luchins, A. (1942). Mechanization in problem solving: The effect of Einstellung. *Psychological Monographs, 54*(6, Whole No. 248).

Middleton, J. A. (1995). A study of intrinsic motivation in the mathematics classroom: A personal constructs approach. *Journal for Research in Mathematics Education, 26,* 254-279.

Mitchell, J. V., Jr. (1968). Dimensionality and differences in the environmental press of high schools. *American Educational Research Journal, 5,* 513-530.

Newell, A., Shaw, J., & Simon, H. (1962). The processes of creative thinking. In H. Gruber, G. Terrell, & M. Wertheimer (Eds.), *Contemporary approaches to creative thinking* (pp. 63-119). New York: Atherton Press.

Picariello, M. L. (1991, May). *The effects of motivational orientation on children's creativity.* Research presented at the meeting of the Eastern Psychological Association, Boston, MA.

Picariello, M. L. (1992, May). *The effects of motivational orientation on children's creativity.* Paper presented at the meeting of the Eastern Psychological Association, Boston, MA.

Pittman, T. S., Davey, M. E., Alafat, K. A., Wetherill, K. V., & Kramer, N. A. (1980). Informational versus controlling verbal rewards. *Personality and Social Psychology Bulletin, 3,* 280-283.

Pollak, S. (1992). *The effects of motivational orientation and constraint on the creativity of the artist.* Unpublished manuscript, Brandeis University, Waltham, MA.

Ramey, C. T., & Piper, V. (1974). Creativity in open and traditional classrooms. *Child Development, 45,* 557-560.

Rosenthal, R., Baratz, S., & Hall, C. M. 1974). Teacher behavior, teacher expectations, and gains in pupils' rated creativity. *Journal of Genetic Psychology, 124,* 115-121.

Ross, M. (1975). Salience of reward and intrinsic motivation. Journal of *Personality and Social Psychology, 32,* 245-254.

Ryan, R. M. (1982). Control and information in the intrapersonal sphere: An extension of cognitive evaluation theory. *Journal of Personality and Social Psychology, 43,* 450-461.

Ryan, R. M., & Grolnick, W. S. (1986). Origins and pawns in the classroom: Self-reported and projective assessments of individual differences in children's perceptions. *Journal of Personality and Social Psychology, 50,* 550-558.

Silberman, C. E. (1970). *Crisis in the classroom: The remaking of American education.* New York: Random House.

Simonton, D. K. (1977). Eminence, creativity, and geographic marginality: A recursive structural equation model. *Journal of Personality and Social Psychology, 35,* 805-816.

Simonton, D. K. (1988). Age and outstanding achievement: What do we know after a century of research? *Psychological Bulletin, 104,* 251-267.

Skinner, B. F. (1938). *The behavior of organisms.* New York: Appleton-Century-Crofts.

Sullivan, J. (1974). Open-traditional—what is the difference? *Elementary School Journal, 74,* 493-500.

Swann, W. B., Jr,. & Pittman, T. S. (1977). Initiating play activity of children: The moderating influence of verbal cues on intrinsic motivation. *Child Development, 48,* 1128-1132.

White, R. W. (1959). Motivation reconsidered: The concept of competence. *Psychological Review, 66,* 297-333.

Williams, T., & Batten, M. (1981). *The quality of school life. ACER Research Monograph No. 12.* Hawthorne, Victoria: Australian Council for Educational Research.

Zuckerman, M., Porac, J., Lathin, D., Smith, R., & Deci, E. L. (1978). On the importance of self-determination for intrinsically motivated behavior. *Personality and Social Psychology Bulletin, 4,* 443-446.

10

Creativity and Whole Language

Michael L. Shaw
St. Thomas Aquinas College

There was a child went forth every day
And the first object he look'd upon, that object he became;
And that object became part of him for the day,
or a certain part of the day, or for many years,
or stretching cycles of years.
  —Walt Whitman (1945, p. 168)

I love everything you do with me and the class.
You're very fun to do things with and have fun with.
You made me believe in myself.
  —Kayla, Grade 4

Research on creativity has been approached from a variety of angles (Hennessey & Amabile, 1988), typically focusing on one or more of the four elements that have been identified with the creative experience: personality, process, product, and/or environment. Early studies highlighted traits of the creative individual by emphasizing personal characteristics (Barron, 1955; Guilford, 1976; MacKinnon, 1970; Roe, 1970) and the importance of heredity (Galton, 1976; Terman, 1970). More recent work has centered on the importance of establishing social contexts that promote intrinsic motivation to learn (Amabile, 1983, 1989; Hennessey & Amabile, 1988) and the creative development of an individual within a given field or culture (Csikszentmihalyi, 1988; Gruber & Davis, 1988; John-Steiner, 1992). Regardless of orientation, many theorists are in general agreement that creativity does not reside in a vacuum; creativity exists as a social process that links the self, which generates new and productive ideas, to the world outside of the self. According to John-Steiner (1985), creativity requires "an intense awareness of one's active inner life combined with sensitivity to the external world" (p. 220).

At the beginning of the 21st century, educators (Brown, 1991; Cambourne, 1993; Fiske, 1991; Harste, 1994; Resnick & Klopfer, 1989), futurists (Toffler, 1990), and even government officials (Reich, 1991), are similarly conceptualizing a vision of literacy as a social process that links an individual to the external world by valuing the ability to construct new and productive ideas. In language that is strikingly similar to the language of creativity, Cambourne (1993) stated that 21st century literacy will enable individuals to exercise creative, critical control over their environments. Similarly, Brown (1991) posed a literacy of thoughtfulness for the 21st century that is not just a set of skills useful for understanding the works and ideas of previous generations; it is a way of creating, here and now, the meanings by which individuals shape their lives and plan their futures. Brown further characterized this new vision of literacy as an ability to conceptualize issues, think critically, take risks, solve problems, and reflect on one's thinking. For Toffler (1990), literate individuals in the 21st century will need to be able to create new networks of knowledge that utilize new languages, images, and relationships. Reich (1991) emphasized the importance of being able to engage in *symbolic analysis* that enables the individual to define problems, assimilate data, make deductive and inductive leaps, and conceptualize solutions.

In every case, as we redefine the kinds of knowledge and skills necessary for individuals to reach their full human potential in the 21st century, we see that literacy and creativity go hand in hand as two interconnected strands of lifelong personal growth and development toward what Maslow (1968) characterized as *self-actualization*. The qualities of thinking or performance that are embedded in literacy are the same qualities of thinking or performance that are embedded in creativity. Consequently, whereas historically the mission of the public schools in the United States has been to assure the literate development of students (Carnegie Forum on Education and the Economy, 1986; Cremin, 1977; Goodlad, 1984), the new demands for achieving success in the world of the future require teachers to also recognize that they must assure the full creative development of students. For me, the place where literacy and creativity meet is whole language.

WHOLE LANGUAGE: THE PLACE WHERE LITERACY AND CREATIVITY MEET

Whole language is a philosophy, or belief system, that builds on the natural way people learn in order to help each child realize his or her full literate and creative potential. Whole language is not a method of instruction, nor can it be represented by a set of lesson plans or marketed as a series of activities. Rather, whole language represents a belief that learning is a lifelong holistic mental process of constructing new understandings (Brause, 1992) that begins at birth within the supportive culture of the primary caregiver, who immerses the learner in authentic, meaningful language-based interactions and experiences (G. Wells, 1986). This dialectical relationship between the individual and his or her culture creates a social relationship that intrinsically motivates the learner to develop new insight, knowledge, understanding, performance skill, and appreciation for the world of possibility being opened.

Whole language creates conditions that support intrinsic motivation to learn by encouraging children to become risk takers, decision makers, and creators of their own learning (K. Goodman, 1986; Harste & Short, 1995; Mills & Clyde, 1990; Weaver, 1990). According to Edelsky, Altwerger, and Flores (1991), whole language can be represented as a *professional theory* that weaves together "a theoretical view of language, language learning, and learning into a particular stance on education" (p. 7) which is committed to the full realization of literacy through the authentic use of language within a natural environment. Weaver (1990) called whole language an *authentic literacy* philosophy that "promotes whole learning throughout students' whole lives" (p. 6). K. Goodman (1986) stated, "Whole language builds around whole learners learning whole language in whole situations" (p. 40). In essence, whole language can be thought of as the *mindset* the teacher brings to the total educational experience that honors the literate and creative potential of each child.

Theoretical Foundations of Whole Language

Whole language is based in large part on Piaget's (1977) theory of learning as a developmentally constructed process, Vygotsky's (1987) theory of learning as a socioculturally constructed process, and Dewey's (1938) theory of learning as meaningful engagements with direct experiences. Although there are differences among the theorists, they share the belief that learning is a lifelong constructed process to realize full human potential.

The first building block of whole language derives from Piaget, who believed that learning was a developmentally constructed process in which the learner forms new knowledge by constructing abstractions that lead to new understandings (London, 1988). As the learner acts on the world, she or he creates meaning from experience by constructing mental maps, or schemata (Rumelhart, 1980), that are based on prior experience. In new situations, the learner engages in a search for coherence (Ferreiro, 1990) that leads to the development of new interpretation systems and novel ways of looking at phenomena. For Piaget, as with many creativity theorists, learning is the growth that takes place as the learner continually reformulates existing knowledge into new frameworks.

The second building block of whole language derives from Vygotsky (1987), who emphasized a sociocultural, dialogic conceptualization of learning. For Vygotsky, learning is socially constructed within a supportive culture as a transaction between a more knowledgeable teacher and a less knowledgeable learner. This creates a mentor-apprentice relationship in which the more knowledgeable teacher guides the less knowledgeable learner to take thoughtful risks in order to move from a level of greater dependence to a level of greater independence. For Vygotsky, the process of learning takes place within the learner's zone of proximal development, which he defined as "the difference between the [learner's] actual level of development and the level of performance that he achieves in collaboration with the [teacher]" (p. 209). This process of learning has been described as *scaffolding* (Bruner, 1985) because the teacher provides essential support, guidance, and assistance to help the learner move to greater levels of productive accomplishment. Vygotsky believed that learning is a socially mediated process that begins first on the interpsychological plane and then proceeds to the intrapsychological plane as new knowledge becomes internalized by the learner (Freeman, 1992). For Vygotsky, as with many creativity theorists, learning centers on supported risk-taking that encourages the learner to generate new and productive ideas.

The third building block of whole language derives from Dewey (1938, 1956) who, as a leader of the Progressive Education movement, initiated child-centered schools that emphasized a curriculum of discovery in which learners were encouraged by teachers to try out ideas and learn from their results (Edelsky et al., 1991). For Dewey, learning centered on meaningful, direct personal experience that took place within a supportive democratic community. Dewey, like many creativity theorists, believed that learning is an intrinsically motivated process of creating that transforms individuals and, ultimately, prepares them to reshape the culture.

Thus, although whole language is sometimes stereotyped as meaning a literature-based approach to reading and process writing, this characterization is short-sighted and incomplete because it does not capture the spirit that drives whole-language philosophy. Whole language represents a paradigm for learning that is based on the way human beings holistically use language to construct knowledge within a supportive social context in order to reach full literate and creative potential. Whole language honors human possibility by recognizing that literacy, like creativity, is more than being able to read a novel, write a term paper, or compute a mathematical problem; it is the empowerment one has to transform the world (Shannon, 1990). Whole language views literacy, like creativity, as liberating (Freire & Macedo, 1987). Smith (1989) described *literacy* as the power that "can raise consciousness and provide a means to fulfill this consciousness" (p. 357). Whole language values the whole learner and celebrates the creativity that is realized in a literate existence.

The Whole-Language Classroom Environment: Supporting the Creative Process

Philosopher, aestheticist, and educator Maxine Greene (1988) powerfully described the type of classroom culture that motivates the creative spirit when she urged the teacher to free the spirit of imagination and take a proactive role to open up the classroom:

> All sorts of things seem possible; things can be different from "the way they are." . . . A space of freedom may open up; the individual, conscious of others around, may experience (unexpectedly, perhaps) a power to choose, to move towards what is not yet. . . . (To learn) is to become different, to see more to gain a new perspective. It is to choose against things as they are. (pp. 48-49)

Whole-language classrooms bring Greene's vision to life by creating a physical, social, and intellectual environment that supports holistic, meaningful, authentic, collaborative, creative learning experiences. Although each whole-language classroom environment is unique, and great variety exists, these classrooms can be described as being *literate* because they provide rich demonstrations of literacy; *trusting* because they are ridicule-free, content-rich, and encourage interdependencies (Brause, 1985); and *creative* because they support intrinsic motivation to learn, individual expression, and divergent thinking.

The cornerstone of the whole-language classroom environment is the commitment to community in which all members believe in one another, trust each other, support each other, and respect individual differences (Hansen, 1987). In a whole-language classroom community, everyone has something to contribute, diversity is celebrated, and uniqueness is honored. Everyone is a learner and everyone is a teacher. There is an honesty and openness that support and encourage individual initiative, risk-taking, and creative expression. Hansen (1987) stated, "The community helps (the learners) realize that they know more than they think they do and gives them the confidence to move ahead more quickly" (p. 64). Routman (1988) noted that in a whole-language classroom, "Trust, respect, support, and high expectations must be generously and genuinely present for all children" (p. 29). This type of classroom environment creates a culture that supports creative development because it is empowering, encourages deep thinking, and honors human possibility (Tardif & Sternberg, 1988).

In whole-language classrooms, this sense of community shapes the physical environment so that it becomes friendlier and more supportive of the creative process. The traditional rows of desks frequently shift into clusters to facilitate conversation and collaboration. There is the emergence of learning centers, including computers, around the periphery of the room that encourage students to independently explore topics of interest in all curriculum areas. Open spaces, frequently carpeted, grow where small groups can informally meet and share ideas. In many whole-language classrooms, cozy easy chairs, beanbag chairs, or even couches serve to overcome the institutional sterility of traditional classrooms. Steadily, the walls begin to sing with a rich variety of environmental support for the process of learning: student work (both in-progress and completed) that learners choose to display; large copies of favorite poems; student-created murals, charts, graphs, and maps; prompts to stimulate reflective thinking (e.g., "Don't be satisfied with your answer . . . explain your reasoning"); rich examples of creative accomplishment; and, perhaps, a message board where students are encouraged to correspond with each other and/or the teacher. Both teacher and learners are totally involved in building the physical setting and assume ownership over its design. Koepke (1991) highlighted this commitment to total involvement when she described the way one whole-language teacher approached setting up a classroom:

> One September, while the other teachers prepared their classrooms for the first day of school, Mary Kitagawa left hers totally unorganized: desks awry and shelves empty. Kitagawa wanted her classroom to be an unusual, dynamic, and stimulating environment where students share in the decision making, so she figured they might as well get involved immediately by designing the physical space. (p. 35)

In whole-language classrooms, this sense of community also shapes the instructional program that is organized to provide ongoing multiple engagements with literacy and creativity. The whole-language instructional program is frequently based on Cambourne's (1988) conditions for natural learning, a model he developed after extensive observation of young children successfully learning to be literate. Cambourne identified seven conditions that he believes must exist for successful learning to occur: immersion, demonstration, expectation, responsibility, use, approximation, and response. Thus, it is important for learners to spend large blocks of time involved with meaningful learning experiences across the curriculum because a disjointed schedule of separate and discrete lessons isolates experience and precludes integration of experience. Furthermore, it is essential for teachers to (a) serve as models by demonstrating the behaviors they want learners to emulate, (b) communicate the message that success is attainable, (c) establish high standards for performance, (d) provide many opportunities for learners to authentically apply new learning, (e) honor learner effort by treating errors as opportunities for new learning, and (f) provide specific feedback that celebrates accomplishment and identifies areas for needed learning.

Cambourne further noted that although these seven conditions for learning are necessary for successful results, they are not sufficient. The essential ingredient for successful literacy learning—and, I would add, creativity—is engagement. In order for a learner to succeed, he or she must totally engage with the learning process. For Cambourne, engagement centers on the learner's belief that participating in the learning process will (a) lead to success, mastery, and achievement; (b) further the purposes of the learner's life; and (c) support the risks associated with taking leaps of learning into the unknown. For Cambourne, like many other literacy and creativity theorists, it is the community of user experts that creates a culture that promotes learner engagement by establishing conditions that intrinsically motivate individuals to want to learn.

Whole-language classrooms typically include curriculum events that serve to bring Cambourne's conditions for learning to life. These curriculum events provide multiple opportunities for learners to explore the world of natural communication through a process of inquiry (Harste & Short, 1995) and frequently serve as classroom rituals, or symbolic transformations of experience (Langer, 1951) that affirm the existence of community and create a definition of what is valued (Peterson, 1992). A review of the literature (Butler, 1987; Cambourne, 1988; Cooper, 1993; Crafton, 1991; K. Goodman, 1986; Mooney, 1990; Routman, 1991) indicates that whole-language classrooms frequently include the following ongoing curriculum events:

Independent Reading. Independent reading, sometimes called Drop Everything and Read (DEAR) Time, Sustained Silent Reading (SSR), or Uninterrupted Sustained Silent Reading (USSR), gives learners and teacher the opportunity to extend knowledge, understanding, and appreciation by providing time and encouragement to independently read in self-selected texts (books, magazines, newspaper, etc.).

Guided Reading. Guided reading, also called reading workshop, has been characterized as the heart of the whole-language instructional program (Routman, 1991) because it is the time when the teacher guides students in the strategies and skills needed for successful reading. Guided reading frequently include *literature circles* (Harste & Short, 1995), where learners and teacher share understandings about texts and response journals, sometimes called *learning logs*, for students to respond to reading through reflective writing.

Reading Aloud. Reading aloud has been reported to be the single most important activity for building the knowledge required for success in reading (Anderson, Hiebert, Scott, & Wilkinson, 1985). In whole-language classrooms, reading aloud of a wide variety of texts by both teacher and students occurs on numerous occasions every day to celebrate literacy and creativity, expand knowledge, stimulate thinking, and explore ideas.

Shared Reading. Shared reading involves a collaborative effort where teacher and learners become co-readers by reading aloud the same text together, either simultaneously or alternatively. For younger children, shared reading frequently includes enlarged text from big books. For all students, shared reading frequently includes poems. Shared reading extends community by inviting all classroom participants to enthusiastically engage with a text in a risk-free setting.

Writing Workshop. Writing workshop gives students the opportunity to write on self-selected topics, either individually or in collaboration with other students. Using a process approach that supports student ownership of text (Atwell, 1987; Calkins, 1986; Graves, 1983), learners are encouraged to create original writing. The teacher typically initiates the writing workshop with a short lesson, also called a mini-lesson (Calkins, 1986), that focuses on essential understandings about writing, and then confers with students while they are engaged with their writing. Students are also encouraged to confer with each other in peer conferences to get response from trusted friends (Atwell, 1987). Writing workshops also frequently include opportunities for student writers to publicly read their work from the *author's chair* (Calkins, 1986; Graves, 1983), a special chair reserved just for author readings. Writing workshops also encourage writers to select particular pieces for publishing as books and/or class magazines. In many whole-language classrooms, publishing serves as an occasion for a publishing party to celebrate effort and accomplishment. At that time, it is common to invite parents and other family members as well as school administrators, other teachers, and even other classes.

Journal Writing. Journal writing is another writing opportunity that encourages students to explore their thoughts, ideas, and feelings (Crafton, 1991) by validating their *life stories* (Routman, 1991). In some whole-language classrooms, journals have been reconceptualized and transformed into writer's notebooks (Harwayne, 1992) that encourage students to generate bits and pieces of many different kinds of writing, both original and copied, that form what can be characterized as *seeds* for more extended writing. Both journals and writer's notebooks value writing as a tool for exploring the meaning of lived experience.

Content-Area Study. In whole-language classes, content-area studies center on a process of inquiry that emphasizes original research (using both primary and secondary sources) across the curriculum. Content-area studies are frequently organized around a theme, or central issue, that is collaboratively developed by teacher and learners. On many occasions, inquiries lead to the development of a culminating project or performance that publicly represents learning, such as setting up a classroom museum, publishing a book or journal, creating an art exhibit or videotape, or presenting a theatrical event.

Share Time. Sharing in whole-language classrooms is an ongoing, integral part of the learning process. During the course of the school day, there are numerous opportunities for students, both in whole-class settings and in small-group settings, to share their reading, writing, personal stories, art, and whatever other projects they are working on with classmates and teacher. In some whole-language classes, students use these occasions to conduct *book sales* in which they recommend favorite books to their classmates. Sharing values learner talk (in contrast to teacher talk!) because it supports the social construction of literacy and creativity.

Thus, in whole-language classrooms the physical layout of the room, the social organization of the learning experiences, and immersion in intellectually demanding content of the curriculum all work together to communicate the implicit message that both teacher and learners are committed to full human literate and creative possibility. Whole-language classrooms embody the type of educational environment that promotes a spirit of inquiry (Barell, 1991), higher level thinking (Perkins, 1991), and as Gardner (1991) stated, "encourage(s) students to represent knowledge in a number of different ways . . . adopt the roles that are ultimately occupied by skilled and adult practitioners, and to engage in the kind of self-assessment that allows one ultimately to take responsibility for one's own learning" (p. 224).

The Whole-Language Teacher: Conductor of the Classroom Orchestra

Every teacher is an unique individual who cannot be reduced to a stereo-typical set of descriptors. In the most idealized sense, however, whole-language teachers can be described as transforming leaders (Burns, 1978) who create purpose, elevate everyone's level of motivation and morality, are committed both to ideas and action (Peters & Waterman, 1982), and define a vision of learning that leads to viewing the world in a new way. Whole-language teachers have *voice* that empowers them to assert themselves in the world (Graves, 1983; Kreisberg, 1992) and engage learners in a pedagogy of empowerment (Simon, 1987). Giroux (1988) described these teacher leaders as *transformative intellectuals* because they engage in critical dialogue to reconstruct the classroom experience in ways that help learners discover their literate and creative voice in the world.

Whole-language teachers are *thoughtful practitioners* (Atwell, 1989) who view themselves as researchers because they have a deep commitment to their own learning and personal growth. They collaborate with students to ask questions, observe, document, study, and draw tentative conclusions that will increase their knowledge and understanding of teaching and learning. They examine their assumptions and engage in reflection, inquiry, and action in order to help learners grow (Newman, 1991; Patterson & Shannon, 1993).

Whole-language teachers believe all children can learn and, more importantly, all children will learn when the classroom culture supports the personal construction of knowledge. They are *kidwatchers* (Y. Goodman, 1991) who honor each child's current level of understanding in order to provide time and opportunity for learners to engage with a multiplicity of meaningful learning experiences.

Thus, the whole-language teacher can be thought of as the conductor of a classroom orchestra who brings all learners together to create a rich, harmonious symphony of literacy and creativity built on the individual strengths and interests of each learner. The teacher, like the conductor, is a leader who sets up the structure, manages the dynamics, inspires, motivates, guides, mentors, instructs, facilitates, models, negotiates, assesses, responds, rewards, and, at appropriate times, evaluates. Like the conductor, the teacher also has high expectations, sets up a system that engages participants in meaningful and authentic work, encourages learners to take risks, empowers learners to take charge of their own learning, and promotes interdependencies. Also like the conductor, the teacher takes great pride and satisfaction in sharing joyful celebrations of effort and accomplishment.

Just like an orchestra conductor, the whole-language teacher *leads from behind* (Newman, 1991) to create a self-sustaining system, fueled in large part by the natural, creative energy of the children and their commitment to learning. This leadership role is best described, perhaps, by the ancient Chinese philosopher Lao Tzu (4th century), who said of the best leaders:

> The best of all rulers is but a shadowy presence to his subjects. . . .
> When his task is accomplished and his work done, the people all say,
> "It happened to us naturally." (p. 73)

Scenes From Whole-Language Classrooms: The Nurturing of Literacy and Creativity

The best way to appreciate how the culture of whole language promotes literacy and creativity is to envision the experience of learning in a whole-language classroom. Take a few moments to peer into these classrooms in an urban whole-language school and imagine yourself as a child:

Scene 1. In Ms. K's third-grade class it is mid-morning. One group of students is sitting in the corridor outside the classroom creating an original play based on *Amelia Bedelia* (Parish, 1963). These students all love the Amelia Bedelia character, who humorously creates havoc by literally interpreting what are intended to be expressions of speech, and they are planning to act out her adventures for the younger children in kindergarten and first grade. Another group has placed in a carton one of the class' two guinea pigs, Wilbur II, named after the pig character in *Charlotte's Web* (White, 1954), a favorite story the whole class read during a literature study. The class is proceeding to weigh the animal on a balance scale. The children will enter the weight on a large graph that is tracking the growth of their pets. A third group is excitedly clustered around the large classroom windows, looking out and writing down observations of street activity in their writer's notebooks. Ms. K had recently attended a poetry workshop by poet, author, and educator Georgia Heard as part of an ongoing series of professional development workshops sponsored by Columbia University Teachers College Writing Project, and she was impressed by Heard's focus on the importance of image in poetry. She had shared her excitement with the class and had invited them to write and/or draw the images they saw as they looked at every day life. Other small groups are similarly engaged in learning activities around the room: One small group is reading independently in the library center; another group is copying favorite poems at the poetry center in preparation for creating personal anthologies; a third group is manipulating math tangrams (geometric shapes) to match patterns and create original designs; and a fourth group is at the computer center, editing an article for the class science journal that grew out of their reading of *The Magic School Bus at the Waterworks* (Cole, 1986). And where is Ms. K? After searching the room for a few moments, she is found tucked away on a carpet in a back corner of the room with a few students clustered around her in a guided reading group discussing character development in the novel *J.T.* (Wagner, 1969).

Scene 2. In Ms. G's first-grade class, the students have just completed a whole-class shared book experience (Holdaway, 1979) in a favorite big book, *Noisy Nora* (R. Wells, 1984). Ms. G's focus for this particular reading was on the language patterns the author had used to create rhythm and rhyme. The class had used their learning from the text to collaboratively create a variation, "Silent Sally," that they had dictated to Ms. G, who then transcribed their story onto a large experience chart. The children had read aloud their own story the way they had read aloud *Noisy Nora*. Now the children have begun to work in small groups. One group of students is working with a parent volunteer, cooking English muffin pizzas in the class toaster oven. The recipe has been written on a piece of chart paper that is tacked to the wall above the cooking center and the children are continually referring to it as they check their preparations. Other students are paired up and *buddy* reading small copies of *Noisy Nora* to each other with great excitement. A third group has moved to the letter writing center and the children are drafting letters to the author Rosemary Wells. Ms. G plans to send out a class set of letters as part of the class' year-long "letters to authors" project. Two students are at the painting easel surrounded with inspiration provided by posters of Monet, attempting to emulate his French impressionism. Throughout the year, Ms. G introduces many famous artists and encourages students to "have a go" at emulating their styles of painting. Still, another group is planting beans in the garden center, while three children are wearing head phones at the listening center and reading along to an audiotape of *Alexander and the Terrible, Horrible, No Good, Very Bad Day* (Viorst, 1972). Still another small group of students is in the dinosaur center arguing over which is the most ferocious looking dinosaur while thumbing through a collection of dinosaur books and preparing to create dinosaur models in clay. During this time, Ms. G is helping three English as a second language (ESL) children (two are Spanish, one is Asian) identify pictures from magazines in preparation for the creation of original alphabet books.

Scene 3. In Ms. L's fifth-grade class it is shortly after lunch. She has just finished reading aloud to the class from *Where the Red Fern Grows* (Rawls, 1961), a story that always brings tears to both Ms. L and the children. Now, the children have moved to group work and individual study. Ms. L sits in a corner of the room meeting with a group of students to talk about the experiences they had interviewing their relatives about their memories of the Vietnam War. She is encouraging the children to compare and contrast their findings with the perspective Nhuong (1982) brought to his autobiographical novel *The Land I Lost.* At the same time, another group of students is creating original board games that got started after Ms. L read the class *Jumanji* by Chris Van Allsberg (1981), a story about a game that magically creates real jungle adventures. A third group is designing travel brochures that highlight features from their family's country of origin that will become part of a project on autobiographies. They have also been audiotaping interviews with their families and photographing them. Still, other children are reading self-selected books from the class library; writing in their journals; or doing independent research on topics *they* chose to investigate because of special interest, including the history of fashion design, horses, and AIDS. One boy is even drawing an original series of cartoons based on a character he created called Stick-O-Man. When the cartoons are ready, he will publish his work as a magazine that will be photocopied for everyone in the class.

These whole-language classrooms are not quiet, but they are not chaotic. A better way to describe these classes is *unquiet* (Kutz & Roskelly, 1991) because they are committed to active, transformational learning. The routines and rituals the teachers and learners have established encourage literate and creative development. In whole language classrooms you will never hear the teacher say, "Now it's time to put on your thinking caps" or "Get ready for creative writing" because these teachers know that thinking and creating can't be turned on and off like so much water from a tap. Nurturing literate and creative growth is a *way of life* in whole-language classes that takes place all the time, orchestrated by a teacher who understands how to best help students reach their literate and creative potential.

CONCLUSION

At a time when whole language is under fierce attack and there are voices calling for "back-to-basics" and "phonics first" ("California Leads Revival," 1996), it is especially important to maintain a focus on classroom conditions that have proved effective in promoting high achievement and successful learning. In his landmark study of educational programs in the United States, Goodlad (1984) noted that in exemplary classrooms, learners are more highly motivated, actively engaged with learning activities, feel good about what is happening in school, and care about learning because their teachers are committed to helping them reach their full human literate and creative potential. In short, Goodlad described the educational culture of whole-language classes. In the 1960s and 1970s, the open classroom provided rich educational environments for developing literate and creative spirit (Houtz, 1990; Ramey & Piper, 1974; Ward & Barcher, 1975). In the 21st century, building on a deeper understanding of language, thought, and learning, it is whole-language classrooms that give voice to a *pedagogy of possibility* (Simon, 1992) by supporting the spirit of literacy and creativity.

STUDY ACTIVITIES

One hopes it is clear that there is no manual of instructions, teacher's guide, or compendium of activities that can offer a recipe for whole language; the road to whole language begins with reflection. Here are a few steps to launch your journey:

1. Keep a journal of your thoughts, ideas, and feelings. Topics to get you started:

    A. Identify teachers who have made a lifelong impact, positive or negative, on you, Why do you remember them? How have they influenced your teaching?

    B. Write a statement of your beliefs about the way children learn. Examine whether your instructional practices are consistent with your beliefs.

    C. Make a list of your instructional goals. By the time your students leave your class, what do you want them to know and be able to do? What do you want your students to appreciate?

    D. For 1 week, write a detailed account of each school day as soon as you get home. Include every detail (with references to specific students) you remember. At the end of the week, read your journal to search for patterns that characterize what it means to be a student in your class. Examine whether you need to make changes.

2. Practice being a keen observer of your teaching. Videotape yourself. Focus on the following questions:

    A. Who talks most in my class? Who talks least? Do students use oral language to express ideas, thoughts, opinions, feelings?

B. How do I organize instruction? How much time do I spend conducting whole class lessons? Facilitating small-group interaction? Conferring with individual students?

C. When do my students appear to be most engaged with learning? When do they appear to be least engaged?

D. How many whole language curriculum events do I include in my daily schedule? My weekly schedule?

Determine whether your findings are consistent with your beliefs. Decide where you need to make changes.

3. Examine how much your curriculum builds on the knowledge and interests of your students? Ask yourself how much you know about the lives of your students and their parents? Create opportunities to learn more by having lunch with small groups of students, inviting parents to visit the class, chatting with parents on a regular basis rather than waiting for scheduled teacher conferences, and meeting families outside the formal setting of the school.

4. Serve as a model for living a literate, creative life. Read when students read during independent reading time. Write when students write during journal writing time. Take risks to learn by collaborating with students on new projects.

5. Keep yourself growing as a professional by joining professional organizations; reading professional books and journals; attending professional development workshops and conferences; studying at colleges and universities, and dialoguing with colleagues about learning, literacy and creativity.

REFERENCES

Amabile, T. M. (1983). *The social psychology of creativity*. New York: Springer-Verlag.

Amabile, T. M. (1989). *Growing up creative: Nurturing a lifetime of creativity*. New York: Crown.

Anderson, R. C., Hiebert, E. H., Scott, J. A., & Wilkinson, A. G. (1985). *Becoming a nation of readers: The report of the Commission on Reading*. Champaign, IL: Center for the Study of Reading.

Atwell, N. (1987). *In the middle: Writing, reading, and learning with adolescents*. Portsmouth, NH: Boynton/Cook.

Atwell, N. (1989). The thoughtful practitioner. *Teacher's Networking: The Whole Language Newsletter, 9*(3), 1-12.

Barell, J. (1991). *Teaching for thoughtfulness*. New York: Longman.

Barron, F. (1955). The disposition towards originality. In P. E. Vernon (Ed.). (1970). *Creativity: Selected readings* (pp. 273-288). Baltimore, MD: Penguin Books.

Brause, R. S. (1985). Classroom contexts for learning. In C. N. Hedley & A. N. Baratta (Eds.), *Contexts of reading* (pp. 23-38). Norwood, NJ: Ablex.

Brause, R. S. (1992). Literacy: A learning resource. In C. N. Hedley, D. Feldman, & P. Antonacci (Eds.), *Literacy across the curriculum* (pp. 15-22). Norwood, NJ: Ablex.

Brown, R. G. (1991). *Schools of thought: How the politics of literacy shape thinking in the classroom.* San Francisco, CA: Jossey-Brown.

Bruner, J. (1985). *Child's talk: Learning to use language.* New York: Norton.

Burns, J. M. (1978). *Leadership.* New York: Harper & Row.

Butler, A. (1987). *The elements of a whole language program.* Chicago: Rigby.

California leads revival of teaching by phonics. (1996, May 22). *The New York Times,* p. B8.

Calkins, L. M. (1986). *The art of teaching writing.* Portsmouth, NH: Heinemann.

Cambourne, B. (1988). *The whole story: Natural learning and the acquisition of literacy in the classroom.* Auckland, NZ: Ashton Scholastic.

Cambourne, B. (1993). Literacy in the year 2000. *Teachers Networking: The Whole Language Newsletter, 12*(3), 1-5.

Carnegie Forum on Education and the Economy. (1986). *A nation prepared: Teachers for the 21st century* (The Report of the Task Force on Teaching as a Profession). New York: Carnegie Corporation of New York.

Cole, J. (1986). *The magic school bus at the waterworks.* New York: Scholastic.

Cooper, J. D. (1993). *Literacy: Helping children construct meaning.* Boston: Houghton Mifflin.

Crafton, L. K. (1991). *Whole language: Getting started . . . moving forward.* Katonah, NY: Richard C. Owen.

Cremin, L. A. (1977). *Traditions of American education.* New York: Basic Books.

Csikszentmihalyi, M. (1988). Society, culture, and person: A systems view of creativity. In R. J. Sternberg (Ed.), *The nature of creativity: Contemporary psychological perspectives* (pp. 325-339). Cambridge, UK: Cambridge University Press.

Dewey, J. (1938). *Experience and education.* New York: Collier Books.

Dewey, J. (1956). *The child and the curriculum: The school and society.* Chicago: University of Chicago Press.

Edelsky, C., Altwerger, B., & Flores, B. (1991). *Whole language: What's the difference?* Portsmouth, NH: Heinemann.

Ferreiro, E. (1990). Literacy development: Psychogenesis. In Y. Goodman (Ed.), *How children construct literacy: Piagetian perspectives* (pp. 12-25). Newark, DE: International Reading Association.

Fiske, E. B. (1991). *Smart schools, smart kids: Why do some schools work?* New York: Simon & Schuster

Freire, P., & Macedo, D. (1987). *Literacy: Reading the word and reading the world.* South Hadley, MA: Bergin & Garvey.

Freeman, C. C. (1992). Shaping reading and writing: Common threads and unique patterns in one fourth-grade (Doctoral dissertation, University of Pennsylvania, 1991). *Dissertation Abstracts International, 52*(7), 2481A.

Galton, F. (1976). Genius as inherited. In A. Rothenberg & C. R. Hausman (Eds.), *The creativity question* (pp. 42-48). Durham, NC: Duke University Press.

Gardner, H. (1991). *The unschooled mind: How children think and how schools should teach.* New York: Basic Books.

Giroux, H. A. (1988). *Teachers as intellectuals: Toward a critical pedagogy of learning.* Granby, MA: Begin & Garvey.

Goodlad, J. I. (1984). *A place called school.* New York: McGraw-Hill.

Goodman, K. (1986). *What's whole in whole language.* New York: Scholastic.

Goodman, Y. (1991). Kidwatching: Observing children in the classroom. In D. Booth & C. Thornley-Hall (Eds.), *The talk curriculum* (pp. 21-32). Portsmouth, NH: Heinemann.

Graves, D. H. (1983). *Writing: Teachers and children at work.* Portsmouth, NH: Heinemann.

Greene, M. (1988). What happened to imagination? In K. Egan & D Nadaner (Eds.), *Imagination and education* (pp. 45-56). New York: Teachers College Press.

Gruber, H. E., & Davis, S. N. (1988). Inching our way up Mount Olympus: The evolving-systems approach to creative thinking. In R. J. Sternberg (Ed.), *The nature of creativity: Contemporary psychological perspectives* (pp. 243-270). Cambridge, UK: Cambridge University Press.

Guilford, J. P. (1976). Factor analysis, intellect, and creativity. In A. Rothenberg & C. R. Hausman (Eds.), *The creativity question* (pp. 200-208). Durham, NC: Duke University Press.

Hansen, J. (1987). *When writers read.* Portsmouth, NH: Heinemann.

Harste, J. C. (1994). Literacy as curricular conversations about knowledge, inquiry, and morality. In M. R. Ruddell & R. B. Ruddell (Eds.), *Theoretical models and processes of reading* (4th ed., pp. 1220-1242). Newark, DE: International Reading Association.

Harste, J. C., & Short, K. G., with Burke, C. (1995). *Creating classrooms for authors and inquirers* (2nd ed.). Portsmouth, NH: Heinemann.

Harwayne, S. (1992). *Lasting impressions: Weaving literature into the writing workshop.* Portsmouth, NH: Heinemann.

Hennessey, B. A., & Amabile, T. M. (1988). The conditions of creativity. In R. J. Sternberg (Ed.), *The nature of creativity: Contemporary psychological perspectives* (pp. 11-38). Cambridge, UK: Cambridge University Press.

Holdaway, D. (1979). *The foundations of literacy.* Auckland, NZ: Ashton Scholastic.

Houtz, J. C. (1990). Environments that support creative thinking. In C. Hedley, J. Houtz, & A. Baratta (Eds.), *Cognition, curriculum, and literacy* (pp. 61-76). Norwood, NJ: Ablex.

John-Steiner, V. (1985). *Notebooks of the mind: Explorations of thinking.* New York: Harper & Row.

John-Steiner, V. (1992). Creative lives, creative tensions. *Creativity Research Journal, 5*(1), 99-108.

Koepke, M. (1991, August). The power to be a professional. *Teacher Magazine,* 35-41.

Kreisberg, S. (1992). *Transforming power: Domination, empowerment, and education.* Albany: State University of New York Press.

Kutz, E., & Roskelly, H. (1991). *An unquiet pedagogy: Transforming practice in the English classroom.* Portsmouth, NH: Boynton/Cook.

Langer, S. K. (1951). *Philosophy in a new key: A study in the symbolism of reason, rite, and art.* Cambridge, MA: Harvard University Press.

London, C. B. G. (1988). *A Piagetian constructivist perspective on curriculum development.* Paper presented at New York Metropolitan Association for Development Education, New York.

MacKinnon, D. W. (1970). The personality correlates of creativity: A study of American architects. In P. E. Vernon (Ed.), *Creativity* (pp. 289-311). Baltimore, MD: Penguin Books.

Maslow, A. H. (1968). *Toward a psychology of being.* New York: Van Nostrand Reinhold.

Mills, R., & Clyde, J. A. (1990). Introduction: The stories whole language teachers tell. In H. Mills & J. A. Clyde (Eds.), *Portraits of whole language classrooms: Learning for all ages* (pp. xxi-xxvii). Portsmouth, NH: Heinemann.

Mooney, M. M. (1990). *Reading to, with, and by children.* Katonah, NY: Richard C. Owen

Newman, J. M. (1991). Learning to teach by uncovering our assumptions. In D. Booth & C. Thornley-Hall (Eds.), *The talk curriculum* (pp. 107-122). Portsmouth, NH: Heinemann.

Nhuong, H. Q. (1982). *The land I lost: Adventures of a boy in Vietnam.* New York: Harper Trophy.

Parish, P. (1963). *Amelia Bedelia.* New York: Harper & Row.

Patterson, L., & Shannon, P. (1993). Reflection, inquiry, action. In L. Patterson, C. M. Santa, K. G. Short, & K. Smith (Eds.), *Teachers are researchers: Reflection and action* (pp. 7-11). Newark, DE: International reading association.

Perkins, D. N. (1991). Educating for insight. *Educational Leadership, 49*(2), 4-8.

Peters, T. J., & Waterman, R. H., Jr. (1982). *In search of excellence: Lessons from America's best-run companies.* New York: Warner Books.

Peterson, R. (1992). *Life in a crowded place: Making a learning community.* Portsmouth, NH: Heinemann.

Piaget, J. (1977). *The development of thought: Equilibrium of cognitive structures.* New York: Viking.

Ramey, C. T., & Piper, V. (1974). Creativity in open and traditional classrooms. *Child Development, 45,* 557-560.

Rawls, W. R. (1961). *Where the red fern grows.* New York: Doubleday.

Reich, R. B. (1991). *The work of nations: Preparing ourselves for a 21st century capitalism.* New York: Knopf.

Resnick, L. B., & Klopfer, L. E. (1989). Toward the thinking curriculum: An overview. In L. B. Resnick & L. E. Klopfer (Eds.), *Toward the thinking curriculum: Current cognitive research* (pp. 1-18). Alexandria, VA: Association for Supervision and Curriculum Development.

Roe, A. (1970). A psychologist examines sixty-four eminent scientists. In P. E. Vernon (Ed.), *Creativity* (pp. 43-51). Baltimore, MD: Penguin Books.

Routman, R. (1988). *Transitions: From literature to literacy.* Portsmouth, NH: Heinemann.

Routman, R. (1991). *Invitations: Changing as teachers and learners K-12.* Portsmouth, NH: Heinemann.

Rumelhart, D. E. (1980). Schemata: The building blocks of cognition. In R. J. Spiro, B. C. Bruce, & W. F. Brewer (Eds.), *Theoretical issues in reading comprehension: Perspectives from cognitive psychology, linguistics, artificial intelligence, and education* (pp. 33-58). Hillsdale, NJ: Lawrence Erlbaum Associates.

Shannon, P. (1990). *The struggle to continue: Progressive reading instruction in the United States.* Portsmouth, NH: Heinemann.

Simon, R. I. (1987). Empowerment as a pedagogy of possibility. *Language Arts, 64,* 370-382.

Simon, R. I. (1992). Empowerment as a pedagogy of possibility. In P. Shannon (Ed.), *Becoming political: Readings and writings in the politics of literacy education* (pp. 139-151). Portsmouth, NH: Heinemann.

Smith, F. (1989). Overselling literacy. *Phi Delta Kappan, 70,* 352-359.

Tardif, T. Z., & Sternberg, R. J. (1988). What do we know about creativity. In R. J. Sternberg (Ed.), *The nature of creativity: Contemporary psychological perspectives* (pp. 429-440). Cambridge, UK: Cambridge University Press.

Terman, L. M. (1970). Psychological approaches to the theory of genius. In P. E. Vernon (Ed.), *Creativity* (pp. 25-42). Baltimore, MD: Penguin Books.

Toffler, A. (1990). *Powershift: Knowledge, wealth, and the violence at the end of the 21st century.* New York: Bantam Books.

Van Allsberg, C. (1981). *Jumanji.* New York: Scholastic.

Viorst, J. (1972). *Alexander and the terrible, horrible, no good very bad day.* New York: Scholastic.

Vygotsky, L. S. (1987). *The collected works: Volume 1.* New York: Plenum Press.

Wagner, J. (1969). *J.T.* New York: Dell..

Ward, W. C., & Barcher, P. R. (1975). Reading achievement and creativity as related to open classroom experience. *Journal of Educational Psychology, 67,* 683-691.

Weaver, C. (1990). *Understanding whole language: From principle to practice.* Portsmouth, NH: Heinemann.

Wells, G. (1986). *The meaning makers: Children learning language and using language to learn.* Portsmouth, NH: Heinemann.

Wells, R. (1984). *Noisy Nora.* New York: Scholastic.

White, E. B. (1952). *Charlotte's web.* New York: Harper.

Whitman, W. (1945). *The portable Walt Whitman.* New York: Viking Press.

11

Counseling Gifted and Creative Students: Issues and Interventions

Merle A. Keitel
Mary Kopala
Mary Ann Schroder
Fordham University

For many years, little attention was paid to the psychological needs of gifted individuals because of a belief, based on past research (Hollingworth, 1942; Terman, 1954), that the gifted were generally well adjusted and not in need of any special services. In recent years, however, there has been recognition of career, family, and personal adjustment issues that might be particularly relevant to gifted individuals. Based on that information, counselors can play a vital role in enhancing the experiences and at times easing the stresses of those whose lives are touched by giftedness.

Before we can discuss how counselors can intervene with the gifted, we must first answer the question "Who is gifted?" Gifted individuals have been identified by intelligence test scores and academic achievement. Intellectual giftedness is probably the most commonly used criteria (Sternberg & Zhang, 1995). Yet, identification may also be extended to those who possess more specific types of giftedness (Sternberg & Zhang, 1995), such as extraordinary talent in specific areas, such as music, visual arts, verbal expression (including writing, acting, and foreign languages), or communication and leadership skills (Kerr, 1991). Although a broad range of talents might theoretically constitute the basis for giftedness, the criteria used in specific circumstances is established by the group doing the evaluating (Sternberg & Zhang, 1995). Therefore, some variability exists across groups in terms of the definition and identification of gifted individuals.

Gifted students in general may benefit from counseling services for a variety of reasons. All students share the same developmental needs, but gifted students may also express concerns that are unique to their giftedness. It is especially important for counselors to understand these latter issues in order to best serve this special population. Counselors have had relatively little to go on in designing and implementing counseling services for the gifted, but information that has emerged in recent decades can be helpful in designing services to fit the needs of gifted individuals. It should also be recognized that most of the research has focused on giftedness as a general category and has not attempted to distinguish factors that may be associated with specific types of giftedness. Clearly, more work in this area is needed before definitive generalizations and recommendations can be made. Given what has been learned in recent decades, it is clear that counseling services for the gifted must become an integral offering in public schools, colleges, and adult education settings. Currently, availability of services is rather limited. Some counselors in private practice, particularly in urban and economically advantaged areas, offer specialized services for the gifted—such as psychological and social adjustment counseling, test-taking strategies, and/or college selection counseling. Unfortunately, these services are not widely available and can be costly. The counseling needs of gifted students are often not met in the school setting, either. VanTassel-Baska (1987) surveyed 200 parents of middle-school aged children. Whereas 68% rated counseling services as the most important school-related service their children might receive, only 9% reported that their children actually received counseling services from the schools. Expansion of services to this population is warranted.

Gifted students can benefit from both direct and indirect counseling services targeted at career issues, personal and affective concerns, and developmental issues. Direct services include individual, group, and family counseling. Group counseling may be particularly beneficial because it provides opportunities for gifted individuals to join together in support of each other and their mutual needs. Indirect services, which are mostly psychoeducational in nature, include consultation with those who are closely involved with gifted individuals. This consultation might include conferring with teachers and administrators about such matters as inservice training, class composition, curriculum design, and specific concerns that arise in classrooms. For example, counselors can suggest to teachers who have students of mixed abilities in their classes how to keep the gifted students stimulated with special projects. Gifted students who are not appropriately challenged may become bored, get turned off to school, and/or perhaps start acting out in the classroom. Indirect services might include programs, such as parent training, tailored to meet the needs of family members. There is, in essence, a broad range of roles, including therapist, consultant, and advocate, that might be played by counselors serving a gifted population.

CAREER ISSUES

For gifted individuals, work is extremely important and a primary source of self-expression and life satisfaction (Perrone, 1986). Nevertheless, it is not unusual for these individuals to report little awareness of the ways in which their interests, values, and abilities relate to career planning (Kelly, 1992; Post-Krammer & Perrone, 1982). This lack of awareness, coupled with the fact that gifted people have the ability to pursue a variety of options, may lead to difficulties with career planning. Possible difficulties include career indecision, based on difficulty in choosing a career, and foreclosure, defined as a premature career decision (Kerr, 1991).

It has been a long-standing assumption that gifted students who possess numerous interests in addition to exceptional abilities, may have difficulty selecting a career (Emmett & Minor, 1993). Achter, Lubinski, and Benbow (1996), however, suggest that this "multipotentiality" is not as widespread as previously thought. In a recent study, Achter et al. (1996) found differentiated patterns of interests and abilities for most gifted adolescents when appropriate measures—those who had high enough ceilings to accurately measure these talented individuals—were used. At this point, the extent of multipotentiality among gifted students, as well as the extent of resulting career indecision, is in question. It may be, as Achter et al. suggested, a problem for a relatively small percentage of gifted students, Nevertheless, it is a possibility that should be kept in mind when working with gifted students who exhibit career decision-making difficulties.

The outcome that is seemingly opposite to that of career indecision is foreclosure or premature career decision making. Gifted individuals may foreclose on a career choice to avoid the decision-making process and the anxiety that might accompany it (Kerr, 1991) or because they focus on a special interest or talent that emerged at an early age.

CAREER COUNSELING

Interventions to address multipotentiality and foreclosure issues have been suggested. The recent work (Achter et al., 1996) that calls into question widespread multipotentiality among gifted students suggests that differentiated patterns of interests and abilities can be determined for most gifted students if the appropriate measures are used. Therefore, it is critical that counselors choose instruments that are appropriate for use with gifted students. As is always the case, individuals must be helped to understand their interest and ability profiles and to base career decisions on them. In cases where multipotentiality does present problems for gifted individuals, however, the use of value-based counseling may prove helpful in unlocking stagnated decision making (Kerr & Erb, 1991). The goal of value-based counseling is to help individuals explore their values and assess potential careers with them in mind. The belief is that commitment to career goals will be greater when decisions are grounded in one's values.

As stated previously, some individuals identify a particular interest or manifest a specific talent early in their lives. An approach for working with these early emergers is twofold—to focus on and encourage the identified interest or talent while simultaneously encouraging exploration of other interests (Kerr, 1991). In line with the first goal, development of the identified interest can be furthered by offering resources and training related to it. These activities can be coordinated, along with messages of encouragement, by counselors, teachers, and parents. With regard to the second goal, early emerging students should be encouraged to identify and pursue other interests and to learn more about alternative careers. It is useful, according to Kerr (1991), to expose the student to this multitude of possibilities while helping to develop the special interest or talent.

It is not just those who face multipotentiality or foreclosure issues, however, who can benefit from career counseling. Indications are that inadequate attention is being paid to the career development needs of gifted students in general. Kelly (1992) studied the career maturity of gifted junior high school students and found that gifted students were not higher in career maturity than their nongifted peers. In fact, they were in need of as much or more career information overall.

The logical conclusion from the existing research is that career counseling should be made available to all gifted students and that it should begin early. Kerr (1991) suggested that career development counseling begin in the elementary school years, continuing through college and into young adulthood. Similarly, Berger (1989) outlined a systematic college planning program that begins in Grade 7 and continues through Grade 12, culminating with the acceptance of a college admissions offer.

Additionally, career counseling programs should address a full range of issues. Overall, the following elements can be considered for inclusion in a comprehensive career counseling program: (a) presentation of career information; (b) experiential career exploration; (c) self-exploration of interests, abilities, and values; (d) discussion of the way in which these individual factors relate to the world of work; (e) help with college selection; and (f) career skills development that continue to be relevant in the years beyond schooling.

There are a number of ways in which each of these components can be presented. For example, career information can be presented by a teacher, a counselor, or when possible, by adults working in selected occupations. Additionally, students can be encouraged to study public figures or famous people, thus providing a look at the motivations and career paths of successful individuals (Pleiss & Feldhusen, 1995). Experiential career exploration, which can provide highly useful information about how it feels to be in particular occupations, can take place through shadowing experiences (i.e., students spend the day with an adult who is working in areas of interest) and role-playing activities (i.e., students engage in career fantasies). Both informational and experiential aspects of career exploration should focus on a wide range of challenging, rewarding, and interesting careers so that students will have opportunities to explore a variety of careers (Fredrickson, 1986).

Self-exploration of values, interests, and abilities is important in the career decision-making process because increased information about one's self appears to decrease career indecision (Schroer & Dorn, 1986). The use of paper and pencil instruments (e.g., vocational interest inventories, values clarification, or aptitude tests) and individual or group discussion can be a vehicle for self-exploration. Fredrickson suggested that the group format is especially beneficial for gifted individuals when fostering discussion of future goals.

In terms of career skills development, the importance of mentor programs has been emphasized (Pleiss & Feldhusen, 1995). Counselors can work with schools, colleges, professional organizations, and businesses to identify potential mentors, establish mentor programs, and match individuals with mentors. Many gifted adults report that mentors helped them to develop their skills and abilities and served to further their careers. Overall, career counseling is a multifaceted endeavor. Attention to each of the aspects noted is important in helping gifted individuals to identify goals and live up to their potentials.

FAMILY ISSUES

The presence of a gifted child in a family is likely to have an impact on parents, siblings, and the family as a unit (Meckstroth, 1992). A gifted child may affect the way family members interact and the way parents and siblings think about themselves and their roles. In some cases, families adapt successfully to these demands. In others, the presence of a gifted child may be a catalyst for difficulties.

For the most part, parenting a gifted child has received little attention in psychological literature, and parents of the gifted have little guidance available to them (Lovecky, 1992). Perhaps there has been an assumption, based on the positive connotation of giftedness, that little guidance is needed. Yet, families of the gifted are often confronted with a number of potentially complex issues (Meckstroth, 1992), and understanding matters common to these families is essential when working in this area.

An initial set of concerns for the family may be related to the child being identified as gifted. The labeling itself brings public recognition of the child as being different from most others, and it is not uncommon for parents to react with mixed feelings (Meckstroth, 1992). For instance, parents may worry that their children may be alienated from peers because of their giftedness. If the parents themselves do not value education or intellectual pursuits, they may feel alienated, intimidated, and perhaps resentful of their children. Parents may also be embarrassed about their children's special status and reluctant to talk with others.

Another common reaction is for parents to question whether the designation is accurate. According to Meckstroth (1992), studies indicate that one third to one half of all parents of gifted students doubt the accuracy of the label for their children. In some cases, the parents may not have seen qualities of giftedness in their children and be surprised by it; in other cases, the parents may have mixed feelings about the prospect of rearing a gifted child. Parental lack of confidence in ability to raise a gifted child could underlie the mixed feelings, as could feelings of personal inadequacy. Parents who are ambivalent about their child's designation as gifted may send double messages, perhaps belittling the value of the child's gift or encouraging the child to succeed while also discouraging a level of achievement that would make them, as parents, feel less successful (McMann & Oliner, 1988).

Recognition by others of their child's giftedness can also cause parents to view their job description differently. Some parents have reported that their parenting role seems to take on a more serious tone after learning of their child's giftedness (Meckstroth, 1992). Along with that, there may be an increased sense of pressure to perform well as parents.

Another set of issues involves marital dynamics. There are a number of points of potential disagreement or misunderstanding between parents. Included are possible disagreements about the existence and extent of the child's giftedness. When parents do not agree on this issue, marital conflict is likely to result (Keirouz, 1990). Parents also may be reluctant or unable to discuss their expectations and standards for the gifted child with one another, perhaps leading to misunderstanding or conflict. Similarly, parents may disagree about the amount of their resources that should be devoted to their gifted child. Raising a gifted child tends to be expensive. Special schools, extracurricular lessons, and activities can be costly (Meckstroth, 1992). Although families of the gifted tend to be child-centered (Lim, 1995; Olszewpki, Kulieke, & Buescher, 1987), sometimes one parent may resent that the gifted child receives high priority in the family. Such disagreement about allocation of resources (e.g., time and money) can lead to marital conflict.

Additionally, gifted children are sometimes given positions of greater power within the family than is typical for children. For example, gifted children may be given more responsibility than they can handle emotionally. Similarly, because these children appear to be mature and have good social skills, parents may depend inappropriately on the children for emotional support. When either of these circumstances occurs, the children's later development may be impeded, and blurred boundaries between parent and child are likely to create problems for the family.

Characteristics of gifted children, such as lower sleep requirements and high activity levels, may exhaust parents. Without careful planning, these characteristics also may leave parents with few opportunities for time together as a couple. Again, the potential exists for the blurring of boundaries between the generations.

Also noted is the tendency of gifted children to display needs for autonomy at an early age (Meckstroth, 1992). This puts parents into the sometimes difficult position of having to make decisions about the amount of independence to allow without having guidelines that are appropriate for their child. In addition to their own struggles with the issue, some parents may also feel conspicuous about giving greater than usual independence to their child, believing that their actions will be met by scrutiny from outsiders who do not really understand the situation.

A final set of difficulties that may be experienced relates to sibling issues. In families with more than one child and with both gifted and nongifted children, parents may be tempted to make comparisons between the children, sometimes resulting in unfair assessments of the nongifted children (Keirouz, 1990). Along with being unfairly assessed, other children in the family may believe that they are inferior to the gifted sibling and may also perceive their position within the family as being inferior. Such perceptions can create feelings of jealousy, lowered self-esteem, and conflict between the siblings.

Although factors that can affect sibling relationships are not well researched or understood at this point, one study (Tuttle & Cornell,

1993) found birth order to be important when considering the quality of sibling relationships. In this study it was found that when the first-born child was identified by the mother as gifted, relationships between that child and siblings were generally warm and close. However, when the second-born child was identified as gifted by the mother, a warm and close relationship was less likely. More work in the area of sibling relationships needs to be done before understanding of this issue can be reached.

UNDERACHIEVEMENT—A SPECIAL PROBLEM FOR THE FAMILY

Gifted children who do not perform at a level equal to their potential are often a concern for their parents (Emerick, 1992; Thomas, 1995), as well as for teachers. Although these children may have performed well on achievement and intelligence tests in the past, their current classroom performance does not match their earlier achievements (Kerr, 1991) or their standardized test scores (Kolb & Jussim, 1994). These individuals, often referred to as *underachievers,* may be perceived as lazy or unmotivated, but it has been suggested that there may be other problems instead that can cause students to perform at lower levels than expected (Kerr, 1985; Kolb & Jussim, 1994; Zuccone & Amerikaner, 1986).

In some cases, tests may have incorrectly placed an individual in the high IQ range when, in actuality, the student's IQ score is within the average range. Because of testing errors, these students may be labeled as *gifted* when in fact they are not. Another possibility is that the student is correctly identified as gifted but is in need of study skills to support academic attainment.

In other cases, the individual may be reluctant to demonstrate abilities in order to avoid social isolation (Kerr, 1985). The work of Gilligan (1982) suggests that adolescent girls are especially likely to hold back in the classroom in order to maintain their popularity.

The source of the problem could also be within the classroom itself. Kerr (1991) suggested that some underachieving students may be unchallenged by the curriculum and bored as a result. Kolb and Jussim (1994) continued the theme of classroom sources of underachievement, writing about the possibility of low expectations for gifted students by the teacher. They indicated that a teacher may develop low academic expectations for the student if the student exhibits behavioral problems in the classroom. Negative attitudes toward the child can then develop and be extended to academic expectations. The teacher's judgments of the child's work may be prejudiced by these negative feelings, and the work itself may actually suffer in the long run. These writers further pointed out that one reason for classroom misbehavior could be boredom with the academic material, leading to a vicious cycle of negative interactions and academic underachievement.

Finally, it is sometimes the case that family factors negatively affect the child's academic performance. Thomas (1995) wrote that family overprotectiveness of a gifted child is not uncommon and is based on a desire to safeguard the treasured child. The overprotectiveness, according to Thomas, can lead to a host of difficulties, including academic underachievement. In another vein, Rogers and Nielsen (1993) pointed out that it is commonly assumed that families of the gifted are stable, two-parent, middle-class families, although such is not necessarily the case. Rogers and Nielsen pointed to divorce statistics that indicate that these families are not sheltered from the possibility of marital difficulties and breakup. The resulting message is that family dynamics and possible difficulties should be explored when problems are exhibited by the gifted child. Indeed, problems such as such as substance abuse, economic hardship, loss, and relational problems within the family may interfere with the child's ability to perform well and achieve in school. One study (Freeman, 1994) found that gifted academic underachievers were more likely to report problems at home than were gifted students performing at their expected level.

Some underachieving gifted students, whatever the source of academic difficulties, tend to manifest characteristics that are more similar to nongifted underachievers than to achieving gifted students. That is, they may have low self-concepts, be socially immature, and exhibit antisocial behavior (Kerr, 1991). When a range of problems such as these are exhibited by the gifted child, the entire family is likely to experience stress.

FAMILY INTERVENTIONS

The home is regarded by many gifted children as a safe haven (Sowa, McIntire, May, & Bland, 1994). Yet, research also suggests that about 15% of families with at least one gifted child experience some difficulties (West, Hosie, & Mathews, 1989).

Given that there are few guidelines available to families of the gifted (Lovecky, 1992) and that a widespread range of issues may come up for these families, it is important for counselors to be informed and prepared to offer interventions that will support the child and family. In some cases, families may benefit from psychoeducation designed to guide them in childrearing, to ease stresses, and to prevent problems. In other cases, they may be in need of therapeutic counseling that remediates existing problems. Ideally, access to both types of services should be made available.

Psychoeducation. Psychoeducational interventions (group or individual) can focus on parenting methods that address the needs of gifted children and their nongifted siblings. Coordinating the needs of all children within the family can prevent or ease existing tensions.

In a study of gifted adolescents and their parents, Strom, Strom, Strom, and Collinsworth (1994), found that adolescents rated their parents as highly successful in the parental role and as more successful than the parents themselves did. It might be helpful for counselors to challenge individuals to reexamine their perceptions of themselves as parents.

Therapeutic Counseling. When serious problems arise, the counselor may meet with family members. The first order of business should be the determination of who will be in therapy at any given time. Although there is no particular formula for determining what is most appropriate, guidelines that are respectful of familial variations in structure and values are suggested. The key consideration is to allow time for parents as a unit to make decisions that are considered within the realm of parental discretion. In some families, it may be useful for parents to discuss issues among themselves. In others, family discussion may be considered a preliminary step to decision making by the parents. The overall goal in either case is to avoid making the child a third partner in the marriage and to encourage parents to see themselves as heads of the household, despite their child's precociousness.

Family communication and decision-making skills may be enhanced with communication training. As a result of research suggesting that family members perceive family dynamics differently, Karnes and D'Ilio (1988) concluded that families should discuss their perceptions regarding a variety of issues, such as family cohesion, independence of members, recreational interests, control mechanisms within the family, and intellectual-cultural orientations. Helping all family members express their perspectives is likely to foster individuation. Additionally, communication between individuals is likely to heighten awareness of each other's feelings, thus enhancing the home environment and encouraging supportive attitudes and behaviors among members.

When underachievement is an issue, counselors can help families to assess possible sources of the problem. When the source of underachievement is school-based (e.g., a lack of intellectual stimulation) counselors can encourage the family to take action with the school system. When family problems underlie the underachievement, interventions can be targeted at the family level. Zuccone and Amerikaner (1986) suggested that counselors view underachievement from a family systems perspective so that the thrust of counseling is not directed solely toward the child. Instead, the counselor attempts to understand what part the child's underachieving behavior plays in the family's behavior patterns, and interventions can be targeted to change the family system rather than the child's behavior alone.

GENERAL EMOTIONAL ADJUSTMENT

The issue of possible maladjustment among gifted students has received some attention. Clinical studies have identified a range of problems among gifted students (Torrance, 1961; Webb, Meckstroth, & Tolan, 1982), including social isolation, low self-esteem, interpersonal sensitivity, and depression and suicidal ideation. Empirical studies, however, have not supported the notion of widespread emotional problems of gifted students, with most empirical studies finding that gifted students are either similar to or better adjusted than their same age nongifted peers (Czeschlik & Rost, 1994; Freeman, 1994; Olszewski-Kubilius, Kulieke, & Krasney, 1988; Richardson & Benbow, 1990; Sternberg & Davidson, 1985; Terman, 1954; Terman & Oden, 1947). Similarly, a study of 8- to 12-year old students found better coping among those who were high in creative thinking (Carson, Bittner, Cameron, & Brown, 1994), and a study of female undergraduates found better psychosocial functioning for those with higher creativity level (Smith & Tegano, 1992).

Overall, evidence suggests that gifted individuals tend to be psychologically and interpersonally well adjusted. Sternberg and Davidson (1985) agreed that IQ and social adjustment are positively related, except at the upper extremes of IQ where the relation between the two seems to break down. There needs to be more research on individuals with extremely high IQs (those above 180) before we can make definitive statements about their adjustment.

Although research studies, for the most part, have shown that gifted students are no worse off, and may even be better adjusted, than nongifted individuals, the myth persists that gifted people, in general, are maladjusted with respect to relationships with peers, interpersonal sensitivity, perfectionism, anxiety and stress, and depression.

Relationships With Peers

The nature and quality of gifted students' relationships with peers has been studied, with similar findings in preschoolers (Austin & Draper, 1981), kindergarten children (Schneider & Daniels, 1992), and elementary school-aged children (Rost & Czeschlik, 1994). The overall conclusion is that the psychosocial adjustment of gifted students generally does not differ significantly from their nongifted peers.

A question still remains about the social adjustment of the extremely gifted students, however. Hollingworth (1942) found that children with IQs above 180 tended to engage in more solitary activities and were not as accepted as their moderately gifted peers. One explanation for this finding has been that teachers may not be able to correctly assess the sociability of gifted students because they may have older friends who are not within the age-segregated classroom (Freeman, 1979). Gifted students who are placed in classes with similarly gifted peers are unlikely to be socially maladjusted.

The question of how adolescent gender and giftedness relate to social adjustment has also been a long-standing one since Coleman (1961) and Keisler (1955) reported that gifted adolescent girls tended to be less popular with boys than nongifted adolescent girls. Although these are dated studies, we cannot ignore them. More recently, Gilligan (1982) suggested that girls "go underground" at around 11 years of age. In other words, girls pretend that they are less knowledgeable or intelligent than they are so as not to sacrifice their social status or popularity. In a study of gifted adolescents, Kerr, Colangelo, and Gaeth (1988) found that although these adolescents appreciate the advantages associated with being gifted (i.e., personal growth and academic ease), they are concerned about the social stigma. Girls, in particular, feel the social disadvantages of their giftedness more strongly than boys. Callahan, Cunningham, and Plucker (1994) suggested that young women may attempt to downplay their academic achievements in order to attain social success.

Interpersonal Sensitivity

There has been a long-standing belief that gifted children are unusually sensitive to interpersonal dynamics and that they develop this sensitivity at an early age (Silverman, 1994). These beliefs are generally supported with case studies or general observations, with little in the way of empirical support.

Perfectionism

Gifted students have been described as having unrealistically high standards for themselves and others, inflexible routines, and indiscriminant acceptance of feedback by external evaluators (Kerr, 1991). The validity of these beliefs, however, remains in question because little quantitative research has been done in this area (Parker & Adkins, 1995). The question arises as to what perfectionism really means and what its psychological connotations are. Parker and Adkins, in their review of perfectionism and the gifted, distinguished between unhealthy perfectionism in which individuals strive to please others and the perfectionism that is based on self-defined standards of excellence. The proposal is that the "shoulds" of the unhealthy type are likely to be associated with feelings of inadequacy, whereas the pursuance of self-defined standards is not necessarily negative. In fact, Hewitt, Flett, and Turnbull-Donovan (1992) found that socially prescribed perfectionism was related to suicidal ideation, whereas expectations of perfectionism for self and others, based on personal standards, was not.

The question, therefore, is whether gifted individuals tend to display higher levels of social perfectionism than nongifted individuals. The answer is likely to be "no." Parker and Adkins (1995) indicated that descriptions of perfectionism in the gifted tended to focus on their self-directed standards rather than on socially prescribed expectations. Furthermore, Roberts and Lovett (1994) found that gifted adolescents were not more likely to evidence unhealthy perfectionism than their nongifted peers. Ochse (1990) reported that devotion to and absorption in one's work was typical of creative achievers and was not necessarily maladaptive. Perhaps "perfectionism" is, as Kerr (1991) offered, not a result of social pressures but an outcome of temperament, a drive to achieve one's personal best.

Anxiety and Stress

Perfectionism has been associated with anxiety and stress. Given the corollary belief that the gifted tend to be perfectionistic, the notion of the gifted experiencing high levels of anxiety and stress is not surprising. As described in the previous section, however, this thinking is flawed. Gifted individuals are probably not more likely to exhibit problematic types of perfectionism, and indeed, studies have not shown increased anxiety levels in the gifted. Jacobs (1971) compared high and average IQ kindergartners on the Rorschach Ink Blot test and found that the gifted children showed greater motivation and interest, less reliance on adults for approval, greater capacity for emotional reactions to the environment, and greater sensitivity to the emotional pressures of the environment than their nongifted counterparts. They were not found to be more anxious. Similarly, Davis and Connell (1985) and Schlowinski and Reynolds (1985) found lower anxiety in high IQ elementary school children. Milgram and Milgram (1976) reported a gender difference with respect to giftedness and anxiety. Gifted fourth- through eighth-grade girls had lower anxiety than nongifted girls but there was no difference between gifted and nongifted boys. There appears to be no merit to the idea that gifted children are more stressed or anxious than nongifted children.

In fact, it may be the case that gifted individuals have coping skills that enable them to take things in stride and actually experience less stress than their nongifted peers. Bland, Sowa, and Callahan (1994) described the concept of *resilience* as protective against stress. Those who are resilient tend to seek out new experiences, to lack fear, to play hard, to be self-reliant, and to be able to create feelings of normalcy for themselves, even in the face of chaos. These characteristics are often observed in gifted individuals as well. Although little research linking the two constructs has been done, these writers speculated that the ability to use cognitive appraisal in the mediation of stress underlies resilience for some gifted individuals. Use of cognitive appraisal helps individuals to reason out their response to stressors rather than to react reflexively. A study by Sowa et al. (1994), in fact, showed that gifted children tended to exhibit more adaptive cognitive appraisals at an earlier age than would normally be expected.

When stress and anxiety are experienced by gifted individuals, two possible sources should be explored. The first is the possibility that the individual is exhibiting high levels of socially prescribed perfectionism, the type that puts one at emotional risk. If a gifted individual has become dependent on external feedback for feelings of self-worth, every endeavor becomes stressful in that it presents, in the person's mind, another opportunity for failure. Another possibility is simply that the individual is taking on more commitments than can be reasonably handled. Because of their special talents and interests in many areas, it is not uncommon for gifted individuals to be encouraged by advisors, parents, and teachers to become involved in many different programs. A combination of poor time management skills and a lack of assertiveness could promote stress in gifted individuals.

Depression and Suicide

Kaiser and Berndt (1985) found that high-ability, high-achieving students did not report more symptoms of depression and loneliness than their nongifted adolescent peers. Webb et al. (1982) theorized that when depression is experienced by gifted adolescents, it is likely to result from a belief that one must live up to different and conflicting standards, isolation, or existential depression. In line with the first, the student who is reliant on external feedback for approval or who is overextended in commitments may feel that it is impossible to live up to all of the expectations and depression may be experienced as a result. In terms of the second issue, feelings of being different may be associated with loneliness and result in depression. In terms of the third issue, the tendency toward moral sensitivity may make gifted children more aware of world events and problems and the potential for injustices at an earlier age and with greater intensity than the typical nongifted child (Silverman, 1994).

Woody Allen vividly portrayed this in his movie, *Annie Hall*. As a young boy, Alvie Singer, an intellectually gifted child, was so depressed that his mother took him to see a psychiatrist, Dr. Flicker. Alvie was dragged to therapy when he withdrew from social interactions and the usual activities he enjoyed. Most disturbing to his mother was that he stopped doing his homework. From Alvie's perspective, there was no point in doing his homework when the world was coming to an end. Apparently Alvie had read that the universe was expanding. In a monotone voice Alvie told the psychiatrist that everything was hopeless. After all, the world was expanding and would ultimately break apart. Alvie's neurotic mother could not understand why her son was so distraught. In her estimation this was not normal behavior for a young boy from Brooklyn. What was it Alvie's business if the universe was expanding. Brooklyn was not expanding. Dr. Flicker tried reassuring Alvie that the universe would not be expanding for billions of years and he should try focusing on enjoying himself in the here and now. The doctor's attempts to cheer him up failed miserably. Alvie, as a gifted child was able to read about a scientific phenomenon that he could not deal with emotionally and psychologically despite a somewhat sophisticated intellectual understanding.

In part, the ability of gifted children to read at an early age enables them to become aware of the world's monumental problems before their defenses are well-enough developed to adequately cope (Kerr, 1991). This juxtaposition of higher order cognition and a childish orientation has been noted by Silverman (1994), who indicated that it is common for gifted children to exhibit asynchronous development, with extraordinary abilities in some areas along with childish reasoning or even immaturity in others. This combination renders a child more vulnerable to distress. For instance, Kerr (1991) suggested that issues such as the meaning of life and the inevitability of death, which do not have clear-cut answers, may provoke anger and despair in gifted students whose cognitive development is still dualistic (seeing things as right or wrong, good or bad). Asynchronous development can also cause others to place on the child disproportionate amounts of responsibility, such as asking a gifted 9-year-old to babysit for younger siblings. If something should happen while the parents are gone, such as an infant becoming feverish, the older child may not know how to handle the situation and may feel overwhelmed and self-critical as a result. In a similar way, adults, particularly parents, may share personal problems or family problems with a gifted child. Despite their apparent maturity in some areas, the gifted child could easily feel overwhelmed and burdened.

With respect to suicide, there are no recent statistics that break down suicide rates by intellectual or creative ability. However, Webb et al. (1982) reported that suicidal college students may be unusually creative, have high overall grade point averages that have recently declined, and attend selective and competitive schools. Because of the seriousness of the issue, suicide potential for any individual, gifted or not, should be carefully evaluated. Kerr (1991) suggested some special considerations for potentially suicidal gifted students. One is that they may develop especially effective suicide plans. It is also possible that these students, when so motivated, can purposely ease the concerns of counselors and other responsible adults by speaking of their problems in an articulate and reasonable manner. When this happens, gifted students may appear to have talked through and be coping with their problems, yet still be intending to kill themselves. These cautions make careful evaluation of the situation imperative.

Special Concerns of Gifted Females

Even though girls continue to receive higher grades than boys throughout their schooling, their intellectual achievements are increasingly devalued over the high school years (Callahan et al., 1994). This may help explain why girls generally have lower vocational aspirations than boys, and adult women have lower job satisfaction than do adult men. Perhaps girls generally have permission to excel in the academic area but not in real life (Stockard & Wood, 1984). Females have been found to be less productive than men with respect to career accomplishments and to be less likely to select careers that are commensurate with their talents and abilities. In a study of creative productivity (Callahan, 1991), it was found that male psychologists were more likely than female psychologists to be employed full time. Of the unemployed females, 51% cited family and domestic reasons as compared with 5% of the men. Male academicians publish more books and articles than their female counterparts; they earn more degrees and produce more works of art. The reasons proposed for this lack of female productivity are numerous.

Callahan et al. (1994) suggested six factors that contribute to female underproductivity. First, they indicated that females often do not have sufficient confidence, tending to attribute their successes to hard work rather than to their abilities. In essence, they discount their own abilities as the source of accomplishments, and messages from parents and teachers often reinforce their perceptions. Second, Callahan et al. indicated that efforts to succeed in the interpersonal domain can interfere with academic functioning. For instance, women may pretend to be stereotypically feminine, with lesser intellectual prowess, in an effort to be attractive to men. Third, they indicated that women often operate on the assumption that if they are well liked they will have more success, thus making the prioritizing of socialization, rather than direct career goals, likely. The fourth factor that they reported is that women tend to be externally, rather than internally, motivated. With that tendency, as well as the tendency to prioritize socialization, women are more likely to choose career paths that are rewarded by others. Additionally, they are inclined to seek out work that serves others. These tendencies may narrow career choices for women and, in some cases, may create stress if external motivations are continually sought. Finally, Callahan et al. pointed out that the excessive demands involved in fulfilling multiple roles, such as wife, mother, and career woman, can overwhelm women and lead them to give up entirely, or make sacrifices, in the career domain,

These factors may affect the career choices and paths of women in general. Gifted women may be especially likely to pursue multiple roles and to be caught up in the dilemmas described because they receive numerous messages from others about their potential. Counselors should be aware of these possibilities when working with gifted women.

Special Concerns of Disadvantaged and Minority Populations

There has been growing recognition in recent years about the issue of identification and inclusion of minority (Griffin, 1992; Scott, Perou, Urbano, Hogan, & Gold, 1992) and disadvantaged (Wright & Borland, 1992) youth in programs for the gifted. It has been widely recognized that these individuals are underrepresented in gifted programs (Swanson, 1995), and efforts to identify and nurture minority and disadvantaged students have taken place.

With this increased recognition has come growing awareness of some of the special issues that might be faced by these youngsters. It should be noted, first, that there are variations in the populations referred to in the works cited here. Two of the works focus on gifted Black students (Ford, 1994; Griffin, 1992). One focuses on gifted minority students, including Black and Hispanic students (Scott et al., 1992). One focuses on gifted students with economic disadvantages (Wright & Borland, 1992), and two focus on mixed categories, such as rural, Black students (Swanson, 1995). Olszewski-Kubilius, Grant, and Seibert (1994), however, identified an element that can be considered a common denominator among the groups: social disadvantage. The individuals referred to in these works generally have less access than gifted students from White middle-class families to people and situations that are conducive to their educational and personal growth.

According to Olszewski-Kubilius et al. (1994), assessing the issues faced by disadvantaged gifted students requires consideration of their individual circumstances. This is essential in order to help these students overcome the obstacles that are likely to hinder their development.

If it can be said that gifted students in general face situations that place them at risk for underachievement (such as has been discussed in previous sections of this chapter), disadvantaged gifted youth face additional risk factors. Black students are disproportionately at risk for underachievement (Ford, 1994) because of factors such as poverty, cultural obstacles, and linguistic differences. Additionally, the family lives of some disadvantaged youngsters may be chaotic, with substance abuse or emotional problems preventing parents from giving appropriate attention to their children (Wright & Borland, 1992). Parents, especially single parents, also may have little time available to them, and some, even with good intent, may have little awareness about how to be helpful.

It is also the case that messages that are conveyed to disadvantaged children by their parents may, at times, not be supportive and appropriate. Instead, these children may receive mixed or negative messages regarding education (Olszewski-Kubilius et al., 1994) because parents hold values that are discrepant with educational attainment or because they fear that achievement will take the youngster away from the family and their culture. If discussion of college attendance takes place at all, parents may expect the child to attend school close to home. They may also expect the child to provide financial or emotional support to the family rather than letting the child separate.

In some cases, discussion of college or career planning may be hampered by parental difficulties with long-range planning. The difficulties could occur because the parents are consumed with day-to-day difficulties or it could be simply that the parents are unaccustomed to planning for the future and are lacking in the skills needed to do so (Olszewski-Kubilius et al., 1994). In either case, the child does not receive needed guidance from his or her parents.

Mixed messages about educational attainment are not limited to the familial environment. There is often pressure from peers as well to reject mainstream values and maintain their cultural identity. Ford (1994) wrote of pressure within the Black culture for students to avoid affiliating too closely with the White culture. Some gifted students fear social isolation and are torn between achievement and their cultural identity.

Overall, there are a variety of circumstances that can place gifted minority or disadvantaged students at risk for underachievement. Careful assessment of circumstances in individual cases is needed in order to help students overcome the many obstacles that may exist.

INTERVENTIONS

Teachers, administrators, and other educational personnel who have contact with gifted individuals need to become aware of possible problems that these children may experience. Although the research clearly shows that the majority of gifted people do not have adjustment problems, some individuals may face issues that interfere with their functioning. In such cases, counseling could be beneficial. Ideally, gifted individuals and their family members should be seen by appropriate professionals who can adequately assess their psychological, social, and emotional needs. Counselors who do not have specialized knowledge and skills should refer the gifted to more qualified counselors or seek appropriate training or knowledge.

As stated previously, few counseling interventions have been empirically tested for use with a gifted population. With the exception of specific interventions that are aimed at career issues, there is a dearth of research comparing treatments for gifted versus nongifted people. In other words, although many authors have described typical behaviors and particular problems that gifted persons might experience, little or no data have been collected to assess the efficacy of intervention techniques with this population.

Instead, suggested interventions reported in the literature are those that appear to be logically related to the problems that have been identified and described. For example, if gifted girls have been found to inhibit the expression of their more scholarly thoughts and opinions in order to maintain popularity, then assertiveness training techniques have been suggested as an appropriate way to intervene. Although this, in fact, may be an appropriate intervention, its efficacy for gifted females, specifically, has not been empirically established. This lack of research regarding counseling techniques is a problem that counselors face whenever they are working with gifted clients. Nevertheless, the following suggestions are provided as a starting point for possible interventions.

Relationships and Interpersonal Sensitivity

When the interpersonal skills of gifted individuals are in need of refining, the traditional counseling methods of social skills training may be appropriate. This training is most effectively done within the context of group counseling so that the clients may receive feedback from others about their interpersonal styles. Assertiveness training may be helpful for those individuals who are hesitant to communicate their ideas for fear they would be ostracized. Often, for instance, very creative people have ideas that are different from those of their peers. Particularly in adolescence, when it is so important to "fit in" with one's peer group, teens may block themselves from sharing thoughts and opinions because their contributions may not be accepted. Assertiveness training may help gifted adolescents to communicate more freely and effectively, thus reducing their chances of alienating others.

Schlichter and Burke (1994) suggested that bibliotherapy (especially in group settings) cap help gifted students move through developmental stages, providing examples of how other people have dealt with developmental issues. They indicated that selecting appropriate books to use in bibliotherapy requires consideration of the qualities of the book (including the thematic dimension, defined as whether the theme is powerful or trite, and the stylistic dimension, defined as whether the book is written in clear or convoluted language) as well as consideration of how effective a vehicle the book would be for discussion of socioemotional themes.

Perfectionism

When unhealthy perfectionism is exhibited by gifted individuals, cognitive therapy techniques may be used to help individuals identify, challenge, and dispute the irrational belief that they must be perfect in order to be cared about and accepted. Students who dread failure, largely because they have no experience with it and therefore imagine the worst, may be asked by counselors to purposely go out and fail at something. In this way, the students learn that they can survive failure and are more likely to take risks in the future. The overall goal for counselors is to help students move away from the need for external approval and to learn to reward themselves instead (see works by Albert Ellis on rational emotive behavior therapy for more details about methods for reducing perfectionism).

Anxiety and Stress

In addition to helping individuals move toward internal motivations, the following interventions for anxiety and stress are suggested: (a) relaxation training to reduce the symptoms of anxiety and stress, (b) time management techniques to prevent gifted individuals from becoming overscheduled and therefore overwhelmed, and (c) assertiveness training to help gifted individuals set limits and to say no when they do not want to participate in certain activities.

Depression and Suicide

If a gifted individual has hinted at suicide and is depressed, a full suicide assessment, including the assessment of lethality, must be completed. If the depression is severe, the individual should be referred to a psychiatrist in order to be evaluated for antidepressant medication. As has been discussed, gifted individuals can be so articulate and competent at rationalizing their difficulties and at offering astute psychological insights that the counselor may be lulled into falsely believing everything is fine. The counselor should consider asking the person to describe his or her daily activities in detail to get a sense of how the individual is actually functioning (Kerr, 1991).

In dealing with depression that is based on irrational beliefs, cognitive restructuring can be used. For example, if a gifted person becomes devastated when someone does not like him or her, the irrational belief that "everyone must like me" can be actively disputed. Thought-stopping can be used to eliminate negative thoughts while these are replaced by positive thoughts. If the person has become withdrawn and isolated, it is important for the counselor to encourage and reinforce more active involvement in activities the individual once found pleasurable.

Special Concerns of Gifted Females

There are three categories of interventions that may be useful when working with gifted females. First, gifted females may be advised that attending an all-female school (high school or college) can be advantageous. Females are more likely to attend graduate school if they have attended an all-female college, and furthermore, many female CEOs of Fortune 500 companies graduated from all-female colleges. An explanation given for this is that females may be better able to express themselves in an environment where they are not concerned about how their scholastic attainment will affect their standing with men. Second, counselors can arrange mentoring opportunities for gifted girls. Mentoring is likely to foster positive personal development and have long-reaching positive effects on professional development. Third, because girls are often socialized to be passive, and let men take the lead, they sometimes lack the appropriate assertiveness needed to succeed. Assertiveness training may be useful in helping girls to speak and act with confidence.

Special Concerns of Disadvantaged and Minority Populations

An initial step to consider in designing interventions for disadvantaged and minority populations is involvement of the parents in parent education groups. Scott et al. (1992) found that parents of Black and Hispanic youngsters, while acknowledging the potential giftedness of their children, were significantly less likely than were White parents to request evaluation for placement in a gifted program. This suggests that these minority parents did not see the value of gifted education for their children. Parent education programs may help to dispel some of the negative images that may be held about gifted education and may also help parents to form an identity as a parent of a gifted child.

A step that might be taken in working with young children was detailed by Wright and Borland (1992). These writers suggested that young disadvantaged potentially gifted students could benefit from access to minority adolescent mentors. These mentors would be older successful students, who might enhance the self-image or encourage the development of a particular talent in the potentially gifted students with whom they were paired.

Ford (1994) outlined a program for fostering resilience to stress among gifted Black students. Parent involvement was an important component because Black students have done better academically when their parents were involved with the school. It was also recommended that an effort be made to have Black role models available. Furthermore, Ford suggested that group experiences be fostered so that gifted Black students can become comfortable with cooperative learning and with close affiliations with members of other racial and ethnic groups.

In terms of counseling needs, Ford (1994) suggested that, given the potential difficulties of being a Black student in a predominately White program, the social and emotional needs of Black students be addressed. With that, Black students can be helped to take on a "bicultural" identity, that is, learning to adapt to differences in cultural experiences while maintaining their cultural identity.

Finally, Olszewski-Kubilius and Scott (1994), after surveying the college counseling needs of gifted economically disadvantaged minority students, identified a wide range of counseling issues. They found that the disadvantaged gifted, although highly motivated to attend college, felt somewhat less prepared for college and less confident about being admitted to college than their more advantaged counterparts. The disadvantaged students also predicted that the college experience might be somewhat lonely for them. Olszewski-Kubilius and Scott recommended that gifted minority students receive early exposure to role models, specifically to minority college students, so that they can develop images of the college experience. Arranging campus visits, as college entry approaches, also may ease tensions about the possible loneliness of campus life. During these visits, students could be oriented to social supports that are available on campus.

Additionally, minority students, like others, can benefit from assistance with college selection and financial arrangements. Olszewski-Kubilius and Scott (1994) found that disadvantaged minority students, like others, often rely on nonacademic criteria (such as attractiveness of the campus) in selecting a school. They also found that Black parents may state that they will help their child finance school while they actually have little idea about how to do that or even what the costs of college will be. Assistance to both child and parent along those lines, then, would be appropriate.

Finally, Olszewski-Kubilius and Scott (1994) recognized that parents of gifted minority students may need help letting their children psychologically separate from the family as they enter college. They recommended that discussion of their feelings regarding their child's transition into college be incorporated into services for the parents.

In conclusion, a number of interventions (individual, group, and family) may be of benefit to gifted minority and disadvantaged students. More empirical research evaluating the efficacy of these interventions is needed.

STUDY ACTIVITIES

1. Interview school counselors at the elementary, middle, and secondary levels about whether they have special interventions or programs for gifted and creative students. If so, ask them to describe in detail the interventions and programs and then share this information with your colleagues.
2. Interview a director of guidance and counseling to identify programmatic interventions implemented throughout the school district to promote the talents of gifted and creative students.
3. Interview the coordinator of a university or college honors program to determine how that school develops the skills, abilities, and talents of these extraordinary individuals.
4. View the film *Little Man Tate,* followed by a group discussion regarding the need for attention to both the intellectual and emotional development of gifted children.
5. Debate whether special counseling programs for gifted and talented individuals is a cost-effective use of resources versus the implementation of counseling programs for all children.
6. Although girls excel academically, we know that they are less likely to produce works of art or to achieve the same levels of success as do men. Facilitate a group discussion that addresses the issue of how society promotes this phenomenon.

7. Working in small groups, have students gather information about enrichment programs available in state and federal programs, colleges and universities, and corporations. Share this information with colleagues. Be sure to include copies of applications and informational pamphlets or brochures.
8. Brainstorm methods that schools and school personnel can use to promote better relationships between creatively gifted students and their nongifted peers.
9. Identify topics and issues that may be of concern to the parents of gifted and creative children. Discuss how these concerns might differ or change at the elementary, secondary, and college levels.

REFERENCES

Achter, J., Lubinski, D., & Benbow, C. (1996). Multipotentiality among the intellectually gifted: "It was never there and already it's vanishing." *Journal of Counseling Psychology, 43,* 65-76.

Austin, A. B., & Draper, D. C. (1981). Peer relationships of the academically gifted: A review. *Gifted Child Quarterly, 25,* 129-133.

Berger, S. L. (1989). *College planning for gifted students.* Reston, VA: ERIC/CEC Clearinghouse on Gifted and Handicapped Children.

Bland, L., Sowa, C., & Callahan, C. (1994). An overview of resilience in gifted children. *Roeper Review, 17,* 77-80.

Callahan, C. (1991). An update on gifted females. *Journal for the Education of the Gifted, 14,* 284-311.

Callahan, C., Cunningham, C., & Plucker, J. (1994). Foundations for the future: The socio-emotional development of gifted adolescent women. *Roeper Review, 17,* 99-104.

Carson, D., Bittner, M., Cameron, B., & Brown, D. (1994). Creative thinking as a predictor of school-aged children's stress responses and coping abilities. *Creativity Research Journal, 7,* 145-158.

Coleman, J. L. (1961). *The adolescent society.* New York: The Free Press.

Czeschlik, T., & Rost, D. (1994). Socio-emotional adjustment in elementary school boys and girls: Does giftedness make a difference? *Roeper Review, 16,* 294-297.

Davis, H. B., & Connell, J. P. (1985). The effect of aptitude and achievement status on the self-system. *Gifted Child Quarterly, 29,* 131-135.

Emerick, L. (1992). Academic underachievement among the gifted: Students' perceptions of factors that reverse the pattern. *Gifted Child Quarterly, 36,* 140-146.

Emmett, J., & Minor, C. (1993). Career decision making factors in gifted young adults. *Career Development Quarterly, 41,* 350-366.

Ford, D. (1994). Nurturing resilience in gifted Black youth. *Roeper Review, 17,* 80-84.

Fredrickson, R. H. (1986). Preparing gifted and talented students for the world of work. *Journal of Counseling and Development, 64,* 556-557.

Freeman, J. (1979). *Gifted children.* Baltimore, MD: University Park Press.

Freeman, J. (1994). Some emotional aspects of being gifted. *Journal for the Education of the Gifted, 17,* 180-197.

Gilligan, C. (1982). *In a different voice: Psychological theory and women's development.* Cambridge, MA: Harvard University Press.

Griffin, J. (1992). Catching the dream for gifted children of color. *Gifted Child Quarterly, 36,* 126-130.

Hewitt, P., Flett, G., & Turnbull-Donovan, W. (1992). Perfectionism and suicide potential. *British Journal of Clinical Psychology, 31,* 181-190.

Hollingworth, L. (1942). *Children above 180 I.Q.: Origin and development.* Yonkers, NY: World Book.

Jacobs, J. C. (1971). Rorschach studies reveal possible misinterpretations of personality traits of the gifted. *Gifted Child Quarterly, 16,* 195-200.

Kaiser, C. F., & Berndt, D. J. (1985). Predictors of loneliness in the gifted adolescent. *Gifted Child Quarterly, 29,* 74-77.

Karnes, P. A., & D'Ilio, V. R. (1988). Comparison of gifted children and their parents' perception of the home environment. *Gifted Child Quarterly, 32,* 277-279.

Keirouz, K. (1990). Concerns of parents of gifted children: A research review. *Gifted Child Quarterly, 34,* 56-63.

Keisler, E. R. (1955). Peer group ratings of high school pupils with high and low school marks. *Journal of Experimental Education, 23,* 375-378.

Kelly, K. (1992). Career maturity of young gifted adolescents: A replication study. *Journal for the Education of the Gifted, 16,* 36-45.

Kerr, B. (1985). Smart girls, gifted women: Special guidance concerns. *Roeper Review, 8,* 30-33.

Kerr, B. (1991). *A handbook for counseling the gifted and talented.* Alexandria, VA: American Association for Counseling and Development.

Kerr, B., Colangelo, N., & Gaeth, J. (1988). Gifted adolescents' attitudes toward their giftedness. *Gifted Child Quarterly, 32,* 245-247.

Kerr, B., & Erb, C. (1991). Career counseling with academically talented students: Effects of a value-based intervention. *Journal of Counseling Psychology, 38,* 309-314.

Kolb, K., & Jussim, L. (1994). Teacher expectations and underachieving gifted children. *Roeper Review, 17,* 26-30.

Lim, T. (1995). Letters to themselves: Gifted students' plans for positive lifestyles. *Roeper Review, 17,* 85-98.

Lovecky, D. (1992). Exploring social and emotional aspects of giftedness in children. *Roeper Review, 15,* 18-25.

McMann, N., & Oliner, R. (1988). Problems in families with gifted children: Implications for counselors. *Journal of Counseling and Development, 66,* 275-278.

Meckstroth, E. (1992). Paradigm shifts into giftedness. *Roeper Review, 15,* 91-92.

Milgram, R. M., & Milgram, N. A. (1976). Personality characteristics of gifted Israeli children. *Journal of Genetic Psychology, 129,* 185-194.

Ochse, R. (1990). *Before the gates of excellence: The determinants of creative genius.* Cambridge: Cambridge University Press

Olszewski, P., Kulieke, M., & Buescher, Y. (1987). The influence of the family environment of the development of talent: A literature review. *Journal of the Education of the Gifted, 2,* 6-28.

Olszewski-Kubilius, P., Grant, B., & Seibert, C. (1994). Social support systems and the disadvantaged gifted: A framework for developing programs and services. *Roeper Review, 17,* 20-25.

Olszewski-Kubilius, P., Kulieke, M., & Krasney, N. (1988). Personality dimensions of gifted adolescents: A review of the empirical literature. *Gifted Child Quarterly, 32,* 347-352.

Olszewski-Kubilius, P., & Scott, J. (1994). An investigation of the college and career counseling needs of economically disadvantaged, minority gifted students. *Roeper Review, 14,* 141-148.

Parker, W., & Adkins, K. (1995). Perfectionism and the gifted. *Roeper Review, 17,* 173-176.

Perrone, P. (1986). Guidance needs of gifted children, adolescents, and adults. *Journal of Counseling and Development, 64,* 564-566.

Pleiss, M., & Feldhusen J. (1995). Mentors, role models, and heroes in the lives of gifted children. *Educational Psychologist, 30,* 159-169.

Post-Krammer, P., & Perrone, P.A. (1982). Career perceptions of talented individuals: A follow-up study. *Vocational Guidance Quarterly, 31,* 203-211.

Richardson, T., & Benbow, C. (1990). Long-term effects of acceleration on the social-emotional adjustment of mathematically precocious youths. *Journal of Educational Psychology, 82,* 464-470.

Roberts, S. M., & Lovett, S. B. (1994). Examining the "F" in gifted: Academically gifted adolescents' physiological and affective responses to scholastic failure. *Journal for the Education of the Gifted, 17,* 241-259.

Rogers, J., & Nielsen, A. (1993). Gifted children and divorce: A study of the literature on the incidence of divorce in families with gifted children. *Journal for the Education of the Gifted, 16,* 251-267.

Rost, D., & Czeschlik, T. (1994). The psycho-social adjustment of gifted children in middle-childhood. *European Journal of Psychology of Education, 9,* 15-25.

Schlichter, C., & Burke, M. (1994). Using books to nurture the social and emotional development of gifted students. *Roeper Review, 16,* 280-283.

Schneider, B., & Daniels, T. (1992). Peer acceptance and social play of gifted kindergarten children. *Exceptionality, 3,* 17-29.

Schlowinski, E., & Reynolds, C. R. (1985). Dimensions of anxiety among high IQ children. *Gifted Child Quarterly, 29,* 125-130.

Schroer, A. C., & Dorn, F. J. (1986). Enhancing the career and personal development of gifted college students. *Journal of Counseling and Development, 64,* 564-566.

Scott, M., Perou, R., Urbano, R., Hogan, A., & Gold, S. (1992). The identification of giftedness: A comparison of white, hispanic, and black families. *Gifted Child Quarterly, 36,* 131-139.

Silverman, L. (1994). The moral sensitivity of gifted children and the evolution of society. *Roeper Review, 17,* 110-116.

Smith, D., & Tegano, D. (1992). Relationship of scores on two personality measures: Creativity and self-image. *Psychological Reports, 71,* 43-49.

Sowa, C., McIntire, J., May, K., & Bland, L. (1994). Social and emotional adjustment themes across gifted children. *Roeper Review, 17,* 95-98.

Sternberg, R., & Davidson, J. (1985). Cognitive development in the gifted and talented. In P. D. Horowitz & M. O'Brien (Eds.), *The gifted and talented: Developmental perspectives* (pp. 37-74). Washington, DC: American Psychological Association.

Sternberg, R., & Zhang, L. (1995). What do we mean by giftedness? A pentagonal implicit theory. *Gifted Child Quarterly, 39,* 88-94.

Stockard, J., & Wood, J. W. (1984). The myth of female underachievement: A re-examination of sex differences in academic underachievement. *American Educational Research Journal, 21,* 825-838.

Strom, R., Strom, S., Strom, P., & Collinsworth, P. (1994). Parental competence in families with gifted children. *Journal for the Education of the Gifted, 18,* 39-54.

Swanson, J. (1995). Gifted African-American children in rural schools: Searching for the answers. *Roeper Review, 17,* 261-266.

Terman, L. (1954). The discovery and encouragement of exceptional talent. *American Psychologist, 9,* 221-230.

Terman, L., & Oden, M. (1947). *Genetic studies of genius, Vol. 4: The gifted child grows up.* Stanford, CA: Stanford University Press.

Thomas, V. (1995). Of thorns and roses: The use of the Brier Rose fairy tale in therapy with families of gifted children. *Contemporary Family Therapy, 17,* 83-91

Torrance, E. P. (1961). Problems of highly creative children. *Gifted Child Quarterly, 5,* 31-34.

Tuttle, D., & Cornell, D. (1993). Maternal labeling of gifted children: Effects on the sibling relationship. *Exceptional Children, 59,* 402-410.

VanTassel-Baska, J. (1987). *Attitudes of parents of gifted students.* Unpublished research report. Center for Development of Talent, Northwestern University, Evanston, IL.

Web, J. T., Meckstroth, B., & Tolan, S. (1982). *Guiding the gifted child.* Columbus: Ohio Psychology Publishing.

West, J. D., Hosie, T. W., Mathews, F. N. (1989). Families of academically gifted children: Adaptability and cohesion. *School Counselor, 37,* 121-127.

Wright, L., & Borland, J. (1992). A special friend: Adolescent mentors for young, economically disadvantaged, potentially gifted students. *Roeper Review, 14,* 124-129.

Zuccone, C. F., & Amerikaner, M. (1986). Counseling gifted underachievers: A family systems approach. *Journal of Counseling and Development, 64,* 590-592.

Part V

Conclusions

The final chapter in this book deals with conclusions. What may we conclude about our knowledge base about creative thinking and creative problem solving? What have we learned about the educational psychology of creativity? There are very few individuals with the stature of E. Paul Torrance to attempt to answer these questions. Torrance has not been the only great figure in the study of creativity, but he may lay claim to being the single most purposeful researcher, writer, and creativity educator of our time. Readers also are referred to a recent biography of Torrance by Garnet W. Millar, titled The Creativity Man: An Authorized Biography.[1]

To be sure, we have incomplete answers and unfinished business. Certainly Torrance expects there to be more questions for current and future researchers. But, in chapter 11, Torrance discusses a number of conclusions about creativity and lessons he has learned over his decades-long career. There is much to study in this chapter and it is fervently hoped that the reader will find it a fascinating and enjoyable enterprise to reread Torrance's paper and other chapters in this book to begin to grapple as fully as possible with the wonders and the promise of the educational psychology of creativity.

---

[1]Millar, G. W. (1996). *The creativity man: An authorized biography.* Norwood, NJ: Ablex.

12

Reflection on Emerging Insights on the Educational Psychology of Creativity

E. Paul Torrance
University of Georgia

The past 40 years have been the most productive in history for new insights into the educational psychology of creativity. I am proud to have been a part of the quiet revolution in education that has been made this possible. It has been exciting to see them emerge and flower. Some of them have come from research and others have emerged from practice. Some have come from the almost forgotten past, while others have come from visioning the future.

In my address in 1960 before the Space Age Conference sponsored by the Minnesota Chapter of the Air Force Association, I (Torrance, 1963) made some predictions about what was likely to happen in this sphere on the basis of the insights that I had at that time. I predicted that the goals of education would change to give more importance to thinking (creative, critical, logical, evaluative). I predicted that educational psychologists would develop a psychology of thinking, not to replace the psychology of learning but to add to it. I also predicted that as a result mankind would become less naive and brutish in future generations. I am glad to have lived long enough to have seen most of these predictions realized. In stating their course objectives, almost all teachers include thinking objectives. There are scores of textbooks on the psychology of thinking and graduate and undergraduate courses in the area. It may seem that we are still as naive and as brutish as ever, but no one can deny that since 1960, we have become less brutish in our treatment of children, women, Blacks and all other races and we have become more willing to negotiate.

I predicted that a great amount of retooling would take place and it has. We now have many tests of creative and other kinds of thinking. Reading books and materials have changed, as have those in every curricular area. As a result, high school students attain higher scores on abstract thinking, creative thinking, and problem solving than they did in the early 1960s (Flanagan, 1976). National and international testing, as well as college and graduate admissions testing have been resistant to these changes. Consequently, society is greatly concerned that today's students are not learning as much.

LEARNING FROM THE PAST AND CONTEMPORARIES

Many insights about the educational psychology of creativity have come from the past. Elizabeth Andrews, Frederick Bartlett, Laura Chassell, S. S. Colvin, John Dewey, Kate Franck, E. A. Kirkpatrick, Hughes Mearns, Johnson O'Conner, T. Ribot, John Rossman, R. M. Simpson, Charles Spearman, M. D. Vernon, George Wallas, Guy Whipple, and Laura Zirbes (Torrance, 1962) were some of these pioneers whose ideas or research findings were ignored at the time. Margaret Mead, the headline speaker at the Space Age Conference, challenged my predictions by asking, "How can we expect creativity to catch on since there have been so many failures in the past?" I responded that we had the experiences, insights, and products of the past. Already, they had given us some tests, the rudiments of a creative problem-solving process, classroom procedures, a philosophy, and curricula.

In 1960, there was already a great deal of research and active practitioners. Among these contemporaries were H. H. Anderson, Manuel Barkan, Frank Barron, Benjamin Bloom, Robert Burkhart, Ruth Carlson, Raymond Cattell, J. E. Drevdahl, Elizabeth Drews, John Flanagan, Norman Fredricksen, J. J. Gallagher, J. W. Getzels, J. P. Guilford, Dale Harris, John Holland, L. S. Kubie, Victor Lowenfeld, D. C. McClellan, D. W. MacKinnon, Joe McPherson, Abraham Maslow, S. A. Mednick, N. C. Meier, Alice Miel, Ross Mooney, Clark Moustakas, Henry Murray, A. F. Osborn, William Owen, Sidney J. Parnes, Catherine Patrick, Pauline Pepinsky, Anne Roe, Carl Rogers, David Russell, M. I. Stein, Calvin Taylor, Irving Taylor, P. E. Vernon, and L. Welch (Torrance, 1979). They were producing tests, problem-solving procedures, classroom procedures, textbooks, and other educational materials. Many of them continued to be active in creativity research and others became famous for their contributions. Some are still active.

With this general overview of how insights on the educational psychology of creativity stood in 1960, we can think of the insights that have emerged. I pay tribute to the insights that emerged from my contemporaries, but it is overwhelming to try to summarize them. Therefore, I have chosen to identify and briefly discuss the insights I have developed during this period.

INSIGHTS ABOUT THE MEASUREMENT OF CREATIVE THINKING ABILITY

Although my deepest concern has been the teaching of creative thinking and creative teaching, I realize that I am best known for my thoughts about the measurement of creative thinking ability and the long-range prediction of creative achievement. This is probably justified because measurement and prediction are the very heart of scientific research.

My objective was to first create an all-purpose test (Torrance, 1962) that could be used from kindergarten through old age. I knew that the test tasks must be open-ended so that the test would be fair to all ages, races, cultures, and both genders; so that subjects could respond in terms of their experiences no matter who they might be. Later, tests could be developed with more specialized but more limited objectives. I realized that one can be creative in many ways and that I must select tasks that would sample the most important ways of thinking creatively. I saw these as hypothesizing, thinking of possible causes and consequences, possible uses, possible changes, and imagining possibilities in impossible situations.

The tasks were factor-analyzed and selected on the basis of these data, selecting those tasks that were most different from one another. This meant that the activities would be task-specific, but I believed that the sampling would overcome this. Later, Cunnington and I created the Sounds and Images Test, which I hoped would be a test of general creativity. It requires the production of images and all creativity requires imagery. This task did prove to be consistently significantly correlated to all of our criteria of creative ability and achievement. However, the Sounds and Images Test has never been widely used. The cumulative bibliography (Torrance, Rose, & Smith, 1996) contains only 40 entries for Sounds and Images, whereas the one for the Torrance Tests of Creative Thinking TTCT; Torrance et al., 1996) contains over 2,000 entries.

The second most used of the TTCT is Thinking Creatively in Action and Movement. The cumulative bibliography (Torrance & Rose, 1992) contained 56 entries in 1992. The biggest insight from using

Thinking Creatively in Action and Movement is that the modality in which the creative thinking is expressed is important. Young children from ages 3 to 6 are not able to respond well verbally or in drawing because they have been talking and drawing for only a short time, but they have been expressing their creative thinking in action and movement all of their lives. Another insight is that economically disadvantaged children, rather than more affluent children, cling to this modality longer. Children are instructed to give movement responses but they are permitted to give verbal or mixed verbal and movement responses. Haley (1984) found no differences between disadvantaged and affluent children in the total responses, but she found that affluent children gave significantly more verbal and significantly fewer action and movement responses.

Some helpful insights regarding motivation in measuring creative ability have also been developed. Two of the tasks in the TTCT were along the lines of Guilford's divergent thinking abilities (Product Improvement and Possible Uses). However, the instructions for the TTCT tell subjects that their creative abilities are being tested and are motivated for fluency, flexibility, originality, and elaboration. This in not done in administering Guilford's tests. I have used the analogy to measuring jumping ability. We would not think of measuring jumping ability by just how high or far they are jumping. We would try to motivate them to jump and we would tell them to see how high or how far they could jump. The TTCT consistently predicts creative achievement whereas the Guilford measures do not.

INSIGHTS ABOUT THE PREDICTION OF CREATIVE ACHIEVEMENT

Two important longitudinal studies of creative achievement have been done. One I refer to as the 22-year study and the other as the 30-year study. There has been significant validity in both studies (Torrance, 1972a, 1972b, 1981, 1993), but the level of prediction has varied as seen in the 30-year study. The first follow-up was of the high school seniors in 1966. The predictive validities were satisfactory for all of the creativity measures (Torrance, 1972a, 1972b). The next follow-up was conducted in 1970 and all the validities were at a higher level. This was an unexpected finding because all previous prediction had shown that correlations are lowered or disappear within a few years. We wondered if they might be even higher in 1990. They were lower in 1990 but still significant. Then we began to study what we called the *beyonders*. We looked for evidence of the beyonder characteristics such as being in love with work, persistence, courage, risk-taking, feeling comfortable with being different, and the like. We constructed a Beyonder Checklist (Torrance, 1991) and applied it in the analysis.

The insight that derived from these findings is that we have to wait long enough (about 10 years after high school graduation) for superior creative thinking abilities to result in creative achievements. However, after 30 years have elapsed, the beyonder characteristics, such as persistence, risk-taking, love of work, and the like, become more important in creative achievements. Those for whom classmates held the highest expectations did attain high creative achievements but not as high as the beyonders. (Great Expectations were determined by five sociometric questions: both the number and quality of the publicly recognized and acknowledged creative achievements as well as their "style of life" creative achievements.)

For numerous reasons, I (Torrance, 1995) maintained that one's image of the future is a better predictor of creative achievement than past achievements. This is an insight that is largely ignored, rejected, and ridiculed. In both my 22-year study (Torrance, 1987) and the 30-year study (Torrance, 1993), future career images proved to be good predictors. In the 30-year study it was the best single predictor (Torrance, in press). Admittedly, further work is needed on the development of measures of future career image but our crude measures yield promising results.

It had long been assumed that having a mentor aided creative achievement, but this insight had never been empirically tested until the 22-year study (Torrance, 1984) and very little had been done to promote mentoring in schools and communities, but in 1996 such programs were commonplace (Torrance, Goff, & Satterfield, 1998). Although I attribute no causal relation between this finding and the great increase in mentoring programs, it is an interesting coincidence.

CULTURE AND CREATIVITY

At least from the time of Aristotle, it had been assumed that creative achievement is influenced by culture. The saying, "What is honored in a culture will be cultivated there" is attributed to Aristotle. We have never had specific insights or research findings about these relations.

My interest in this problem began when I tried to understand the "fourth-grade slump" in creative thinking. In the early 1960s I undertook a large-scale study involving about 1,000 subjects in Grades 1 through 6 in the following cultures: India, Norway, Germany, Western Samoa, Australia, mainstream U.S. culture, and the segregated Black U.S. culture. Later, I collected other data to explore specific issues from the following cultures: France; Greece; Mexico, and the Chinese, British, Malay, and

Tamil cultures in Singapore. One of the problems I wanted to investigate was the different attitudes concerning divergency.

This study yielded many insights regarding creativity and culture. Almost all of the children in these cultures did experience a slump in creative thinking ability but at different times. The U.S. mainstream culture showed this discontinuity earliest but Germany and India did not experience a discontinuity until Grade 5 for verbal and in Grade 6 for figural. The other cultures experienced very little discontinuity, but neither did they show much growth. In Western Samoa, the children in the native schools followed this same pattern, but those in schools operated by the Mormon missions with U.S.-trained teachers showed the same discontinuity, although a later time than in the United States.

Gender differences in levels of creativity were also influenced by culture. Boys in the Western Samoan and Mexican cultures excelled girls in figural creativity. On further examination it was found that in Mexican culture only males are permitted to paint the pottery, the chief product of the area. In Western Samoa, males are the official artists of the culture. In India, males excelled females in verbal creativity. Much of the curriculum is devoted to languages and boys are expected to excel to carry on the business of the culture and they have to know three or more languages to succeed and everyone knows this.

We derived two indexes that I believed would be related the level of creativity of children being educated in that culture. One of these indexes was based on the diversity of the occupational aspirations expressed by the subjects. I thought that this would reflect the opportunity they had for the expression of their creativity. The other index was based on teachers' responses to the Ideal Child Checklist, which required teachers to rate the extent to which they encouraged or discouraged each of 60 characteristics that had been found to be related to creativity (Torrance, 1965).

Data were available on the following cultures and subcultures: mainstream U.S. Minnesota, mainstream California, and U.S. Black Georgia; West Germany (Berlin); Norway; Chinese, Tamil, and Malay Singapore; India (New Delhi), and Western Samoa. The 11 cultures and subcultures were ranked on the creativity of the subjects and each of the predictor indexes. The results are summarized in Table 12.1.

Rank-order correlation was used. It should be noted that there is almost perfect correlation. The only slight deviations were western Australia and the Singapore cultures. The Australian children perceived limited occupational opportunity in creative occupations. The Australian teachers were also a little harsh in discouraging creative characteristics. The Tamil and Chinese subcultures in Singapore were also harsh in discouraging creative characteristics.

Table 12.1. Ranking of Cultures and Subcultures by Three Criteria.

Culture or Subculture	Creativity Level	Creative Characteristics	Creative Occupational Aspiration
Minnesota, U.S.	1	1	1
California, U.S.	2	2	2
West Germany	3	3	3
Norway	4	—	6
Chinese, Singapore	5	7	7
Tamil, Singapore	6	7	6
West. Australia	7	8	4
Malay Singapore	8	5	8
Georgia Black, U.S.	9	7	9.5
India, New Delhi	10	10	9.5
Western Samoa	11	9	11

Raina (1996), by synthesizing my cross-cultural studies, derived several new insights. In his conclusion, he wrote the following:

> Multicultural exposure provides vast and variegated foundations to salvage some neglected and complex facts. It provides sensitive respect for others' values and facilitates communication between members of different cultures by recognizing and accepting the deep seated complexes which color our own outlook as well as those of other interlocutors.
>
> . . . giving the world a better understanding of creativity within all of us will revivify the mind and open up a whole horizon that celebrates the manyness of Lord Vishvakarma. (p. 164)

Among the more specific insights discussed by Raina (1996) are the following:

- Creativity is an infinitely endlessly diverse phenomenon that provides meaning and purpose to many in life and a sense of purpose in relation to cosmos.
- The drops in creativity found in some cultures and the failure to reach a higher level of creativity are culturally and not biologically related.

- One's conceptualization can get broadened and illuminated as a result of positive understanding of international insights.
- A worldview that grants genuine legitimacy to those beliefs and values can inspire a sense of connection.
- International networks of creative people can be a very powerful force for keeping world peace and for dealing with other threats that exist tomorrow.

These insights that emerged from a synthesis of my cross-cultural studies add strength to my findings.

CREATIVE PROBLEM SOLVING

Many insights concerning creative problem solving have emerged since the 1950s. One of the most basic is that willingness to disagree promotes the production of creative ideas and problem solving. This insight emerged and was tested in a variety of ways when I was engaged in survival research in the 1950s (Torrance, 1957). During this period, we were in a somewhat paradoxical situation regarding willingness to disagree. On one hand, much importance was placed on maintaining harmony and agreement in groups—business, industry, family, education, military, government, and so on. On the other hand, many were bemoaning the fact that we seemed to be living in an age of conformity and that controversy was a lost art. We found in a study of air crew effectiveness in combat over Korea that the more effective crews in comparison with less effective crews were characterized by greater participation, initially wider divergence of expressed ideas, and greater acceptance of decisions.

It seemed obvious that if people do not communicate their creative ideas and opinions, there are likely to be misunderstandings that affect group processes and performance. Our research in both survival training and actual survival in emergencies and extreme conditions showed that willingness to disagree meant the difference between survival and failure. There remained a need for new insights about the factors that impede expression of disagreement. In our research, it was demonstrated that power or status differences impede the expression of disagreement. This has to be handled in a nonsuppressive manner. Basic perhaps is a clear demonstration that disagreement will not be punished. When there is a need for creative thinking, permanent groups with power differences should not be used. In fact, this was clearly demonstrated in some of my experiments. A parent, teacher, supervisor, manager, superior officer, or other power figure must learn to identify with the group's decision rather than his or her initial opinion.

These insights are still not widely accepted. However, vast progress has taken place. In December 1996, I heard senators, congressmen, cabinet members, diplomats, and other politically powerful figures expound the values of disagreement and creative solutions. This boded well for the U.S. government, international relations, and society in general.

These insights were basic to Osborn's (1952, 1953) formulation of the principles of brainstorming and creative problem solving. His famous four rules for brainstorming were a calculated procedure to produce disagreement and conditions conducive to the production of original ideas. His first rule forbids criticism. This was based on the insight that the creative mind and the judgmental mind cannot function at a high level at the same time. This insight led to the principle of suspended judgment in brainstorming and creative problem solving.

Parnes (1988, 1992) refined and elaborated many of Osborn's insights. Perhaps the greatest leap by Parnes is found in his visionizing program. This program consists of the following five steps: exploring dreams, expanding options through imaging, expanding and clustering possibilities, focusing on options and improvements for action plans, and committing to action. The primary advance springs from the insight that imagery is involved in all creative thinking. This is probably the reason that Sounds and Images has been such a consistent predictor of creative behavior and creative achievement.

Several disciplined procedures for creative problem solving in addition to Osborn's emerged—synectics (Gordon, 1961), de Bono's (1970) lateral thinking, Torrance's (1975) sociodramatic approach, the Japanese methods (Kawakita, 1967; Nakayama, 1977), and the like. Several hundred studies were analyzed (Torrance, 1972c, 1987), including the use of art, dramatics, creative reading programs, complex programs involving packages of materials, motivational programs and devices, and the like. All of these methods usually produced growth in creative ability or achievement as assessed by various criteria. However, the disciplined problem-solving method produced the most successful results. Some of the investigators in these experiments were inexperienced and lacking in skills themselves. Success seemed to depend more on the skills of the experimenter than on the method of creative problem solving or other procedure.

THE INCUBATION MODEL OF TEACHING

Several insights about teaching for creativity have emerged in the process of developing and perfecting the Incubation Model of Teaching. I identify and discuss a few of these insights.

These insights started coming when I was asked by an educational publisher to serve as creativity consultant on a new program of reading materials. There would be the reading books, teacher's manuals, and skills books with exercises. I realized that to prepare the teachers manuals the writers were limited to suggestions of what they could do before, during, and after the reading. Then came the insights about what could be done to accomplish this. Before reading, the task is to heighten anticipation by creating the desire to know, to get the attention of the readers, to arouse curiosity, to tickle the imagination, and to give purpose and motivation. During the reading, the teacher's task is to continue to deepen expectation. This could be done by doing something to make the reader "dig deeper," to "look twice," to use all their senses, and the like. At the end or after the reading, the task is to keep the creative process going, by relating it to the reader ("singing in one's own key"), to imagine and fantasize ("building sand castles"), plugging into other resources and putting forth more effort ("plugging in the sun"), and thinking of future uses of the information read.

After working through this, insights emerged about how to put it all together and the Incubation Model of Teaching was born (Torrance & Safter, 1990). This is expressed in Figure 12.1. The fundamental insight underlying the entire model is that creating incompletenesses results in motivation for creative learning.

The publisher and I had focused on creative learning skills and had not given much thought to other outcomes. When field reports began to come in, these outcomes began to unfold. Everyone was surprised that so many of the children in the entire school began to check out more books from the school library. One school reported that more than twice the number of books were checked out than during the previous year. Teachers said they never knew when a reading lesson ended. Children conducted experiments, asked questions of their parents and others, and applied insights about what they had read.

Insights also came from the interactions of the writers, editors, artists, and graphics people. The chief editor was enthusiastic from the outset, but the in-house editor was doubtful. She did not think that she was creative. She learned that she was creative and sparked the creativity of the artists, graphics people, and writers. The writers wrote stories that led beginners through the creative problem-solving process. The graphics people used print in new ways. The artists used pictures to facilitate the creative process. The entire staff apparently bonded as a result of their creative interaction. I attended the unveiling celebration and their pride in the product was visible.

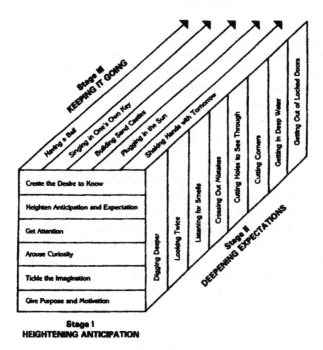

Figure 12.1. The incubation model of teaching

INSIGHTS FROM OTHER DISCIPLINES

Many of the insights from other disciplines are useful in the educational psychology of creativity. For example, in physics it was found that the most productive and creative physicists had read more of the old literature than their less productive and creative counterparts. Insights that had been advanced in the past that had been ignored, ridiculed, or rejected had been later tested and were proved correct and were accepted. I have always encouraged my doctoral students to examine the old literature even though some of my colleagues in educational psychology counseled their doctoral candidates to be concerned only with the last 5 or 10 years of research.

Insights may come from any discipline, but I think the discipline of psychology has produced the most insights applicable to the educational psychology of creativity. Barron (1990, 1995) and Amabile (1989, 1996) have been two of the most productive psychologists over a long period. Barron's insights have been primarily in the areas of measurement, personality characteristics, and mental health. Amabile's insights have been in the areas of development, personality characteristics, and contexts. Although I and other educational psychologists had advanced and presented evidence favoring the insight that "Extraordinary talent, personality, and cognitive ability do not seem to be enough—it's the labor of love aspect that determines creativity" (Amabile, 1986, p. 12). It was Amabile who gained general acceptance of the insight.

CONCLUSION

This chapter has reviewed many of the insights that have emerged since the 1950s concerning the educational psychology of creativity. Tribute was paid to past and contemporary investigators, but this chapter has been concerned with the insights I have developed. The insights have been about the measurement of creative thinking ability and other creative characteristics, the prediction of creative achievement, culture and creativity, the creative problem solving, the Incubation Model of Teaching, and insights from other disciplines.

REFERENCES

Amabile, T. (1986). The personality of creativity. *Creative Learning, 15*(3), 12-16.

Amabile, T. M. (1989). *Growing up creative: Nurturing a lifetime of creativity.* Buffalo, NY: Creative Education Press.

Amabile, T. M. (1996). *Creativity in context.* Boulder, CO: Westview Press.

Barron, F. (1990). *Creativity and psychological health.* Buffalo, NY: Creative Education Press.

Barron, F. (1995). *No rootless flower: An ecology of creativity.* Cresskill, NJ: Hampton Press.

de Bono, E. (1970). *Lateral thinking.* New York: Harper & Row.

Flanagan, J. F. (1976). Changes in school levels of achievement: Project TALENT ten and fifteen year retests. *Educational Researcher, 5*(8), 9-12.

Gordon, W. J. J. (1961). *Synectics: The development of creative capacity.* New York: Harper & Row.

Haley, G. L. (1984). Creative response styles: The effects of socio-economic status and problem solving training. *Journal of Creative Behavior, 18*, 25-40.

Kawakita, J. (1967). *Hasso-ho: Abduction procedure.* Tokyo: Chuko Shinso.

Nakayama, M. (1977). *NM method.* Tokyo: Sanno College Press.

Osborn, A. F. (1952). *Wake-up your mind.* New York: Charles Scribner's.

Osborn, A. F. (1953). *Applied imagination: Principles and procedures of creative problem solving.* New York: Charles Scribner's.

Parnes, S. J. (1988). *Visionizing.* East Aurora, NY: D.O.K.

Parnes, S. J. (1992). *Visionizing.* Buffalo, NY: Creative Education Foundation.

Raina, M. K. (1996). The Torrance phenomenon: Extended creative search for Lord Vishvakarma. *Creative and Innovation Management, 5,* 149-168.

Torrance, E. P. (1957). Group decision-making and disagreement. *Social Forces, 35,* 314-318.

Torrance, E. P. (1962). *Guiding creative talent.* Englewood Cliffs, NJ: Prentice-Hall.

Torrance, E. P. (1963). *Education and the creative potential.* Minneapolis: The University of Minnesota Press.

Torrance, E. P. (1965). The creative personality and the ideal pupil. *Teachers College Record, 65,* 220-229.

Torrance, E. P. (1972a). Career patterns and peak creative achievements: High school students twelve years later. *Gifted Child Quarterly, 16,* 15-88.

Torrance, E. P. (1972b). Predictive validity of the Torrance Tests of Creative Thinking. *Journal of Creative Behavior, 6,* 236-252.

Torrance, E. P. (1972c). Can we teach children to think creatively? *Journal of Creative Behavior, 6,* 114-143.

Torrance, E. P. (1979). *The search for satori and creativity.* Buffalo, NY: Creative Education Foundation.

Torrance, E. P. (1981). Predicting the creativity of elementary school pupils (1958-1980). *Gifted Child Quarterly, 25,* 55-62.

Torrance, E. P. (1984). *Mentoring relationships: How they aid creative achievement, endure, change, and die.* Buffalo, NY: Bearly Limited.

Torrance, E. P. (1987). Teaching for creativity. In S. G. Isaksen (Ed.), *Frontiers of creativity research.* Buffalo, NY: Bearly Limited.

Torrance, E. P. (1991). The beyonders and their characteristics. *Creative Child and Adult Quarterly, 16,* 69-79.

Torrance, E. P. (1993). The beyonders in a thirty year longitudinal study of creative achievement. *Roeper Review, 15,* 131-134.

Torrance, E. P. (1995). Insights about creativity: Questioned, rejected, ridiculed, ignored. *Educational Psychology Review, 7,* 313-322.

Torrance, E. P., Goff, K., & Satterfield, N. B. (1998). *Multicultural mentoring of the gifted and talented.* Waco, TX: Prufrock Press.

Torrance, E. P., & Rose, L. (1992). *Cumulative bibliography on Thinking Creatively in Action and Movement.* Athens: Georgia Studies of Creative Behavior.

Torrance, E. P., Rose, L. H., & Smith, R. (1996). *Cumulative bibliography: Thinking Creatively with Sounds and Words (TCSW)*. Athens: Georgia Studies of Creative Behavior.

Torrance, E. P., & Safter, E. P. (1990). *The incubation model of teaching*. Buffalo, NY: Bearly Limited.

Torrance, E. P. et al. (1996). *Cumulative bibliography on the Torrance Tests of Creative Thinking*. Athens: Georgia Studies of Creative Behavior.

About the Contributors

Teresa Amabile, PhD, was originally educated and employed as a chemist. Dr. Amabile received her PhD in psychology from Stanford in 1977. Since then, she has been a psychology professor at Brandeis University, conducting research on the ways that social environments can influence the verbal, artistic, and problem-solving creativity of both children and adults. Currently, Dr. Amabile is professor of business administration at Harvard University. Dr. Amabile is a fellow of the American Psychological Association and the American Psychological Society (APS), a member of the Board of Trustees of the Creative Education Foundation, and a member of the editorial board of the *Creativity Research Journal*. She is co-editor of *Psychological Research in the Classroom,* and author of *The Social Psychology of Creativity* and *Growing Up Creative.* Recently, she appeared in the PBS Television Series *Creativity.*

Giselle B. Esquivel is professor of school psychology and chairperson of the Division of Psychological and Educational Services in the Graduate School of Education at Fordham University. She is past coordinator and director of training for Fordham's APA-accredited school psychology programs. She is co-founder of the bilingual school psychology program, one of the few such programs in the United States. Giselle has a bachelor's degree in psychology from Rutgers University and a master's degree in educational psychology from Montclair State College. Since earning her doctorate in psychology from Yeshiva University in 1981, Giselle has pursued her research and clinical interests in identification and education of linguistically and culturally diverse gifted and creative children. She is a frequent presenter at professional conferences and publishes in such sources as *Best Practices in School Psychology,* the *Creativity Research Journal,* and *Professional Psychology: Research and Practice.* Giselle is also a nationally certified school psychologist and licensed psychologist.

John F. Feldhusen is professor emeritus of education and psychology at Purdue University. Dr. Feldhusen received his PhD from the University of Wisconsin-Madison and has enjoyed a long and distinguished career as a scholar and educator. He was the long-time director of the educational research and psychology training programs at Purdue, a department chairman, dean, and past president of APA's Division 15 (Educational Psychology). He is the author and co-author of more than 200 journal articles and an equal number of papers presented at various professional associations. He is the author/editor or co-author/editor of *Teaching Creative Thinking and Problem Solving* (Kendell/Hunt, 1984), *Toward Excellence in Gifted Education* (Love, 1985), and *Talent Identification and Development* (Center for Creative Learning, 1995), and numerous other books and monographs in the fields of giftedness, creativity, and problem solving. Dr. Feldhusen is the founder and past director of the Purdue Gifted Education Resource Institute.

Traci G. Hodes earned a bachelor of science degree in special education at New York University and her doctoral degree in school psychology at Fordham University in New York City. She has been a teacher of children with multiple handicaps and currently is a school psychologist and clinical director for an early intervention program. Her research interests concern the evaluation and efficiency of early intervention programs with infants and toddlers and teachers' sense of self-efficacy as it relates to school consultation.

John C. Houtz is professor of educational psychology in the Graduate School of Education at Fordham University's Lincoln Center Campus, Manhattan, New York. He is past chairman of the Division of Psychological and Educational Services and currently is coordinator of Fordham's Master of Science Program in Creative Studies. He received his baccalaureate in mathematics at Bucknell University in 1969 and a master's degree in educational research at Bucknell in 1970. After Bucknell, John studied at Purdue University and completed his doctorate in educational psychology in 1973. At Purdue, John developed his interest in creativity and problem solving as a student of John Feldhusen and Don Treffinger and was a member of the team that developed the *Purdue Elementary Problem Solving Inventory*. John is co-editor of the book *Cognition, Curriculum, and Literacy* and has contributed articles to such journals as *Contemporary Educational Psychology, Educational Psychology Review,* the *Creativity Research Journal,* and *Educational Research Quarterly.*

Merle A. Keitel received her PhD in counseling psychology from the State University of New York at Buffalo. She is currently associate professor and director of counseling psychology programs in the Graduate School of Education at Fordham. Her major research interests are in the areas of stress and coping. She is an active member of APA's Division 17 (Counseling Psychology), a past chair of the Committee on Special Interest Groups, and member of the Committee on Public Interest. She has presented numerous papers in counseling of individuals and families dealing with health crises and in professional supervision of counselor training.

Mary Kopala received her master's of education in counseling in 1980 and a PhD in counseling psychology in 1987 from Penn State University. She has taught at Fordham University and currently she is associate professor of counseling at Hunter College of the City of New York. Dr. Kopala is widely published in such professional journals as *Counselor Education and Supervision,* the *Journal of Counseling Psychology, Counseling and Values, Psychotherapy,* and the *New York State Journal for Counseling and Development.* Dr. Kopala has contributed work to *The Counseling Sourcebook: A Practical Reference on Contemporary Issues,* currently in press. She also has worked as a clinician and has provided direct service to clients at the University of Delaware, Drexel University, and Georgia State University.

Emilia C. Lopez graduated from Fordham University's doctoral program in school psychology in 1989. She has worked as a school psychologist at the preschool, elementary, and high school levels. Currently, she is associate professor of school psychology at Queens College. Her research and teaching interests include the assessment of linguistically and culturally diverse students, language development and second language acquisition, the use of interpreters in the assessment process, and school consultation.

William B. Michael, a native southern Californian, earned his PhD in psychology at the University of Southern California in 1947, with J. P. Guilford serving as chairperson. Dr. Michael has held academic appointments at Princeton University and the University of Southern California, where he is currently professor of counseling and educational psychology. He also has held research assignments at the Educational Testing Service and the RAND Corporation. In addition to serving as editor-in-chief of *Educational and Psychological Measurement,* Dr. Michael regularly contributes articles to the professional literature that deal with measurement, evaluation, and creativity. His recreational interests center around extensive travel, classical music, and visitations to establishments featuring ice cream of gourmet quality.

Martha L. Picariello holds master's and doctoral degrees from Brandeis University and is a Phi Beta Kappa graduate of Wellesley College. She has presented lectures at major universities and conferences in areas of children's creativity, motivation, and intersections between psychology and business. Dr. Picariello has been guest speaker at the opening ceremonies of Inventure Place, home of the National Inventors Hall of Fame, where she spoke about the influences of the work environment on innovation and the creative process. Currently, Dr. Picariello is education director of Edutainment World Wide, a global enterprise devoted to developing and promoting quality entertainment.

Mark A. Runco, professor of psychology and education at California State University–Fullerton and fellow of the APA, received his bachelor of arts from Claremont Men's College in 1979 and the master's doctorate (1984) in cognitive psychology from Claremont Graduate School. He is founder and editor of the *Creativity Research Journal* and director of the Creativity Research Center of Southern California. Mark is past-president of APA Division 10 (Psychology and the Arts) and author/editor/coauthor of more than 50 books, monographs, and journal articles on gifted and creative children, including *Divergent Thinking, Problem Finding, Problem Solving, and Creativity, Theories of Creativity,* and *The Creativity Research Handbook.*

Mary Ann Schroder received her bachelor's degree in psychology from Bard College, a master's degree with a counseling specialization from the State University of New York, New Paltz, and the doctorate in counseling psychology at Fordham University. Her research is focused on family topics, including coping with infertility and the relationship between adult children and their elderly parents. Her work on the needs of elderly parents has been presented at the APA and published in *Psychological Reports.*

Michael L. Shaw is assistant professor of education and director of the graduate reading program at St. Thomas Aquinas College in 'Sparkill, New York, a suburb of New York City. He also serves as a literacy consultant to a number of school districts, including Community School District 11, Bronx, New York, where he works with classroom teachers to implement instructional programs that support the literacy and creativity of each child. Dr. Shaw also has been an elementary classroom teacher and has served as a reading specialist, writing specialist, and communications arts program director. Dr. Shaw speaks at numerous local, state, and national conferences on classroom practices that support high standards. He has published articles on the role of the teacher, parent involvement, and professional development.

Elizabeth Tighe is a social psychologist trained at Carnegie-Mellon University, Brandeis University, and Brown University. She has held research positions in the department of psychology and the Heller School at Brandeis and in the departments of psychology and education at Brown and has taught undergraduate and graduate level methodology courses at Brandeis, Brown, and at Wellesley College. Her research has focused on motivation, emotion, creativity, and attitude structure and change. She is currently a senior research associate at the Heller School for Social Welfare at Brandeis.

E. Paul Torrance is professor emeritus of Creative Studies at the University of Georgia. He is an internationally known scholar and advocate of creativity research and education. He has authored hundreds of books, monographs, chapters, and articles during his career. He has been the author, developer, or motivator for creativity training programs and activities that have impacted thousands of pupils from childhood through college and adulthood. A recent biography, called *The Creativity Man*, is currently available. He began his study of creativity in 1943 when he developed his first creativity test and administered it to elementary and high school students at Georgia Military College. This interest was nourished through his experience during World War II, counseling disabled veterans at Kansas State University, and as director of survival research at the U.S. Air Force Advanced Survival School. When he became director of the Bureau of Educational Research at the University of Minnesota in 1958, he began his scientific research on creativity, which he continued at the University of Georgia until 1984. He is especially known for the Torrance Tests of Creative Thinking and for his longitudinal studies of creative achievement beginning in 1958 and continuing through the present.

Donald J. Treffinger is founder and president of the Center for Creative Learning, Inc., in Sarasota, Florida. He received his bachelor of science degree in education and sociology from Buffalo State University College and the Master's and PhD degrees from Cornell University. Dr. Treffinger is a member of many professional organizations in education and psychology. He received the National Association for Gifted Children's E. Paul Torrance Creativity Award in 1995 and NAGC's Distinguished Service Award in 1984. He has served as a member of the faculty at several universities, including appointments in the Educational Psychology and Research departments at the University of Kansas (where he was department chair), Purdue University, and in the Center for Studies in Creativity at Buffalo State College. Dr. Treffinger is the author or coauthor of more than 250 books, chapters, monographs, and articles on creativity, creative problem solving, giftedness, and talent development.

Erik Westby received his bachelor's degree in psychology from Union College in 1993. During his program, he was awarded a fellowship to study at Brown University and develop a computerized video testing system to examine children's perceptions of interpersonal situations. He also has conducted grant-supported research on teachers' perceptions of creativity, which has led to publications in *The Creativity Research Journal*. Currently, Erik is a graduate research assistant in the master's degree program in educational psychology in the Department of Educational Studies at Purdue University.

A Bookshelf of Creativity

The following books contain collections of articles about creativity from a variety of authors. Over the years, these books have been published to summarize the various theories and applications of creativity and creative thinking principles at the time. Experts as well as the novice can get a fairly broad sampling of views by using these books.

Anderson, H. (Ed.). (1959). *Creativity and its cultivation*. New York: Harper & Row.

Anderson collected the papers presented at several symposia on creativity conducted at Michigan State University from 1957 to 1958. The papers ranged from theory to applications, including contributions from Henry Eyring, Edmund Sinnott, Alden Dow, Erich Fromm, Carl Rogers, Abraham Maslow, J. P. Guilford, Ernest Hilgard, Henry Murray, George Stoddard, Harold Lasswell, Margaret Mead, and Anderson, himself.

Barron, F. (Ed.). (1965). *Creative person and creative process*. New York: Holt, Rinehart & Winston.

Chapters in this volume focus on classic research by Barron and others on personality and development of creativity.

Glover, J. Ronning, R., & Reynolds, C. (Eds.). (1989). *Handbook of creativity research*. New York: Plenum Press.

The creators of this volume intended to accomplish three objectives: (a) critique the existing literature, (b) identify an agenda for future research, and (c) organize what they felt was a disparate and "declining" field.

Gowan, J. C., Khatena, J., & Torrance, E. P. (Eds.). (1981). *Creativity: Its educational implications* (2nd ed.). Dubuque, IA: Kendall/Hunt.

This volume includes 37 articles from many sources focusing on schools and classrooms. They are representative of the broad range of issues in creativity from the 1960s and 1970s.

Gruber, H., Terell, G., & Wertheimer, M. (Eds.). (1962). *Contemporary approaches to creative thinking.* New York: Atherton Press.

These editors include the papers from a symposium held at the University of Colorado in 1958. Jerome Bruner, Mary Henle, Allen Newell, John Shaw, Herbert Simon, Richard Crutchfield, David McClelland, and Robert MacLeod are the contributors.

Isaksen, S. (Ed.). (1987). *Frontiers of creativity research: Beyond the basics.* Buffalo, NY: Bearly Limited.

Isaksen is the former director of the Center for Creativity Studies at the State University at Buffalo, New York. This book includes articles reflecting on the history of creativity research and training and on needed areas for future research.

Isaksen, S. G., Murdock, M. C., Firestein, R. L., & Treffinger, D. J. (Eds.). (1993). *Understanding and recognizing creativity: The emergence of a discipline* and *Nurturing and developing creativity: The emergence of a discipline.* Norwood, NJ: Ablex.

This is two-volume work of papers developed from the 1990 International Working Conference on Creativity organized and hosted by the Center for Studies in Creativity at the State University College at Buffalo, New York.

Montuori, A., & Purser, R. E. (1999). *Social creativity* (Vols. 1 & 2). Cresskill, NJ: Hampton Press.

This is a collection of 24 chapters by more than 30 contributors, including the editors, concerning creativity in the social context, including artistic and organizational settings. Volume 1 focuses on how we have come to understand creativity as a social phenomenon, while Volume 2 focuses on how social forces affect the development and encouragement of creativity.

Parnes, S., & Harding, H. (Eds.). (1962). *A source book for creative thinking.* New York: Charles Scribner's Sons.

This is a collection of papers from institutes on creative problem solving conducted at the Creation Education Foundation at the University of Buffalo and from other sources. It is an excellent survey of the field in the early years, including articles on the importance of creativity for the "space age," theories, identification and training of creativity, and reviews of famous creative problem-solving courses or programs. The most recent edition of this book is edited by Sidney Parnes and is entitled: *Source Book for Creative Problem Solving: A Fifty Year Digest of Proven Innovation Processes* (Buffalo, NY: Creative Education Foundation, 1992).

Parnes, S., Noller, R., & Biondi, A. (Eds.). (1977). *Guide to creative action: Revised edition of the creative behavior guidebook.* New York: Charles Scribner's Sons.

This volume describes the course on creative problem solving developed and promoted by the Creative Education Foundation in Buffalo, New York. Individual training sessions are outlined, with content and activities described for participants. Extensive references are provided, including the tests available to assess creativity and problem solving. Individual articles from issues of the *Journal of Creative Behavior* also are reprinted to supplement the material from the training sessions. The volume provides an excellent survey of major issues in the field.

Rothenberg, A., & Hausman, C. (Eds.). (1970). *The creativity question.* Durham, NC: Duke University Press.

This volume contains an exceptionally comprehensive group of readings, including selections from Plato and Aristotle, Freud, Galton, Kant, and writers and scholars describing thinking and creating, a wide selection of psychodynamic, cognitive, and humanistic authors, and articles pertaining to educational issues.

Runco, M. A. (Ed.). (1997). *The creativity research handbook* (Vol. 1). Cresskill, NJ: Hampton Press.

This first volume of a planned three-volume set contains 12 papers by 17 authors. The contributions to Volume 1 cover major theoretical views of creativity and the creative process, plus special topics, including current research on the structure of intellect, mental imagery and creativity, humor, mental illness and deviance, and brain lateralization and creativity.

Runco, M., & Albert, R. (Eds.). (1990). *Theories of creativity.* Newbury Park, CA: Sage.

Contemporary theoretical views of creativity, the creative person, and the creative environment are the focus of this volume. Contributors include Runco, Albert, John Gedo, Ravenna Helson, Teresa Amabile, Dean Keith Simonton, Robert Epstein, David Harrington, Donald Brenneis, Mihaly Csikszentmihalyi, and Roberta Milgram.

Runco, M. A., & Pritzker, S. (Eds.). (1999). *Encyclopedia of creativity.* New York: Academic Press.

This mammoth, two-volume sourcebook, includes selections on more than 180 topics and their connections to human creativity and selected biographical articles of noted individuals of significant creativity in their respective domains.

Russ, S. (Ed.). (1999). *Affect, creative experience, and psychological adjustment.* Philadelphia, PA: Taylor Francis/Brunner Mazel.

This volume contains 12 chapters by 14 authors dealing with the role of affect in the creative experience and creative expression. Authors include Stephanie Dudek, Gregory Feist, Isaac Getz, Beth Hennessey, Alice Isen, Geir Kaufmann, Kimberly McCarthy, Ruth Richards, Mark Runco, Sandra Russ, Melvin Shaw, David Shuldberg, Todd Lubart, and Suzanne Vosburg.

Sternberg, R. (Ed.). (1988). *The nature of creativity: Contemporary psychological perspectives.* New York: Cambridge University Press.

Sternberg extends his triarchic theory of intelligence to creativity in one selection of this book and includes several more articles organized traditionally into psychometric and cognitive views, creative person, and environment. Also, several contributors write in terms of a more integrated, systems approach to creativity.

Taylor, C., & Barron, F. (Eds.). (1963). *Scientific creativity: Its recognition and development.* New York: Wiley.

This volume is a collection of papers from the first three University of Utah Conferences on the Identification of Creative Scientific Talent (1955, 1957, 1959). These papers reflect the major developments and research efforts in the field during the 1950s. The major research questions remain relevant today.

Vernon, P. (Ed.). (1970). *Creativity: Selected readings.* Baltimore, MD: Penguin.

This is a classic anthology of readings organized in the following sections: (a) pioneer empirical studies, (b) introspective accounts of creativity, (c) distinctive theoretical approaches, (d) psychometric approaches, (e) personality studies, and (f) teaching and training for creativity. This book reflects the seminal influences in the field prior to 1970 and may be very useful to the beginning student looking for a basic structure to the field as well as an understanding of important foundational concepts.

Wallace, D. B., & Gruber, H. E. (1989). *Creative people at work: Twelve cognitive case studies.* New York: Oxford University Press.

This volume details Gruber's "evolving systems" approach to the analysis of the creative enterprise. It includes fascinating case studies from science, poetry, psychology, literature, art.

The following books are "single subject" works by individual authors. They are of major influence and/or usefulness to students of creativity.

Amabile, T. (1983). *The social psychology of creativity.* New York: Springer-Verlag.

A comprehensive text about the social psychological foundations for the study of creativity. This volume includes assessment and environmental factors. It presents Amabile's research and theory concerning the influence of intrinsic motivation on creative development.

Arieti, S. (1975). *Creativity: The magic synthesis.* New York: Basic Books.

Arieti's theory of tertiary process is the subject of this enlightened summary of theories of creativity, research on creative persons, and environmental influences of culture and society. Included are many clinical examples from fields such as writing, art, science, philosophy, religion.

Csikszentmihalyi, M. (1996). *Creativity: Flow and the psychology of discovery and invention.* New York: Harper/Collins.

Csikzentmihalyi describes the results of detailed interviews of 91 contemporary, acknowledged creative persons from a variety of disciplines and occupations. The theory of "flow" is described as it pertains to the creative process. Chapters review the theories and accumulated knowledge base of creativity, including analysis of the development of creativity through the lifespan of the interviewees. To complete the volume, Csikszentmihalyi also discusses several domains of creativity and principles for increasing one's personal creative potential.

Gardner, H. (1993). *Creating minds: An anatomy of creativity seen through the lives of Freud, Einstein, Picasso, Stravinsky, Eliot, Graham, and Gandhi.* New York: Basic Books.

This is a biographical case study of seven creative geniuses illustrating Gardner's theory of multiple intelligences.

Getzels, J. W., & Csikszentmihalyi, M. (1975). *The creative vision: A longitudinal study of problem finding in art.* New York: Wiley-Interscience.

In this study of young artists in training and those several years into the development of productive careers, the authors suggest with their research that problem-finding abilities are as important, if not more, than any others in predicting creative success.

Guilford, J. P. (1967). *The nature of human intelligence.* New York: McGraw-Hill.

This is a classic work, in which Guilford presents his research and structure-of-intellect model. Extensive literature reviews of cognitive skills are included. Guilford's tests are described.

Khatena, J. (1982). *Educational psychology of the gifted.* New York: Wiley.

The history and study of the creatively gifted is the focus of this volume. Khatena's work on imagination, imagery, education, and guidance of creatively talented children and youth is described. The title of Khatena's text served as the "inspiration" for *The Educational Psychology of Creativity.*

Millar, G. W. (1995). *E. Paul Torrance, "The Creativity Man"—an authorized biography.* Norwood, NJ: Ablex.

This volume presents a biography of the career of E. Paul Torrance, his youth, education, and professional life. Torrance's lifetime publications are presented.

Osborn, A. F. (1963). *Applied imagination: Principles and procedures of creative problem solving* (3rd rev. ed.). New York: Charles Scribner's Sons.

Another classic, this is an in-depth look at brainstorming and group problem solving. Osborn's theory, research, and training principles are discussed.

Prentky, R. A. (1980). *Creativity and psychopathology: A neurocognitive perspective.* New York: Praeger.

A detailed examination of the research and theory relating genius, creativity, and mental illness is presented. More than a research summary, this volume includes many examples and interpretations in modern cognitive and neurocognitive theory.

Stein, M. (1974, 1975). *Stimulating creativity. Vol. I: Individual procedures, and Vol. II: Group procedures.* New York: Academic Press.

Morris Stein is a long-time scholar and researcher in the field of creativity. These volumes provide exceptional reviews of the literature on all aspects of creativity study and enhancement as well as Stein's own theoretical approach.

Sternberg, R. J., & Lubart, T. I. (1995). *Defying the crowd: Cultivating creativity in a culture of conformity.* New York: The Free Press.

This book describes Sternberg and Lubart's investment theory approach to creativity, and the role of intelligence, knowledge, personality, thinking styles, motivation, and environmental factors in the creative process.

Torrance, E. P., & Myers, H. (1970). *Creative learning and teaching.* New York: Dodd, Mead.

A summary of Torrance's work on training and development of creative thinking is provided. Extensive recommendations are given for educators on classroom structure and learning activities to promote children's creativity. Torrance has published many books, before and since this volume, but this book deals most directly with education.

SELF-HELP BOOKS

Another category of resources available to teachers (as well as everyone else) is what may be termed *self-help books.* These books are written to describe particular theories or models of creative problem solving, typical problems and methods of solution, and techniques to overcome blocks to problem solving. Many of these books are available in trade bookstores.

Ackoff, R. (1978). *The art of problem solving.* New York: Wiley-Interscience.

Adams, J. (1979). *Conceptual blockbusting: A guide to better ideas* (2nd ed.). New York: Norton.

Bransford, J., & Stein, B. (1984). *The IDEAL problem solver.* New York: W. H. Freeman.

Brown, S. I., & Walter, M.I. (1990). *The art of problem posing* (2nd ed.). Hillsdale, NJ: Lawrence Erlbaum Associates.

deBono, E. (1970). *Lateral thinking: Creativity step by step.* New York: Harper & Row.

deBono, E. (1992). *Serious creativity: Using the power of lateral thinking to create new ideas.* New York: Harper Business.

Kim, S. (1990). *Essence of creativity: A guide to tackling difficult problems.* New York: Oxford

Levmore, S., & Cook, E. (1981). *Super strategies for puzzles and games.* Garden City, NY: Doubleday.

Olson, R. (1978). *The art of creative thinking: A practical guide, including exercises and illustrations.* New York: Barnes & Noble/Harper & Row.

Polya, G. (1957/1973). *How to solve it: A new aspect of mathematical method* (2nd ed.). Princeton, NJ: Princeton University Press.

Raudsepp, E., & Hough, Jr., G. (1977). *Creative growth games.* New York: Harvest/Harcourt Brace Jovanovich.

VanDemark, N. (1991). *Breaking the barriers to every day creativity: A practical guide for expanding your creative horizons.* Buffalo, NY: Creative Education Foundation.

von Oech, R. (1983). *A whack on the side of the head: How you can be more creative* (rev. ed.). New York: Warner Books.

Wickelgren, W. (1974). *How to solve problems: Elements of a theory of problems and problem solving.* San Francisco, CA: Freeman.

PARENT EDUCATION

The following books were written with parents in mind. They offer suggestions for understanding children's giftedness and how parents and other adults may help encourage the development of children's gifted and creative abilities.

Amabile, T. (1988). *Growing up creative: Nurturing a lifetime of creativity.* New York: Crown.

Dunn, R., Dunn, K., & Treffinger, D. (1992). *Bringing out the giftedness in your child: Nurturing every child's unique strengths, talents, and potential.* New York: Wiley.

Khatena, J. (1978). *The creatively gifted child: Suggestions for parents and teachers.* New York: Vantage Press.

Lehane, S. (1979). *The creative child: How to encourage the natural creativity of your preschooler.* Englewood Cliffs, NJ: Prentice-Hall.

IDEA BOOKS FOR TEACHERS

The following books represent those that have been written for teachers and other school personnel containing ideas for curriculum and classroom activities. Their intent is to improve the range of creative thinking and feeling activities available to teachers and pupils.

Eberle, B., & Hall, R. (1975). *Affective education guidebook: Classroom activities in the realm of feelings.* Buffalo, NY: Disseminators of Knowledge.

Krulik, S., & Rudnick, J. A. (1987). *Problem solving: A handbook for teachers* (2nd ed.). Boston: Allyn & Bacon.

Kruse, J. (1988). *Classroom activities in thinking skills.* Philadelphia, PA: Research for Better Schools.

Schaefer, C. E. (1973). *Developing creativity in children: An ideabook for teachers.* Buffalo, NY: Disseminators of Knowledge.

Stephens, L. S. (1983). *Developing thinking skills through real-life activities.* Boston: Allyn & Bacon.

Williams, F. (1970). *Classroom ideas for encouraging thinking and feeling.* Buffalo, NY: Disseminators of Knowledge.

Williams, L. V. (1983). *Teaching for the two-sided mind: A guide to right brain/left brain education.* New York: Simon & Schuster/Touchstone.

CREATIVITY IN BUSINESS AND INDUSTRY

The following books were intended for adults in business and industrial settings. Although the obvious focus is on developing creative problem-solving skills in adults, these books contain many of the same explanations and activities as the self-help books just listed.

Brightman, H. J. (1980). *Problem solving: A logical and creative approach.* Atlanta: Georgia State University Business Press.

Davis, G. A., & Scott, J. A. (Eds.). (1978). *Training creative thinking.* Huntington, NY: Robert E. Krieger. (Original work published 1971)

Henry, J. (Ed.). (1991). *Creative management.* Newbury Park, CA: Sage.

Miller, W. C. (1986). *The creative edge: Fostering creativity where you work.* Reading, MA: Addison-Wesley.

West, M. A., & Farr, J. L. (Eds.). (1990). *Innovation and creativity at work: Psychological and organizational strategies.* New York: Wiley.

Creativity and Related Organizations

There are a number of organizations that specialize in developing research and training activities concerning creativity and problem solving and/or disseminating information about creativity. A brief description and address of a few of these organizations are offered here.

THE CREATIVE EDUCATION FOUNDATION (CEF)

The Creative Education Foundation (CEF) is a multipurpose organization founded in 1954 by the late Alex Osborn, one of the original partners of the advertising agency, Batten, Barton, Durstine, and Osborn. CEF sponsors numerous workshops and creative problem-solving courses and seminars for academics and for individuals in business and industry. Its annual Creative Problem Solving Institutes are attended by hundreds of educators, business leaders and executives, researchers, and scholars each year. The CEF publishes the *Journal of Creative Behavior*, and numerous occasional books, pamphlets, monographs, and newsletters. The current mailing address of the CEF is 1050 Union Road, Buffalo, NY 14224. Its website is: http://www.cef-cpsi.org/

THE CENTER FOR STUDIES IN CREATIVITY AT BUFFALO STATE COLLEGE, BUFFALO, NEW YORK

The Center for Studies in Creativity (CSC) is an academic unit within the State University College at Buffalo, New York. It offers a master of science degree in creative studies and contributes to an undergraduate major in creative studies within the college and to other certificate and degree

303

programs. The faculty of the center conduct research, sponsor confer-ences, and promote creativity through a variety of professional activities in addition to their teaching and writing. One of the center's resources is the Creative Studies Library, a collection of more than 5,000 books, dis-sertations, and papers, including some archival documents from the Creative Eduction Foundation. The Center for Studies in Creativity is an independent outgrowth and expansion of the original mission and activi-ties of the Creative Education Foundation dating back to the 1960s. The address of the CSC is Chase Hall 244, Buffalo State College, 1300 Elmwood Avenue, Buffalo, NY 14222-1095. The internet address in http://www.buffalostate.edu/~creatcnt/

THE CENTER FOR CREATIVE LEARNING, INCORPORATED

The Center for Creative Learning, Inc. was founded by Donald J. Treffinger in 1981. The center sponsors both training and research activi-ties on a broad range of topics related to creative growth and develop-ment. Dr. Treffinger and other individuals associated with the center develop and sponsor a regular program of national courses, workshops, and seminars. Additionally, the center offers numerous books, pamphlets, educational materials, and monographs for teachers, business people, aca-demics, and others interested in developing creative talent. The center publishes the *International Creativity Network Newsletter*. The current address of the center is PO Box 14100, NE Plaza, Sarasota, FL 34234. Phone: (941) 351-8862. The website is: http://www.creativelearning.com/

NATIONAL ASSOCIATION FOR GIFTED CHILDREN (NAGC)

The National Association for Gifted Children (NAGC) is composed of educators, parents, and people from the larger community who are inter-ested in discovering and encouraging the special abilities and talents of children. NAGC is primarily an information dissemination network, pub-lishing a journal, the *Gifted Child Quarterly,* a newsletter, the *Communique,* and numerous pamphlets, monographs, and educational materials. NAGC sponsors institutes and an annual conference. The cur-rent address is 1707 L Street NW, Suite 550, Washington, DC 20036. Its website is: http://www.nagc.org/

ASSOCIATION FOR SUPERVISION AND CURRICULUM DEVELOPMENT

The Association for Supervision and Curriculum Development (ASCD) is a professional organization of educators, researchers, and community people who are very much concerned with teacher education, school organizations, and curriculum development. ASCD publishes *Educational Leadership Journal,* and numerous other books, monographs, and educational materials. ASCD also sponsors a full program of workshops and institutes on a variety of topics during the year. Most relevant to this book, however, are ASCD's institutes and conferences on building problem solving and critical thinking into school curricula. The current address is 1703 North Beauregard Street, Alexandria, VA 22311. The ASCD website is: http://odie.ascd.org/

AMERICAN CREATIVITY ASSOCIATION

The American Creativity Association (ACA) was founded in 1989 by noted scholars and professionals interested in increasing the awareness of the importance of creativity in society. The ACA provides a national network of individuals interested in promoting greater personal and professional creativity, a newsletter, a journal, and various educational materials. The ACA also holds an annual conference and sponsors special seminars in the professional areas. The website is: http://www.BeCreative.org

THE NORTHWOOD UNIVERSITY'S ALDEN B. DOW CREATIVITY CENTER

Located in Midland, Michigan, the Creativity Center sponsors conferences, seminars, and summer research fellowships on creativity, including an annual conference on creativity in U.S. colleges and universities. Northwood University is a business management college, for whose students the Creativity Center offers creative problem-solving coursework. Information about the Creativity Center can be obtained by writing to Alden B. Dow Creativity Center, 3225 Cook Road, Midland, MI 48640. The website is: http://www.northwood.edu/

RESEARCH FOR BETTER SCHOOLS

Begun in 1966, Research for Better Schools (RBS) is a private, nonprofit educational research and development organization. RBS is also a mid-atlantic regional educational laboratory, supported by the U.S. Department of Education. RBS sponsors research and policy studies and offers numerous research and professional development services and products to schools and other educational organizations. Of particular relevance to this book has been RBS' efforts in development and study of higher level thinking skills, problem solving, and critical thinking. One notable publication is Janice Kruse's (1989) *Resources for Teaching Thinking: A Catalogue.* The website is: http://www.rbs.org/

THE NATIONAL RESEARCH CENTER ON THE GIFTED AND TALENTED

The National Research Center for the Gifted and Talented is located at the University of Connecticut and directed by Drs. Joseph Renzulli and E. Jean Gubbins. The center sponsors research and national and international conferences, provides resources and disseminates information on gifted and talented education, including creativity, for parents, educators, researchers, and the general public. Books, monographs, research reports, position papers, video training tapes, practitioners' guides, and other materials are available from the center. In addition, the National Research Center is a clearinghouse on major research and training activities for the gifted and talented and coordinates activities and connects scholars at other universities, including Yale, Stanford, the University of Virginia, and the City University of New York. The address is 362 Fairfield Road, U-7, Storrs, CT 06269-2007. Phone: (203) 486-4676. Fax: (860) 486-2900. The website is: http://www.ucc.uconn.edu/~wwwgt/nrcgt.html/

THE CENTER FOR TALENTED YOUTH (CTY)

Located at the Johns Hopkins University in Baltimore, Maryland, the Center for Talented Youth (CTY) is part of the Institute for the Academic Advancement of Youth (IAAY). The Office of Talent Identification and Development (later to become the CTY) was originally founded in 1979 with the goal of promoting the academic ability of children and youth. The various activities of the CTY include national and international talent searches, in- and out-of-school programs in mathematics, the sciences, and the humanities. The CTY organizes conferences and symposia, publishes books and materials, and maintains a network of supporters, scholars, and program alumni. The address is Johns Hopkins University, 3400 North Charles Street, Baltimore, MD 21218. Phone: (410) 516-0337. The website is: http://www.jhu.edu/~gifted/

THE CENTER FOR CREATIVE LEADERSHIP

The Center for Creative Leadership, with additional sites in Brussels, Belgium, Colorado Springs, Colorado, and San Diego, California, was originally founded in 1970 in Greensboro, North Carolina, and continues to maintain headquarters there. The center is an international, nonprofit educational institution whose purpose is the development of managerial science. The center conducts research, assessment, and training activities, organizes conferences, and publishes books and materials. The address is PO Box 26300, Greensboro, NC 27438-6300. Phone: (910) 545-2810. The web address is: http://www.ccl.org

ODYSSEY OF THE MIND

Odyssey of the Mind (OM) is an international not-for-profit organization that promotes team-based creative problem solving for children from kindergarten to college age. Schools join the OM program and become involved in local-to-national creative problem-solving tournaments, where teams of five to seven students, led by coaches, compete to solve challenging problems in creative ways. OM began in 1978 and now has members in all 50 of the United States and many countries, involving thousands of students each year. Local OM associations are chartered by the parent organization. An annual creativity conference for educators, researchers, and other professionals also is held.

THE FUTURE PROBLEM SOLVING PROGRAM AND THE TORRANCE CENTER FOR CREATIVE STUDIES

Begun by E. Paul Torrance in 1974, the *Future Problem Solving Program* is a national network of creative competitions. The *Program* involves problem-solving teams of four to six students who must address futuristic problem situations. There are junior, intermediate, and senior divisions, corresponding to upper elementary, junior-, and senior-high school grades. Teams have coaches and practice problems and compete with other teams locally or from schools across the country (or in different countries). Trained judges evaluate team responses in terms of a number of creative problem-solving criteria (quality, feasibility, level of sophistication, etc.). The internet address is www.fpsp.org/overview.html. The phone number is 1-800-256-1499. Also available are books and creative problem-solving materials, lesson plans, classroom activities, posters, tapes, and research articles.

The mission of the Torrance Center for Creative Studies in the Department of Educational Psychology at the University of Georgia is to support scholarly inquiry into creativity and giftedness among diverse populations of all ages. The center supports a number of activities and programs, including various "Challenge Programs" for school-age children and their teachers, workshops, seminars, research by students and faculty, a visiting scholars program, an annual lecture series, and technical assistance services to schools. The center also houses the Torrance library and archives. The web address is http://www.coe.uga.edu/torrance/problem-solving/html. The telephone number is (706) 542-5104/5. E-mail: torrance-center@coe.uga.edu.

DESTINATIONIMAGINATION

DestinationImaginNation is a relatively recent organization designed in a manner similar to that of Odyssey of the Mind and the Future Problem Solving Program. It is an international, nonprofit educational corporation whose mission is to teach life skills and expand creative imaginations through team problem solving. DestinationImaginNation is supported by affiliate groups in many states and countries which offer problem-solving tournaments at various levels for kindergarten through college-level students and community groups. Membership includes "instant" as well as "team challenges," a "passport license" to enter tournaments, training sessions, a quarterly newsletter, curriculum guides, access to DestinationImagiNation for questions and suggestions, and an annual conference, at which a culminating tournament is held. The home address is PO Box 547, Glassboro, NJ 08028. The website is http://www.destinationimagination.org.

Author Index

Subject Index